Women & the Historical Jesus

Women & the Historical Jesus

Feminist Myths of Christian Origins

Kathleen E. Corley

Women & the Historical Jesus

Published in 2002 by Polebridge Press, P. O. Box 6144, Santa Rosa, California, 95406.

Library of Congress Cataloging-in-Publication Data

Corley, Kathleen E., 1960-
Women & the Historical Jesus : feminist myths of Christian origins / Kathleen E. Corley.
p. cm.
Includes bibliographical references and index.
ISBN 0-944344-93-3 (alk. paper)
1. Women in Christianity--History--Early church, ca. 30-600. 2. Bible. N.T.--Criticism, interpretation, etc. 3. Christianity--Origin. 4. Feminist theology. I. Title: Women and the Historical Jesus. II. Title
BR195.W6 C67 2002
255.9'5'082--dc21

2002034581

To my mother
In Loving Memory

Dagmar Neick Meyers
1936–2000

Contents

Acknowledgements

This book is the end of a long process of personal and professional struggle. The beginnings of the book come from a discussion with Elizabeth Castelli over my contribution to Burton Mack's Festschrift. In our discussion, she suggested that there was a "feminist myth of Christian origins," and her comment led to my article for that collection. I am indebted to her for sharing her unpublished work on this with me. My own research on women in early Christian meals suggested that early Christian women, and thus the women of the Jesus movements, were participants in a larger process of innovation which incorporated the inclusion of women in various social and religious contexts. In my own acknowledgements for that volume, I suggested that the ramifications of my study on meals for other early Christian communities were obvious. This suggested strongly to me that such would also be the case for the group centered around Jesus himself. Given the popularity of the feminist myth which posits a generating moment of Christian feminism, I decided to embark on an interaction with scholarship on the Historical Jesus to test my larger theory on the changing roles of women in the Greco-Roman period in more detail.

This led to my involvement in the Jesus Seminar, before which several articles in this volume were originally presented. I am indebted to the fellows of the seminar for their welcome and critique of my work. I would particularly like to thank Robert Funk and John Dominic Crossan for their encouragement to publish the results of my research. I should mention other fellows as well: Arthur Dewey, Hal Taussig, Perry Kea, Marvin Meyer, Marcus Borg, Daryl Schmidt, Gerd Lüdemann, and the many others, who made me welcome to the work of the seminar. I am indebted to several other scholars for their support and comments on this work over the years that it has taken me to complete it, including Amy-Jill Levine, Ross Kraemer, Jane Schaberg,

Burton Mack, Karen Torjesen, Richard Pervo and John Kloppenborg. As always, my best friend and conversation partner Diana Bailey, contributed her invaluable critical efforts throughout the process. I have endeavored to revise my manuscript with the help of these many thoughtful readers, though the final responsibility is of course my own.

As I could not have accomplished the completion of this project without the firm support of my University of Wisconsin-Oshkosh colleagues over several years of adversity, I would like to thank them as well. More recently, my husband John C. Harris has been unwavering in support of this project's completion. I am sorry that my mother did not live to see the publication of this book which I dedicate to her, in loving memory.

Several of these chapters are updated and revised from earlier published versions. Chapters 1 and 5 appeared in the Jesus Seminar *Forum* volumes of 1998. Chapter 2 appeared in *A Feminist Companion to Mark* (Sheffield: Sheffield Academic Press) edited by Amy-Jill Levine, in 2001. Chapter 3 will also appear in abbreviated form in *Profiles of Jesus*, edited by Roy Hoover for Polebridge Press in 2002.

Kathleen E. Corley
University of Wisconsin-Oshkosh
January 2002

Introduction

Soon after the death of Jesus, controversy over the role of women arose in various Christian groups. For decades scholars have argued that Jesus' teaching itself fostered inclusive communities and the full participation of women. Thus, the baptismal creed found in Paul, "in Christ there is neither Jew nor Greek, neither slave nor free, neither male nor female" (Gal 3:28) had its roots in a message that was uniquely Christian and reflective of an aspect of Jesus' own message, and in effect repudiated earlier Jewish restrictions on women. Eventually, this egalitarian social arrangement was challenged and overcome by the influence of Hellenistic patriarchalism. This book argues that such a reconstruction of Jesus' preaching and practice can function as a foundational myth for modern Christian feminism. While this study affirms the role of women in Jesus' own community and in subsequent Jesus movements, it challenges both the assumption that Jesus himself fought ancient patriarchal limitations on women and the hypothesis that the presence of women among his disciples was unique within Hellenistic Judaism. Rather, an analysis of Jesus' teaching suggests that while Jesus censured the class and status distinctions of his culture, that critique did not extend to unequal gender distinctions. The notion that Jesus established an anti-patriarchal movement or a "discipleship of equals" is a myth posited to buttress modern Christian social engineering.

To support this reconstruction of Jesus' teaching and the role of women in his movement, it will first be necessary to reconceive the social, religious, and political lives of women in Greco-Roman antiquity, Hellenistic Judaism and Roman Palestine. This will be done in chapter 1. First, recent research on women in Hellenistic Judaism will be reviewed in order to establish that Jewish women in both the Diaspora and Palestine, although living in a male dominated culture, participated in the changing social environment of the Imperial age which afforded women access to certain legal rights (such as divorce), social contexts (such as communal meals), religious contexts (such as synagogue and Temple), and political power (as patronesses and synagogue leaders). Economic and status distinctions between women will be also be assessed so as better to understand the diversity of women's experience, and the likelihood of their presence in the context of the open road, at meals, and in various religious and philosophical groups. Jewish women's lives in both the Diaspora and Roman Palestine probably differed little from those of their Greco-Roman counterparts throughout the Roman Empire. It is plausible that Jesus traveled with and joined women at table, since that comports with recent research on women in Roman Palestine indicating that women were far more active in Palestinian religious, political and social life than has previously been assumed. Women were not only active members of synagogues and ascetic societies of the Diaspora, but women can also be located within the community of Qumran, the Zealot band of Simon b. Gioras, and among the disciples of John the Baptist in first century Palestine.

In chapter 2 we will see that women did indeed number among Jesus' followers or disciples. In addition to the testimony from the Zealot, Baptist and Essene movements, evidence derived primarily from Mark's gospel strongly suggests that Jesus' own movement included several women, in particular Mary Magdalene, Jesus' mother Mary, and Salome. Luke mentions a woman named Joanna. Still, the presence of women among Jesus' disciples does not differentiate his movement from Jewish groups in either the Diaspora or Palestine, but rather reflects the newer presence of women in the wider Greco-Roman context of clubs, philosophical societies and newer religious groups. The presence of women on the road with Jesus may also be an indication of a social constituency of which Jesus was a part. Once it is understood that the majority of women in antiquity were not homebound or like the rich in need of chaperones while travelling, the presence of women in many gospel scenes becomes more everyday – a fact of life for the vast majority of ancient working people. Further, although it is true that the presence of women at Jesus' meals brought social disapproval, it also reflects changing fashions of Greco-Roman society, for during the early Imperial period women are more often found at meals with men, even in formerly all male philosophical symposia and formal banquets. This social trend, although controversial, affected Jewish groups as well, even in Palestine. Thus, neither the presence of women among Jesus' disciples, nor the inclusion of women among his table associates distinguishes Jesus from either his Greco-Roman or his Jewish Palestinian environment.

The larger presence of women within both Greco-Roman and Hellenistic Jewish contexts also makes it less likely that the appearance of women in the Jesus movement was a direct outgrowth of his vision of the Kingdom of God. In chapter 3, we will see that the parables and teachings of Jesus reflect no real interest in the role of women in his culture, nor do they defend the rights of women to participate in his movement or in inclusive meals. Rather than directly addressing the inequality between the sexes, Jesus' open commensality and concern for the poor had a secondary significance for women, who for the most part belonged to the poor and the working classes. Further, Jesus' basic theological concern is for other matters. "Call no man Father" (Matt 23:9) is not Jesus' attack upon patriarchy. In its Matthean context "call no man Father" is a Matthean addition to Mark (Mark 12 :37b–40; the question about the primary commandment) which Matthew then connects to Q where Jesus attacks the custom of the veneration of dead prophets who, like the Patriarchs (the "Fathers") were venerated at tomb shrines. Nor does the parable of the feast reinforce the invitation of women to meals, but rather the plight of the poor (Luke 14:16–24; Matt 22:1–14; Thom 64:1–12). Women are of course among the poor, but the parable in no way points to the presence of women among them, and thus does not function as an ideological support for the presence of women at table.

The familial conflict caused by Jesus' teaching is not gendered, but generational: a father is turned against his son, a mother against her daughter (Q 12:52–53; Thomas 16). Indeed, it seems likely that the anti-family animus of Jesus' teaching was more an attack on popular burial practices than a critique of patriarchy or the opression of women. Jesus declares to a young man on the way to rebury his father's remains in an ossuary, "Let the dead bury their own dead" (Q 9:60), thereby deprecating continued attention to one's ancestors in family tombs. Jesus' concern in this instance is ultimately religious, and secondarily social. Cultic practices associated with graveyards and tombs had long been considered at odds with Hebraic monotheism from the time of the classical prophets. In short, Jesus' concern here is more likely to have been idolatry than patriarchy; the conflict he precipitated stemmed from his censure of ongoing burial rites for family not from the peripatetic or mixed nature of Jesus' group (Q 10:1–12). The issue of gender becomes secondary to Jesus' larger concern of the worship of one God as "Father" in the context of Roman Imperial domination. Thus Jesus' theological concerns express an interest in basic Hebraic monotheism, and his social concerns express an interest in class and rank; but he did not address the concern most central to modern women – inequality between the sexes. In fact he reaffirmed marriage, the major hierarchical social relationship between a man and a woman that was considered the bedrock of the state in antiquity (Mark 10:1–12 par.; 1 Cor 7:10–13). The one possible sign that Jesus recognized the presence of women among his followers as controversial is that he repeated a cultural stereotype to defend them by calling the women who sought the Kingdom of God "whores" (Matt 21:31–32).

Chapter 4, dealing with the earliest layer of gospel tradition, the Q document, will further buttress the evidence for the presence of women among Jesus' listeners and followers by establishing the presence of women as disciples at Jesus' meals and among his peripatetic entourage on the basis of early and pervasive gospel traditions. In particular, Jesus was known for eating and drinking with "tax collectors and sinners" (Mark 2:17; Q 7:29–35), as well as for associating with "prostitutes," a tradition that I will argue was originally found in Q (Q 7:29–30). This language functions as a form of slander and polemic, and reveals the presence of women among Jesus' dining companions and disciples. Stories such as the Last Supper, which exclude women, are late creations whose stereotypical literary banquet motifs reflect Hellenistic literary tradition which therefore cannot be used as evidence against women's presence among the closest circle of Jesus' disciples. Q indicates that the memory of the presence of these women among Jesus' disciples was controversial because of the associations of lower class women with servitude and sexual promiscuity, or the associations of independent or even elite women with liberated social behavior.

Further, Q includes Jesus' criticism of common burial practices of family ancestors, as well a critique of the veneration of dead prophets at tomb shrines (Q 11:47). This indicates that although these early Palestinian followers of Jesus considered Jesus and John in the line of dead prophets, and therefore as special figures for their community, they did not associate the veneration of either with a particular tomb location. This can be seen to reflect Jesus' own sentiments about burial practices proper (Q 9:60) and John's criticism of an over-reliance on the Patriarch Abraham, a long-dead "Father" figure commonly venerated in Palestine during the first century at a public shrine (Q 3: 8). Women's participation in these practices related to tombs is not singled out for special criticism in Jesus' teaching, neither is it singled out in Q. Nonetheless, we do see in the imagery of the "Children of the Marketplace" parable in Q 7:31–32, reference to the funerary roles of piping and mourning that were often performed by women; and here is yet another indication that aspects of Jesus' teaching precipitated family controversies over funerary practices among his contemporaries. The role of women in funerary lamentation and professional mourning suggests that women were involved in this conflict, as well as in the creation of the Wisdom oracle found in the "Lament over Jerusalem" (Q 13:34–35).

Chapter 5 investigates the burial and empty tomb traditions, especially in the Gospel of Mark. In the context of historical-critical inquiry, the tradition linking Mary Magdalene to a resurrection appearance is commonly set aside in favor of Paul's earlier description of an appearance to Peter mentioned in the early creed found in 1 Cor 15:3–11. However, aspects of the tradition linking Mary Magdalene to a resurrection appearance are too early and striking to be ignored. The account of the appearance to Mary in John 20 clearly contains an early element in Mary's declaration, "I have seen the Lord" (John 20:18; compare 1 Cor 9:1). The empty tomb traditions in Mark and John which affirm an appearance to Mary Magdalene are arguably late fictions. However, even the first recorded empty tomb narrative found in Mark's gospel, although late and driven by fictional narrative themes, was in part suggested by the early and pervasive creedal formulation that Jesus "was buried" and then "was raised on the third day;" and this in turn no doubt reflected the common connection of women to tomb visitation and funeral lamentation on the third day after death or burial. The repeated affirmation that Jesus was "buried" and "raised on the third day" in 1 Cor 15:4 makes it likely that Jesus was indeed buried, and that in spite of his own objections to certain burial customs, some of his followers (including women) fulfilled basic burial obligations to Jesus following his death, including a "third day" visit to his burial site. They at least conducted mourning rites even if the location of his body was unknown. This is not unexpected, given the conservative nature of burial customs generally, and the tendency of women in antiquity to fulfill their ongoing obligations to the deceased even in spite of prohibitive legislation. Further, the connection of women to corpses, tomb visitation and magic in ancient culture and literature no doubt contributed to the marginalization of Mary's claim to have "seen" the risen Christ. The empty tomb narrative also functions to discourage tomb visitation and cult of the dead practices among Christians. Although it is inaccurate to claim that the women's witness was rejected due to Jewish legal sensibilities, it is quite likely that the witness of Mary and the other women was rejected due to cultural stereotypes concerning women's ritual lamentation for the dead at tombs.

As is the case with any study of the gospels, the review of gospel traditions concerning women thus moves us beyond the historical Jesus, and well into the world of competition for authority in early Christian groups. However, when viewed in this wider cultural and religious context, Jesus' message, the social composition of his movement, and the disputes over the nature of the resurrection and the locus of community authority in the aftermath of Jesus' death are easily placed within a Hellenistic Jewish and Greco-Roman framework. Traditions about Jesus developed within particular cultural, liturgical, and religious contexts, which in part determined the depiction of women within the gospels and development of later resurrection theologies. The fact that women played a role in Jesus' movement, in the development of gospel and liturgical traditions, and in contests for authority in early Christian groups means that we can place Jesus' movement and the early Christianities solidly within Jewish Palestinian and larger Greco-Roman environments, both of which were far more open to women's involvement in religion, society and politics than has previously been assumed.

Chapter 1

Jesus, Women, & the Social & Religious Environment of Palestine

The feminist project on Christian origins, which really began in the 1970's, has already generated a number of much needed corrections to the historical formulations which preceded it. The presence and participation of women in ancient society and religions, including the Jesus movement, has been firmly established; suggestions continue to be made for the agency of women in the development and passing on of gospel traditions.[1] These reflect crucial advances in our discipline which have had far reaching consequences for biblical studies generally. Continued feminist analysis of the role of gender in the development of gospel tradition will have a tremendous impact on the project of Christian origins overall, and remains crucial to correcting modern discourse on the relationship between Judaism and Christianity as well as to exploring the significance of Jesus as a religious figure, a pursuit which all too often continues to operate at the expense of Judaism.

Since the early 1970's those working for justice and equality for women in modern society and the church have enlisted Jesus on their side, claiming that he had a special concern for women's equality. Further, many Christian feminist and womanist scholars assume the egalitarian nature of the Jesus movement, as do Christian feminist scholars engaged in historical Jesus studies.[2] Recently, such prominent historical Jesus scholars, including Marcus Borg, John Dominic Crossan, Robert Funk, Joachim Gnilka, Richard Horsley and Gerd Theissen and Annette Merz have agreed.[3] Even the corporate decisions of the skeptical Jesus Seminar reflect this growing consensus that Jesus preached a kind of social egalitarianism that pitted him against the social and religious hierarchies of his day.[4] Notably Crossan and Horsley and to a lesser degree Borg, have been influenced by the work of

Elisabeth Schüssler Fiorenza, whose groundbreaking book, *In Memory of Her*, charted the course for subsequent feminist reconstruction of Christian origins and made the claim that the Jesus' movement was remembered primarily as a "discipleship of equals."[5] For once mainstream biblical scholarship and feminist scholarship find themselves in agreement on at least this one issue: Jesus called women to be disciples and treated them as equals.

However, problems remain with this reconstruction. In spite of the hard work of certain Christian and Jewish feminist scholars to try to correct the formulation that Jesus was a feminist within a negative Jewish environment, many Christian writers continue to use a narrative of primitive Christianity which posits a time of pristine origins followed by decay – a discourse that ultimately serves an anti-Judaic function. In this view the Edenic time of the Jesus movement is followed by a Fall when the patriarchal Christian church eventually reverses an egalitarian ethic present at the time of Christian beginnings. Elizabeth Castelli and I have labeled this narrative, which could be called an apologetic or a foundational story, as a myth of Christian origins that posits the motivation for modern Christian inclusivity in Jesus' movement and message.[6] Castelli suggests that this reconstruction can be described as a "myth of Christian origins" in that it functions as a foundational narrative for modern Christian feminism.[7] This is not the first time similar reconstructions of Jesus' relationship to women have been called "myths."[8] In its more extreme forms, this reconstruction of Christian origins claims that the practice and teachings of Jesus established an unprecedented and revolutionary model for the full acceptance of the personhood of women, reversing earlier Jewish codes which defined women as mere chattels. Many Christian and Jewish feminist scholars, among them Amy-Jill Levine, Judith Plaskow, Elisabeth Schüssler Fiorenza and Susan Brooks Thistlethwaite, have challenged the continued tendency of Christians to contrast Jesus with a negative Jewish foil.[9] However, these efforts have not yet been successful in overturning the traditional reconstruction of Jesus' relationship to women in the context of his Jewish environment. The continued predominance of this understanding of Jesus in scholarly literature, seminary classrooms, and the popular press calls for further analysis of its apologetic function in Christian discourse, and requires an ongoing reassessment in light of new historical evidence.

The Standard Christian Reconstruction

Most Christian reconstructions of Jesus' relationship to women begin with discussions of the position of women within ancient Mediterranean cultures – usually Greek, Roman and Jewish – which serve as a background for the emergence of Christianity.[10] In these discussions the portrayal of women in Judaism is profoundly negative. Jewish women of antiquity are described as having no rights in inheritance, marriage, or divorce – indeed, they can be dismissed by their husbands for burning their suppers. These women, it is argued, were not allowed to serve meals or eat with men, and were unduly burdened by restrictive purity regulations surrounding childbirth and menstruation. Not persons before the law but mere chattels, women are portrayed as being unable to serve as witnesses in Jewish courts. Women's roles in Jewish institutions are portrayed as equally restricted, and it is commonly noted that they were exempt from such religious obligations as study and prayer, were segregated from men in special women's "courts" in the Jerusalem temple and in "galleries" in synagogues, and were banned not only from studying the Torah, but from any form of education generally. Furthermore, it is regularly asserted that the restriction of Jewish women to household roles led to their virtual absence from public places, or at least to laws prohibiting men from speaking to them in public, and to the exclusion from all leadership functions in ancient synagogues. Although the diversity of Jewish women's experience particularly in the Diaspora is sometimes acknowledged, this rarely affects the overall characterization of women's place in Jewish communities. Most often invoked as the culprits in this overwhelming Jewish patriarchy are "rabbis," identified either individually or as a group, or alluded to by a continued appeal to Rabbinic sources in the Mishnah or the Talmud. Such Jews, it is suggested, arose every morning to thank God that he had not made them a Gentile, a slave or a woman.[11]

This terrible fate of Jewish women is then compared to that of Greek, Roman and other Hellenistic women, who were also oppressed, but not as badly as their Jewish sisters. During the Roman period non-Jewish women gained increased rights in inheritance and divorce proceedings, had freer access to education, and could own, inherit and transfer property. They are also seen as active participants in various philosophical groups, voluntary associations, and such new and interesting religions as the Isis cult in which they even held leadership roles. In contrast, Jewish women were largely unaffected by the legal and cultural changes which swirled around them, and if they were so affected, it was only in the Diaspora. Palestine is characterized as a conservative enclave or Jewish backwater. Even should the possibility of Hellenistic influence be acknowledged for parts of Palestine, such influence is then confined to urban areas, or perhaps to Jerusalem; it is never imagined to have affected rural areas, and especially not Galilee.[12]

Jesus is then projected against this drastically negative cultural background. His attention to the concerns of women is noted, as is his willingness to talk to women or even to touch them in public. Other aspects of the gospels' portrayals are rehearsed: Jesus heals women and uses them as examples in his parables and teaching. In a Jewish culture which devalues women, Jesus allows women to be his disciples, even to join his male disciples on their journeys in the Palestinian countryside. Especially popular is the story of Mary and Martha (Luke 10:38–42), commonly described as showing Jesus' acceptance of a woman as a rabbinical student: in complete opposition to Jewish tradition, Mary sits at Jesus' feet and receives instruction. Jesus' prohibition of divorce is considered equally challenging to Jewish restrictions on women since it presumes the equal responsibility of men and women for maintaining the marriage bond. For these and other positive actions toward women, Jesus is called a "feminist,"[13] and his level of acceptance of women labeled "revolutionary,"[14] "radical,"[15] "unique,"[16] "reformational,"[17] or even "unprecedented"[18] in the ancient world, especially in Palestine. Even those find Jesus uninterested in social revolution still maintain this basic reconstruction insofar as Judaism is concerned.[19] Jesus' treatment of women is thus highlighted against the bleak and stultifying tapestry of ancient Judaism, whether it be Rabbinic or Palestinian. Thus, according to many Christian writers, Christianity began with a revolutionary surge that quite reversed the preceding history of women's oppression.

But the all too familiar myth continues, this time of pristine origins did not last. This revolutionary teaching was eventually overcome, either by a reasserting of Jewish tradition (especially in the case of Paul),[20] or by the encroachment of pagan or Hellenistic conservatism,[21] or because of the threat of gnosticism, which afforded more roles for women.[22] By the second or the third centuries the reversal is seen as complete. To attain acceptability, the church finally succumbs to the dominant cultural values of the Roman world.[23] The result is the transformation of a revolutionary, egalitarian movement into an institutionalized church controlled by "bishops,"[24] a "male monopoly,"[25] "male hierarchies"[26] "orders,"[27] or a leadership structure patterned after the "Jewish priesthood."[28] The struggle over the role of women in early Christianity is thus portrayed as an intrinsically Christian struggle against other cultural patterns, pagan and Jewish alike, which have not benefitted from similar revolutionary insight.

Historical Reconstruction or Foundational Myth?

We have seen this story before. In his discussion of Christian comparisons of early Christianity to the mystery religions, Jonathan Z. Smith has shown that Protestant anti-Catholic apologetics and Protestant historical models shape Christian reconstructions of early Christianity. True pristine Christianity (Protestantism) gives way to pagan sacramental mysteries (Catholicism).[29] Similarly, Christians appeal to gospel traditions about Jesus to define the true teaching of the church before it became corrupted into the male monarchical episcopate of Roman Catholicism. In this model Christian origins are partly shaped by the rhetoric of Protestant anti-Catholic apologetics. Reformation history is projected back on to early Christian history.[30]

Second, Smith shows that Christian comparisons between Christianity and its pagan environment claim uniqueness for the "Christ event."[31] Similarly, the majority of Christian descriptions contrast Jesus' views on women to those of all other cultures during his time. While the language of incomparability is most often used to characterize Jesus' death and resurrection, recent reconstructions of the female roles in early Christianity employ this same language to describe his attitudes toward women. The ontological value of Jesus (i.e., as "revelation") is transferred to the historical level.[32] Jesus is "unique," "unprecedented," or "revolutionary," because his ideas about women set him apart from his environment. This view of Jesus' relationship to women has even filtered into the popular press. For example, according to theologian, priest, sociologist, and novelist Andrew M. Greeley:

> Jesus treated women with so much respect and so much awareness of their fundamental equality that he was virtually unique among the leaders and teachers of his own time. Indeed, some

> theologians suggest that this uniqueness is in itself enough to prove the special relationship with God that Christianity claims for Jesus.[33]

Once again the theological assertion of the unprecedented disclosure of God in Christ is transmuted into an historical claim for Jesus in relation to his environment.

Such uniqueness requires isolation. Jonathan Z. Smith has further illustrated the role of Jewish "backgrounds" in Christian claims for the singularity of the early church within its social and historical context. Smith writes,

> In this latter endeavor, Judaism has served a double (or, duplicitous) function. On the one hand it has provided apologetic scholars with an insulation for early Christianity, guarding it against 'influence' from its 'environment.' On the other hand, it has been presented by the very same scholars as an object to be transcended by early Christianity.[34]

Not only has the second function – that of a negative foil over against Christianity, long been recognized as a major source of Christian feminist discourse,[35] but Smith's discussion of the use of Judaism as a vehicle of insulation against "Hellenism" is particularly illuminating in understanding what is ultimately at stake in recent disputes over the Hellenization of Palestine, especially Galilee. Smith shows how theories about the insulation of Judaism from its Hellenistic environment contribute to the protection of Christian uniqueness.[36] Thus, in reconstructions of early Christian origins, Christian scholars often distinguish between the categories of "Judaism" and "Hellenism" as well as between "Palestinian Judaism" and "Hellenistic Judaism." Likewise, New Testament scholars posit historical development from "Palestinian" Christianity (early, insulated, genuine) to "Hellenistic" or "Gentile" Christianity (late, influenced by its environment). As an intra-Jewish movement earliest Christianity is also pictured as being culturally distinct from its larger environment, thereby assuring the uniqueness of its message.[37]

When viewed in this larger context of Christian discourse on Judaism and Hellenism, discussions of Jesus' relationship to women can be seen to use Judaism in precisely the same manner. The Judaism of Jesus' day is characterized as "Jewish" not "Hellenistic." In the interests of Christian apologetics, Judaism must seem utterly "Jewish" and patriarchal so that Jesus can supersede it. But since research continues to show how thoroughly Hellenistic culture pervaded Diaspora communities, "Palestinian Judaism" must also seem free of Hellenistic influence: Jesus supersedes a Judaism which is unaffected by the presumabley freer habits of Jewish women in the Diaspora. Moreover, as archaeological evidence continues to illustrate the impact of Hellenistic culture on Palestine, Galilee must then be shown as insulated from Hellenistic culture. The pattern continues with the increasing finds of scholarship: the difference between Lower Galilee and Upper Galilee must be emphasized, assertions made that rural areas were insulated from urban areas, and so on.

It is possible, of course, to recognize regional differences between Galilee and Judea without suggesting that there was no interaction, travel, or trade between the two.[38] To say that Roman Palestine by the time of Jesus had been Hellenized is not to imply that Jewish culture or identity was obliterated, but rather to illustrate that there was a diversity of Jewish culture even in Palestine, which mirrored a diversity that had always existed in Judaism more generally.[39] There was never a singular monolithic Judaism to begin with. Biblical texts illustrate ongoing social interaction between Israel, Judah and cultures that flourished both within and along their borders.[40]

This does not mean that there were not strategies of resistance against certain customs or ideas perceived as foreign, especially idolatry.[41] Post-Maccabean art in particular, while employing Hellenistic artistic motifs, also clearly reflects Jewish cultural nuances, in that it avoids human and animal representation. It is the art of pre-Maccabean Palestine and Late Antiquity, not Second Temple Herodian Palestine, that features extensive use of Hellenistic figurative motifs.[42]

The point remains, however, that Hellenistic culture became a part of the cultural mix of Palestine and fostered further cultural diversity by the time of Jesus. Greek language, customs and certain cultural institutions became part of the Jewish cultural landscape hundreds of years before Jesus was born. Continued haggling over the extent of Hellenization does not erase the inscriptional, material, literary, and documentary evidence that exists in both Judea and Galilee. Even if the population estimates for Galilee have been exaggerated, making a large cosmopolitan environment less likely in this area,[43] and even if we cannot imagine a full blown market economy in ancient Palestine,[44] the evidence of the widespread use of Greek as the dominant, culturally privileged language throughout Palestine, even in Galilee, and the great likelihood that Jesus was at least bilingual (in Greek and Aramaic) cannot be ignored.[45] Not only do texts like the Wisdom of Solomon or Ben Sira demonstrate the inroads of Hellenistic philosophy and rhetoric into Jewish scribal contexts, but Rabbinic literature also reflects engagement with Hellenistic rhetoric, mythology and culture.[46] The sharp distinctions among "Hellenistic," "Jewish" and "Palestinian" cultures thus create a false picture by obscuring the cultural and religious complexity of ancient Judaism. This complexity also allows for greater cultural affinity between the Jerusalem church and the Hellenistic mission, as well as between Jesus and Paul.

Furthermore, it must be recognized that discussion about the position of Jewish women in Roman Palestine are shaped in no small degree by what is ultimately at stake. If some Jewish women in Roman Palestine enjoyed the freedoms of other Roman women, then Palestinian Jewish women were not singularly oppressed. If women in Roman Palestine weren't singularly oppressed, then Jesus' attitude towards women was neither "revolutionary" nor "unique." However, given the clear apologetic function of this reconstruction of women in early Christianity, its basic outlines must be abandoned both because it serves a theological rather than historical purpose and because it does so at the expense of Judaism. The reconstruction of the Jesus movement as a time of Edenic equality and egalitarianism for women is a myth of Christian origins which follows set narrative pattern common to a number of foundational myths. As an historical reconstruction of Christian origins, therefore, it is difficult to sustain.

Correcting the Myths

Certain feminist scholars, especially Bernadette Brooten, Ross Kraemer, Amy-Jill Levine and Elisabeth Schüssler Fiorenza have attempted to correct aspects of this reconstruction of early Christianity and Judaism, particularly because of its anti-Judaic bias.[47] These scholars have emphasized the diversity and progressivism present within ancient Judaism, both in Palestine and the Diaspora. When it comes to Christology, however, despite this ongoing discussion among Jewish and Christian feminist scholars, most Christian writers, even some Christian feminists, continue to contrast Jesus with his Jewish environment. Susan Brooks Thistlethwaite suggests that this tendency in

Christian theology is difficult to overcome in a society that remains structurally anti-Semitic.[48] Many books promoting Jesus' revolutionary stance in regards to women remain popular in Christian seminaries, particularly books by biblical (Evangelical) feminists.[49] Recent books and articles on women and Jesus or the New Testament continue this trend and perpetuate an outdated understanding of women's role in Hellenistic Judaism.[50] General textbooks now widely used in women's history courses American colleges and universities repeat the above outlined reconstruction of Jesus' message and his relationship to women, and clearly contrast him with a Jewish environment, rather than place him in the Greco-Roman world he inhabited.[51] According to these texts, the gospel stories about Jesus reflect a "marked change" and "break from Jewish custom."[52] Or, Jesus' words and actions in regards to women were "new and surprising" in that he "rejected much that earlier cultures had taken for granted" by preaching "the equality of all believers" in the context of "Roman dominated Hebrew Palestine"[53] and "for a brief moment egalitarianism reigned" in early Christianity.[54] Thus, the basic thesis that Jesus had feminist leanings has gone largely unchallenged.[55] This has muted the critique of the mythic function of "Jesus the feminist" reconstructions in feminist and womanist Christological constructions,[56] and has contributed to the continued uncritical acceptance of the basic outlines of this thesis in women's history textbooks.[57]

The most significant advance from the "Jesus the Feminist" reconstructions of the 1970's is the work of Elisabeth Schüssler Fiorenza. Schüssler Fiorenza's groundbreaking book *In Memory of Her* was the first to begin a reconstruction of early Christian origins from a critical feminist perspective with the assumption of women's active agency in early Judaism and Christianity. She also included a critique of anti-Judaism in Christian feminist discourse. Since the publication of *In Memory of Her* new information about women in Hellenistic Judaism has confirmed her assumption of a progressive tendency within ancient Judaism.[58] Following her lead, many Christian writers and biblical scholars now modify, or at least nuance their discussions comparing Judaism and early Christianity.[59] In particular, certin Christian feminist and womanist theologians now modify their Christological formulations.[60] Research into Hellenistic Jewish women's history has buttressed such modifications: recent scholarship provides an analysis of the images of women in Jewish Hellenistic literature and documentary sources, and brings a continued challenge to the uncritical use of Rabbinic sources. Many scholars of Hellenistic Judaism now argue that these sources, reflecting as they do later halakhic ideals, do not reflect first century Jewish and Palestinian practice,[61] and in any case they contain diverse opinions on women's roles.[62]

Yet, despite Schüssler Fiorenza's intentions to the contrary, the reconstruction of Jesus' movement in *In Memory of Her* reinforces the "Jesus the feminist" model that preceded her.[63] First, since Schüssler Fiorenza is unable to demonstrate a more progressive Judaism, her reconstruction still sets Jesus apart from his environment and does so to make a theological point in order to establish a biblical foundation for modern feminist theology. As such, as Elizabeth Castelli has suggested,[64] her reconstruction functions as a foundational narrative for modern Christian feminism. Second, although Schüssler Fiorenza claims that Jesus' movement was one among several renewal movements of his time, Jesus' "discipleship of equals" remains without real parallel in first century Palestine.[65] She identifies no other comparable renewal movement within ancient Judaism.[66] Neither does she document the "critical feminist impulse" nor the "emancipatory Jewish framework" that her own work presupposed,[67] save by means of an appeal to the book of Judith.[68] Judith is not only a fictional work that likely tells us little about the lives of real ancient Jewish women, but the narrative leaves us at the end of the story with a domesticated heroine.[69]

Third, Schüssler Fiorenza still juxtaposes Jesus over against Judaism by emphasizing Jesus' reinterpretation of the Jewish understanding of election, as well as his rejection of purity, particularly in his open table practice. According to Schüssler Fiorenza, Jesus' Sophia inspired message fostered an inclusive community of the Kingdom for all Israelites: he preached "wholeness" in contrast to "holiness:" "Not the holiness of the elect but the wholeness *of all* is the central vision of Jesus."[70] In her view this central egalitarian message forms the ultimate basis for early Christian equality "in Christ."[71]

From this a fourth problem emerges. If Jesus preached an explicitly egalitarian message that benefitted women, this would not necessarily make him un-Jewish, although it seems doubtful that in first century Judaism or Greco-Roman culture there existed any examples of egalitarianism as moderns understand it. Thus it is doubtful that

Jesus' message directly fostered an egalitarian program directed toward women as women, although his message addressed issues important to women (as to men).[72] Finally, Schüssler Fiorenza still attributes the decline of the status of women in early Christianity largely to the encroachment of Greco-Roman social institutions.[73] It is more likely that political, economic, and social changes affecting all of Greco-Roman society contributed to the conservative trends in social morality from the first to third centuries which occasioned subsequent changes in women's roles in early Christianity. These changes are not specifically Christian.[74] Thus, in spite of the organizing metaphor of "ongoing struggle" that is central to her book,[75] and her stated intent to displace earlier paradigms of Christian uniqueness,[76] the book *In Memory of Her* still creates the illusion that early Christianity was a special (albeit Jewish) emancipatory movement founded on the liberating message of Jesus which later fell into institutionalized decay. Although her stated task was to distinguish between Jesus and the subsequent Jesus movements behind the gospels,[77] she in fact went on to make claims for the theology of Jesus, locating a challenge to patriarchy, and thus the theological basis for feminism, in Jesus' teaching itself.[78]

Jesus, Miriam's Child, Sophia's Prophet develops themes from *In Memory of Her* in its elaboration of Schüssler Fiorenza's method of feminist critical hermeneutics, a continued critique of anti-Judaism in Christian theology, and a fuller development of the significance of Sophia in the construction of feminist Christology. Although Schüssler Fiorenza now acknowledges that Jesus' teaching had patriarchal aspects,[79] she still maintains her basic thesis that Jesus as the prophet of Sophia sought to abolish the patriarchal family, challenged the oppressive Roman imperial system in his proclamation of the "Kingdom of God," and performed healings of women as well as welcomed them, the poor and other disenfranchised groups to his inclusive table community.[80]

Schüssler Fiorenza has resisted critiques of her work on the basis that she did not intend to reconstruct "the historical Jesus" (or even early Christianity) in view of the subjectivity of such an undertaking: scholars who attempt this task merely reconstruct a Jesus "in their own image and likeness" without making clear their own ideological interests.[81] *Jesus, Miriam's Child,* is particularly critical of recent discussions in historical Jesus studies, which she characterizes as exercises in "historical positivism" that rely on questionable theories of layering in Q and create un-Jewish Jesuses.[82] Because of her suspicion that feminist work is easily co-opted by "malestream" academic theories, in this recent work Schüssler Fiorenza maintains a critical distance from mainstream historical biblical criticism on the one hand, and post-modernism on the other.[83] Women who take over historical-critical methodologies common in the academy, she argues, are in danger not only of being co-opted by "malestream" political interests inherent in these methods but of reinscribing the androcentrism of the biblical texts themselves.[84] Elizabeth Castelli has criticized Schüssler Fiorenza's similar sentiments concerning feminist scholars in religion who use "malestream" postmodernist theories.[85] Thus, Schüssler Fiorenza distances herself from the work of both historical-critical feminist scholars on the one hand, and post-modernist feminist scholars on the other. The Bible and Culture Collective has argued that by doing this Schüssler Fiorenza creates a dichotomy between "good feminists" who follow her method of theological reconstruction, and "bad feminists" (so-called "gender feminists") who do not.[86] This in turn creates what historian Joan Scott has called a false dichotomy between theory and politics.[87] Schüssler Fiorenza has attempted to answer these criticisms by claiming that she has not rejected the use of postmodern or other "malestream" theories, as her own work is "firmly rooted in historical and rhetorical biblical method as well as feminist theory."[88] Rather she advocates filtering these methods "through a critical feminist lens before using them."[89] What this means is that scholarship characterizing itself as feminist must produce research that is useful for effecting change in modern society.[90] I would contend that for Schüssler Fiorenza such scholarship must be a theological force in the community or a catalyst for change in society in order to be called "feminist."[91] Even the classic "Jesus the feminist" reconstruction – which she has attempted to replace because of its anti-Judaic overtones – remains for Schüssler Fiorenza such a force.[92]

Further, Schüssler Fiorenza's criticism of the methods of "malestream" biblical scholars is inconsistent with her own appropriation of these methods to produce her reconstructions. For example, one of her sharpest attacks on current "Newest Quest" scholars such as John Dominic Crossan and the other Fellows of the Jesus Seminar is that they are dependent on a particular stratigraphy of Q that was established (admittedly not without controversy) by John Kloppenborg's meticulous textual analysis.[93] Yet, large portions of her own reconstruction, especially her reconstruction of the role of women in the transmission of the "words of Sophia" by Q prophets, presupposes the reality of Q as a document and the existence of the "Q community" assumed by Q scholars.[94] Further, she puts forward her own layering of the Q document based on a dichotomy of male and female transmitters of tradition, by claiming the exclusivistic language of Jesus' relationship to the "Father" as "Son" found in QMt 11:25-27 is a later masculinization of an earlier feminine sophialogy found in Q. Although she fully acknowledges that this masculinization of Wisdom can be traced back to Jewish Wisdom speculation,[95] this does not deter her from suggesting that QMt 11:25-27 is a late introduction into Q traditions without any textual or analytical support. Here Schüssler Fiorenza ignores Luise Schottroff's rejection of the usefulness of Wisdom traditions for feminist reconstructions of Jesus traditions, given the *Sitz im Leben* of Wisdom speculation in the instruction of wealthy young men.[96] The understanding of Wisdom as "Son" in relationship to a "Father" is a component of Wisdom speculation generally, and it should not be viewed as an indication of a separate "layer" of Q traditions merely on the basis of its masculinized nature. Schüssler Fiorenza also tries to show that the "empty tomb" traditions featuring women are as early as the list of male witnesses to the resurrection found in the Pauline creed (1 Cor 15:3-11) by connecting them to the Q matrix of Sophia's prophets.[97] Not only is this unlikely, given that the empty tomb stories have no tradition historical connection with Q, originating as they do with Mark, or perhaps independently in John, but by making this argument Schüssler Fiorenza shows that she accepts the very "commonsense" reasoning of historical priority which she claims to reject.[98]

Finally, Schüssler Fiorenza continues to express puzzlement over the inability of certain feminist scholars to accept her reconstruction of Jesus' movement in terms of particularity within an emancipatory Jewish framework.[99] She resists historical-critical challenges by other feminist scholars to the basic tenets of her reconstruction of an egalitarian movement. Within her framework of the ekklesia of wo/men, "we can no longer argue that, for instance, women might not have been members of the communities that produced the Sayings Source Q."[100] However, given that her Jesus remains unique in Palestine in his teaching of egalitarian reform, there appears to be merit in the continued concern of certain feminists that Schüssler Fiorenza's reconstruction remains somewhat structurally anti-Judaic, although clearly an advance from the "Jesus the feminist" reconstructions of the 1970s, in spite of Schüssler Fiorenza's obvious intent to the contrary.[101] (Books can, after all, prove to have discursive functions contrary to an author's purpose).

Her continued defense of this thesis in light of the identification of her reconstruction as an exercise in Christian mythmaking does nothing to respond to this critique, nor does she address the clear evidence presented of the pervasive presence for social change throughout the Greco-Roman world.[102] She admits her reconstruction of a "discipleship of equals" is merely "possible" to imagine, yet asserts that a "possible" reconstruction should be given equal weight to what is probable or plausible.[103] The assertion that Jesus fostered an egalitarian movement targeting social inequality between the sexes not only flies in the face of evidence to the contrary, but still reinforces a structurally anti-Judaic model.[104] Some reconstructions are more probable than others, and not all projects define themselves as theological in intent, as hers does. Although it is possible that Jesus was a teacher of an egalitarianism that fostered a vision of social equality, it is unlikely. A review of much of the evidence, even the evidence used by Schüssler Fiorenza, Crossan and others, belies the reconstruction of Jesus as a Sophia inspired prophet who fostered a new egalitarian movement of social equality.[105] Schüssler Fiorenza claimed a "critical feminist impulse that came to the fore in the vision and ministry of Jesus."[106] Crossan proposed that Jesus' "radical egalitarianism" extended to women.[107] A review of the evidence about the historical Jesus in the context of ancient Palestinian Judaism is in order.

Women and Ancient Judaism

The evidence indeed suggests that in first century Judaism women lived lives similar to those of their Gentile counterparts, and that a monolithic view of Jewish women's experience based on a few sources is no longer possible to maintain. Since all contemporary Mediterranean societies were highly patriarchal, it is no longer possible to claim that Jewish women were more oppressed than others of the time. Jewish families were indistinguishable from other Greco-Roman families insofar as their basic relationships are concerned. Cultural values governing relationships between Jewish mothers and daughters, parents and children, masters and slaves are quite in line with those of Greco-Roman society.[108] Hellenistic Jewish meal customs and ideology are also indistinguishable from those of other Greco-Roman people, and furthermore reflect perceptible cultural changes affecting all of Hellenistic society.[109] Even the communal meals at Qumran reflect the basic patterns of Greco-Roman communal meals.[110] There is evidence that some Jewish women had the right to divorce their husbands as did their Roman counterparts;[111] some were leaders and patronesses of their synagogues;[112] some Jewish women were educated in philosophy;[113] some daughters were instructed in Torah and other biblical texts, perhaps to the point that they could cite scripture;[114] other Jewish women, even in Palestine, knew Greek.[115] Moreover, new research on Hellenistic Jewish literature demonstrates not only its richness and diversity, but also the potential for social progressivism within Hellenistic Judaism.[116] Finally, not only is the declaration of the equality before God of men, women, slaves, Jews, and Gentiles (comparable to Gal 3:28) to be found in Rabbinic contexts, but the tripartite distinction of the Jewish benediction declaring gratitude for not being born a woman, a slave, or a foreigner is also found in Hellenistic settings.[117] Thus, it is probable that both formulations are proverbial and reflect a diversity of attitudes about women, slaves and foreigners in the Greco-Roman world, rather than positive Christian or negative Jewish ethics respectively.

Nor is it the case that Jewish women were completely segregated from religious life and practice. There is no evidence that they were segregated from men in ancient synagogues.[118] Furthermore, the Women's Court in the Jerusalem temple was an innovation of Herod's restoration,[119] and in light of the temple layout of progressively more restricted courtyards, would require gender segregation in only a single sacred courtyard. In the so-called "Women's Court" women would have mixed freely with men, even priests.[120] That means that before 4 B.C.E. women would have had freer access to the temple precincts and suggests that the exclusion of women from the court of men was a Hellenistic innovation.[121] It seems likely that women participated in the religious life of the Temple, and visited Jerusalem for pilgrim festivals and prayer.[122] Moreover, although Rabbinic literature reflects great interest in regulating male contact with menstruants,[123] there is little evidence either way about whether Hellenistic Jewish women adhered to laws of ritual purity surrounding menstruation and childbirth.[124] Further, since such regulations were created to protect the purity of the temple, at the time of Jesus they may well have affected women only when residing in or visiting Jerusalem.[125] Many of the baths from the Second Temple period identified as "ritual baths" (*miqva'ot*) outside of Jerusalem, such as those in Jericho, Sepphoris, and Masada, were probably not baths used for ritual purification, but are rather modifications of Roman style cold stepped pools (*frigidaria*).[126] Thus it is difficult to maintain that Palestinian Jews of Jesus' time exhibited deep concerns for the ritual purity of women. After all, ritual purity is a common element of many ancient religions, including early Christianity.[127] Purity regulations regarding contact with corpses and bodily emissions, particularly before the entrance to holy sanctuaries and in preparation for prayer, were not only common in other ancient religions, but applied to men as well as women.[128] Further, the limitation of women's sexuality in this manner might not have seemed oppressive to ancient women whose birth control options were limited.[129]

The notion that Jewish women were somehow protected from Hellenization is impossible to maintain. It has long been recognized that a distinction between "Hellenism" and "Judaism" cannot be made for Hellenistic Judaism generally, even for Palestinian Judaism. The work of Martin Hengel, which canvassed literary, archaeological and inscriptional evidence, has shown that by as early as the mid-third century B.C.E. Hellenism pervaded Palestine to the extent that the daily lives of Jews there would have been all but indistinguishable from those of their Diaspora counterparts.[130] Many scholars in historical Jesus studies now recognize the extent to which Hellenistic culture had pervaded first century Palestine. This point has become important for several recent reconstructions of the historical Jesus.[131] It is significant that independent scholarly discussions among both historical Jesus scholars and scholars of Jewish women's history have reached similar conclusions concerning the Hellenization of Palestine in the first century and the uncritical use of late and diverse Rabbinic sources in reconstructing the social situation of its people. Archaeological evidence continues to confirm the presence of Hellenistic culture in Palestine, even in Galilee.[132] Although there is far less of a Hellenistic presence in upper Galilee and in rural areas than in lower Galilee and in urban areas, Hellenistic culture is by no means absent.[133] Indeed, given the accessibility of places like Sepphoris by means of major trade routes, it seems unlikely that villages like Nazareth which were in walking distance of such cities would have been somehow cut off from Hellenistic contact.[134] Given the economic interconnectedness of rural and urban areas in agrarian societies, it is more likely that rural people in Galilee would have traveled back and forth to urban centers to sell their goods and services.[135] This would be particularly the case for rural women, who are most often the members of peasant families to engage in the bartering, marketing of household goods.[136] In spite of Rabbinic ideals excluding women from the marketplace, incidental stories even from Rabbinic sources indicate that women – especially poor women – shopped and sold their own goods and produce in marketplaces and served as shopkeepers with their husbands, or even as innkeepers in their own homes.[137] To deny the existence of a full-blown market economy in Roman Palestine does not imply the complete isolation of Galilee from Judea or rural areas from urban areas, nor does it require a virtual negation of common marketing habits of peasants, especially peasant women, which are essential to their economic survival.[138] Thus, the notion that Galilee and Palestine were somehow "conservative enclaves" of Judaism unaffected by the cultural changes of the Greco-Roman world now seems impossible, or at very least highly unlikely.[139]

Thus, in view of the diversity of Jewish women's experience in the Diaspora, it is more reasonable to assume a similar diversity for Jewish women living in Roman Palestine.[140] Although it may well be that most Jewish women could not initiate divorce, evidence suggests that some Jewish women in Palestine exercised the right to divorce their husbands. Herod's sister Salome sent her husband Costobarus a bill of divorce, though admitedly this may be more a reflection of Roman legal practice.[141] And in a newly published early second century document from Palestine, a woman named Shelamzion acknowledges the receipt of several items from her former husband Eleazar, including a divorce bill she had sent to him.[142]Jewish marriage contracts from Elephantine Egypt dated from the fifth century B.C.E. and the Babatha archives from the Bar Kochba period (135 C.E.) which suggest similar marital rights of Jewish women have clear ancient Near Eastern antecedents.[143] And in Palestine women appear in supposedly unexpected political, religious and social contexts. Josephus records that the Zealot band of Simon bar Gioras included his wife and other women, as well as peasants and runaway slaves. In fact, Simon's wife and some of these women were at one point held hostage by a rival faction.[144] Although probably a member of the old ruling class,[145] Simon proclaimed freedom for slaves and the abolition of debt, a move which Josephus describes as tactical rather than altruistic.[146] It is interesting that Josephus nowhere criticizes Simon bar Gioras for the mixed nature of his band of revolutionaries, although the inclusion of women in Simon's entourage may have led other *sicarii* to view him with some suspicion.[147] We should also record that Pharisees were known for their influence among aristocratic women;[148] 6000 men, women and children followed an unnamed charismatic prophet into the Temple in 70 C.E.;[149] and that a few women numbered among John the Baptist's disciples.[150]

Moreover, evidence for the participation of Jewish women in communal meals with men also comes from Palestine. Herod's fortress as Machaerus had two dining rooms immediately alongside one another, one for women, and one for men.[151] This suggests at least on some occasion that men and women dined separately.[152] But Ben Sira mentions the presence of married women at meals with men.[153] Josephus records Imperial decrees securing funds for common meals among Jews that included women and children,[154] as well as complaints of Jewish envoys to Rome following the death of Herod the Great concerning the presence of Jewish wives and daughters at Roman style orgies.[155] This is probably an exaggerated description of respectable elite Jewish women attending court banquets. Although written in Egypt, both Third Maccabees and the Testament of Job also know of communal meals among Jews that included women and children.[156] The Passover Seder, of course, was celebrated by Jews everywhere and was one such communal meal that required the presence of both women and children for the meal. Wives are directed to recline alongside their husbands for the Seder meal, following progressive Hellenistic and Roman style.[157] Both the Mishnah and the Talmud indicate that the meal is to be taken reclining,[158] and while this evidence does not necessarily reflect first century practice, there may be good reason to consider it in this instance. G. H. R. Horsley cites the comment of E. Ferguson:

> It might be thought that this evidence is too late to confirm first-century practice; but the reason given for this posture in the Talmud, namely as a sign of freedom, is such a thoroughly Greek reason that one should conclude that the practice dates from the Hellenistic period.[159]

Other cultural influences from the Diaspora affected the private customs of women in Palestine. Some Jewish women in Roman Palestine even chose to represent themselves sporting the changing hairstyle fashions of the Imperial court.[160]

Furthermore, new appraisals of the sect at Qumran, although a matter of heated debate, have strongly questioned the characterization of this sect as an all-male monastic community.[161] In fact, women and children represent over thirty percent of all burials so far excavated at the Qumran site. These burials are not on the periphery of the regular graveyards as has previously been supposed, but are interspersed throughout the major gravesites.[162] Although the excavations represent only a small percentage of the total number of graves, the presence of women and children among those buried at Qumran has gone long ignored and unexplained. And yet, the texts of the Dead Sea Scrolls mention the presence of women and children in certain assemblies and liturgical celebrations[163] and regulate marriage and sexual intercourse for members of the group, especially by restricting polygamy and incest.[164] The Qumran texts further attest to the ability of women to give judicial testimony in corporate assemblies,[165] and contain elaborations of stories of heroines of the Hebrew Bible, such as an expanded song of Miriam, the sister of Moses[166] and a lengthy description of the beauty of Sarah.[167] Several Qumran scholars suggest that the Miriam expansion indicates a joint liturgy was practiced by men and women in the Qumran community, comparable to that which Philo suggests was practiced by the Therapeutae in Alexandria.[168] Other Qumran scholars have suggested that the clear references to women in the community indicates their full membership in the sect[169] and thus implies the presence of women and children at certain community meals, at least the Passover Seder.[170] Although it is possible that the references to women in the Scrolls could be theoretical or a mere reflection of Deuteronomic antecedents which presuppose their presence,[171] the mortuary evidence suggests the opposite.

Recent scholarly controversies over the nature of the Qumran community underscore the likelihood of cultural and social mixture like that increasingly being suggested for Palestine more generally. The communal meal structures of the Qumran community are thoroughly Greco-Roman.[172] The role of women in the group increasingly leads Qumran scholars to compare that community – if indeed monastic – with the Therapeutae of Alexandria, Egypt,[173] a Jewish monastic group that practiced communal meals including both men and women, followed by corporate worship and liturgy in after-dinner choirs.[174] Although the Dead Sea Scrolls also demonstrate that this was a community thoroughly immersed in a Jewish apocalyptic heritage and intensely interested in creating a ritually pure community patterned after the Temple priesthood it is fair to insist that recent studies of women's social roles confirm not only the inapplicability of many Rabbinic sources for determining first century Palestinian attitudes and practices, but demonstrates the powerful influence of Hellenistic and Roman culture on the women of Palestine.

Finally, as many have emphasized, it must not be forgotten that the movement initiated by Jesus was both Jewish and Palestinian. Both Jesus' teaching and the social configuration of his movement further illustrate the cultural diversity present in the Greco-Roman world and first century Palestine. This belies simplistic attempts to label Jesus, or Palestine more generally as either "Jewish" or "Hellenistic." While it seems likely that Jesus associated relatively freely with women, the pervasive presence of women in Jewish, Roman and Hellenistic societies generally serves to undermine the contention that this is a special characteristic of Jesus' movement or an outgrowth of his message of the Kingdom of God. The constituency of Jesus' movement may rather be seen to reflect changes in the larger Hellenistic society, or the social constituency of which he was a part.[175] Still, the coexistence of Graeco-Roman meal customs with an all-encompassing dedication to community purity and an apocalyptic eschatology in Qumran should caution us against exaggerating the apparently Hellenistic aspects of Jesus' teaching. Alas, in some recent reconstructions, Jesus no longer seems Jewish, but almost completely Greek.[176] This too seems to involve a blurring of the evidence, for which the work of G. Vermes, E. P. Sanders, Paula Fredricksen and others provides a needed balance.[177] In the end, it seems more reasonable that the diversity of Jewish women's experience found in the Diaspora should be assumed for some women in first century Palestine as well, and that a recognition of the wide variety of the evidence should caution us against simplistic portraits – whether of Jesus or the life of first century Palestinian women – on the basis of a false Hellenistic/Jewish dichotomy.

Chapter 2

Working Women in the Gospel of Mark

While some remain unconvinced, the gospel evidence has persuaded the majority of historical Jesus scholars that Jesus had women disciples who traveled with him as well as joined him for meals.[1] One major early gospel tradition, the Gospel of Mark, identifies Mary Magdalene, Mary the mother of James and Joses and Salome, as women who traveled with Jesus from the beginnings of his ministry in Galilee. The Markan material also suggests that the presence of women among Jesus' followers was a controversial characteristic of his movement. Mark 2:14–17 records both that Jesus was accused of reclining at table with "tax collectors and sinners" (the latter is a euphemism for "prostitutes") and that a group of women "followed and served" Jesus throughout his entire ministry (Mark 15:40–41). The accusation that Jesus associated with "tax collectors and sinners" also occurs in Q.[2] Mark's elaboration of this accusation into a narrative, however, is probably his own literary creation.[3] The descriptions of these women suggest that at least Mary Magdalene and Salome came from the lower classes of antiquity, and were either working women, hired servants, slaves or runaway slaves. No so, apparently, a woman named Joanna, who is reported to have left her husband at the court of Herod to follow Jesus. But the social class of Mary and Salome and the consequent implications concerning the social class of Jesus raise a problem. They render the social stratification of pre-industrial agrarian societies by Gerhard E. Lenski, so popular among New Testament and Historical Jesus scholars as a sociological model for first century Palestine, inappropriate for understanding the complexities of ancient society. This is particularly problematic given his omission of any slave or freedmen classes or any attention to the function of gender as well as class.[4] Reliance on Lenski's model among New Testament scholars has obscured the social diversity of Jesus' movement, the class concerns inherent in his teaching and activities, and the reasons for the presence of women disciples among Jesus' followers.

Women who Follow and Serve (Mark 15:40–41)

Discussions of women in Mark's narrative generally begin with Mark 15:40–41. This pericope can be shown to connect women not only to Jesus' group of disciples, but to meals with Jesus,[5] and it contains the one early gospel attestation that women followed Jesus during his ministry.[6] The introduction of the women into the events of the Passion narrative in Mark 15:40 is noticeably abrupt, and the lists of the women vary: 15:40–41 (three women), 47 (two women) and 16:1 (three women). This suggests that some source may lie behind the account of the women, or one or more pre-Markan traditions. Some scholars argue that Mark here relies on an early Passion source he shares with the Gospel of John. [7] Yet, since the lists of the women show only partial correspondence, and lists of two and three are common in folk narratives, [8] some have been inclined to see the had of the evangelist here. [9] However, I would argue against both a Passion story source and Markan invention on the grounds that the reference to the women constitutes and intrusion into the narrative flow, and that the women play no significant roles in Mark's gospel. Further, since it is true that lists of two and three are found in other oral traditions,[10] and since Mark's depiction of the women does not conform to the literary stereotypes of women in the noble death traditions he presupposes, the mention of the women here is best seen as the evangelist's adaption of an element of oral tradition.[11]

Like their male counterparts, the women form a subset of Jesus' followers with a core group of three (Peter, James and John/Mary Magdalene, Mary the Mother of James and Joses, Salome). Like the men, the women flee the scene, are frightened by a vision (the transfigured Jesus or the angel at the tomb), and do not do what they are told.[12] These women are said to both "follow" (ἀκολουθέω) him and "serve" (διακονέω) him, along with "many others" (ἄλλαι πολλαί).[13] Thus, like the male disciples, at least three women have accompanied Jesus throughout Galilee and all the way to Jerusalem. In Mark the group of the three named women is clearly distinguished from the many other women (Mark 15:41b, ἄλλαι πολλαί) who join Jesus for his final journey to Jerusalem. The "many other women" may have included a number of those who commonly traveled to Jerusalem for yearly festivals like the Passover.[14] However, this suggestion that crowds of women flocked along with Jesus on the way to Jerusalem may be an exaggeration.[15] Traditional evidence for the presence even a few women among Jesus' entourage could have been perceived by Mark as a crowd. John records no such crowd of women in John 19:25.

Mark's list of women is probably the earliest, and almost certainly the literary source for the lists of women in Matthew 27:55–56, Luke 8:1–3 and John 19:25. Matthew's list is most easily argued to be dependent on Mark's.[16] In fact, Matthew enhances the role of the women at the cross as disciples by moving forward the Markan reference to the large group of women (γυναῖκες πολλαί, Matt. 27:55, cf. Mark 15:41b) whose position he underscores with an emphatic αἵτινες in place of the Markan αἵ.[17] Even the lists of women in John and Luke often considered independent of Mark, can be argued as stemming from Mark 15:40–41. A gender analysis of John's accounts of the crucifixion, burial and empty tomb makes it unlikely that John preserves an independent witness to the women's presence at the crucifixion.[18] For example, in John's list of the women at the cross, Mary Magdalene is listed last, rather than being in her usual primary position. This presupposes the Markan list and serves to weaken her importance (John 19:25, cf. 15:40, 47; 16:1). Further, the nearness of the women to the cross and the emphasis on Jesus' mother are often considered Johannine constructions, theologically motivated, and historically implausible.[19] John has thus expanded a list of three women into four to correspond to the four soldiers (John 19:23).[20] Yet while John 2:12 clearly states that Jesus' mother traveled with him and his other disciples, Mary Magdalene is conspicuous by her absence early in the narrative. This is a further indication that John wishes to limit her significance among Jesus' retinue.[21]

Luke 8:1–3 may also be a Lukan redaction of Mark 15:40–41.[22] First, Luke omits any reference to the names of the women at the crucifixion scene proper, preferring to generalize the group of women gathered to view Jesus' death (Luke 23:49). Further, in the same verse Luke adds a group of Jesus' male acquaintances or friends to those witnessing the crucifixion: a group of male dining companions (lit. "friends," οἱ γνωστοί) joins the group of (unnamed) women (Luke

23:49).[23] In Luke these women are part of a larger group that includes men and women, but they are no longer part of a separate special group of women disciples. In fact, the significant correspondence between Mark 1:17 and Mark 15:41 that allows for the discipleship of the women in Mark all but disappears in Luke.[24] The absence of the women's names in Luke 23:49, combined with the use of διακονέω ("to serve") in Luke 8:1–3 makes it highly likely that Luke has split Mark 15:40–41 into two sections: 1) Luke 23:49, where a group of unnamed women "follow" Jesus (συνακολουθέω) at a distance at the crucifixion, and 2) Luke 8:1–3 where a group of named women and "many others" (ἕτεραι πολλαί, cf. Mark 15:41) join Jesus and the Twelve during their travels in the cities and villages of Galilee.[25] These women "provide" (διακονέω) not only for Jesus (as in Mark 15:41), but also the Twelve out of their personal resources (ἐκ τῶν ὑπαρχόντων αὐταῖς).[26] Luke also includes a list of three women at the scene of the empty tomb (Luke 24:10): Mary Magdalene, Mary the mother of James, and Joanna; but the mention of Mary the mother of James shows Luke's reliance here on Mark 16:1, not on Mark 15:40–41. In 8:1–3 then, rather than relying on special material, Luke is reworking Mark 15:40–41, representing the service of the women as acts of charity. They are not table servants as in Mark, but more akin to Greco-Roman patronesses. In Luke, this shift serves to limit the function of the women providing charity (διακονέω), while restricting them from leadership roles defined as διακονία ("ministry") which are reserved for men.[27] His narrative thus further reinforces a distinction between the women and the all male Twelve.

One of these women, named Joanna, is described as being respectably married to a steward of the court of Herod. This does not indicate that she is one of the elite, but rather a member of the "retainer class" according to Lenski's model. Retainers were dependent upon the aristocracy for their wealth.[28] However, here Lenski's model again needs modification, since in antiquity such retainers would not necessarily number among the elite; stewards of large households like that of Herod were commonly slaves or freedmen.[29] Lenski's model, although helpful, fails to illustrate the complexity of ancient society – particularly, as noted earlier, since Lenksi does not factor the institution of slavery into his analysis.[30] It is possible that Joanna could be the wife of a highly placed slave or freedman in Herod's court.[31] The name Chuza occurs in Nabatean and Syrian inscriptions in Aramaic as *Kuza* which suggests an Aramean connection. It is possible that Chuza, by means of his position at court, could have "married up" by wedding a well-to-do Hebrew free woman. Luke may thus intend for us to understand that the money Joanna contributes is her own. This description of the women as philanthropists conforms to Luke's overall interest in portraying Jesus' group and the early church as a quite socially acceptable movement. According to Luke even Jesus is no longer an artisan or carpenter, but spends much of his time hob-nobbing with the rich.[32] Therefore, since the Jesus movement and the early church are respectable, but by no means upper class,[33] these named women are not of the aristocracy, and hence their presence on the road with Jesus is not so scandalous as is usually supposed. This is in contrast to the clear overtones of scandal in the story about the sinful woman in Luke 7:36–50.[34] Here we find no indication that the presence of women is controversial or unusual.[35] The shift from the language of table service (in Mark) to that of charitable service (in Luke) erases the undertones of scandal present in the Mark 15:40–41 which connects the women followers of Jesus to meals, domestic service, and the lower classes.[36]

In short, the overall picture of Jesus' women followers as being able to support the movement financially shows Luke's own bias, and is unlikely to be historical. This depiction of the women among Jesus' followers as coming only from a higher social level is unparalleled in earlier sources such as Q, which at least suggests the socially mixed nature of Jesus' group.[37] In Luke's narrative these women are wealthy enough to provide financial support for Jesus and the Twelve out of gratitude for their having been healed of ailments or delivered from demonic possession.[38] The only name common between Luke 8:1–3 and Mark 15:40–41 is Mary Magdalene, which no doubt was fixed in the tradition.[39] Joanna and Susanna, however, should be seen as Luke's own additions to the narrative,[40] and may have been names of prominent women in his own community or chosen for literary reasons. Joanna is a Hebrew name for Hellenistic Jewish women and is attested in Palestine (occurring at least eight times).[41] The Hebrew name Susanna appears for Hellenistic Jewish women only in two inscriptions from Italy, outside of its use here and in the story of Susanna in the Apocrypha.[42] Luke 8:1–3 thus gives us little additional historical information about the actual names, status or situation of the women who followed Jesus during his lifetime. Of the two named women not found in Mark, only Joanna is likely to have been a real person from

Palestine who followed Jesus. The inscriptional evidence renders the reality of Susanna unlikely.[43]

To sum up, then, Mark remains our earliest source for the names and identity of the women who followed Jesus. Mark lists by name three women who were known to have followed Jesus from the very beginnings of his ministry in Galilee: Mary Magdalene, Mary the mother of James and Joses, and Salome (15:40–41). The other women, if not Markan exaggeration, seem to have journeyed with Jesus only for this last Passover visit to Jerusalem (15:41). Matthew's and John's lists vary from Mark's.[44] Matthew lists Mary Magdalene, Mary the mother of James and Joseph and the mother of the sons of Zebedee (Matt 27:55–56). John expands this list into four, including Jesus' mother, Jesus' aunt, Mary (wife of) Clopas, and Mary Magdalene.[45] Mark, in 15:47 and 16:1, varies the identification of the second Mary, by first calling her the mother of Joses and afterward the mother of James respectively. Matthew simplifies this to "the other Mary" (Matt 27:62; 28:1). In spite of these apparent similarities in the lists of women, it is unwise to conflate the names.[46] Nearly 50% of the women in second temple Palestine were named either Mary (Mariamne) or Salome. This means that every second woman in Palestine at the time of bore one of these two names.[47] Their popularity may well have been due to their association with the royal Hasmonean family: Salome derived from Queen Salomezion Alexandra, and Mariamne or Mary after Mariamne the Hasmonean, Herod the Great's beloved wife. A similar tendency is evident in male names: five early Hasmoneans (John, Simon, Judas, Eleazar, Jonathan and their father Mattathias) account for nearly 40% of men's names during the same period.[48] This reinforces the likelihood that Mark preserves the earliest and best list in terms of reflecting the Palestinian situation of Jesus, naming two Marys and one woman named Salome. Luke may plausibly provide us with a fourth, Joanna.

The Identity of the Women

About these women Mark tells us little. Mary Magdalene is the most fixed name of a woman disciple of Jesus in the tradition. She is named consistently in all four canonical gospels, as well as in the Gospel of Peter, the Gospel of Thomas, the Gospel of Mary, and numerous other non-canonical texts. In Gnostic literature Mary Magdalene is commonly Jesus' closest companion and an active participant in dialogues between the disciples and the spiritual Christ.[49] Rather than identifying her by the more common means of a male relative, Mary's name indicates that she came from Magdala, a village on the northwest shore of the Sea of Galilee, about three miles north of the city of Tiberias.[50] The identification of Mary with a particular geographical location puts emphasis on the character of that location, rather than on her family, father or a husband as a means of identifying her.[51] Magdala was one of the better known fishing towns along the Sea of Galilee, and was known to Josephus by the name Tarichea, meaning "salt fish." Josephus also mentions that the city had a hippodrome, which indicates its Hellenistic character.[52] Since Mark records that many of Jesus' first male followers came from the ranks of fishermen who worked along the Sea of Galilee (Mark 1:16–20), and that Mary Magdalene was with Jesus from his earliest travels in Galilee (15:40–41), it is quite likely that Mary Magdalene was a fisherwoman herself.[53]

Women among the working poor practiced many trades in antiquity; women could be shopkeepers, butchers, innkeepers, weavers, waitresses, shoemakers, prostitutes, professional mourners and musicians, or fishers. In rural areas women could run farms with their husbands, engage in a trade, or run inns in their homes; in towns and cities women shared the responsibility of managing small businesses.[54] Women rarely earned enough money to secure financial independence, but rather worked to support their families; poorer families usually required the labor of all family members in order to survive. In times of economic hardship, working women could be driven into prostitution (often, apparently, as a form of barter)[55] or even obliged to sell their children.[56] Household work was divided on the basis of gender – with women responsible for the management of the household and children, including grinding, baking, washing, cooking, textile production and the like, while commonly men worked in the fields (cf. Luke 17:34–35; Matt 24:40–41). This distinction was not absolute, however, as rural women and children also performed farm labor.[57] The realities of life for lower class women contributed to the elite perception and devaluation of their character, and led to the stereotyping of lower class women as promiscuous, whether this reputation was realized in the form of prostitution or not.[58] The association of Jesus with both working class women and at least one woman of a higher position could further explain the tradition associating him with "sinners/prostitutes" (Matt 21:31–32). Despite her standing, a woman like Joanna might well have been labeled a whore for her association with other women and men beneath her station.[59]

However, Mark gives no indication that Mary Magdalene or any of the women around Jesus are by actual vocation prostitutes. It is more reasonable to conclude on the basis of Mary Magdalene's town of origin that she met Jesus along the Sea of Galilee as did Simon Peter, Andrew James and John (Mark 1:14–20).[60] The longer ending of Mark records that Mary Magdalene was a former demoniac (Mark 16:9), a tradition that Luke also repeats (Luke 8:2).[61] Reports of Jesus' cure of those characterized as demon-possessed (see e.g. Luke/Q 11:14–23) support Luke's assertion that certain women in his company were healed of various mental illnesses or madness (Q 11:20).[62] In spite of this repeated theme, however, there is no narrative in the gospels in which Jesus cures Mary Magdalene or any other woman of madness, although Luke records Paul's casting out of a spirit of fortune-telling from a slavegirl in Jesus' name (Acts 16:16–18). The association of Mary Magdalene with demon possession serves to connect her to frequent tomb visitation and the contact with spirits of the dead (necromancy).[63] In Mark, this association devalues her witness to the resurrection, and functions to bar her from any connection to the Twelve (c.f. the rejection of the Gerasene demoniac in Mark 5:18–19).[64] However, given that in antiquity possession by gods or spirits was associated with creativity and prophetic powers, any such narrative portrayal of Jesus' women followers would likely be problematic.[65] In view of the reports that Jesus himself was thought to be mad (John 8:48; Mark 3:20–21) and possessed by a demon – indeed the prince of demons, Beelzebul (Mark 3:22), this charge of demon-possession places Mary Magdalene not in the category of the Peter and Twelve, but that of Jesus, or even John the Baptist (Q 7:33). Since men with such characteristics were commonly labeled as prophets,[66] this charge against Mary Magdalene strongly suggests that she might be identified not merely as a follower of Jesus, but as a prophet who was later demoted by an early Christian tradition that also demoted John.[67] Jesus, John and Mary would then have all exhibited similar erratic behavior at an early point in their lives.[68] Although she is likely only one of many to have received exorcism from Jesus' hand, Mary's prominence in early Christian tradition sets her apart from others merely healed by Jesus. If indeed she was a prophet similar to Jesus and

John, her words and sayings either were simply lost, or were incorporated into the Jesus tradition itself. She too began her life in a Galilean village, as a fisherwoman from the village of Magdala, who fished alongside men on the shores of the Sea of Galilee as did many working women of the area. Fisherwoman or not, such a working class woman was one of the several kinds of women who joined Jesus and his retinue.

Of the other two women named by Mark we know even less. Mark probably intends for us to understand Mary the mother of James and Joses to be the mother of Jesus (cf. Mark 6:3),[69] according to which Mary also had two other sons, Jude and Simon, and an unspecified number of unnamed daughters. If this is the case, then her presence at the crucifixion with Mary Magdalene and her subsequent desertion of the empty tomb would contribute not only to Mark's theme of the failure of the disciples, but the Markan theme of the failure of Jesus' family as well.[70] The association of this Mary with Jesus' mother in Mark 6:3 would in part explain John's placement of Jesus' mother both among Jesus' traveling retinue in John 2:12 and at the cross in John 19:25. The Acts of the Apostles also attests to the presence of Mary among Jesus's disciples (Acts 1:14), as do several extra-canonical works.[71] The only other Markan report concerning Jesus' mother is that her son bore her name and not his father's: Jesus is a "carpenter" (or 'artisan,' τέκτων), the son of Mary" (Mark 6:3). Several other manuscripts, including p45, read, "Is this not the son of a carpenter and Mary? (τοῦ τέκτονος υἱός or τοῦ τέκτων ὁ υἱός).[72] The intent of the question is to underscore the ordinariness of Jesus' origins and birth. He is the son of well-known locals.[73] The identification of Jesus by his mother's name could imply that Mary was from a higher social class or held a higher social status than her husband, or it may simply reflect her status and position in the early church. It was common in Second Temple Judaism for a man to be known by his mother's name when his mother was of a higher rank than his father. In antiquity, status was a matter of birth, not necessarily wealth. This Markan designation may in part explain Luke's connection of Mary to a priestly family (Luke 1–2) as well as later legends suggesting that Mary came from the city of Sepphoris rather than the paltry village of Nazareth.[74] This might suggest that Jesus came from a socially mixed background, a not uncommon occurrence among the ranks of slaves, freedmen, and the free poor.[75] Here again the Lenski model, which creates an illusion of unbending categories of class, does not really illustrate the more fluid situation of the lower classes in Greco-Roman antiquity.[76] It is thus less likely that the designation of Jesus as "the son of Mary" suggests the stain of illegitimacy.[77] This is not to deny that a first century illegitimacy tradition concerning Jesus arose (cf. Thomas 105; John 8:41; Matt 1), but the designation "son of Mary" in Mark 6:3 may not be the source of the rumor.[78] The infancy narratives of Matthew and Luke (Matt 1–2; Luke 1–2), which contain later legendary material about Jesus' birth, probably give us little further historical information about Jesus' mother. Later infancy gospels, such as the *Protevangelium (Infancy Gospel) of James* or *Pseudo-Matthew*, give us even less.[79]

About Salome we also know very little, though after Mary Magdalene, she is the most often mentioned woman disciple of Jesus in early Christian literature. She is mentioned in the Secret Gospel of Mark as being associated with Jesus' family,[80] she appears in the Gospel of Thomas on a dining couch with Jesus,[81] and like Mary Magdalene she engages in dialogues with Jesus in extra-biblical sources, most notably in the Gospel of the Egyptians quoted by Clement of Alexandria.[82] In a Q like section of the Manichaean Psalms, Salome joins Mary Magdalene and other women in a group of wandering, ascetic itinerants.[83] Later stories found in such books as the Infancy Gospel of James, which identify the disciple Salome as Mary's midwife at the birth of Jesus, are no doubt legendary.[84] We can only speculate about Salome's relationship to Jesus or her family background. Still, it seems reasonable to conclude that two women named Salome and Mary Magdalene traveled with Jesus during his lifetime and were among his closest followers. Since they are here joined by Jesus' mother, Mark's theme of enmity between Jesus and his family serves to diminish the role of women, and especially that of his mother, among Jesus' disciples.[85] This further suggests that in 15:40–41 Mark is preserving a tradition about women disciples which he finds uncomfortable, but cannot deny.[86] Mark underscores their discipleship by his use of ἀκολουθέω ("follow") and διακονέω ("serve"). The two Marys and Salome follow and serve Jesus from the time of his early ministry in Galilee.

Service and Social Class

Still, the undercurrent of discomfort behind this description of the women's discipleship is evident.[87] The very description of discipleship likens the activity of these women to that of slaves, hirelings, or table servants. First, slaves or servant women would characteristically "follow" (ἀκολουθέω) along behind their master, as would a female lover or sex slave.[88] A quote from Philostratus' *Life of Apollonius* makes this image clear:

> And as they fared on into Mesopotamia, the tax-gatherers (τελῶνες) who presided over the Bridge (Ζεῦγμα) led them to the registry and asked them what they were taking out of the country with them. And Apollonius replied: "I am taking with me temperance, justice, virtue, continence, valour, discipline (σωφροσύνην, δικαιοσύνην, ἀρετήν, ἐγκράτειαν, ἀνδρείαν, ἄσκησιν)." And in this way he strung together a number of feminine nouns or names. The other, already scenting his own perquisites, said, "You must then write down in the register these female slaves (τὰς δούλας)." And Apollonius answered, "Impossible, for they are not female slaves that I am taking with me, but ladies of quality" (δεσποίνας).[89]

The assumption of the tax-collector in this scene is that a large number of women traveling with a man in this manner would be his slaves. Apollonius' response underscores that a man's traveling companions could stereotypically be characterized as slaves, and therefore as unvirtuous or promiscuous women. Apart from this underlying connection between slave women and promiscuity, Apollonius' witty remark would have been nonsensical. Smilarly, the women in Mark 15:40–41 could easily have been mistaken by an ancient reader, not as Markan disciples, but sexually available slaves. Although Mark's description of the women may involve mere caricature, it cannot be ruled out that either Mary Magdalene or Salome are servants, runaway slaves or hirelings of Jesus, his family or servant escorts of his mother. Mark's use of these women as examples of his theme of discipleship does not rule out the possibility that one or more of them was a runaway slave, a slave, a hired servant of Jesus' or his family or that the women provided mundane service for Jesus.[90] In fact, Mark is careful to distinguish between Jesus' women disciples and women like Herodias and her daughter, portrayed by Mark as a bawd and her fledgling courtesan daughter in a fictional scene laden with Greco-Roman banquet stereotypes.[91] This makes it improbable that the description of the women in Mark 15:40–41 is mere caricature.

Slave ownership and the use of domestic servants was common in Greco-Roman antiquity. Many peasant households in antiquity owned at least one male/boy slave or maidservant, who was by custom sexually available to all men in the household, as well as to visitors.[92] Like all slaves in antiquity, women slaves were subject to rape and various forms of violence and abuse.[93] Boy slaves could be similarly victimized.[94] Even ordinary people in antiquity rarely traveled without at least one servant.[95] Tasks assigned to slaves in either rural or urban households often followed gender lines, but slavewomen could also serve as fieldhands, or be trained as secretaries or household stewards or managers.[96] Slavewomen could also end up working in textile making or other trades – or in brothels.[97] Slavewomen connected to households could also engage in prostitution to earn extra money or their freedom; poor free women and slavewomen could be forced by economic hardship to sell not only their bodies but even their children.[98] Among the lower classes, slavery, poverty and high indebtedness were inseparable socio-economic realities in Greco-Roman antiquity.[99]

Although Jewish law put restrictions on the enslavement of other Jews, particularly Jewish males, Jewish families owned slaves as did other Greco-Roman people. In fact, cultural values governing relationships between Jewish masters and slaves are virtually indistinguishable from those of their Hellenistic counterparts in the Greco-Roman world.[100] The pervasiveness of slavery as an institution in Palestine, although hotly contested for apologetic reasons, is widely accepted as a plausible assumption in reasonable discussions.[101] Foreign slaves were cheap and easily available, although there is no evidence for the widespread use of slaves in Palestine, even for agricultural purposes.[102] Slave labor was therefore less common in Palestine, and then utilized mostly for domestic service, as in Egypt.[103] However, this means that first century Palestinian Jews of varying financial means did hire and buy household or agricultural servants, especially Gentile slaves, although more modest farmers might be forced to sell their slaves during times of economic hardship.[104] Gentile slaves were rarely manumitted, a tradition which is likely to have persisted throughout the first century.[105] When increases in manumission did occur during the Second Temple period, the motivation was often the financial benefit for the owner, not the well being of the slave.[106] Although leasing land to tenant farmers was by far the most common arrangement in Palestine, both richer landowners and modest householders applied mixed solutions to their labor needs, and could own slaves, hire laborers for the short or long term, as well as lease their land to tenants or sharecroppers.[107] Jesus' parables clearly reflect the presence not only of day laborers and tenants in Palestinian society, but also of slaves, who more often served as household stewards and servants, but could also be fieldhands. Jesus' parables use terms like *δοῦλος*, "slave" (Matt 18:23; Luke 14:17; Matt 21:34/Luke 20:10; cf. Thomas 65; Luke 19:13/Matt 25:14), *οἰκόνομος*, "steward" (Luke 16:1), as well as *ἀμπελουργός*, "vinedresser" or "gardener" (Luke 13:7), *γεωργός*, "tenant" (Matt 21:34/Luke 20:10; cf. Thomas 65), *ἐργάτης*, "worker" (Matt 20:1), and *μίσθιος*, "hired laborer" (Luke 15:17).[108] Josephus also makes clear references to servants who are indeed slaves, not hired laborers. Furthermore, Josephus does not distinguish between Jewish slaves and non-Jewish slaves – both are *δοῦλοι*.[109]

Family hardship could lead to the enslavement of even Jewish men in Palestine. The pervasiveness of debt slavery in Palestine is a widely disputed topic, particularly since it is commonly assumed that Jewish law requiring the manumission of Hebrew slaves after six years (Exod 21:2–6) was generally followed.[110] However, during times of impoverishment and crop failure, the self-enslavement of men and the sale of their children, or perhaps even their wives, was not uncommon.[111] Enslavement as a punishment for theft was also practiced.[112] If the poor would resort to selling their children to satisfy debts, it is hardly surprising that they would turn to thievery to survive. Thus, in spite of the tendency in Palestine towards the forfeiture of land and property as a means of settling a debt, it was often the case that the debtor himself, or members of his family, became his creditor's slave.[113] Debt slavery was an ever-threatening possiblity in first century Palestine, although the availability of cheap foreign slave labor may have kept it from being widespread.[114] The reality of the practice is reflected in Jesus' teachings as recorded by Matthew. When a slave is unable to pay a king (his master) what he owes him, the king orders the slave, his wife, his children, and all his belongings to be sold to pay the man's debts (Matt 18:23–35).[115]

Not usually considered in this discussion, however, is the fact that Exod 21:7–11 did not require the manumission of Jewish girls 6 years after enslavement, although Deuteronomic legislation extended this privilege to women and girls (Deut 15:12–18); girls could also be sold into concubinage, i.e., as slave-wives.[116] Thus, in spite of the minimal evidence for the sale of Jewish girls by their families,[117] it seems likely that young girls would be far more subject to debt slavery than were boys or adult men.[118] Women and girls could also be just as likely to be driven to thievery as men. Later *halakhic* sources assume the existence of slavewomen in Jewish households, as well as discussing their duties and the problems arising from their sexual availability.[119] Slavewomen owned in Palestine could be Gentile women owned by Jewish families, Jewish women sold to non-Jews, or even Jewish women owned by Jewish families.[120] It seems doubtful that girls sold in this manner would have been liberated when they came of age,[121] although women were more often manumitted than men elsewhere in the Roman world.[122] If liberated, they would be less valuable as marriage partners, due to the stain of their sexual availability during enslavement whether realized or not.[123] Notably, Simon b. Gioras' entourage included his wife and her attendants as well as runaway slaves, and his proclamation of slave emancipation was combined with a call for the abolition of debt.[124] Female slaves, even young girls, could run away from their masters; some ancient novels portray well-to-do women running away from their husbands with their slaves.[125] Jesus' admonition concerning the forgiveness of debts (Q 11:4) would thus have had direct significance for the well being not only of impoverished families generally, but for the well being of children, especially girls, who were probably the ones most often sold into slavery to cancel family debts[126] or even to raise money for the purchase of farm animals and other household goods.[127]

In view of the socio-economic context, it seems reasonable to suggest that one or more of the women described as being in Jesus' service in Mark 15:40–41 is a runaway slave or servant in spite of the fact that their names are of Hebrew derivation.[128] Mary the mother of James and Joses, Jesus' mother, is unlikely to be a slave or servant; Mary Magdalene seems to be associated with the fishing trade. Of the three, Salome is the most likely to be a slave or domestic servant, given that in The Secret Gospel of Mark she is closely associated with Jesus' family, but not identified as a family member.[129] Mark identifies only "table service" as Salome's primary occupation, though as a slave or hired servant she would probably have performed domestic or other services in the family as well. She could be both a servant and a disciple; indeed this suggestion concerning her likely vocation would not detract from Salome's significance in the tradition as one of Jesus' disciples, but enhance it. For given a slave's presumed sexual availability and the prevalence of women forced into prostitution due to economic hardship or to earn their freedom, the possiblity that Jesus' group included slavewomen or runaway slavewomen could explain the accusation in Q that Jesus associated with or reclined at table with "sinners/prostitutes" (Q 7:28–29; Mark 2:16).[130] The accusation against Jesus then suggests that he is lowering himself by eating with those who are beneath his station. This confirms Dennis Smith's suggestion concerning the significance of the "tax collectors and sinners" tradition for Jesus' social class. If correct, it calls into question the identification of Jesus as a peasant, at least a destitute or homeless one: his social status is higher than that of some of his disciples.[131]

Here again the Lenski category, "artisan," which according to his model denotes a dispossessed peasant or non inheriting son subsequently forced into manual labor,[132] does not accurately reflect the situation of a τέκτων (artisan) in antiquity, nor allow for the kind of interaction between the various lower classes in antiquity. First, the landowners in the gospels are described as splitting their wealth and property between sons, not following a law of primogeniture (cf. Luke 15:11–32). Artisans and the members of various trade guilds in antiquity could be freeborn or freedmen/women, but many were slaves, and they were not always destitute, nor devoid of all influence in politics or society. Some freedmen could be described as wealthy.[133] Further, the situation of many of the working poor is not comparable to the serfs and other peasants of early Europe that strongly influenced Lenski's study. In antiquity there was a distinction between πένης (day laborer, poor) and πτωχός (poor, destitute, beggar) that remained constant from Greek through Roman times. Day layborers were those who needed to work in shops or in the fields, but still had a voice in the community. The basic concerns, and therefore the categories, of the rich gentry and the day laborers overlapped. It was the πτωχοί (the destitute) who remained truly on the margins of society and were often objects of pity. Antipathy between the rich and the working poor stemmed in part from their mutual competition for status.[134] Moreover, in antiquity merchants (an upper class category according to Lenksi's model) might be freeborn, but were often freedmen and women – former slaves.[135] Retainers (another upper class category according to Lenski's model), such as scribes, secretaries or stewards of large households, could also be slaves or freedmen, men or women.[136] Although there is little evidence for a freed class in first century Palestine,[137] one Roman governor of Judaea, Festus, was an ex-slave, and therefore lacked social status and prestige in spite of his Imperial appointment.[138] Further, rather than suggesting an absence of slaves in first century Jewish society, the lack of evidence for a large freed class in first century Palestine may simply confirm that the later prejudice against manumission found in Rabbinic sources existed in Palestinian Judaism at an earlier time. This is the more reasonable conclusion when even the sayings of Jesus presuppose their presence. While testamentary manumission upon the death of the owner might also have been practiced,[139] the manumission of Gentile slaves was discouraged, ostensibly lest non-Jewish elements be set loose in the community.[140] Certain slaves could own property, or even other slaves.[141] Lenski's class categories are thus inadequate to account for these social and economic complexities of ancient society, even ancient Palestinian society.

Jesus is a case in point. Mark 6:3 and the description of the women disciples in Mark 15:40–41 may imply that Jesus had family ties to both the poorer working classes and a social class that was elevated, either by wealth or status of birth or by means of his earned prestige as a teacher/prophet (i.e., his popularity).[142] By this I do not mean to suggest that Jesus was an aristocrat, or even on the level of the Lenski "retainer class," but to make the point that there was a complex economic and social range to even the lower classes in antiquity, and that perhaps more interaction existed between Lenski's "peasant" and "retainer" classes than has previously been assumed. If Jesus was an artisan or carpenter, we cannot be sure how long he had been in that vocation, under what circumstances he became an artisan, and whether or not he or his family had worked, leased or owned land in the past.[143] In fact, Eusebius records in an early church tradition that in the late first century two surviving members of the family of Jesus were spared execution under Domitian due to their humble land holdings. They are described as farmers, but small landowners who could pay their taxes nonetheless.[144] Further the reference in Mark 6:3 to Jesus' vocation as and artisan is a piece of evidence that should be carefully scrutinized over against other evidence as well as the social location and concerns suggested in those of his teachings and deeds that can reasonably be considered authentic. Paul remarks to the Corinthians that Jesus had been "rich" (πλούσιος) but "became poor" (πτωχεύω) (2 Cor 8:9) on their behalf.[145] Celsus understood Jesus to be πενίαν ("poor" as a workman), not πτωχός (destitute).[146] In fact, the very message of the "Parable of the Feast" (Q 14: 16–23) recommends a pooling of resources that would be possible if some in the community, including Jesus, his family, or even someone like Joanna, had resources to share.[147] While some of Jesus' parables concern rich landlords,[148] others tell about small landowners who own only 100 sheep (Luke 15:3–7), as well as poor women who do their own housework and have only 10 silver coins (Luke 15:8–10).[149] Thus, scholarly assumptions concerning Jesus' social location and family background need serious re-examination.

The social mixture of Jesus' movement could easily explain the accusation that Jesus associated with "tax collectors and sinners/prostitutes," given that some of the women disciples or even some of the men would have been perceived as being either beneath his station or acting beneath their own. This makes it less likely that Jesus' women followers included actual prostitutes, given that such language can be shown to function more as slander and caricature, than social description (Matt 21:31–32).[150] Further, the Hellenistic evidence suggests that whether the women described in Mark 15:40–41 were working class women, slaves, or runaway slaves, whether single or married, they could be equally undeserving of such blanket accusations of sexual promiscuity and prostitution.[151] Such an insult would have been particularly demeaning to Jesus' mother. The subjection of Jesus' mother to negative gender stereotyping due to the mixed company of her son's friends could explain the stain upon her character present in early Christian tradition without assuming that Jesus' birth may have been illegitimate (cf. Thomas 105, "child of a whore," *πόρνη*). Matthew's inclusion of Tamar, Rahab, Ruth and Bathsheba in his genealogy could thus be seen as an attempt to defend the reputation of Mary by connecting her to other women in Jewish tradition who, despite doubtful reputations, are examples of Jewish faithfulness nonetheless.[152] It may be Mark's concern for Greco-Roman propriety that causes him to have the women view the crucifixion "from afar,"[153] although he is probably influenced by literary precursors as well:[154] the women are probably waiting to perform the burial tasks often assigned to women in antiquity.[155]

The language of this passage also suggests the presence of these women at meals with Jesus. *Διακονέω*, "serve," calls to mind the image of women who serve Jesus at table, a task often assigned to household servants or slaves, or if there were no servants, to women or children in a household.[156] In households that could afford one or two slaves, table service was provided by slavewomen or pretty young slaveboys, although in poorer homes the women of the family could provide this service.[157] In large banquets of the wealthy, such table service was usually provided by handsome young male slaves.[158] In Mark, it is only the women and angels who serve Jesus (Mark 1:29–31; 14:3–9), and even the job of the angels is apparently to bring him food at the end of his fast in Mark 1:13.[159] Thus, there is a clear connection between the service rendered by these women and the preparation and service of food in meal settings.[160] Mark 15:40–41 can thus be read as indicating that these women were present with Jesus for meals, at least as table servants. In combination with the tradition that Jesus ate with "tax collectors and sinners" (Mark 2:17), this could also imply that the women joined Jesus for meals.[161] The convergence of the lower class images of slavery, table service, and sexuality in Mark 15:40–41 would not have been lost on Hellenistic audiences familar with Greco-Roman meal protocol. Yet in spite of these associations, Mark incorporates this description of the women into his larger theme of discipleship.[162] It is these overtones of scandal and the association of these women with the lower classes that Luke erases by raising the social rank of the women and characterizing their service as philanthropic (Luke 8:1–3).

Why does Mark incorporate this description of Jesus' women disciples into his narrative in spite of the significance of the tradition which he inherits? Although most scholars place the composition of Mark in Syria,[163] this inclusion may indicate that the gospel was written somewhere in the Western Empire, where the social mobility of women was more accepted than in the Greek East. Further, although sharing meals with men and frequent travel were controversial for ladies of the elite, travel by women of most social classes was not. In spite of the Greco-Roman cultural ideal that women should remain in the home, even before the building of Roman roads it was not uncommon for women to travel with their husbands, particularly to popular religious festivals or sacred sites. Women could also travel long distances with servants to meet their husbands elsewhere. Women also obviously traveled *as* servants; some traveled by becoming runaway slaves.[164] Only wealthy women lived secluded lives; the rest of population probably couldn't afford to keep the women of their families idle and in the home.[165] Further, there is little direct evidence from Palestine that women were kept in seclusion in women's quarters as in the Greek East; the limited evidence that exists applies only to the upper classes.[166] Travel for unmarried women and younger virgins may have been more restricted,[167] but this would not necessarily apply to all young or unmarried women; the practice of debt slavery makes it difficult to imagine that girls thus victimized would have their potential rendering of service limited by travel restrictions.[168]

Some ancient governments, however, did have an interest in restricting the travel of women, especially prostitutes. These restrictions were enforced by exorbitant fares or taxation for travel services. Presumably, if women or their husbands could pay the fares charged by ship captains, they would be allowed on board. Men were charged higher fares for their wives than for themselves, but these fares were not nearly so high as those charged for prostitutes.[169] Such a policy probably affected unescorted women, regardless of their true vocation, although even men rarely traveled alone, but usually took along at least one servant.[170] Travel for pure pleasure and sight-seeing was only done by the extremely rich,[171] but even elite married women known for too frequent holiday trips to seaside resorts or well known spas could be characterized by their peers as pleasure seeking courtesans or sexually loose, since such holidays were seen as possible occasions for adulterous liaisons.[172] The many women mentioned in the Pauline letters who traveled either as missionaries or as the result of imperial edicts like the Edict of Claudius (Acts 18:2),[173] should not be considered out of the ordinary for their time or for their social class. Rather, Paul's letters give us additional evidence for the general mobility of women like Junia, Priscilla, or even Phoebe. Paul himself shows no discomfort with the fact that women he knows travel long distances or that the apostles from Palestine are known to take along a sister/wife on their journeys. In fact, he asserts their right to do so (1 Cor 9:5). He even uses Phoebe, whom he calls his "patroness," as a courier (Rom 16:1–2).[174] Again, although it may be unwise to assume that Paul's information concerning the Jerusalem church is applicable to the Palestinian situation more generally, the evidence suggests that on the whole women did travel, especially to religious festivals like the Passover in Jerusalem, or from town to town to engage in barter and trade,[175] rendering Mark's description of the women on the road with Jesus in Mark 15:40–41 quite explicable in spite of the undertones of scandal associated with terms ἀκολουθέω ("follow") and διακονέω ("serve"). The inclusion of the wife of Simon b. Gioras and other women attendants in his Zealot retinue gives further evidence for the traveling habits of Palestinian women.[176] The authenticity of Mark 15:40–41 is even more probable if two of the women are associated either with Jesus' family (his mother/and or Salome) or the families of the other male disciples (cf. Matthew 27:56). Only Mary Magdalene seems completely unconnected to Jesus or the other disciples by any familial tie, and she may well be connected to the fishermen in the group by means of her trade, just as Priscilla shared a trade with Paul.

Marriage and Social Class

It is difficult to determine the marital status of the women in Mark 15:40–41. That no husbands are mentioned, in particular for Salome or Mary Magdalene, may indicate either that they were not married[177] or that they were divorced. It is also possible that they simply left their husbands and children for a freer life, with or without a divorce. Salome, if a runaway slave or domestic servant, may have been single, given the difficulties involved in the marriage of women formerly enslaved or in domestic service due the stain of assumed sexual activity. Still marriages of manumitted slavewomen to their masters or to others are recorded in later sources.[178] Mary Magdalene, if an ordinary working woman, could well have been married, even perhaps involved in a business with her husband or family members. Mary the mother of James and Joses was probably married or divorced, given that she is the mother of sons.[179] If as Mark 6:3 indicates she is Jesus' mother, it would appear that she was married, and either of a higher social class than her husband or simply better known than her husband.[180] However, since Matthew and Luke do give independent attestation that Mary was married to a man named Joseph (Luke 2:4; Matt 1:16), it seems equally possible that she was separated, divorced or widowed.[181] All such suggestions remain conjecture. There is no evidence in Luke 8:1–3 that Joanna's husband or children are with her, but exemplifies those women most able to leave her family behind with servants to care for them.

Here one must give consideration to the cost paid by mothers and especially fathers who undertook the often romanticized step of deserting their families and children to follow a prophet like Jesus.[182] The lack of references to the women's husbands in Mark 15:40–41 is often taken as an indication that these or other early Christian women were celibate and eschewed marriage.[183] This is unlikely. It is Matthew, not Mark who records the harsh statement about becoming eunuchs for the Kingdom (Matt 19:1–12). And Mark, by reporting the full divorce prohibition without exceptions (Mark 10:2–12), reinforces the value of marriage for both women and men. In spite of the oft-mentioned lack of fathers among those Jesus calls his true family in Mark (3:31–35),[184] in view of the importance placed on marriage in Mark 10:2–12, Mark's lack of interest in "fathers" is unlikely to reflect a repudiation of marriage or an anti-patriarchal ethic.[185] The emphasis on the fatherhood of God has little or no relation to the description of the "true family" as consisting of mothers and children, but no fathers (Mark 3:31–35; Mark 10:29–31).[186] It is far easier to make a case for an interest in celibacy on the part of Matthew and even more so Luke.[187] Jesus himself was hardly known for asceticism, but was perceived as a libertine, and left the ascetic movement of John the Baptist in order to start his own group (Mark 2:17; Q 7:34).[188] Given the tendency of the gospels to neglect personal details about even key individuals, it is also quite possible that like most first century Jewish women Salome and Mary Magdalene were indeed married, and that Mark did not find details about their marital status to be of much importance.[189] Still, it is notable that unlike Philostratus' Apollonius, Mark does not assert that Jesus' travel companions are truly virtuous women (as does Luke 8:1–3) rather than mere servants. Mark records their presence, but in no way defends it.[190] Winsome Munro's original contention that Mark deliberately postpones his reference to the women to obscure or suppress their role in Jesus' movement may thus be correct.[191] Mark's picture of the women completely silent at the cross and the grave in combination with his narrative in which the women are chased away from an *empty* tomb indeed suggests an overall Markan reluctance to associate women disciples not only with Jesus' movement, but with his death, burial and resurrection as well.[192] Mark is uncomfortable with this early oral tradition, it embarrasses him, but he cannot deny it. This further increases the probability that the association of Jesus with women disciples, and the identification of at least two of these women as coming from the lower classes, is historically authentic.

Jesus, Tax Collectors, and Sinners in Mark (Mark 2:14–17)

In Mark 2 Jesus reclines at table with Levi the tax-collector and a group of his friends.[193] The call to Levi has long been considered a Markan composition. Mack has suggested that Mark expands an earlier chreia by creating a scene in which Jesus actually eats with a tax-collector named Levi.[194] The pun implied by the verb καλέω ("to invite") could indicate that in a pre-Markan form the saying pictured Jesus as the host of the meal rather than the guest.[195] Thus, Mark portrays Jesus as engaging in the kind of behavior of which the Pharisees accuse him: "Why does he eat (ἐσθίω)[196] with tax-collectors and sinners?" (τῶν τελωνῶν καὶ ἁμαρτωλῶν) (Mark 2:16). This verbal swipe at Jesus' table practice also occurs in Q 7:34 where the association of Jesus' behavior with banquet revelry is clear. There Jesus' is called a "wine-bibber" (οἰνοπότης) and a "glutton" (φάγος). The accusation that Jesus reclined at table with "tax collectors and sinners" recalls typical slander against those known for dining with promiscuous women at public banquets. Tax collectors were stereotypically connected to slave trafficking and brothel keeping; "sinners" were connected to the lower classes and prostitutes.[197] Mark, however, connects Jesus' meal to his own themes of calling and discipleship.[198]

It is notable that both Luke and Matthew interpret the phrase "tax collectors and sinners" found in Mark and Q to include women. Luke describes a woman as an example of a "sinner" (Luke 7:36–50) and for this reason is hesitant to portray Jesus as clearly reclining with "tax collectors and sinners" in a scene. This indicates that Luke is careful to conform his narrative to standards of Greco-Roman propriety as well as ancient literary conventions.[199] In Matthew the phrase "tax collectors and sinners" even more explicitly includes women, in that Matthew retains the parallel construction of "tax collectors and prostitutes," which I argue preserves Q (Q 7:29; Matt 21:31).[200] Consistently, Matthew expands the guest lists of the Eucharistic feasts in the miraculous feeding narratives to include both women and children, and strengthens the characterization of the women as disciples at the end of his gospel (Matt 27:55–56).[201] Thus both Luke and Matthew's narratives display authorial ramifications of the basic picture evoked in both Mark 2:16 and Q 7:34.

In Mark 2 this traditional slander is transformed into a narrative involving a later church conflict with the Pharisees over a more developed notion of ritual purity in the context of meals. It seems unlikely that Jesus himself would have been in conflict with Pharisees over purity and table fellowship. The general purity regulations which governed all Jews had less effect on everyday, communal, or celebratory meals, than on Temple practices.[202] Ritual impurity incurred in the course of everyday life, for example from contact with a dead family member, menstrual bleeding or sexual emissions, affected both men and women. Being in a state of ritual impurity did not constitute "sin." Ritual impurity was easily remedied by ritual cleansing; immersion pools were located around the Temple precincts for this very purpose.[203] In spite of Mark's statement that "all the Jews" were concerned about the washing of hands (Mark 7:6–9), only the *haberim* ("associates") were strict about infusing priestly rules into the everyday handling of foodstuffs. But *haberim* are not easily equatable with the "Pharisees," and they were no doubt a very small minority within Judaism before 70C.E..[204] Thus it remains doubtful that the concern of Jesus' contemporaries for his table practice reflects disputes over Jewish purity regulations.[205]

Therefore, Mark's representation of the situation as a conflict over purity is probably less an indication of the situation of Jesus' day, than a manifestation of later conflicts between Judaism and early Christian groups following the fall of the Jerusalem Temple. In light of the Hellenistic evidence, the original accusation against Jesus functions as a form of slander, and reflects a concern not for purity, but for propriety. This suggests that Jesus' table companions included members of the lower classes, including women, as well as possibly one wealthier woman.[206] This would be far more indicative of the concerns of Jesus' real day-to-day opponents, who would have been local leaders from the ranks of wealthy landowners, old prominent families, local government officials, and local priests and scribes. A few Pharisees could have numbered among these groups in Galilee during Jesus' lifetime, but cannot be imagined to dominate them.[207] The possibility that Jesus stood a step higher on the social ladder than many of his followers would help explain concern for his behavior on the part of the local leadership. The accusation that Jesus "eats with tax-collectors and sinners" makes better sense if Jesus' social standing is somehow above some of those he joins for meals.[208] Thus, the concern over Jesus' dining habits more likely reflected a conflict over his challenge to Greco-Roman class structures, as Marcus Borg and John Dominic Crossan have suggested,[209] than a conflict over purity.[210] Unless Jesus failed to cleanse himself before entering the Temple, it is hard to imagine that even the most conservative Jews would have accused him of abrogating Jewish purity regulations let alone objected to his dining habits.[211]

What these early traditions do suggest, however, is that Jesus was perceived as challenging Greco-Roman ideals of rank and privilege by means of his actions. This increases the likelihood that although a member of the peasant class, Jesus was not from the lowest ranks of that class, but from a level of the peasantry able to exercise resistance to authority on behalf of those beneath his station. Resistance to authority by means of overt action is a common tactic of political resistance among the lower classes.[212] One could argue on the basis of Mark 2:15–17, which preserves the accusation that Jesus ate with "tax collectors and sinners," and Mark 15:40–41, which names Jewish women from the lower classes as Jesus' disciples, that the mixed social constituency of Jesus' meals suggested by the "Parable of the Feast" (Q 14:16–24; Thomas 64) included household slaves, hirelings, runaway slaves, debt slaves and/or day laborers, among them women.[213] The image in the parable of the "Returning Master" is also notable, given that it contains an inversion of the master/slave (δοῦλος) roles at table (Luke 12:35–38; cf. also Mark 10:42–45; John 13:1–16).[214] The inclusion of servants, especially slaves, at meals was considered particularly controversial among the elite, since inviting a slave to recline for a meal was an informal means of manumission (*per mansam*).[215] Only a few Hellenistic philosophers advocated such an innovative table ethic.[216] Such a social mixture, however, was again more common among the lower classes, in which the mixture of the free poor, freed and slaves was relatively common in social situations, communal meals and clubs.[217] Jesus' challenge to Greco-Roman ideals of rank in the "Parable of the Feast," although not a direct challenge to Greco-Roman notions of gender, could have had further significance, albeit a secondary one, for women among the lower classes.[218] However, this suggests that Jesus' real concern was class inequity, not gender inequity. The table ethic of the "Parable of the Feast" could reflect a common lower class resistance mentality,[219] a Hellenistic philosophical ethic,[220] as well as the Hebraic ideal of charity.[221] Given the Hellenistic milieu of Greco-Roman Palestine, the "Parable of the Feast" may in fact reflect all three. This conclusion seems consistent with the complexity of first century Judaism and the syncretic social and religious environment of Jesus' day.[222]

The accusation that Jesus dined with "tax collectors and sinners/prostitutes" is highly credible as a charge leveled against Jesus during his lifetime, and reflects the presence of women and the lower classes at Jesus' own meals. Few scholars doubt the authenticity of at least the accusation itself.[223] Dennis E. Smith, however, has consistently argued that this tradition is inauthentic for two reasons: 1) the sectarian nature of the language reflects a level of social formation that fits better the situation of early Jewish Christians in conflict with other Jews and 2) the "tax collectors and sinners" tradition reflects the "heroizing" of Jesus in early gospel tradition, in that it functions as a literary motif in much the same manner as gospel narratives which portray Jesus as reclining for meals as the primary setting for his teaching. Hence, according to Smith, the tradition that Jesus reclined with "tax collectors and sinners" is an early Christian literary invention which idealizes Jesus as the hero figure presiding over banquets.[224] Although it is true that many narratives involving banquet motifs do apparently reflect the heroization of Jesus in developing Christian tradition,[225] it is unlikely that the "tax collectors and sinners" tradition is an example of such a development – precisely because reclining with the scum of Hellenistic society is decidedly unheroic behavior.[226] Moreover, not only is the tradition found in two early streams of gospel tradition, Mark and Q, but the gospel writers who inherit this tradition consistently show discomfort with the ramifications of the accusation. This strongly suggests that the accusation itself is authentic and not an idealization of Jesus' table practice.

Moreover, although it is true that the accusation reflects a situation involving mutual polemics, such polemics do not necessarily reflect sectarian formation, but are highly consistent with group conflict.[227] It is fully plausible that Jesus gathered a small group of disciples around him, among them women, slaves, debt slaves, and hired laborers, and that he and his friends came into conflict with other Jews over the socially mixed nature of his entourage as well as certain religious concerns. The charge against Jesus is thus not pure fiction, but "distortion of the truth."[228] If Jesus' teaching had not engendered conflict with other Jews during his lifetime, it is highly unlikely that he would have met with the kind of resistance that led to his crucifixion and death. Thus, the accusation that Jesus dined with "tax collectors and sinners/prostitutes" can be justifiably seen as an authentic gospel tradition which reflects the socially mixed nature of the Jesus movement.

Women Disciples and the Historical Jesus: Some Conclusions

It remains plausible in light of all the evidence we have that Jesus dined and traveled with women named Mary Madgalene, Salome and his mother. That he traveled with a woman named Joanna is less certain, although the slander leveled against Jesus strongly suggests that relatively elite women were among those women in Jesus' company. In spite of the fact that the gospels themselves indicate that Jesus' association with women was controversial, this association pervades the early layers of the gospel tradition, and is therefore difficult to explain except as an historically reliable element of Jesus' movement. This suggests that Jesus suffered social criticism from his contemporaries in part because of his association with women, especially women of the working classes and the free poor.[229] These early traditions linking women disciples to Jesus' meals strongly suggests that the "Last Supper" traditions which limit his intimate circle to men are later literary creations which cast Jesus' meals with his disciples as all male *symposia*, or "drinking parties," in accordance with stereotypical Greco-Roman literary conventions.[230] Since upper-class wealthier women could be branded whores for social unconformity, and lower class women could be assumed to have been forced into prostitution, it is less likely that the women around Jesus were actual prostitutes. The accusation that Jesus dined with "tax collectors and sinners/prostitutes" can therefore be seen as a form of slander against Jesus and his companions, and remains suggestive of a socially mixed group which included slaves, runaway slaves and/or day laborers, as well as the freeborn poor

Chapter 3

Gender & Class in the Teaching of Jesus

Certain scholars explain the presence of women followers in Jesus' retinue on the basis of his teaching of the Kingdom of God: Jesus' message would have been clearly understood as an explicit challenge to the patriarchal bias of his culture. Elisabeth Schüssler Fiorenza calls this aspect of his message a "critical feminist impulse that came to the fore in the vision and ministry of Jesus."[1] Both John Dominic Crossan and Marcus Borg see Jesus' message of the Kingdom similarly and cite his "radical egalitarianism" in the midst of a culture that devalued both women and the poor peasant underclass.[2] Yet little in the sayings generally considered authentic merits such elaborate claims insofar as women are concerned. Although his teaching demonstrates a clear awareness of poverty and a critique of class inequity in ancient Palestine, it does not show an equivalent critique of patriarchy, nor a similar interest in gender concerns. Thus, although there is reason to describe aspects of his message concerning the Kingdom of God as "egalitarian," this egalitarianism does not extend to the concerns of women, nor was it aimed at a clear social program geared towards major social change for women.

Women in the Parables of Jesus

The parables of Jesus have long vexed New Testament scholars. Only recently freed from centuries of misleading allegorical interpretations, the parables continue to attract the attention of many serious commentators, and books on the subject have become legion.[3] Most scholars now agree that the parables were not intended to be complex allegories containing several points of reference, but are stories that create their own narrative world.[4] The allegorization of Jesus' parables began early in Christian tradition, a tendency that can be seen in Mark's version of the parable of the Sower (Mark 4:3–20) or Matthew's version of the parable of the Banquet (Matt 22:1–14). Other parables went through a process of alteration either in oral retelling or in written redaction. In spite of this, the parables remain the bedrock of historical information concerning Jesus, as well as the defining center of his proclamation of the Kingdom of God.

Since the parables use images drawn from everyday Palestinian life, women and women's activities occasionally figure as the point of comparison to the Kingdom of God. This leads certain scholars to posit an anti-patriarchal or egalitarian ethic for Jesus' teachings overall. Upon closer analysis, however, the images and roles of women in Jesus' parables are unexceptional. Stories involving women simply reflect the presence of women in Jesus' social environment; they are told to make points about the Kingdom of God, not the status of women. Activities such as kneading bread, carrying grain jars, sweeping floors, and grinding meal not only reflect traditional roles of women in ancient society, but their juxtaposition in the gospels over against typical male roles such as planting seeds, shepherding sheep, parenting sons, and reclining on couches for meals reinforces gender roles rather than challenges them.[5] This arrangement of parables in gendered pairs is arguably secondary to the tradition and reflects either the legal interests of a document like Q,[6] or simply the tendency in that social environment towards a gendered division of labor among peasants and the lower classes.[7] Such images reflect everyday situations from ancient Palestine and force the hearer to active thought concerning either the Kingdom of God or the situation described in the story itself.

Recent feminist analysis has drawn attention to the feminine imagery of Jesus' parables, which can be viewed in either a positive or negative light.[8] However, in spite of the tendency among certain feminist scholars to characterize Jesus' overall teaching as anti-patriarchal, the evidence of the parables reveals that Jesus was part of the patriarchal society in which he lived and that he evinced similar patriarchal biases. For example, as Nicola Slee has pointed out, among Jesus' parables and sayings in the Synoptic gospels, of the 104 in Matthew, 47 involve human actors, with 85 characters in all. Of the 85, 73 are men and 12 are women – 5 of whom are foolish maidens. In the 94 parables and sayings in Luke, 51 concern human actors, with 108 characters. Of those 108, 99 are men and 9 are women. Slee is right to caution that the predominance of male characters in Jesus' parables and sayings by itself suggests that Jesus, like other speakers and writers of his day, was by nature predisposed to re-imagine in his narratives a world dominated by men and their concerns and shows little interest for women and women's concerns.[9] There are in fact only five parables now arguably considered authentic which utilize images of women: the Leaven (Matt 13:3/Luke 13:20–21/Thomas 96), the Lost Coin (Luke 15:8–9), the Empty Jar (Thomas 97), the Unjust Judge (Luke 18:2–8) and the Prodigal Son (Luke 15:11–32). And of these only four focus upon actions of women, since in the last case women are mentioned only briefly as the prostitutes (πόρναι) upon whom the Prodigal Son squanders his money (Luke 15:30). Indeed, the Empty Jar from the Gospel of Thomas has only recently been considered in these discussions – a fact which reflects the increasing tendency to include evidence for Jesus' teachings from Thomas as equally significant for reconstructions of the historical Jesus.

In spite of the presence of images of women in these parables, it is difficult to argue that the first three demonstrate any subversion of gender roles. Rather, the parables of the Leaven, the Lost Coin and the Empty Jar underscore common gendered roles from antiquity by creating images of women engaged in everyday activities. Further, the feminine activities described in these parables are not themselves referents for the Kingdom of God.

The parable of the Leaven is assuredly an authentic parable of Jesus.[10] Since Thomas has introduced a contrast of the small amount of the leaven with the large size of the leavened loaves (Thomas 96),[11] the version found in Luke 13:20–21/Matt 13:33 (Q) is arguably the earliest. The original parable thus compares the Kingdom of God (or Heaven) to leaven (ζύμη) which a woman (γυνή) takes and hides (ἐγκρύπτω) in a very large amount of flour until the leaven spreads throughout. The use of "to hide" is surprising in combination with leaven. The verb φυράω ("to knead") is more to be expected (cf. Hos 7:4, LXX). Scholars have suggested various interpretations of the parable by emphasizing the smallness of the beginnings of the Kingdom in contrast to its later size,[12] the mysterious nature of the Kingdom's growth,[13] the reversal of expectations of the nature of the God's reign,[14] the culmination of the Kingdom of God in Jesus' ministry,[15] or the domestic work of women as an example of the activity of God.[16] In any case, however, the parable clearly highlights the images of the leaven and the meal as the point of comparison for the reign of God, rather than the woman herself. Thus, even though the image is one of women's domestic work, the focus is still the leavening, not the woman. Since leaven was regarded in Judaism as a symbol of corruption (Exod 12:15; Mark 8:15; 1 Cor 5:7), Jesus' comparison of leaven to God's Kingdom is very provocative.[17] Indeed he quite reverses the expectations of his hearers. What appears to be the activity of corruption – the overproduction of leavened bread[18] – is essential and characteristic of divine activity, the reign of God. Thus, the parable turns not on the fact that this is a woman's activity, but rather on the unexpected comparison of leaven to God's activity – a possible allusion to the presence of lower classes and outcasts in Jesus' close circle of followers.[19]

The Lost Coin (Luke 15:8–10) contains what may be a similar story of domestic incompetence followed by the surprising joy of rediscovery.[20] A woman loses (ἀπόλλυμι) one drachma of the ten she has, searches for it, and upon its rediscovery rejoices with her women neighbors. This parable is coupled in Luke with the parable of the Lost Sheep and followed by the parable of the Prodigal Son. In Luke the parable concerns the joy in heaven over human repentance, an interpretation that is widely considered secondary.[21] The image is again unexpected. A woman searches diligently for something that on the face of it is of limited intrinsic value. A drachma was a Greek silver coin equal in worth to a denarius, which was a day's pay for a male fieldhand.[22] Of course the drachma may be worth considerably more to her, since women workers made barely half as much as men for the same amount of manual labor. The single drachma is thus enough for roughly two days of subsistence level support for one person.[23] Some interpreters have proposed that the money was part of the woman's dowry, but nothing in the text suggests this.[24] And given Luke's context and interpretation, it is difficult to consider the woman a feminine image for God or Jesus. As Dominic Crossan has said, there is no tradition comparable to John 10:11, "I am the good shepherd," declaring "I am the good housewife."[25] Still, such a reading remains popular, essentially following the Lukan interpretation in which the shepherd, the woman and the father all represent images of insistent divine activity.[26] Apart from its Lukan context, however, this parable further associates the reign of God with the unexpected. What appears to be of little value is highly prized, and the kingdom is again associated with the poor, and one might add, the incompetent.[27]

The parable of the Empty Jar contains yet another image of womanly inattention or incompetence (Thomas 97).[28] The Kingdom of "the Father" is compared to a woman carrying a full jar of meal:

> Jesus said: The [father's] kingdom is like a woman (ϩιⲙⲉ) who was carrying a [jar] full of meal (ⲛⲟⲉⲓⲧ). While she was walking along [a] distant road, the handle of the jar broke and the meal spilled behind her [along] the road. She did not know it; she had not noticed a problem. When she reached her house, she put the jar down and discovered that it was empty (ϣⲟⲩⲉⲓⲧ).[29]

In the gospel of Thomas, the Empty Jar is set between the parables of the Leaven (Thomas 96) and the Assassin (Thomas 98). The image of the woman is also one of domesticity and failure. Although hardly a clear image of uncleanness simply due to her femaleness,[30] the woman does not notice when her jar is broken and thus loses all of her grain, the basic means of subsistence for the poor in antiquity.[31] The tension inherent in this story is underscored by a well known parallel in the Hebrew Bible, the story of the widow of Zarephath (1 Kgs 17:8–16).[32] In a time of famine Elijah is told to go to the widow of Zarephath who has been commanded to feed him. When Elijah finds her, she tells him that she has nothing prepared and only a small amount of meal and oil. Miraculously, the grain in her jar does not run out and she, her child and Elijah subsist on cakes baked from her supplies for many days. Thus, the Empty Jar parable reverses the story of the Elijah and the widow Zarephath. No prophet comes to the woman's aid; her jar remains empty. Once again, expectations for the reign of God are reversed.[33] The images of women in these three parables are hardly complimentary. One loses a coin worth two days sustenance, another spills her grain without noticing it, another overproduces bread; the point of the parable is made at each woman's expense.

The final authentic parable which employs the image of a woman is usually called the Unjust Judge (Luke 18:2–8).[34] Although occasionally named after the widow in the story, the main character in the story is the man.[35] In this engaging story, a woman receives justice at court, not because her cause is just, nor because the judge she approaches is just, but because she is persistent to the point of threatening the judge with a black eye ("she will wear me out," lit. "give me a black eye" or "bruise" [ὑπωπιάζω]). The image is striking to the point of being humorous. The contrast between the social and economic circumstances of the two characters in the story is stark: the judge would be a member of the urban elite, the woman of the urban poor.[36] Further, in a long history of Jewish tradition, widows belonged to a category of persons who needed special protection from God: "widows, orphans and foreigners." Israelites were commanded to protect these classes. Just as God protected the Israelites while they were in bondage in Egypt, so he is the patron of the most needy of the Israelite community.[37] Indeed, the treatment of widows, orphans and foreigners amounted to a gauge for determining the faithfulness of the Jewish people.[38]

Many commentators see the parable in terms of an analogy between the judge and God: if a widow can get justice from an unjust judge, how much more likely will God respond to persistent prayer? Luke's appended interpretation encourages this reading (Luke 18:6–8),[39] but is probably secondary.[40] Read without this Lukan interpretation, the parable takes on a quite different meaning. The emphasis falls upon the woman's unflagging insistence for vindication, not upon the action of the judge whose motive is self interest. The parable thus portrays a disadvantaged widow gaining justice by her own means, without reliance upon God.[41] It might fittingly be likened to Luke's parable of the Unjust Steward (Luke 16:1–8), in that the overwhelmingly aggressive and even insubordinate behavior the widow achieves her intended result. Her actions border upon harassment. Jesus' description of this woman, although hardly complimentary, is in marked contrast to the images of domestic failure in the parables of the Leaven, the Lost Coin, and the Empty Jar. Such a story surely reinforces shrewd, calculated and resistant behavior on the part of the oppressed and is not merely a metaphor for the continuation of the kingdom.[42] Still, since the internal monologue is that of the judge, the story reflects not the the woman's perspective, but the man's.

Open Commensality and the Parable of the Feast

Insofar as gender issues and women are concerned, the above parables do not substantiate modern feminist claims for Jesus. Rather, they suggest a male-centered outlook that tends to portray women characters in less than complimentary ways. Nor do these parables focus on the acceptance of women as women into the kingdom, but rather on their status as members of a larger class of outcasts whose acceptability as God's children underscores the unexpected nature of the reign of God. One parable, however, when read in conjunction with the tradition that Jesus welcomed "tax collectors and sinners" to his table does seem to suggest the invitation of women to the Kingdom of God, and that is the parable of the Feast (Matt 22:2–13; Luke 14:16–24). Here the theme of the unexpected nature of the Kingdom of God has its clearest expression. In this parable Jesus overturns ancient social paradigms of honor and wealth in a depiction of a Feast for the lowly and the derelict, rather than one for the customary guests of rank and privilege. Borg, Crossan, and Schüssler Fiorenza all focus on the message of the parable of the Feast and Jesus' table practice as a sign of his egalitarian ethic.[43] Both Borg and Schüssler Fiorenza see Jesus as opening up the banquet of the Kingdom to the unclean: Jesus overturns purity regulations by eating with women.[44] Dominic Crossan and Luise Schottroff see Jesus' egalitarianism as reflective of a peasant mentality or a consequence of impoverishment. Jesus' parable of the Feast thus portrays the Kingdom of God as a large inclusive meal to which are invited people from all levels of society, including women (Luke 14:16–24; Matt 22:1–14; Thom 64:1–12).[45]

Such arguments require some nuance. First, the argument that Jesus here challenges purity regulations is unlikely since, as was noted earlier, Jews may not have been overly concerned with purity outside of the Temple, and because Rabbinic sources emphasizing purity issues post-date the New Testament. Recent reconstructions of the Qumran community suggest that even the purity-conscious sectarians at Qumran could have allowed women to join certain ritual meals. Thus concern over Jesus' table practice is more likely to have been a matter of propriety than purity.[46] Second, the point of the parable of the Feast does not hinge on the issue of gender, but on that of class or rank. Any application of the parable to the situation of women would therefore have been strictly secondary. One could argue that women are invited as those among the poor, the sick, and the street people, but the point of the parable is not to invite *women* to the Feast, but the underclasses. Jesus here does not defend the right of women to join him at table. Given the strong liklihood that Greco-Roman culture pervaded Palestine, and with it the customary presence of women at meals with men, it seems more plausible that inclusion of women at Jesus' meals reflects progressive (although controversial) cultural practices found throughout Greco-Roman society and in Hellenistic Judaism, rather than a peasant egalitarian ideology or Sophia – inspired prophetic vision.

In fact, later gospel portrayals of Jesus at meals do not show him taking a particularly radical stance. For example, in the story of his meal with Mary and Martha (Luke 10:38–42), Jesus does encourage Mary, who is seated at his feet. However, although such a position does indicate that Mary is receiving instruction, her posture reflects a more conservative, matronly role, and she remains silent throughout the scene. The more radical stance would have been to invite Mary to recline with him like an equal on a banquet couch, as Jesus does with Salome in the Gospel of Thomas (Thomas 61). In these Lukan stories Jesus does not appear radical in his relationships with women; it is the women who are bold, not Jesus.

In order to derive from the Feast parable an egalitarian meaning, it must be read in conjunction with one other piece of evidence from the Jesus tradition, the accusation that Jesus dined with "tax collectors and sinners" (Mark 2:15; Q 7:34). This accusation, as we have seen, reflects typical characterizations of those known for banqueting with tax collectors, pimps and prostitutes. The very imagery of disreputable banquet behavior calls to mind the presence of lewd women, slaves, and courtesans – the kind of women present in a typical Hellenistic banquet scene. This accusation should thus be seen as a standard charge of Hellenistic rhetoric, and not necessarily indicative of the occupations or morals of Jesus' actual table companions. Both Mark and Q imply that Jesus is eating with women, and thus a participant in the social progressivisim of his day.[47] Again, however, the force of this tradition maintains between Jesus and his dining companions a distinction that remains one of class, not necessarily sex-differentiation. Jesus is here accused of dining with those who are beneath his station. Dennis E. Smith writes:

> The strongest evidence for the open commensality theme in the Jesus tradition is the theme that Jesus dined with tax collectors and sinners. Yet, this theme only works best if Jesus is not of the same social level with tax collectors and sinners. If all parties involved, including Jesus, are peasants, then the motif fails, for there is no experience of social stratification at table.[48]

If Jesus or all of his followers are of the same low social class, then the force of the insult leveled against him is lost. Smith argues that John Dominic Crossan, although having made a good case for an egalitarian table ethic in Jesus' movement undercuts his proposition by turning Jesus into a peasant.[49] Still, it is possible to maintain a lower social location for Jesus as long as it is recognized that there would have been those even beneath his social station in ancient Palestine, particularly slaves.[50] The Feast parable would then reflect Jesus' resistance to authority on behalf of those beneath his station, including perhaps women of the lower classes, even though they are not the focus of the Feast parable proper.

That said, it is still possible to identify one tradition considered by some scholars both early and authentic, that suggests Jesus himself defended the presence of women among his followers by deflecting slander leveled against them. Probably going back in some form to Q[51] is the statement of Jesus that links women to both his movement and to John the Baptist's:

> Truly I say to you, the tax collectors and the harlots go into the kingdom of God before you. For John came to you in righteousness, and you did not believe him, but the tax collectors and the harlots believed him; and even when you saw it, you did not afterward repent and believe him (Matt 21:31b–32; RSV).

Here Jesus calls the women entering the Kingdom of God "whores." As I have suggested, taken as a repeated form of slander leveled against Jesus and his table companions, rather than as a social description of some of his followers, this would indicate that he was well aware of the controversial nature of his group, including the presence of women. He accepted the label of the women around him as "whores," possibly in bitter jest, even as the basis of a bitingly sarcastic riposte. His opponents accused him of consorting with "tax collectors and whores," but those so labeled will enter the Kingdom of God first. To claim an insult robs it of its power. Of course, Jesus' use of snide humor implies discomfort as well as acceptance. By using the gender stereotypical label of "whores" for the women in his group, Jesus identifies the underlying cause of the tension aroused by the presence of women among his followers – their difference. So employed, humor seeks to relieve tension through laughter, while at the same time serving to incorporate women in a predominantly male group.[52] In sum, this saying does not identify the women in Jesus' group as actual prostitutes, but merely repeats a slander leveled against women whose bad reputations are due either to their socially progressive behavior, or to their low social status.[53] That Jesus could have expressed his discomfort with the presence of women in his company by means of snide humor suggests either the resistant attitude of lower class peasants, or a wit informed by the currents of Greco-Roman philosophy present in first century Palestine, or both.[54]

Thus, the parable of the Feast in combination with the typical characterization of his dining companions as "tax collectors, sinners and whores," suggests that Jesus' teaching on open commensality was inclusive of women and those beneath Jesus' station, such as domestic servants and slaves. Yet the critique of Greco-Roman ideals of rank and privilege (and by extension the system of slavery) remains central to the Feast parable and this theme can be shown to be far more significant than gender within Jesus' overall message.

Slavery, Ethics and the Kingdom of God

Although obscured in most translations due to the use of terms like "servant" and "steward," slave imagery abounds within the parables and sayings of Jesus far more than feminine imagery. For example, Jesus' parables use terms like δοῦλος, "slave" (Matt 18:23; Luke 14:17; Matt 21:34/Luke 20:10; cf. Thomas 65; Luke 19:13/Matt 25:14), οἰκονόμος, "steward" (Luke 16:1), as well as ἀμπελουργός, "vinedresser" or "gardener" (Luke 13:7), γεωργός, "tenant" (Matt 21:34/Luke 20:10; cf. Thomas 65), ἐργάτης, "worker" (Matt 20:1), and μίσθιος, "hired laborer" (Luke 15:17).[55] Josephus makes clear references to servants who are real slaves, not simply hired laborers, and he does not distinguish between Jewish slaves and non-Jewish slaves – both are δοῦλοι.[56] Although not as crucial to the economy as elsewhere in the Roman empire, the presence of slaves as workers, especially as domestic workers or even debt slaves should be assumed for first century Palestine. The use of tenant farmers and sharecroppers was more common, but slaves were used in both agricultural contexts and in the trades.[57] The so-called "Servant" parables of Jesus and several of his sayings are thus better understood within the context of the institution of Greco-Roman slavery.[58] As Crossan has pointed out, a total of nine parables from the gospels have servants as central characters and involve a "master-servant relationship *and* a moment of critical reckoning therein."[59] Two parables usually considered authentic illustrate Jesus' attitude toward slaves and the servant/master relationship: the parable of the Dishonest Steward (Luke 16:1–8) and the Unmerciful Slave (Matt 18:23–24).[60]

The parable of the Dishonest Steward continues to puzzle commentators. In this story the manager of a rich man's estate is dismissed for supposed financial mismanagement. Following his dismissal, the steward calls in his master's debtors and reduces the amount of their debts to his employer with the understanding that in return they will care for him in his time of need. He is subsequently praised by his master for his shrewdness. The original parable probably ended at this point (16:8a), as the κύριος here easily refers back to the ὁ κύριος in vv. 3 and 5.[61] The three appended explanations to the parable in Luke demonstrate the difficulties of its interpretation even in antiquity.[62] In past years many scholars saw the meaning of the parable centered on the prudent behavior of the steward during a time of crisis, a course of action analogous to the appropriate response to the preaching of the Kingdom.[63] More recent scholars have questioned an apocalyptic interpretation,[64] and rightly refocus upon the social word evoked in the parable itself.[65] The audience of the parable would have assumed that the steward (οἰκονόμος) was a slave or freedman.[66] The steward is dismissed from his post, and faces the prospect of hard manual labor (Luke 16:3). In quick response, the steward acts to protect his own interests. The difficulty of interpretation lies in the master's praise for a servant, who has in effect twice defrauded him of large amounts of money.

Mary Ann Beavis has proposed that the best context in which

to understand the steward is in his resemblance to Aesop the crafty, trickster slave of the *Life of Aesop*. In episode after episode, this Greco-Roman picaresque hero[67] finds himself in similar crises, in trouble with his master or mistress, takes quick action to protect himself – usually by means of his quick wit, and subsequently gets the better of his superiors. Seen against this backdrop, the story of the Dishonest Steward would be both funny and familiar. The steward is in trouble with his master, he acts to remedy the situation behind his master's back, and then succeeds and receives the praise of his master for doing so. The charges leveled against the steward may be exaggerated, as a character like Aesop is often quickly punished on the basis of false accusations without the opportunity to defend himself.[68] In any case, the sympathy of the hearers of this parable, especially those from the lower classes, would have been with the steward and the other debtors, not the master.[69] The story thus has a subversive function, in that it praises the self-interested, resistant actions of a slave or freedman steward, whose actions help him survive in economically threatening circumstances. Neither the institution of slavery nor economic exploitation is directly challenged; rather the survivalist actions of the steward are praised.[70]

The parable of the Unmerciful Servant (Matt 18:23–35) is found only in Matthew's gospel where it concludes the discourse on community discipline. As Matthew presents it, the parable concerns the nature of the Kingdom of Heaven, the mutual forgiveness required in the community, and the subsequent judgment in light of moral failure. Interpreters have generally argued that the connective διὰ τοῦτο (therefore) and introductory formula "the kingdom of Heaven is like" (v. 23a) are Matthean, as is the final reference to judgment at the end of the parable proper (v. 35).[71]

The story hinges on the intricate relationships between patrons and their clients among the upper classes.[72] The servant in this case is clearly a slave (δοῦλος, v. 23) as is demonstrated by the king's ability to sell not only the servant, but his wife and children (v. 25). His entire family is owned by the king, although this particular slave has obviously risen to a high level within the court bureaucracy. The forgiveness of the slave's unimaginably large debt by the king is the most surprising feature of the story (v. 27), as one would expect the king to keep the debt in place as a means to exert control over his well-placed underling. For this reason Herzog's suggestion that the king's action is meant to recall the messianic jubilee has merit.[73] However, it is clear from the story that the actions of a king are not sufficient to initiate the jubilee; persons within each level of the bureaucracy must also be willing to forgive the debts owed to them. As Jeremias has suggested, the story is thus a negative example of discipleship[74] and its message comports with Jesus' exhortation to pray for mutual forgiveness of debts (Matt 6:12; Luke 11:4a–b). High levels of indebtedness led inexorably to increased enslavements of the lower classes, who could be forced to sell themselves or their children in order to meet the terms of outstanding loans.[75] The parable of the Unmerciful Servant thus suggests to Jesus' hearers the surprising solution of the forgiveness of debts, even those among the lower classes, who should not merely wait for a coming messianic jubilee.

Since other servant parables attributed to Jesus are less unsettling in their implications, gospel traditions that attempt to reverse the implications of these parables by picturing slaves behaving in expected and obedient ways are thus rendered historically suspect. In later traditions slaves watch eagerly for their returning master (Mark 13:34–37),[76] are punished accordingly for good or bad behavior (by dismemberment [διχοτομέω] Matt 24:45–51/Luke 12:42–46),[77] and should not expect their master to wait upon them upon his return (Luke 17:7–10).[78] Moreover, it must be explicitly stated at a later point that slaves are not above their masters (Matt 10:24; John 13:16).[79] This trajectory in the gospel tradition suggests that the gospel writers needed to temper Jesus' authentic teachings in order to deflect the controversial nature of earlier traditions concerning slavery and slave/master relations.

In light of Jesus' interest in his parables to challenge his hearers to consider slave/master relations, I would like to introduce into this discussion two traditions that have gone unnoticed for their probable significance for Jesus' social interests: the welcoming of "children" into the Kingdom of God (Mark 10:14/Matt 19:14/Luke 18:16) and the cryptic reference to those who make themselves eunuchs for the Kingdom (Matt 19:12). Both suggest Jesus maintained a subversive attitude towards slavery. In Mark 10:14–15 Jesus says,[80]

> Let the children (παιδία) come to me, do not hinder them; for to such belongs the kingdom of God. Truly I say to you whoever does not receive the kingdom of God like a child (παιδίον) will not enter it.

Virtually all commentators assume that Jesus here refers to children, and refer at some length to the low familial and social status of children in antiquity.[81] Children are those last who shall be first (Matt 20:16; cf. Mark 10:31; Matt 19:30; Luke 13:30; Thomas 4). However, children were not the lowest in prestige in ancient society unless they were slaves. Further, free children were not marginalized in antiquity, and were involved in many rites and festivals of public and private life.[82] Indeed, in Mark servitude is the model for discipleship, not childhood. Mark clearly identifies the "last" in prestige as slaves or servants. Whoever would be first (πρῶτος) must become the slave (δοῦλος) of all (Mark 10:44);[83] whoever would be first (πρῶτος) must be last and servant (διάκονος) of all (Mark 9:35).[84] In light of these observations, the saying probably has a quite different meaning, especially in Mark. The cognates παῖς and παιδίον have another meaning that goes unnoticed here. Both can mean slave or young slave, and can include boys, girls and handsome young men. This meaning is well attested in both Hellenistic literature, including Josephus and Philo,[85] and in papyri contemporary with the New Testament.[86] It is eminently reasonable, then, to propose that Jesus' hearers are told to identify themselves with the enslaved or those in positions of servitude. In fact, the reign of God belongs especially to them. Given that according to Mark Jesus is scolded by his disciples for blessing παιδία brought to him (Mark 10:13), Jesus' saying makes more sense if it refers to slaves, not children. Surely the statement that young slaves were of God's kingdom would have been met with surprise or even shock by his hearers, especially the free, even if they were poor.[87] Any who had been forced to sell children into servitude, however, would have appreciated Jesus' subversive speech.

The Eunuch saying carries this admonition to an even further extreme (Matt 19:12a). One of the most difficult of Jesus' sayings, it is probably authentic.[88] Since it can be easily detached from its Matthean setting, it probably circulated separately from the discussion concerning divorce (Matt 19:4–10). It is usually assumed that the reference here is to a celibate lifestyle, a recommendation which would have been hard to accept.[89] However, eunuchs were not necessarily celibate, merely sterile. In fact, eunuchs were often castrated as young boys in order to maintain their appeal as sex objects. Hence, I would like to suggest an alternative interpretation. Not only were eunuchs in a category segregated and devalued in Jewish life[90] but virtually all eunuchs were slaves or freedmen, having been cruelly emasculated before puberty. Although like all slaves eunuchs could rise within estate and royal bureaucracies, they were still the objects of derision and scorn.[91] Thus in a clear use of hyperbole, Jesus declares that some will "castrate (εὐνουχίζω) themselves for the sake of the kingdom of heaven" (Matt 19:12) – i.e., they will become like slaves. What could this mean? I would like to suggest that it be understood in light of the kind of self-sacrifice recommended in 1 Clement:

> We know that many among ourselves have given themselves to bondage (εἰς δεσμά) that they might ransom others. Many have delivered themselves to slavery (εἰς δουλείαν), and provided food for others with the price they received for themselves.[92]

This would place this saying well within the context of other ethical statements of Jesus found in other well known sayings: lend without interest (Thom 95:1–2/ Matt 5:42b; Luke 6:34–35),[93] always give to beggars (Matt 5:42/Luke 6:30),[94] offer the other cheek, give the shirt off your back, walk that extra mile (Matt 5:39–41)[95] and sell all you have and give to the poor (Mark 10:21).[96] The first shall be last and the last shall be first (Matt 20:16; cf. Mark 10:31; Matt 19:30; Luke 13:30; Thom 4);[97] whoever would be first (πρῶτος) must become the slave (δοῦλος) of all (Mark 10:44);[98] whoever would be first (πρῶτος) must be last and servant (διάκονος) of all (Mark 9:35).[99] Jesus' could be espousing either a radical Hebrew ideal of charity[100] or a Hellenistic philosophical ethic.[101] The social environment of Palestine and the Galilee allows for both.[102] Thus, both the Eunuch and the Young Slave sayings are highlighted by a saturnalian inversion of rank, and encourage this behavior as an ongoing altruistic ethic in the Kingdom of God. Mark interprets Jesus' ideal of service in terms of his suffering and death, an ideal which the Markan community should emulate during times of persecution (Mark 10:45) and in positions of leadership (Mark 10:35–45). John portrays Jesus as actually performing the service of a slave by washing the disciples' feet at a meal (John 13:1–20).

Conflicts in the Family

Such teachings inevitably created social conflicts, their nature and intensity depending in considerable part on the social class of the hearers. Contemporary dissension over Jesus' teachings has certainly left its mark on the gospel record in the form of an anti-familial theme and an emphasis on the primacy of a heavenly Father, not an earthly one. Jesus' true relatives are not his real family, but those who do the will of the Father (Matt 12:48–50/Thomas 99; cf. Mark 3:33–35/Luke 8:21);[103] one must be ready to hate one's own family for the kingdom (Luke 14:26; cf. Thomas 55; Matt 10:37/ Thomas 101);[104] and in Luke those who come after Jesus must revoke "father and mother and wife and children and brothers and sisters" (Luke 14:25–27).[105] Certain scholars have argued that Jesus' remarks concerning both the family and God's true fatherhood reflect an anti-patriarchal ethic in his teachings.[106]

However, it is highly unlikely that family disruption caused by Jesus' movement can be explained on the basis of a direct challenge to the inequality between men and women in the family. Peasant families and marital relationships are characterized by their gendered division of labor.[107] Further, the family conflict described in the two following passages derived from Q is clearly generational, not gendered:

> "For henceforth in one house there will be five divided, three against two and two against three; they will be divided, father against son and son against father, mother against daughter and daughter against her mother, mother-in-law against her daughter-in-law and daughter-in-law against her mother-in-law. (Q 12:52–53).[108]

And again:

> Whoever loves father and mother more than me is not worthy of me; and whoever loves son or daughter more than me is not worthy of me. (Matt 10:37)[109]

Thomas' version of the first saying, which is no doubt an earlier form, omits the reference to women altogether, and keeps the conflict strictly between father and son (Thomas 16).[110] Further, conflict between mothers-in-law and daughters-in-law is customary in extended families, since the daughter-in-law is not tied to her new family by blood, and mothers-in-law generally rule over their daughters-in-law sternly.[111] This underscores the secondary nature of Q 12:52–53 and makes it more likely that someone unfamiliar with women's intimate relationships – a scribe, perhaps – has expanded the saying on the basis of Mic 7:5–6.[112] The Lukan counterpart of Matt 10:37 has likewise expanded the familial conflicts to include those between men and women, as well as those between parents and children: one must "hate his own father and mother and wife and children and brothers and sisters" (Luke 14:25–27 RSV).[113] The Lukan version, omitting the reference to wives and children and requiring hatred of the family, is probably more authentic.

This anti-familial theme in the gospel record suggests that women and men did leave their families to follow Jesus; their usual household concerns became secondary to their commitment to his vision. This caused dissension, divisions, and probably separations. The potential for family crisis is clear from the fact that for members of the working classes and the peasantry, survival depended on close interdependence between husband and wife.[114] Jesus' teachings on marriage show sensitivity to this reality of lower class life. Thus, although Jesus acknowledged the family dissension and divisions caused by his message, he seems to have upheld the marriage and family bond between men and women by restricting divorce and remarriage.

Marriage and Divorce

Jesus' teaching on divorce occurs in three separate strands of early Christian tradition: Mark (Mark 10:5–10/Matt 5:32), Q (Luke 16:18/Matt 5:32), and Paul (1 Cor 7:9–11). This triple attestation makes it likely that Jesus made a pronouncement on divorce. Unfortunately, the great discrepancy among the three traditions makes Jesus' actual words irrecoverable.[115] Matthew has added the exception clause for cases involving adultery or fornication (πορνεία, Matt 5:32, 19:9), an addition that is widely considered Matthean.[116] The unqualified moral prohibition found in Mark is probably earlier. Both Mark and Paul assume that either the man or the woman has the legal right to initiate a divorce; Q assumes that right is only the man's. The significant variations in wording found among the divorce sayings suggest early Christians found Jesus' teaching on marriage and divorce difficult. It is best then to conclude that Jesus did prohibit divorce and remarriage.[117] The Markan version will be a convenient point of departure, since it is the earliest of the Synoptic versions.

Mark sets Jesus' comments on divorce in the context of a dialogue with Pharisees who have questioned him about divorce. Jesus responds by challenging Mosaic law (Deut 24:1–4), which allows a man to dissolve his marriage by simply presenting his wife with a certificate of divorce. Portrayed here as a point of contention with Jewish authorities on the Law, Jesus' teaching may be viewed in terms of the debate between the schools of the conservative Shammai and more liberal Hillel.[118] The use of Genesis to support the security of the marriage bond sounds strikingly similar to discussions found in the Dead Sea Scrolls, which seem to prohibit both polygamy as well as remarriage.[119] The dialogue between Jesus and the Pharisees ends with an aphorism: "Therefore what God has joined together let no one separate" (χωρίζω) (Mark 10:9). Such aphorisms are characteristic of Jesus' authentic words. In an aside to his disciples, Jesus categorically prohibits divorce and remarriage (Mark 10:10–12). Here Jesus' views are reminiscent of Mal 2:10–16.[120] His comments also suggest that both men and women could initiate divorce proceedings, and thus be equally culpable of adultery. Although many scholars argue this saying assumes Roman and not Jewish law, it is clear that some Jewish women did sue for divorce in first century Palestine.[121] It is also the case, however, that Cynic-Stoic philosophical writers were similarly supportive of marriage, and therefore probable that we have here another theme in Jesus' teaching which reflects the multi-cultural environment of first century Palestine.[122]

One could argue that in his affirmation of the sanctity of marriage Jesus reinforces the main hierarchical relationship between the sexes in ancient society rather than disrupts it. Whether this prohibition of divorce would be restrictive of women depended on their individual situations. It may have limited some Jewish women, by denying a legal right they enjoyed; others, dependent on their husbands for their equal share in the economic unit of a peasant household, may have welcomed it. Nor should it be forgotten that such a proscription would have been even more restrictive of men, since first century men enjoyed a high degree of sexual freedom as well as legal access to divorce. The fact that Jesus spoke to the matter at all suggests that divorce and separation were facts of life among his followers.

Jesus' teachings thus contain an anti-familial theme and suggest that family divisions and even marital separations occurred within the families of those who responded to his message. However, there is little evidence that Jesus challenged family solidarity on the grounds that the family was inherently patriarchal or was characterized by the inequality between sexes; rather it seems to have been the case that the radical commitment required by his teachings diminished the relative importance of other matters. The proof of this is twofold: he did not attack marriage, the central hierarchical relationship between a man and a woman in his society, and the divisions caused by his message were primarily between the generations, not the sexes. Finally, Jesus seems to have been critical of the reverence children accord fathers, or even parents. Jesus' ideal family requires husbands and wives, but it does not include fathers: Jesus' true relatives do the will of the Father in heaven (Matt 12:48–50/Thomas 99; cf. Mark 3:33–35/Luke 8:21). Yet even this appears to reflect not an anti-patriarchal theme in Jesus' teaching, but a Hebraic reaffirmation of the fatherhood of God, a faith that had ramifications for relationships between the generations, rather than between women and men.

Call No Man On Earth Father

Few dispute that Jesus addressed God as Father.[123] Based on the work of Joachim Jeremias, many Christian scholars have affirmed the special nature of Jesus' relationship to God on the basis of this title and have argued that Jesus' use of the term *abba* set him apart from both Hellenistic Judaism and the early church.[124] Robert Hammerton-Kelly further asserted the anti-patriarchal nature of Jesus' theology in the wake of feminist critiques of the use of titles like "father" for God.[125] Certain feminist scholars followed Hammerton-Kelly's example in their reconstructions of the message of Jesus.[126] Mary Rose D'Angelo has documented this discussion, and successfully called all aspects of it into question.[127] Jewish texts in first century Palestine, most notably from Qumran,[128] give evidence for the use of the term "father" as an address to God both in general declarative statements, and in prayer. Further, linguistic analysis of the use of the Aramaic *abba* does not support a specialized meaning conveying the intimacy between father and child.[129] Rather, the title "father" evoked the power, divine authority and kingship of the Jewish God in the face of Roman Imperial propaganda.[130] D' Angelo argues that presupposing as it does the superiority of men within society, it cannot convey an anti-patriarchal meaning. "Father" is the highest title of authority only within a social system in which privileged men have power over women, children, and such lesser males, as slaves, freedmen and clients.[131] Therefore, if Jesus addressed God as his father, he did so within the context of a Hellenistic Judaism that revered its God as king in an empire that demanded fealty to the emperor (cf. Mark 12:17/Luke 20:25/ Matt 22:21; Thomas 100:2–3).

Yet the evidence that Jesus applied the title "Father" to God is slight. It is limited to Mark 14:36 when Jesus prays to God in the Garden of Gethsemane, the Lord's Prayer in Q (Luke 11:2b/Matt 6:9), and also from Q the so-called "Johannine Thunderbolt" (Luke 10:21–22/Matt 11:25–27).[132] But only with great difficulty can one ascribe to Jesus the use of "*abba*" for God in Mark 14:36, given that it occurs in a section of Mark which is undeniably Markan composition. For one thing Jesus is alone; no one can witness to his words. Second, Mark casts Jesus as one in a line of Jewish martyrs.[133] Further, since "abba" was used liturgically in the early church (the spirit causes believers to cry out "Abba, father!" [Αββα ὁ πατήρ] [Gal 4:6; Rom 8:15]),[134] the use of Aramaic does not suggest that here we have Jesus' actual words. Thus, the cry of Jesus in the Garden of Gethsemane almost certainly does not go back to Jesus. Similarly, Jesus' claim of a special relationship with the Father in Luke 10:21–22/Matt 11:25–27 reflects Q's identification of Jesus with the figure of Wisdom, and is therefore not likely to represent Jesus' understanding of God or himself.[135] The Lord's Prayer, derived from Q, thus remains the only identification of God as πατήρ ("father") that can reasonably be attributed to Jesus himself. Yet there is no compelling reason to assume that the Aramaic "Abba" lies behind this address. No recensions of the Lord's Prayer read "Abba," nor is there any evidence that the Lord's Prayer was composed in anything but Greek.[136] Given that "Father" appears as an address in Jewish prayer of the period, D'Angelo is right to conclude that it is not surprising to find Jesus employing in prayer "an address to God that called Caesar's reign into question and made a special claim on God's protection, mercy, and providence."[137]

Still, D' Angelo's discussion accounts neither for the absence of fathers from Jesus' ideal family nor for the generational nature of the dispute fostered by Jesus' message. The context of a Jewish anti-imperial theology does not by itself explain either Jesus' address of God as father, or the incidence of family conflict created by his message.

However, another controversy within Judaism could well explain Jesus' interest in God as the true father. In Judaism, as in other religions of the ancient Mediterranean, there existed a complex of family rituals surrounding the burial of family members; it is commonly referred to as the cult of the dead. This family cult was usually dominated by women, although within Judaism men were also active in mourning rites. Ceremonies included funeral liturgies and feasts, frequent visits to the burial place, and the offering of foodstuffs to the deceased, who was thought to be in need of sustenance following death.[138] These practices were condemned by a number of Jewish prophets and assailed in other biblical writings. The Deuteronomist, for instance, declared that such practices were in conflict with Yahwism and centralized worship of Yahweh in the Jerusalem Temple. Laceration of the flesh, practiced by the prophets of Jezebel (1 Kgs 18:28), is condemned in Deut 14:1.[139] Elsewhere we find denunciations of the customs of leaving food in tombs and funerary feasting with the dead.[140] Isaiah denounces the continued invocation of the spirits of the dead, as well as other related customs such as eating with the dead in tombs.[141] Neither Jeremiah nor Ezekiel participated in funerals; Ezekiel did not even mourn the death of his wife.[142]

In Jesus' day care of the dead included rites of reburial; after the body of a loved one had decayed, the bones were carefully placed in a bone-box called an ossuary, which was then placed in a niche in the family tomb. Rather than being restricted to a particular group of Jews, such as the Pharisees or the upper classes, such reburials are now considered to have been performed more generally.[143]

Even the High Priest Caiaphas and his family were re-buried in ossuaries.[144] Inscriptional evidence for the naming of children after family members rather than popular biblical figures may reflect Hellenistic influence, but it clearly shows an interest in Jewish ancestral lines among Palestinian Jews of the Second Temple period.[145]

The veneration of special prophets and patriarchs was a well established practice in first century Palestine. Extant at the time of Jesus were tombs dedicated to the Patriarchs and Matriarchs, Rachel, the Maccabean martyrs, the prophetess Hulda, the prophet Isaiah, the prophet Zechariah ben Judah and a necropolis of kings near Jerusalem.[146] Making pilgrimages to these tombs and monuments[147] is precisely the custom that is being criticized in Q 11:47–51(Luke 11:47–51/Matt 23:29–36).[148] Several of these special tomb monuments, such as Zechariah's, are still standing in the Kidron valley.[149] In Bethlehem a tomb monument to Rachel still remains.[150] Depictions of these tombs of the special dead can be found as ossuary decorations, further attesting to their popularity during the first century.[151] Jewish writers are found debating the efficacy of prayer to prophets and "fathers." Deborah is portrayed in the first century *Biblical Antiquities* as saying right before her death: "Do not hope in your fathers (*patres*)," an exhortation which correctly – if ironically would discourage veneration of her as a dead prophetess and matriarch.[152] In Second Baruch the writer envisions a future in which such prayers to the ancestors and prophets will cease.[153] John the Baptist warned his contemporaries not to depend on Abraham as their Father (Matt 3:7–10/Luke 3:7–9).

Within this context I would like to place a series of sayings attributed to Jesus which suggest both a generational dispute over burials and disapprobation of practices involving veneration of the dead:

> To another (Jesus) said, "Follow me." But he said, "Lord, let me go first and bury my father." But he said to him, "Leave the dead to bury their own dead; but as for you, go and proclaim the kingdom of God (Luke 9:59/Matt 8:21).[154]
>
> Where the corpse is, there the eagles with be gathered together (Luke 17:37/ Matt 24:28).[155]
>
> Become passersby (Thomas 42).[156]
>
> Woe to you! for you are like unmarked graves, and people who walk over them do not know it (Luke 11:44/Matt 23:27).[157]

> Woe to you! for you build the tombs of the prophets but it was your fathers that killed them (Luke 11:47/Matt 23:29).[158]

> Call no man your father on earth (Matt 23:6–11).[159]

The saying on the dead burying their dead is usually considered authentic. Since burial rites for parents were a special responsibility, this saying would have been particularly offensive to many. Accordingly, most scholars have interpreted this saying to mean "let the (spiritually) dead bury the (physically) dead."[160] However, Byron McCane has argued persuasively that this saying refers not to initial burial, but to reburial, particularly the practice of reburial in ossuaries. Jesus would then be saying, "let the dead (in the tombs) re-bury their own dead," and thus denouncing special attention to the dead as contrary to his teaching of the Kingdom of God.[161] The saying from the Gospel of Thomas can also be read to betray a similar critique of the over attention to graves: "Become passersby" (ϣⲱⲡⲉ ⲉⲧⲉⲧⲛ̄ⲣ̄ⲡⲁⲣⲁⲅⲉ) may well allude to the phrase "passersby" common in ancient grave epitaphs. The point would be to keep on walking.[162] The saying on eagles and corpses seems to express a similar distaste for burials; vultures were birds of carrion, in the same class with ravens and crows.[163] This teaching of Jesus is the most likely to foster a family generational dispute, as it denies the legitimacy of burial practices traditionally owed to parents by their children. Excessive concern with tombs, corpses, and burials – to one's "fathers" or ancestors – was regularly censured by biblical writers and prophets as being at odds with true Hebraic monotheism. Jesus' concern was similar.

But this does not fully explain the witty harshness of these sayings, which fit better in a Hellenistic context. Cynic, Epicurean and Stoic philosophers also considered such solicitude for the dead superstitious, and were fond of quoting Theodore the Atheist to Lysimachus who was threatened with death without burial: "What matters it if I rot on the earth or under it?"[164] Socrates, of course, was also notable for his lack of concern for his own burial. When asked how he would like to be buried, he replied, "However you please, if you can catch me."[165] Other philosophers, especially Cynics, expressed a similar lack of concern for the disposal of their remains.[166] Thus, Jesus' saying has a clear Hellenistic flavor to it, although the underlying concern is Hebraic, not Greek.

Likely enough, Jesus also rejected the practice of venerating the dead at tombs. The woes against the Pharisees involving graves and the tombs of the prophets should be reconsidered as evidence for the historical Jesus. Many scholars reject these sayings because they betray the influence of a Deuteronomic view of history and therefore tend to presuppose the situation following Jesus' death.[167] While that is certainly the case for Luke 11:49–51/Matt 23:34–36, there are several reasons to consider the less complex sayings in Luke 11:44, 49/ Matt 23:27, 29 as authentic. First, Q 11:47–48 is not so obviously Deuteronomic, and is detachable from Q 11:49–51.[168] Second, O. H. Steck has argued that by the first century C.E. two themes in prophetic thought had coalesced: 1) the Deuteronomic view of history which assumed that God's judgment was precipitated by Israel's disobedience to God's law, and 2) the notion that prophets were habitually killed by Israel (cf. Neh. 9:26). According to Steck this blended theme was an oral tradition, widespread in Palestinian Judaism between 200 B.C.E. and 100 C.E. [169] Hence Jesus' words in Q 11:47–48 do not presuppose his death, and may make good sense for the situation following the death of John the Baptist. It is therefore not necessary to consider the entire section of the woes against the Pharisees in Matt 23:27–36/Luke 11:44–51 inauthentic. Jesus could well be reproaching the Pharisees for participating in a documentable and popular institution from first century Palestine, the veneration of popular prophets and patriarchs at special tomb-sites. This scenario accords well with the widespread view that Jesus was a prophetic figure who defended a strict view of Hebraic monotheism.

Clearly, Matthew so understood these imprecations. As a precursor to the woes against the Pharisees, he quotes Jesus as saying:

> Call no man your Father on earth, for you have one Father who is in heaven (Matt 23:9) (RSV).

This is a Matthean addition to Mark 12:37b–40, the question concerning the greatest commandment, which Matthew connects to one of the Q passages in which Jesus attacks the popular veneration of the prophets (Q 11:47–48). This suggests a concern not for family, marriage, or patriarchy, but for monotheism.[170] Here, emphasizing and expanding on a theme that I suggest was fundamental to

Jesus' own teaching, Matthew reasserts Hebraic monotheism according to classic prophetic style: God sends prophets who preach repentance, but Israel persecutes and subsequently kills them.

Jesus' concern for the veneration of prophets at tombsites readily comports with the saying "let the dead bury their own dead," which criticized the reburial of "fathers" as contrary to the vision of the Kingdom of God. Both would reflect an ongoing concern within Judaism going back to Exilic times. The presence of such a prophetic theme in Jesus' teaching would best explain the repeated characterization of Jesus as a prophet[171] without denying the Hellenistic flavor of many of his sayings.[172] Further, according to Q Jesus taught that the judgment would come unnoticed in the midst of everyday activities (Luke 11:26–32/Matt 24:37–39; Luke 17:34–35/Matt 24:40–41).[173] That is, most would not notice that there was anything amiss. Similarly, burial customs were so much a part of the culture it is easy to imagine that few would have considered them objectionable.

That Jesus repudiated extravagant burial practices for parents and the veneration of patriarchs and special prophets at tombs makes better sense of his omission of fathers from the ideal family (Mark 3:33–35) and the generational nature of family divisions fostered by his message as found in Q (Luke 12:52–53/Matt 10:35–36; Luke 14:25–27; Matt 10:37). Burial customs are essential to the workings of any culture, and Jesus' challenge to traditional practices, even ancient practices considered at odds with Jewish monotheistic tradition, would have been highly offensive and caused deep divisions within households.[174] This theme of Jesus' teachings demonstrates both the Hebraic aspects of his message, and its Hellenistic flavor, reflecting as it does both prophetic monotheistic interests and the often mordant wit of Hellenistic aphorisms expressing a lack of interest in burial. The easy intertwining of these two influences in Jesus' message should warn us against glibly characterizing him as either a prophetic character or a Cynic, but it does allow for his assimilation in the culturally eclectic environment of Palestine and Lower Galilee. Further, this interpretation of Jesus' message does not permit an anti-patriarchal characterization either for Jesus' emphasis on the fatherhood of God or for the absence of fathers in the ideal family. Rather, Jesus' interest was focused on other matters entirely, particularly the fatherhood of the one God within his kingdom.

Gender, Class and Jesus: Some Conclusions

Women obviously joined the Jesus movement, although interest in that presence is largely absent from Jesus' teaching itself. A few women belonged to the Jesus movement just as they were present in small numbers among the Cynics, Epicureans, Pythagoreans, Stoics, Therapeutae, the Zealot group led by Simon son of Gioras, the disciples of John the Baptist and the sectarians at Qumran. So why were women in Jesus' movement? Why did they join? Their presence no doubt reflects the fact that women then, like women now, had diverse interests.[175] It is inappropriate to stereotype first century women in such a way that we cannot imagine the true diversity of their experience. For example, wealthier women could have been attracted by Jesus' challenge to the ancient notion of rank, having experienced the often close relationship between women and their house slaves (Q 14:16–24; Thom 64:1–12). Poor women might have been attracted to Jesus' saying, "Blessed are the poor" (Q 6:20). Both girls sold into debt slavery and their parents might have been attracted to his declaration about the forgiveness of debts (Q 11:2–4; see also Matt 18:23–34). Some working women would have been attracted by the motif of lower class resistance to authority explicit in parables such as the Unjust Judge and the Dishonest Steward. Others may have responded, as did a number of men, to Jesus' criticism of traditional burial practices and his emphasis on God as Father. Although women's particular interests are secondary to such concerns, it can be argued that the social resistance inherent in Jesus' reign of God, and the enactment of that resistance in the context of open commensality and renewed emphasis on the Fatherhood of God must have contributed to women's interest in becoming disciples of Jesus and in joining early Christian communities.

Chapter 4

Women, Gender & Lament in Q

The Sayings Source Q, a collection of traditions about Jesus, was known to both Matthew and Luke and contains primarily Jesus' teachings and parables. Q was probably compiled in Palestine in two stages between the years 50–70 C.E. Just as evidence from Mark's gospel reflects the presence of women within his movement, evidence from this earlier layer of the gospel tradition further suggests that women who joined Jesus for communal meals were branded "whores." Further, Q suggests that women participated in early Palestinian controversy over funeral lamentation and burial rites, a debate which affected the Q community. These traditions linking Jesus to women followers and table companions show that the association of women with Jesus was not only a characteristic of his movement, but also a controversial one. Further, the relevant material from Q suggests that women were among the disciples of John the Baptist, which in turn intimates that women were among those disciples of John who reportedly left John to follow Jesus (cf. John 1:35–37). Not only does Q retain Jesus' concern for customs like secondary burial (9:60), but it further extends his critique to tomb veneration, and thus reflects a Jewish aversion to idolatry reflected in the prophetic literature and the disdain for comon funerary rites common among Hellenistic philosophers (Q 11:47–48; cf. Q 11:44).[1] This controversy over burial rites and the veneration of the tombs of the prophets in Q is explicable following the death of Jesus and John, both perceived by the Q community to be prophets of Sophia who were killed (Q 7:35). In response to their deaths, women may have participated in the creation of traditions like the Wisdom oracle which prophesied the destruction of

Jerusalem (Q 13:34–35), a lament that may have originated in the context of ritual lamentation before being transferred into its scribal context in Q.

Feminist Analysis of Q

Because of the ongoing interest in the question of Jesus' relationship to women, the sayings source Q has become a new focus for feminists and others engaged in exploring both the presence of women in early Christian groups and gendered theological themes in early Christian literature.[2] Furthermore, various elements from Q have been incorporated as background for recent discussions of the "Historical Jesus." This undergirds the argument that aspects of Jesus' teaching and social program challenged the ancient social hierarchy and with it the secondary role of women in the ancient world.[3] This understanding of Q and subsequent historical reconstruction of Jesus, however, have not gone unchallenged.[4] The characterization of Q as a sapiential document, and its attendant focus on the figure of Sophia has proven to be a fruitful avenue of research for scholars interested in developing modern feminist theological readings of both early Christian history and New Testament texts.[5]

Although the matter is indeed complex, it is possible to argue from Q that women played a role in the Jesus movement. For example, women are included in the implied audience of Q, in that women's roles, particularly domestic roles, are often paired with those of men in various sayings and parables.[6] Women are equally affected by the household strife alluded to in Q, to the extent that even relationships between women may fall into disrepair.[7] It is usually proposed that the family discord suggested in Q is linked to the itinerancy fostered by the so-called "mission" in Q,[8] which in turn is used to argue the presence of women in that "mission," however that mission is conceived.[9] Yet since the household conflict in Q is not gendered (i.e., pitting women against men), but clearly generational (pitting parents against children) (Q 12:52–53; 14:26–27), it seems more likely that the disruption reflected in Q stems from conflict over traditional burial rites, a more plausible source of generational dispute (Q 9:59–60). It is Luke's rendition of Q 14:26 which expands the household dispute across gender lines, making it a disruption of marriage by requiring the rejection of wives and children rather than intra-generational strife between parents or children (Luke 14:26; Matt 10:37–39). In fact, in view of the short distances between towns and villages in ancient Galilee, homelessness, or true itinerancy may not be what the Q document implies.[10] In any case, if Q advocates the outright desertion of the extended family, the interdependence of lower class families was such that this would hardly have benefited those most likely to be left behind: women and children.[11]

Although women are nowhere excluded (Q 10:2–12), evidence for women's presence in the "Q mission" as prophets or missionaries remains inconclusive, at least on the basis of Q itself.[12] Paul's reference to the apostles, Cephas and the "brothers of the Lord" taking along a "sister/wife" (1 Cor 9:5), may refer to the Palestinian missionary situation,[13] though less likely to that of the Jerusalem church, [14] given Q's apparent antipathy towards Jerusalem (Q 13:34–35). Yet, the possibility that members of this Jesus movement were engaged in shorter trips buttresses the argument that women might have participated. Cross-cultural studies indicate that lower class women, particularly peasant women, have a greater degree of mobility than their elite sisters, and commonly travel from town to town to engage in trade, barter or other business of the day.[15] Thus the kind of travel implied in Q may reflect everyday life in ancient Palestine rather than some sort of organized itinerancy with the sole aim of preaching. In that case, of course, the participation of women in any kind of missionary activities would not likely have caused the household disruptions recorded in Q 12:52–53 and 14:26.[16] Still, given current discussions on the social location of Q, the first layer of Q,[17] and the process of Q redaction,[18] questions about the likely social status of women participants in the Jesus movement reflected in Q are not easily resolved. For example, given that the mission instructions imply voluntary, not involuntary poverty, not all in this movement would fall under the category of "peasants."[19] In fact, it may be unrealistic to assume an impoverished social location for the Q source at all, as it is the product of scribal activity and its writers/redactors are involved in a scribal argument.[20] Scribal communities in agricultural societies often adhere to very traditional gender roles.[21] We will see that the context of scribal argumentation may at have bearing on the implications of Q for the presence of women in the Jesus movement.

Q assumes women at least in the audience and perhaps as mission participants need not imply an overall predisposition in favor of women or the feminine in Q. For example, even though the parables in Q depict the roles of women as well as men, they do not describe those roles in positive ways.[22] And the unrelentingly androcentric character of all the gendered couplets in Q seems likely to be patterned after legal or quasi-legal formulae found in Greco-Roman law which functioned to regulate men and women's behavior within the patriarchal state.[23] This in turn suggests that the scribal village administrators responsible for the compilation of Q were exclusively male.[24] Moreover, although possibly fruitful for constructing feminist theologies, the Jewish Wisdom theology in Q seems completely traditional and consistent with other uses of Sophia mythology in Jewish Wisdom schools.[25] And while Q 10:21–22 clearly reflects wisdom motifs, [26] it also characterizes Jesus' relationship with God as one between father and son, and implies an exclusive relationship between Wisdom as "Son" and God as "Father."[27] Finally, wisdom writers or other authors employing Sophia mythology in their larger theological constructions of God were hardly known for their elevation of real women in the social realm.[28] Thus, we should not overlook the overall male-centered mindset of Q when using it to reconstruct the place of women in early Christianity and in Jesus' own movement.[29]

Yet there is further evidence that Q knows of women's participation in this Jesus movement, for material from Q 7 implies that women were present at meals with Jesus. In Q 7:33–34 Jesus is accused of being a "wine bibber and a glutton" and a "friend of tax collectors and sinners" – slanderous imagery that implies immoral behavior with women at meals. Furthermore, the so-called "Children in the Marketplace" pericope, – which has been interpreted as alluding to the lack of response to Wisdom's envoys, such as John, Jesus and the Q prophets, – uses imagery implying activities characteristic of men and women in banquet and funerary contexts (piping and mourning). In light of this imagery in Q 7:31–35, the possibility that Q 7 also included an actual reference to women "prostitutes," the kind of women stereotypically linked in Hellenistic literature to public meals, needs serious examination. Although a seemingly minor matter, the presence of women at meals with men was one controversial aspect of the overall social progress of women which developed during the Hellenistic era.[30] The presence of women in meal contexts would place the Q depiction of the Jesus movement squarely within the context of the social progressivism of the Roman age as well as one trajectory of Jewish tradition which allowed for the presence of women in communal and celebratory meals.

Meals with "Tax Collectors and Sinners" (Q 7:33–34)

In Q 7:34 Jesus is insulted for his table practice, one that supposedly features "wine bibbing and gluttony." He is also accused of being a "friend of tax collectors and sinners." This characterization of Jesus' activities appears also in Mark (2:14–17) and is considered by most Historical Jesus scholars to be an authentic tradition,[31] since they are persuaded that these passages involve groups that can be identified within the social environment of first-century Palestine.[32] "Tax collectors" (or "toll collectors"),[33] are usually identified as despicable because of their relationship with the Roman occupational forces,[34] their connection with "robbers,"[35] or their basic dishonesty.[36] For Jews to eat with them would therefore have been considered scandalous, not only in view of their occupation and lifestyle, but out of concern for becoming ritually impure in their company.[37] Or such behavior could simply have been considered immoral.[38] The term "sinners" is similar. Many scholars identify "sinners" with those who would have been considered ritually impure, particularly by Pharisees. These would have been the 'amme ha'ares, i.e., all non-Pharisees with whom Pharisees would have been prohibited from eating, though the number of Pharisees actually affected by such restrictions would have been small. [39] Narrower definitions of "sinners" have also been suggested, such as those known for habitual sin, or those unwilling to repent.[40] Still others suggest these "sinners" were Jews who lived like Gentiles or rejected the practice of the Law.[41] "Sinners" were also associated with all those involved in lower class service occupations, including former slaves.[42] Some scholars have even argued that the category of "sinners" would have included women generally, or particularly those with bad reputations, or prostitutes.[43] However, it cannot be substantiated that the practice of eating with those characterized as "sinners" would in and of itself have been contrary to Jewish purity regulations.[44] It is further unlikely that the mere presence of women at meals would have violated Jewish purity regulations, and especially not in the context of everyday or celebratory meals.[45] Rather, as was previously noted, the complaint of Jewish envoys to Caesar that Herod allowed their women to participate in Roman orgies suggests that their concern was not purity, but propriety.[46]

In fact, since eating with "tax collectors and sinners" was probably less a purity issue than a matter of propriety, "tax collectors" and "sinners" may not be a designation for two historically identifiable groups at all. Rather, "eating with tax collectors and sinners" may be simply a stereotypical way of insulting someone's way of life in terms of one's customary behavior at meals.[47] The accusation in Q may simply be a swipe at Jesus' table etiquette. For example, that Jesus is "friends" with tax collectors and sinners certainly implies that he eats with them. "Friendship" is a common banquet theme.[48]

Such a characterization also reflects typical depictions of those known for banqueting with "promiscuous" women and pimps, for in antiquity tax collectors were often linked to prostitution. In ancient Greece, state revenue was collected by special tax gathers known as πορνοτελῶναι who kept lists of licensed harlots.[49] Prostitutes were not taxed during the Roman period until the reign of Caligula (37–41 C.E.), but they were still required to register to ply their trade.[50] Thus, tax collecting and keeping a brothel still remained linked in Hellenistic literature. This association can also be found in first century Palestine.[51] Because of these stereotypical associations, tax collecting and brothel keeping were also taken up by rhetoricians and others as a means to slander groups or individuals. Thus Plutarch remarks that the Spartans slight the Athenians for collecting taxes and keeping brothels,[52] and Dio Chrysostom remarks of rulers, "Is it not plain to see that many who are called kings (βασιλεῖς) are only traders, tax collectors (τελῶναι) and keepers of brothels (πορνοβοσκοί?).[53] Brothel-keepers, of course, would be expected to have prostitutes in their company.[54]

Not only was the term "tax collector" associated with those who kept company with promiscuous women, prostitutes and pimps, but the term "sinner" likewise held connotations of sexual impropriety. Certain behavior identified Hellenistic persons as "sinners," and the term was particularly applied to those who participated in sexual misconduct, such as drunkards, male prostitutes, men who chased women, and adulterers.[55] In Hellenistic literature, ἁμαρτωλός usually designated either a person's lack of education or moral failure of some kind,[56] and as such appears in Hellenistic catalogues of virtues and vices, where it is roughly equivalent to the Latin *sceleste*.[57] Plutarch uses it in the first sense as slander against his Stoic opponents.[58] Luke uses the term to designate a "woman of the city" (i.e. a prostitute) who anoints Jesus at a meal (Luke 7:37).[59]

This background reinforces the recent suggestion that "sinners" (ἁμαρτωλοί) is best understood in the context of Jewish sectarianism and philosophical debate, where it is used as rhetorical slander to denounce fellow Jews who do not belong to one's particular sect.[60] Dennis Smith has suggested that both "sinners" and "tax collectors" should be understood in this manner. Thus, according to Smith, the entire phrase, "tax collectors and sinners" should be categorized as a *topos* in Greco-Roman Jewish polemic.[61] Although the use of the term "sectarian" to describe first-century Jewish groups may not be helpful for understanding the relationship of these groups to one another,[62] it remains the case that these groups engaged in polemic and verbal exchange.[63] Thus, the accusation that Jesus associated with "tax collectors and sinners" is an example of the caricature of polemic and not social description.[64]

As was noted above, the connection between these two terms and their use as slander against Jesus' or his followers' table practice is apt, as tax collectors are connected in Greco-Roman literature to those who trafficked in prostitution and slavery, particularly to brothel keepers and pimps, those most responsible for supplying women and slaves for banquets.[65] And it was common for demeaning portraits of individuals to include insults leveled against their table practice and dining companions. To malign Verres, for example, Cicero pictures his degenerate behavior at banquets with lewd women.[66] In view of such a model, it is hardly surprising to find τελῶναι combined with πόρναι (Matt 21:31), nor startling that Luke should portray a prostitute at a meal in staging his dramatic narrative about Jesus' attitude toward "sinners" (Luke 7:36ff).[67]

Certain scholars of Q have remarked that Q 7:34 makes Jesus out to be some kind of "party boy" or "party animal."[68] However, the Hellenistic evidence suggests that this kind of language in Q 7:34

is merely the language of insult, and tells us little about Jesus' actual behavior, nor can it be used to identify Jesus table companions in Q as being real "tax collectors" or "sinners."[69] Even the accusation against Jesus' lifestyle in Q 7:31–35 as a "wine-bibber and glutton" reflects the Deuteronomic theme of the "rebellious son" who keeps company with "harlots." Far from being a trivial allegation, being a "rebellious son" is a serious indictment.[70] The "wine bibber and a glutton" charge and the accusation of eating with "tax collectors and sinners" are similar insults. The force of "tax collectors and sinners" is connotative rather than denotative, and mainly identifies Jesus or his followers as opponents.[71] It is said of John "He has a demon." No one has ever taken seriously the reported claim that John had a demon (Luke 7:33), or speculated about what kind of demon he had.[72] Both attacks are simply insults disparaging the respective lifestyles of Jesus and John.[73]

Given the links between "tax collectors" and prostitution, "sinners" and sexual impropriety, and banqueting and consorting with lewd women at meals, such slander also suggests that Jesus is here being accused of eating with "promiscuous" women. Women were often accused of promiscuity for public behavior generally, particularly when they participated in unorthodox table etiquette or engaged in free association with men in the public sphere.[74] In fact, the accusation of meretricious behavior is also found in the context of philosophical repartée, in particular as a term bandied about by philosophical groups in the habit of slandering one another when debating the relative merits of one another's philosophical systems.[75] The use of this kind of slander reveals the presence of women in certain philosophical groups. The Cynic school in particular was notable for its inclusion of women like Hipparchia and for their defense of women's ability to study philosophy and achieve moral virtue.[76] Women were included in Epicurean circles[77] and had diverse social backgrounds; some were slaves and courtesans, others were respectably married.[78] The Stoic philosopher Musonius Rufus also encouraged teaching women philosophy, albeit for the purpose of making them better housewives and mothers.[79] Given the rivalry between philosophical groups, and the controversial nature of the presence of women in groups usually restricted to men, it is not surprising that these groups used cultural stereotypes of women to insult each other. Since the attainment of a philosophical education was common among ancient Greek courtesans, women in these groups could be called "prostitutes" by rival philosophical sects.[80] Various religious groups in antiquity were also accused of sexual immorality, particularly on the part of women members. Groups so accused include early Christianity and Judaism, as well as the adherants of Isis and Dionysius.[81] The term "prostitute," then, as well as the general accusation of sexual promiscuity on the part of women in a group, should be recognized as a common form of insult leveled against women in antiquity, and therefore numbered among the Hellenistic *topoi* of Greco-Roman polemics.[82]

Hence the report in Q 7:34 implies that Jesus was slandered for eating with women, and thus is a participant in the social progressivism of his day, as were Cynics, Epicureans, Stoics, and others who allowed women to attend philosophical symposia and other public or religious meals. It further betrays the presence of women in the Q community, and identifies the Jesus movement as one of the numerous Jewish and other Hellenistic groups that were affected by changing Greco-Roman meal customs.

Furthermore, this kind of slander fits well with the consensus view of the redaction of Q, particularly the layer known as Q2. This stratum is considered to be particularly characterized by rhetoric leveled against "this generation," and Pharisees.[83] In fact, in light of John Kloppenborg's recent suggestion that the compilers of Q were lower level scribes in opposition to a higher level of more elite scribes, like the Pharisees,[84] this kind of rhetoric on both sides becomes completely explicable. The opponents of the Jesus movement use stereotypical language and accuse them of being a bunch of "tax collectors and sinners" who run around with women and pimps, and in return the Q scribes call their opponents "this generation," "white washed tombs," a "brood of vipers," and the like. If this language is understood within the context of first century Jewish inter-sectarian polemics, one may conclude that the boundary creation was well underway in the Jesus movement as early as the time of the compiling of Q.[85]

Jesus, John and the Courtesans

In light of the foregoing discussion, the possibility that Q 7 included a reference to "prostitutes" (πόρναι) needs further examination. Immediately preceding the "Children of the Marketplace" pericope, Luke offers a further comparison of those who accept Jesus and John with those who reject them:

> I tell you, among those born of women no one is greater than John; yet the least in the kingdom of God is greater than he." (And all the people who heard this, including the tax collectors, acknowledged the justice of God, because they had been baptized with John's baptism. But by refusing to be baptized by him, the Pharisees and the lawyers rejected God's purposes for themselves) (Luke 7:28–30)(NRSV).

There is an enticing parallel to this in Matthew 21:31–32:

> Jesus said to them, "Truly I tell you, the tax collectors and the prostitutes (*πόρναι*) are going into the Kingdom of God ahead of you. For John came to you in the way of righteousness, and you did not believe him, but the tax collectors and prostitutes believed him; and even after you saw it, you did not change your minds and believe him" (NRSV).

The Matthean version suggests that women were numbered among the disciples of John the Baptist, were baptized by him, and then subsequently joined Jesus' movement. The Gospel of the Nazoreans known to Jerome also suggests the presence of women disciples, including Jesus' mother, among John's followers.[86] Matthew thus records an ancient tradition linking women to the Baptist's movement.

There are good reasons for arguing that some form of this pericope might have been present in Q. Several scholars in the past have suggested this, most recently William Arnal of the International Q Project.[87] In spite of the consensus that Q did not include this saying,[88] some commentators remain persuaded that here Matthew and Luke are drawing on an earlier written source.[89]

Given the stereotypical imagery found in Q 7:31–35, which becomes explicable in the context of ancient gendered ideology, some form of Matt 21:31–32 would easily cohere with the slander about Jesus the "wine bibber and glutton."[90] This would mean that the theme of Jesus' connection to the stigmatized is clearly a theme grounded in Q, and not just a later development of the evangelists Matthew and Luke.[91] Furthermore, the "Children of the Marketplace" contains a similar depiction of the lifestyles of both Jesus and John, as Q 7:34–35 and can be read to link them both to the "marginalized," namely to women and/or slaves.[92] Thus, not only is this theme found in Q, it is found precisely in Q 7:31–35 – the context in which Arnal has argued 7:29–30 should be placed – since it reflects a parallel attack on the lifestyles of Jesus and John, not just a rejection of their preaching.[93]

Furthermore, given the scribal context posited for Q and Q redaction,[94] it is not all that surprising to find evidence of the obverse of the Q group's claim to be "children of wisdom" (Q 7:35) found in a Q section which contains slander and polemic leveled against them (Q 7:33–34). The opposite of "Lady Wisdom" in Jewish sapiential tradition is of course "Lady Folly," the whore.[95] Another example of this kind of rhetoric is found in the "Woe" of P Oxy 840, which contains an accusation of Jesus against a chief priest/Pharisee:[96]

> Woe unto you blind that see not! You have bathed yourself in water that is poured out, in which dogs and swine lie night and day and you have washed yourself and have chafed your outer skin, which prostitutes (πόρναι) also and flute-girls anoint, bathe, chafe and rouge, in order to arouse desire in men, but within they are full of scorpions and of (bad)ness (of every kind).

Thus, associating John and Jesus (via John) with "tax collectors and prostitutes" in Q 7 would be cutting and ironic. The accusation against Jesus associating with "tax collectors and sinners," which would include women (obviously such women would be labeled "whores")[97] is here turned on its head. Even so-called "tax collectors and prostitutes" (πόρναι) have precedence over the opponents of Jesus and John. As has been noted, to claim an insult robs it of its power.[98]

Once this thematic correspondence between Luke 7:29/Matt 21:31–32 and Q 7:31–35 is recognized, then the hints of verbal agreement between Luke 7:29 and Matt 21:31 become more significant.[99] The basic antithesis of the passages is the same: John's teaching was well-received by two groups, "tax collectors" (τελῶναι) and either "all the people" (πᾶς ὁ λαός) (Luke) or "prostitutes" (πόρναι) (Matthew) but rejected by the Pharisees. Luke 7:29 shares vocabulary with its Q context (δικαιόω), cf. Q 7:35) and τελῶναι (cf. Q 7:34). These correspondences have usually been used to argue for Lukan composition of 7:29 on the basis of Q 7:31–35.[100] However,

Matt 21:31–32 also contains catchword connections with *Luke's* Q context, despite the fact that Matthew has removed this pericope from its original context (Matt 11:7–11; 11:16–19 = Luke 7:24–28; 31–35) and placed it into a Markan section (Matt 21:23–27 = Mark 12:27–33). Yet it still retains the words ὁδῷ ("way, road," cf. Q 7:27), βασιλεία ("kingdom," cf. Q 7:28) and ἦλθεν γὰρ Ἰωάννης ("for John came," cf. Q 7:33). Thus, the thematic correspondences between Luke 7:29/Matt 21:31–32 and Q 7:31–35, the structurally analogous content they display, and the catchword associations linking both Luke 7:29–30 and Matt 21:31–32 to Q 7:24–28; 31–35 all give weight to the argument for placing this material in Q.

Both Luke 7:29 and Matt 21:31–32 show signs of heavy redaction.[101] This is not surprising given the controversial nature of the term πόρνη. There were many euphemisms for "whore" or "prostitute," and many literary images of the kind of women and slaves found in banquet settings; but the term πόρνη was the most indelicate, coarse and insulting term for common whores in antiquity. It was used for the lowest of the prostitute classes, designating not the higher class courtesans, but rather the lowest kind of street hookers, flute-players and harpists.[102] The inclusion of the phrase "tax collectors and prostitutes" (πόρναι) in Q is thus a clear case of *lectio difficilior potior*.[103] The connotations of this epithet would no doubt have motivated great redactional effort on the part of Matthew and Luke. However, the redactional activity of the evangelists indicates that they are working with a common written source.

From Luke's version of this pericope, there are several arguments which would favor his reliance on a source before him which included πόρναι as we find in Matthew 21. First, an occurrence of πόρναι in Q 7 would explain Luke's variation from the Markan chronology to include the anointing story at this point (Luke 7:36–50)[104] as well as his reinterpretation of the woman as a prostitute (πόρνη).[105] Here Paul Hoffmann misses the clear connotation of the phrase used by Luke to describe this woman which is in fact a euphemism for "prostitute." She is γυνὴ ἥτις ἦν ἐν τῇ πόλει ἁμαρτωλός, "a woman who was a sinner in the city" (Luke 7:37). Combining the term "sinner" with the phrase "known in the city" to describe a *woman* results in the colloquial gendered epithet much like "streetwalker" or "public woman."[106] Since Hoffmann and

Robinson miss this connotation, they insists that the woman is not called a "prostitute," but merely a "sinner"[107] and therefore see Luke 7:36–50 as Luke's elaboration of Q 7:33–35, which shows Jesus to be a "friend to sinners."[108] This seems highly unlikely given Luke's clear interest in portraying the women in his narrative as respectable Greco-Roman matrons.[109] In fact, this concern is particularly evident in his scenes involving women at meals. Luke tends to redact passages in such a way as to keep Jesus from dining with "sinners" (5:29; 7:34; 15:1ff; 19:1–10). This is probably because he interprets "sinners" to include women, particularly a woman like the one described in Luke 7:37 as *ἁμαρτωλός* ("sinner").[110] Although he records that Jesus is accused of dining with *τελῶναι καὶ ἁμαρτωλοί*, "tax collectors and sinners" (Luke 5:30), when he turns this into a narrative Luke depicts Jesus eating with "tax collectors and others" (*ἄλλοι*), not "tax collectors and sinners" (*ἁμαρτωλοί*) (cf. Mark 2:15 and Lk 5:29).[111] Luke's shift from Mark's *ἁμαρτωλοί* ("sinners") to *ἄλλοι* ("others") in Luke 5:29 would thus correspond neatly to a shift from *πόρναι* ("prostitutes") (in Q) to *πᾶς ὁ λαός* ("all the people") in Luke 7:29. Thus a Lukan shift from "tax collectors and prostitutes" to "all the people and the tax collectors" is all but predictable, given Luke's tendency to avoid depicting Jesus joining women for meals and his tendency to cast the women around Jesus as respectable.[112] The occurrence of the term *πόρναι* in a written source, however, would fully explain both Luke's recasting the story of the anointing (Mark 14: 3–9) as a story about a repentant hooker, and his placement of this story in the middle of this particular section of Q 7. Given Luke's general conservative attitude about women, and his reticence about the meal tradition concerning "sinners," it seems highly unlikely that he would take a story devoid of erotic overtones in Mark[113] and deliberately transform it into a scandalous story about a streetwalker who comes in and caresses Jesus' feet unless some (undeniable) written tradition suggested it. Hoffmann presents no adequate explanation for Luke's transformation of Mark 14:3–9 in Luke 7:36–50 and Luke's placement of this pericope immediately following Q 7:24–28 and 7:31–35.[114] Luke shows additional discomfort with this story, by avoiding the term *πόρνη* and suggesting that this woman had repented of her sinful life long before she approaches Jesus at a meal.[115] Although it is true that a call to the poor and the marginalized is often claimed as a Lukan theme,[116] Luke's Jesus spends the bulk of his time lounging around with the rich (not the poor) and rarely associates with "sinners" directly, unless they are specifically described as previously repentant.[117] Hence the scene in Luke 7:36–50, particularly the depiction of the woman, cannot be explained on the basis of Lukan theology alone.

Finally, Luke clearly connects the "children" in the marketplace in Q 7:32 to this woman "sinner" who "weeps" in Luke 7:36–50.[118] A clear reference to *πόρναι* "prostitutes" in Q 7 would give him further motivation for making this connection. Moreover, a Q passage contrasting the response of "prostitutes" to Jesus and John and the lack of response of their opponents would also explain Luke's setting the anointing in the home of "Simon the Pharisee" who is subsequently unmoved by the weeping (*κλαίω*) (7:38) of the sinner/prostitute, just as "this generation" is unmoved by the "piping" and "mourning" of Jesus, John, and their followers.[119] Thus, Luke's interpretation of the "Children of the Marketplace" pericope, his use of the story about the woman who anoints Jesus, and his redactional activity all suggest that the version of Q used by Luke contained a reference to "tax collectors and prostitutes" (*πόρναι*) in Q 7.[120]

Elements of Matthew's gospel also suggest that some form of Matt 21:31–32 might have been present in Q. First, it is difficult to show that Matthew has some special interest in prostitutes that adequately explains Matt 21:31–32 on the basis of Matthean redaction.[121] Hence, Matt 21:31 is often assumed to be traditional material.[122] However, Matthew has never been characterized as bringing special materials involving women to his gospel as has Luke.[123] Given that various passages in Luke not paralleled in Matthew seem surely derived from Q on the basis of their coherence with other sections confidently assigned to Q,[124] the possibility that Matt 21:31 preserves Q should remain open.[125] Since Matt 21:31 coheres with Q 7:31–35, its origin in Q is plausible. The occurrence of the non-Matthean phrase "kingdom of God" (*βασιλεία τοῦ θεοῦ*) in v. 31 has often puzzled commentators.[126] Given the other catchword associations between Matt 21:32 with the Q context of Q 7:24–28; 31–35[127] it is not impossible that here Matthew preserves Q.

Although "kingdom of God" does occur once as Matthean redaction (Matt 21:43)[128] it is derived in another instance from Q (Matt 12:28).[129] Thus, it is reasonable to suppose that this uncharacteristic "kingdom of God" in Matt 21:31 indicates a pre-Matthean source, namely Q. Although the occurrence of this phrase in Matt 21:31 may have less bearing on whether Matt 21:32 was in Q, this is only the case if Matt 21:31 is assumed to be from Matthew's special material and hence considered separately.[130]

The Matthean context does not influence the basic order of responses found in Matt 21:32. The "Parable of the Two Sons" (Matt 21:28–31a), which immediately precedes Matt 21:31–32 and is supposed to explain the parable (but does not)[131] lists the positive response first (the first child says "no" but does the "will his father" thereby obeying) and the negative response second (the second child says "yes" but disobeys). Matt 21:32 preserves the opposite order: the negative response of the Pharisees to John appears first; the positive response of the "tax collectors and prostitutes" second.[132] This implies a fixed structure of responses in Matt 21:32.[133] Furthermore, even though Matthew removes Matt 21:31–32 from its Q context, Matthew's use of the "Children of the Marketplace" pericope from Q (Matt 11:16–19) still reflects the connection between Jesus and John's followers to at least a few women who are characterized as prostitutes.[134] Matthew also interprets the category "sinners" to include women, even to the point of identifying "sinners" with "prostitutes."[135]

Finally, recent scholarship on Q and Matthew suggests that Matthew continues an egalitarian tradition which may predate him. James M. Robinson suggests that Matthew's tradition may be traced back to his own community's roots in the Q community.[136] If there is a trajectory from Q which allows for the merging of the Q community into Matthew's own, then one aspect of that trajectory might have included the characterization that Jesus and John welcomed women to their circles.[137] After all, it is Matthew who adds women to the crowds who sit down for the miraculous feedings (14:13–21; 15:32–39).[138] Thus it seems unnecessary to fabricate a common "oral topos" to account for the similarities between Luke 7:29/Matt 21:31–32.[139] Such an "oral topos" seems inadequate to account for the retention of this vulgar tradition which linked Jesus (via John) to prostitutes. Rather, the similarities between Matt 21:31–32 and Luke 7:29–30 are better explained on the basis of a common written source, namely Q.

It seems probable that Q contained a reference to "prostitutes" among Jesus' followers via John's. Why would we find this odd characterization of Jesus' and John's followers here in Q? Why does Q even bother to repeat this apparently insulting material? The controversial nature of this imagery certainly favors its antiquity. First, its inclusion may be explained on the basis of the Deuteronomic character of Q, which is in fact presupposed as the overriding context for the second redactional layer of Q,[140] and has been previously noted as a thematic presence in Q 7:31–35.[141] The very accusation against Jesus' lifestyle in Q 7:31–35 as a "wine-bibber and glutton" reflects the Deuteronomic theme of the "rebellious son" who keeps company with "harlots."[142] Not only are these women (usually Gentiles) found in the D-History, but their faith and contribution to the history of Israel are often placed in opposition to the unfortunate lack of true Yahwism found among the Israelites.[143] The classic examples of this are Rahab the Harlot[144] and the Queen of Sheba.[145] Moreover, the D-history features women as judges and prophets, and the book of Deuteronomy itself is said to have been interpreted by the prophetess Huldah.[146] In spite of Rahab's scandalous background, the faith of Gentile women from the D-History was repeatedly admired in subsequent Jewish literature.[147] The image of the Queen of Sheba underwent a similar mixed development in both Jewish and Christian literature.[148] In early Christian literature she first represents Gentile acceptance of Christianity; she later becomes a type of the Church.[149] In light of the mention of the Queen of Sheba in Q 11:31 as an example of Gentile responsiveness to the announcement of the coming judgment, the function of female characters from the D-History and their subsequent function in Q needs more attention. The influence of Deuteronomic themes may in part explain the presence of stereotypical slander leveled against Jesus and his followers in Q 7. That other Jewish Christian groups considered sexually suspect women like Rahab the Harlot as being worthy of emulation can be seen in both the Matthean genealogy[150] and in lists of the faithful both in the book of Hebrews (11:31) and in James (2:25). Not only is Rahab the Harlot in the famous roll call of the Christian faith found in Hebrews, but she is the only female one.[151] Furthermore, in the Gospel of Thomas the phrase "child of a whore" (πόρνη) serves as a positive designation (Thomas 105).[152] Thus, the repetition of this characterization of Jesus, John and their followers functions to defuse it, by transforming it into a positive characterization of community faith, especially among Gentiles. Once again, to repeat and claim an insult robs it of its power.[153]

Despite the positive allusion to these fallen women inherent in the slander of Q 7:31–35, the repetition of this negative sex stereotyping implying that such women are "whores" still functions ultimately to reinforce the positive notions of chastity and virginity which in turn function to control women's behavior. This is, of course, not unique to Judaism,[154] as the polarization of women into two stereotypes (good wife/mother and whore) is common in most ancient literature. Karen Jo Torjesen writes:

> The whore is an important symbol whose negative stereotype functions to underscore the values associated with female chastity. She represents the woman whose sexuality is uncontrolled. By not belonging to one man, she becomes available to all. Thus her uncontrolled sexuality is perceived as dangerous, corrupting both men and women and threatening the social order itself.[155]

This is the case in Q. In spite of the implications of Q for the presence of women in the Jesus movement and possibly in the Q "mission," Q prohibits divorce (Q 16:16–18) and warns against causing scandals (Q 17:1–2). The divorce prohibition in Q, unlike that in Mark (10:2–9) is directed only towards men. Since there is limited evidence that Jewish women in Palestine could initiate divorce[156] it is possible that the prohibition of divorce in Q reflects concern for the kind of social instability associated with the greater social mobility of women during the Roman period, rather than as some kind of anti-patriarchal ethic.[157] However, although divorce prohibitions serve to control the behavior of women more than men – by functioning to keep women in marriages even when such arrangements are emotionally or physically debilitating – the Q limitation does not restrict women's sexual behavior, but men's, and restricts their behavior at a time of relative sexual freedom for men. The concern for divorce in Q thus suggests a social location for Q that is not limited to the peasantry, since only men of some means could buy or marry a second wife, or afford prostitutes.[158] Further, although women of various social strata as well as slaves may be argued to be included in Q's version of the "Parable of the Feast" (Q 14:16–24) – particularly in its mention of the kind of riff-raff from the streets implied in the "Marketplace" pericope and among the "tax collectors and sinners" (Q 7:31–35) – Q does not take the extra step found in other Hellenistic literature by arguing openly for women's newer social roles by defending their behavior as respectable.[159] Rather, it moves to restrict women, and even more so men, in marriage.[160] In fact Q may reflect more conservative (i.e. gendered) meal practice, at least at the eschaton (Q 17:34–35):

> I tell you, in that night there will be two on one couch (κλίνη); one will be taken and the other left. There will be two women grinding together; one will be taken the other left (RSV).

The *δύο ἐπὶ κλίνης μιᾶς* ("two on one couch") probably refers to two men reclining on a banquet couch.[161] Thus Q does not uniformly reinforce with subsequent theological statements the inclusive table practice of which Jesus' followers are accused. One could argue that the "Parable of the Feast," (Q 14:15–24) which more clearly challenges Greco-Roman ideals of rank, does not necessarily challenge Greco-Roman notions of gender.[162] Thus, while the insulting language leveled against the Q group is repeated and so defused, it is never directly challenged.

The Children of the Marketplace (Q 7:31–32)

Another passage found in Q which further associates Jesus with banquet revelry and thus women, is the so-called "Children of the Marketplace" pericope in Q 7:31–32. This passage immediately precedes the accusation of Jesus' dining with "tax collectors and sinners." The rejection of Jesus and John reported in Q 7:33–34 is also implicit in Q 7:31–32. John came fasting, and he was not accepted, Jesus came "eating and drinking" and he was not accepted. Again, this implies that the criticism of John and Jesus was a criticism of not their preaching but of their respective lifestyles.[163]

The Q redactor uses the "Marketplace" pericope to elaborate this comparison:

> To what will I compare this generation?
> They are like children sitting in the marketplace (παιδίοις τοῖς ἐν ἀγορᾷ καθημένοις) and calling to one another:
>
> "We played the flute for you and you did not dance; we wailed (θρηνέω) and you did not weep" (κλαίω) (NRSV).

The "children" in both 7:32 and 7:35 have been variously interpreted. However, in spite of the lack of parallelism between the two sections, it seems clear that the activities of the "children" in 7:32 (piping and mourning) roughly correspond to the activities of Jesus and John in 7:33–34 (feasting and fasting), at least in this Q context.[164] In Q, however, Jesus and John are the "children" (τέκνα) of Wisdom (v. 35).[165] Thus, those who refuse to respond are "this generation," i.e., the same opponents who accuse John of having a demon and Jesus of being a "wine bibber" and "glutton." Likewise, the followers of Jesus and John, are "children" of Wisdom who "call" out to others who also refuse to respond.[166] In Luke those who respond to the call of Jesus and John are likened to the woman "sinner" who "weeps" (κλαίω) at the feet of Jesus (Luke 7:38).[167] Thus, according to Luke, implicit in the "Marketplace" pericope is some kind parallel between women such as this sinner/prostitute and the followers of Jesus and John.

Although it must be admitted that without the necessary historical and social background the image seems anomalous, Luke's understanding of this section of Q can be easily explained. First, it is unlikely that the image in Q 7:32 is meant to call to mind children acting like adults seated in judgment in the marketplace, as Wendy Cotter has suggested.[168] Although the diminutive of παῖς can indeed mean "child," either a boy or a girl up to the age of seven or so, the activities of these "children" do not really suggest children at play so much as banquet or funeral musicians. These could men or women, free or slave. In Judaism hired mourners were more commonly women.[169] In fact, one could expect to find slaves or day laborers waiting in the marketplace to be hired, especially since slave owners often sent their unoccupied slaves to the marketplace to look for extra work.[170] Here they display their wares, as it were, by piping and wailing. A tomb painting from Marissa nicely illustrates this social custom. The painting depicts two funerary musicians, a man and a woman, both dressed in funerary attire. The man leads playing the flute, while the woman follows with a harp.[171] The activities of these "children" (piping and mourning) certainly explains the use of the diminutive of παῖς (τὸ παιδίον, "young child" but also "servant" or "slave") in this instance.[172]

Flute playing and mourning were stereotypically associated with women.[173] Public mourning of this nature was often performed by women.[174] Many of whom came not only from the family of the deceased, but from the ranks of prostitutes, and were especially found among the lower class of skilled slavewomen or day laborers who were often hired to serve, entertain and play musical instruments for banquets.[175] However, such women would similarly be hired to play instruments and mourn at funerals.[176] Flute-players could also be men.[177] This kind of banquet or funeral help may have been young, but it is it not their youth that catches the attention of the Q redactor, but the similarities of their activities (piping and mourning) to Jesus and John's (eating and drinking/fasting). Thus, although τέκνα in 7:35 tends to indicate young children,[178] the παιδία of 7:32 are still best understood as slaves or day laborers watting in the marketplace to be hired for banquets or funerals. Furthermore, even if this group of musicians and mourners is understood as we now have it to be children and not hired adults or slaves, the mixed gendered nature of this image still remains: boys *and girls* pipe and mourn in the marketplace, not simply boys.[179] The redactor of Q has used this parable as an example of the contrast between the lifestyles of Jesus and John: Jesus "feasts" (pipes) whereas John "fasts" (mourns) (cf. Mark 2:18–19). Jesus' activity is likened to that of flute-players awaiting hire to play at a dinner party, whereas John's is likened to professional mourners awaiting hire to mourn at a funeral.[180]

The accusation leveled against Jesus in Q 7:34 fits neatly with the characterization of the situation of the opposition to Wisdom's envoys by "this generation" in Q 7:32. Both sections of this Q passage employ stereotypical banquet imagery. Subsequently, as the "children/servants" of Wisdom can also be understood to include those who have responded to the message of Wisdom's prophets, especially Jesus, these new envoys of Wisdom or the Q "mission" are likewise compared to those hired either to play music for a dinner party, or mourn at a funeral. Thus, both John and Jesus are here tacitly accused of having women, hirelings and slaves among their followers, John in the context of a funeral, Jesus in the context of a banquet. As this implies the presence of women among their followers, it subsequently associates women, hirelings and slaves with both "envoys" of Wisdom, Jesus and John. The parallel between Jesus and John found in Luke 7:29/Matt 21:31–32 is thus already presupposed in Q 7:33–34.[181] The controversial nature of the image notwithstanding, it is one that is inclusive of, and one could argue, even more characteristic of women's roles than men's. It must be admitted, however, that the Q redactor shows little interest in the gendered overtones of the "Marketplace" parable, nor does he use this parable explicitly to identify Jesus' followers or the Q prophets with women. The attention in the text falls on the similarity of the activities described in Q 7:31–32 and Q 7:34–35, not its gendered overtones. The mourners suggest fasting (John's activity), the pipers represent feasting (Jesus' activity). Both Jesus and John are emissaries (children; τέκνα) of Wisdom.

Still a problem is the fact that the parable likens the activity of these children/servants to "this generation" which is usually a designation of Jesus' opponents in Q, as well as a sign of the Q redactor's hand.[182] The lack of parallelism between Q 7:31–32 and Q 7:34–35 is often taken as an indication that the placement of this parable in Q is secondary.[183] This case can be strengthened if the parable is taken out of its Q context entirely and considered on its own terms. Without Jesus' "eating and drinking" and John's "fasting" (Q 7:34–35), the image of the pipers and mourners become an image of mourning activities alone, not banqueting and mourning activities respectively. The antiphonal nature of the piping and mourning may be the key to its original meaning. The lack of response inherent in the image of the parable is better understood in the context of ritual lamentation, in which calling back and forth between mourners was commonplace. Seen in this light, there are two sides to this encounter in the marketplace.[184] One side of mourners criticizes the other for refusing to participate in antiphonal mourning: "we piped to you, and you did not dance, we wailed and you did not weep" (Q 7:31–32). The stronger term for mourning found in the Matthean version (Matt 11:17; "you did not beat your breast in grief" [κόπτω]), long a problem for translators and interpreters in relationship to the play of children, is thus probably earlier, original to Q, and a designation for mourning, not childplay.[185] "This generation," usually a designation of those opposed to Jesus and the Q prophets, objects to those who do not participate in mourning rituals. Although the Q redactor has used this parable for another purpose, once it is removed from its Q context its meaning is clear, for it corresponds nicely with early traditions that indicate Jesus (and his subsequent followers) rejected certain burial customs (Q 9:60).

Lamenting the Deaths of the Prophets

As well as retaining Jesus' harsh statement about burial customs, Q elaborates the theme of the rejection of the ongoing veneration of dead prophets (Q 11:47). Q 11:47–48 is often taken to reflect the situation following the deaths of Jesus and John, who were considered by the Q community to be the prophets of Sophia (Q 7:35).[186] While Q has an even higher regard for Jesus than for John, since he represents the way to the "Father" by means of his status as Wisdom or "Son" (Q 10:22), Q understands the deaths of Jesus and John within the framework of a Deuteronomic-prophetic view of history: God sends prophets who preach repentance, but Israel persecutes and subsequently kills them (cf. also Q 13:34–35).[187] Q criticizes Israel for venerating dead prophets on the one hand while killing prophets (like Jesus and John) on the other (Q 11:47–48). This Q passage has gone unexplained.[188]

However, there is ample evidence that a Jewish equivalent of "hero" and "heroine" cults of the special or holy dead continued from ancient times through the Greek and Roman periods. Tombs extant at the time of Jesus include tombs dedicated to the Patriarchs and Matriarchs, Rachel, the Maccabean martyrs, the prophetess Hulda, the prophet Isaiah, the prophet Zechariah ben Judah and a necropolis of kings near Jerusalem.[189] Throughout New Testament times there remained a deep rooted belief among Jews in the incorruptibility of these special dead. The Jewish holy dead could be solicited for intercessory prayer on behalf of the living and to work wonders and magic. Jews made pilgrimages to their tombs and monuments.[190] It is precisely this custom that is being criticized in Q 11:47–51(Luke 11:47–51/Matt 23:29–36).[191] Several of these special tomb monuments, such as Zechariah's, are still standing in the Kidron valley.[192] In Bethlehem a tomb monument to Rachel still remains.[193] Busloads of pious Jewish women still visit these ancient tombsites as sacred places where they venerate Jewish saints, prophets, matriarchs and patriarchs, pray for healings of various sorts, and socialize with other women at elaborate picnics.[194] As previously noted, depictions of these tombs of the special dead can be found as ossuary decorations, further attesting to their popularity during the first century.[195]

Jewish literature from second century B.C.E. through the first century C.E. also attests to the continuation of practices connected with the cult of the dead, especially feeding the dead and requesting the prayers of dead ancestors or "fathers" and prophets. When combined with archaeological evidence, literary evidence buttresses the argument that in post-exilic times and into the Greek and Roman periods Jews continued these family religious practices. Most references to these rituals are negative, some are not. During the early Greek period, Zechariah may reflect restrictions similar to those enacted in Solon's legislation, in that formal funerals require the segregation of the sexes (Zech 12:11–14). Second Maccabees attests to the acceptability of sacrifices for the dead, and assumes that Onias and Jeremiah could perform intercessory prayer for Jerusalem.[196] Other Jewish writers dispute the efficacy of such prayer to prophets and "fathers."[197]

Once the practice of the veneration of special prophets and Patriarchs can be assumed for first century Palestine,[198] it makes good sense to place Q 11:47–48 following the death of Jesus and John as well as within the Q community which understood both Jesus and John to be dead prophets. Q 11:47–48 suggests that these early followers of John and Jesus did not encourage the veneration of Jesus and John at tombsites following their deaths, in spite of the fact that they considered Jesus and John prophets, and in spite of the fact that during the first century dead prophets and the Patriarchs (the "Fathers") were revered as special and powerful dead in tombsites in Palestine.[199] There is no evidence that Jesus or John were venerated at tombsites in Palestine; Jesus' so-called tomb did not become a Christian tourist site until the fourth century.[200]

In light of the absence of such evidence in first century Palestine, Q 11:47–48 could reflect a continuation of Jesus and John's own teachings as they were understood by the Q community: when asked about burying one's father, Jesus said "Let the dead bury their own dead" (Q 9:60) and taught his disciples to pray to God alone as their "Father" (Q 11:2, πατήρ);[201] John warned his contemporaries not to rely on Abraham as their "Father" (πατήρ; Q 3:8). Jesus himself may also have rejected the practice of venerating dead prophets at tombs, particularly since Q 11:47–48 is hardly Deuteronomic, and is arguably detachable from Q 11:49–51.[202] The retention of Q 11:47–48 could thus reflect the other side of a controversy reflected in the "Children of the Marketplace" parable – a controversy among Palestinian Jews and Jewish Christians over funerary rites and the veneration of Jewish heroes at tombs.

This in turn implies that Jesus, and subsequently some of his followers rejected these mourning practices, and that some of Jesus' followers rejected such rites on behalf of Jesus himself. Such a rejection of mourning rituals would have been more restrictive of women's religious roles in first century Judaism than men's, and this would help explain the lack of evidence for the veneration of Jesus at a tombsite in Palestine until post-Constantinian times.[203] Again, women are not singled out in the "Marketplace" parable, but religious roles commonly practiced by women are assumed, and rejected. Given the perseverance of women's lament rituals throughout antiquity, the fact that professional mourners were commonly women, and Q's extension of generational household disruption to women's relationships, it is not unreasonable to suggest that women were included both in "this generation" (who encouraged lamentation and mourning) and in the Jesus movement (which rejected them). It would logically follow that Q 7:31–32 reflects an aspect of Jesus and John's *preaching* that formed a basis for their rejection by "this generation," and not simply the disapproval of their lifestyles reported in Q 7:33–34.[204]

And, following Mark, Matthew adds to Jesus' refusal to fast a refusal to mourn (πενθέω), which further serves to distance Jesus himself in later gospel tradition from any such ritual lamentation of the dead (Matt 9:14–15; cf. Mark 2:18–20; Luke 5:33–35). Likewise, in miracle/resurrection stories Jesus calls for an end to lamentation and weeping, dismisses hired mourners and flute-players, or shows up too late for the funeral altogether.[205] In Luke, Jesus even dismisses the women who have come to lament his own death (Luke 23:28).[206] This suggests that on the one hand some of Jesus' followers continued the practice of lamenting Jesus' death[207] whereas other rejected practices like "piping and wailing," created stories which distanced Jesus from such funerary rituals, and followed Jesus' example and let "the dead bury their own dead" (Q 9:60).

Coinciding with the evidence of the "Marketplace" parable, Q also contains a formal lament over Jerusalem which is usually considered to be an oracle of Wisdom pronounced by Q prophets or prophetic wisdom teachers following Jesus' death (Q 13:34–35 cf. also Q 11:49).[208] Such an oracle would have been prophetic for the Q community, a proclamation that the second destruction of the Temple indicated God's response and judgment against Israel for the death of Jesus (so also Mark 13).[209] Although still placed on the lips of Jesus, in Luke this lament is eventually enacted by women, the "Daughters of Jerusalem" who proleptically mourn Jesus' death on his way to the crucifixion (Luke 23:27–31). Given the common transference of women's ritual laments into scribal contexts,[210] it is not improbable that this lament over Jerusalem began in the Q community as an actual lament by women over Jesus' and John's deaths.[211] In fact, the lament genre, which can encompass a sung oracle of vengeance, fits easily into a context of Q community prophecy; laments were often sung to express protest against violent or unjust deaths. The lament contains feminine imagery of the hen brooding over her children (Q 13:34), reflects wisdom motifs, Deuteronomic themes, and ends with an allusion to the Septuagint's version of Psalm 118:26. Scribal activity is often suggested to account for these features.[212]

However, although laments over the destruction of cities developed into a formal scribal genre in the Hebrew Bible and the Ancient Near East generally,[213] of the wisdom prophecies in Q, the

"Lament over Jerusalem," has a good chance of having originated in a woman's prophetic utterance and subsequently revised and transferred into its scribal context in Q. Professional mourners are called to lament the destruction of nations in biblical texts, and women are described as lamenting the destruction of cities in other Ancient Near Eastern contexts. Oral lament forms seem to have been known by both male and female singers.[214] Further, the entire book of Lamentations may have been used liturgically following the first destruction of the Temple, and as such would provide evidence for an oral form of city laments accessible to rich and poor, men and women.[215] Moreover, it is hardly to be supposed that Jewish women were completely ignorant of the Jewish scriptures; likely they were familiar at least with the book of Genesis and the Psalms, which were no doubt used in Jewish liturgical contexts.[216] For example, there is evidence that Psalm 118 was recited by Jerusalemites to incoming pilgrims visiting Jerusalem for yearly festivals like the Passover.[217] Finally, O. Steck's study of the Deuteronomic theme of murdered and martyred prophets throughout biblical, Second Temple and Rabbinic literature concludes that it was not a direct literary use of biblical motifs like Nehemiah 9 that led to the eventual interpretation of the destruction of the Temple in 587 B.C.E. and 70 C.E. as divine punishment for national sin, but rather a popular oral tradition that had formed by the first century C.E.[218] Thus, community grief over the deaths of Jesus and John, and expressions of God's possible retribution by the devastation of Jerusalem would most naturally have been expressed first by women in the community by means of oral ritual lamentation, although that was not the sole province of women, especially in Israel. However, this in turn suggests not a "Q misson," but rather community lamentation as the original context of this oracle. Given the absence of evidence that either Jesus or John was venerated at a tombsite, the setting of such community lamentation would have been either in a home or meeting place other than a tomb, or on the occasion of another community member's funeral. The "Lament over Jerusalem," although showing signs of scribal composition, may thus reflect the practice of the ritual lamentation of Jesus and John's death in the Q community. This makes further sense inasmuch as the "Marketplace" pericope suggests that such funerary practices became a source of community controversy and boundary formation. Some applied Jesus' harsh statement, "Let the dead bury their own dead" (Q 9:60) even to Jesus and John themselves, whereas others did not. This controversy among early Palestinian Christians would be even more explicable if Jesus himself questioned the practice of venerating dead prophets at tombs.[219]

A controversy over ritual lamentation and burial among Christians, especially the ritual lamentation of Jesus's death, and gendered power struggles over the significance and location of his resurrection, may be reflected in later Markan narratives of the both the crucifixion and the "empty" tomb (Mark 16:1–8), and may help explain the disjunction between "Galilean" appearances apart from a tomb (to men) and "Jerusalem" appearances at an *empty* tomb (to women).[220] This same debate suggests a *Sitz im Leben* of cultic lamentation for the development of certain prophetic wisdom sayings in the Jesus tradition other than the context of itinerant radicalism of early Christian prophets suggested by Gerd Theissen.[221]

Jesus' lack of attention to burial rites is thus understood in Q to place him within a line of persecuted prophets, and further illustrates the syncretic nature of certain of Jesus' teachings.[222] This ethic could be compared with Cynic critiques of burial customs.[223] However, criticism of practices associated with the cult of the dead can be found not only in the prophets, but in Hellenistic Jewish texts before the time of Jesus, even in Palestine; and the harshness of Jesus' critique is not limited to Cynic discourse. The saying, "Let the dead bury the dead," is thus essentially syncretic (Jewish/prophetic and Hellenistic), rather than specifically Cynic, and in part reflects a Hebraic repudiation of idolatry.[224] The "Children of the Marketplace" parable should be therefore be re-examined as a source of authentic information about an element of Jesus' mission and message than his table practice. Rather, it reflects Jesus' denunciation of customary burial and mourning rites for family members, and possibly even for dead prophets, a condemnation which, ironically, was subsequently rejected by a number of his followers.[225] This rejection of burial practices is understood in Q to include a rejection of the veneration of dead prophets at tombshrines in Palestine.

Women, Lament and Q: Some Conclusions

Q confirms the presence of women, albeit by means of slander, among the earliest converts to the Q community. At this early layer of the tradition, Jesus is slandered for his table practice, one which includes the presence of "tax collectors and sinners" for meals and features "wine-bibbing and gluttony." Such characterizations reflect stereotypical slander used against those known for dining with "promiscuous" or "liberated" women. Furthermore, there is reason to suspect that Q might have contained a reference to the presence of "prostitutes" among Jesus' followers. The presence of women among the disciples surfaces in this polemic leveled against the group. In its Q context, the "Children of the Marketplace" pericope also highlights those who acknowledge Jesus and John by "wailing" or "piping," both customary activities of those hired for banquets and funerals. However, once removed from its secondary placement in Q, this parable has strong overtones of funerary practice and antiphonal mourning. This suggests that Jesus' repudiation of many common funerary rituals led to controversy over funerary rites among Palestinian Jews. The "Lament over Jerusalem," may retain some elements of an actual ritual lament, in the form of a prophetic oracle of Wisdom before being transferred into the scribal context of Q. Below the surface of Q may be echoes of the lamentation of Jesus' death by women and other early Palestinian Christians. Q would then reflect the cultural discomfort with women's lamentation rituals common throughout Greek, Roman and Jewish societies.

That Q suggests the presence of women in the Jesus movement shows its continuity with other later layers of the Jesus tradition. Women's presence is presumed, even at community meals. This is a controversial aspect of the Jesus movement in later gospel traditions.[226] That even Q itself betrays discomfort with these traditions does not detract from its significance for our understanding of the place of women the development of early Christianity and in Jesus' own movement.

Chapter 5

He Was Buried, On the Third Day He Was Raised

While all four canonical gospels attest to the presence of women at the crucifixion, the question of the historicity of that report is a complex one. In these narratives the women serve as an important witness linking the stories of Jesus' death, burial, and empty tomb. However, when viewed in light of ancient women's roles in death and burial rituals, especially their role in lamenting the dead, the behavior of the women as described in most of these gospel scenes is rendered implausible. Furthermore, their presence of in these scenes can be accounted for both on the basis of the evident centrality of the Psalms to the Passion tradition and in light of ancient narratives of the death of heroic individuals, particularly those accounts influenced by the stories of the "noble" deaths of Socrates and Herakles. Far from fitting the stereotypical role of the *women* in these stories, the behavior of the women at the crucifixion, befits that of the close associates, disciples, or friends of the dying hero – who are usually men. Close attention to the function of gender in ancient tales of dying heroes as well as to the roles of women in ancient burial rites will therefore contribute to the overall task of testing the historicity of the Passion narratives.

The Role of Women in Greek, Roman and Jewish Burial Customs

In many cultures women play an important role in the customs surrounding the care for the dead. Women often wash and prepare the corpse for burial, lead the community and family in bereavement for the dead, and prepare festive meals for the enjoyment of both the living and the departed. This connection of women to death leads in many cultures to a degree of anxiety about women, not only because a corpse is often considered a source of pollution, but because women's role in funeral proceedings potentially gives them control over two of the most important "rites of passage" in a culture, birth and death.[1] It is not surprising then that over the centuries women's control over funerals and mourning rituals has often been challenged and sometimes abrogated. In spite of this, women have retained key roles in certain burial rituals, most notably the tradition of formal lamentation still practiced in rural Greece.[2]

Women, Death and Burial in Ancient Greece

In ancient Greece women played a central role in the burial and lamentation of the dead. Females of the family customarily washed and anointed the corpse (the laying out of the body, or *prothesis*).[3] In Homer, the duration of the *prothesis* is indefinite, but in classical Athens it lasted only 24 hours.[4] Ritual laments were conducted during this time, primarily by women. The grief expressed during the *prothesis* was thought to confirm that the person was really dead, and not merely sleeping.[5] In literature, ritual lament of the *prothesis* is sometimes described concurrently with the burial proper.[6] Following the *prothesis* (or wake) was a formal funeral procession to the gravesite (the *ekphora*). Women mourners also figured prominently in this procession[7] and subsequently went to visit the tomb on regular occasions, usually on the third and ninth days after death, and then monthly and annually.[8] Men may be described performing such tasks as washing, anointing, and lamenting the dead, but this is often in battlefield situations where womenfolk would not ordinarily be present.[9] It also seems that attitudes about the respectability of masculine grief underwent a change in ancient Greece, so that masculine grief depicted in Homer eventually became unacceptable.[10] In vase-representations, women are certainly majority participants in mourning processions and dirge-singing; they are depicted putting both hands to their heads and tearing their hair, whereas men are shown holding one hand to the head, but not tearing the hair.[11] Funeral processions were often very public affairs which occurred during the daylight hours and made various stops along the way to the burial grounds.[12] Women joining in these proceedings could be family members and friends, as well as household slaves or professionals hired for the occasion. Hired musicians, especially fluteplayers are depicted.[13] Rites at the gravesite performed by women included calling to the dead, which was accompanied by various offerings (often food) and libations. These rituals, especially the cries and wailings, were thought to raise the spirit of the dead from the grave.[14] Communal meals with the dead were also held, at which the deceased was believed to be a participant.[15] These rites did not presume later notions of an afterlife or "resurrection" for the deceased, but rather functioned to establish a sense of connection or continuity with the dead.[16] Finally, many Greeks practiced cremation, although inhumation was probably also done, especially among the poor.[17]

However, there were ancient attempts to curb the prominence of women in Greek funerals, particularly their role as mourners. In a relatively short time, and in spite of the conservative nature of burial customs, legislation restricting various funeral practices was enacted in a number of places in the Greek world from the seventh to third centuries B.C.E.[18] Although restrictions varied from place, those placed on women have such uniformity that some scholars have come to see women as the special target of this legislation.[19] At Athens they restricted the number of women mourners, confined female participation to immediate kinswomen or women over sixty years old, limited offerings brought to the gravesite, and required that women march behind the men in funeral processions. Excessive signs of grief, such as laceration of the flesh were banned, as were excessive displays of wealth. Tombs of non-relatives were not to be visited except at the time of their burial, and participants were prohibited from mourning any except the person being buried. The procession was to proceed quickly to the gravesite and be completed before sunrise. Notably absent are any such restrictions to the numbers of male mourners. [20]

In other places similar restrictions on women were enacted. At Delphi the funeral procession itself was to be conductes in silence and, to prohibit mourning along the way, the bier was not to be put down at various stopping points. Laments and mourning at the grave on customary days following the funeral and on the anniversary of death were also prohibited.[21] Alexiou suggests that these restrictions on women are related to the shift of emphasis in inheritance laws from clan to family, in that women played a role in the determination of inheritance by means of their funeral participation.[22] Following Plutarch's discussion of the Solonian legislation, which implies the use of funerals to encourage rivalries between clans, Alexiou comments: "In the inflammatory atmosphere of blood feud between the families of Megakles and Kylon that was raging in Solon's time, what more effective way could there be to stir up feelings of revenge than the incessant lamentation at the tomb by large numbers of women for "those long dead"?'[23]

At the same time that women's public mourning was restricted, a new male genre was created, the funeral oration (*epitaphios logos*), which declared that men who died on behalf of the state were not to be mourned, but praised.[24] Women's mourning, which focused on the pain of the loss and the continued connection with the loved one, became negatively coded, whereas male praise of the dead took on positive value. Male grief was characterized by restraint and praise for the dead, whereas women's mourning was considered "uncontrolled" and "unmanly," in spite of the apparent orderliness of their religious rites.[25] In this way public funerals came under the firm control of men, and the state.[26] Subsequently, women mourners could be called upon to restrain their grief, or are even summarily dismissed from death and mourning scenes.[27]

In spite of these legislative restrictions and cultural disparagement, however, women continued to participate in funerals and mourning, and continued regular visits and food offerings to the dead. Some funeral proceedings may have been moved indoors. Later representations of funeral proceedings are lighted by torches, suggesting that processions eventually were held before dawn.[28] Holst-Warhaft demonstrates the continued connection of women to laments in subsequent Greek literature. In the context of Greek literature, especially tragedy, women's laments could still function as calls for revenge and violence, create a sense of continuity with the dead, as well as serve to protest the various inequities and sufferings of women.[29] That does not mean that these protests changed the social situation in which women found themselves all that much, but it does help explain the continued need to control women's self-expression. The powerful potential of funerals for complaint and protest through the mourning of women and kin is no doubt one reason why criminals and traitors were usually denied burial rites and mourning and their bodies either dumped into mass graves or simply left to rot unburied outside the city walls. In spite of legislation banning tomb visitation at unspecified times, women continued to accompany friends to visit tombs of non-relatives and take offerings to their dead.[30]

Women, Death and Burial in Ancient Rome

The connection of women to burial, funerals and mourning can also be found in Roman culture. Although Greek customs influenced the west, the connection of women to funerals and mourning also has Etruscan antecedents.[31] As in Greek culture, death brought pollution, but providing a proper burial for the deceased was essential.[32] Family and friends usually gathered at the death bed, and the nearest relative gave the dying a last kiss, ostensibly to catch the soul as it left the body with the last breath.[33] Catching this last breath was very important to the bereaved, and Cicero reports that mothers even spent the night outside prisons hoping to give their sons this final kiss before execution.[34] Upon death, the eyes and mouth were closed by a close relative, often a woman or mother,[35] a coin was placed in the mouth to pay the fare for Charon's ferry (also a Greek custom),[36] the corpse was washed and anointed,[37] and a wreath placed around the head.[38] These tasks were usually performed by women kin or other close relative, but at times by domestic servants or an undertaker. Perfumes could also later be placed in tombs or sprinkled on the ashes of the remains.[39] Women began mourning immediately at the time of death (the *conclamatio mortis*), calling out to the dead. Not only did this establish a sense of continued contact with the deceased, but some supposed the wailing and crying would awaken the person if they were not really dead.[40] Funeral arrangements were often made by a male slave, the *Pollinctor*, a slave of the *Libertinarius*.[41] Women, however, were still featured prominently as mourners at the wake held in the home and in processions for public funerals. They are found in this role in artistic representations of wakes and funeral processions, beating their breasts or stretching out their arms towards the deceased. The tearing of hair is also an expression of grief in Roman art.[42] The mourning of women throughout the funeral proceedings continued the *conclamatio* which immediately followed the death.[43] Grief was expressed both by laments (Gr. θρῆνος, Lat. *nenia*) and by gestures (Gr. κοπετός, Lat. *planctus*).[44] The kinswomen of the dead lamented, as well as women hired to mourn along with mothers, daughters and sisters.[45] Again, flute players were often featured in funerals: they could be either men or women, but were usually slaves.[46] As in Greek custom, a funeral oration (the *laudatio funebris*) was delivered by a prominent man, but even in the case of war dead, eulogies were not collective but individual.[47] Bodies were generally cremated, and the ashes kept in urns in the family tomb, but inhumation was also practiced, particularly among the poor.[48] Eventually, the entire Roman empire took up the practice of inhumation.[49] The poor could not afford their own tombs, and were often buried in common graves or public cemeteries.[50] Others joined guilds or burial societies, which provided proper burials for members of the poorer classes.[51] Following the funeral homes were purified.[52] Romans also visited the graves of their family members, and funerary feasts were held at the tomb on the day of the funeral,[53] on the ninth day after the funeral, and at the end of the mourning period, as well as at various times throughout the year. The deceased was thought to be present for these meals and food was set out for the dead, or even poured into the burial site.[54] Some tombs even had kitchens.[55]

As in ancient Greece, attempts were made to limit what were considered the excesses, both emotional and financial, of funerary rituals. Restrictions on expenditure were introduced, as well as limitations on the expression of grief by women. Cicero writes that because the Solonic restrictions on funerals were written into Roman law, similar funeral restrictions appear in the *Twelve Tables*.[56] He also mentions later regulations, such as on the size of the crowd or the attendance of non-family members. Funeral orations were allowed only at public funerals, and could be delivered only by appointed orators.[57] Although these regulations surely reflect an interest in curbing expenditure,[58] the interest in controlling the potential disruptive power of funeral proceedings is also evident. It is the case, however, that the expensive individual monuments so characteristic of the Late Republic eventually gave way to simpler family plots and group burials with standardized accessories. The burial practices of the poor eventually mimicked the simplified funerary conventions of the rich.[59] The simplification of Roman burial practices, however, was part of the larger effort to consolidate the power of the state through newer art and imagery which created a homogeneous culture of "uniformity and prosperity" in the Imperial age.[60] As in Greek areas it is questionable how successful these efforts were in controlling the behavior of women at Roman wakes and funerals. Lucian continues to parody women mourners in the second century, arguing that surely the deceased received no benefit from such behavior.[61] In the role of the departed he comments:

> What good do you think I get from your wailing, and this beating of the breasts to the music of the flute and the extravagant conduct of the women in lamenting? (*ἡ τῶν γυναικῶν περὶ τὸν θρῆνον ἀμετρία*) Or from the wreathed stone above my grave? Or what, pray, is the use of your pouring out the pure wine? You don't think, do you, that it will drip down to where we are and get all the way through to Hades?[62]

Later church writers also complain about extravagant behavior of women at wakes and funerals, particularly on the part of non-Christian women. Again, the focus falls upon controlling women mourners. Eventually churches gained control of funerals by bringing them into the church proper. Laments were replaced with the singing of Psalms.[63]

Funeral rites were often denied to criminals and traitors, but as previously mentioned, family members and close associates of the condemned sometimes went to great lengths to secure the remains of their loved ones, either by purchase or even theft.[64] Although some form of funeral rite, however perfunctory, was performed if at all possible.[65] The vast majority of the condemned were no doubt consigned to mass graves or cremations. Indeed, the denial of burial and funeral rites was an important component of the punishment meted out to the condemned.[66] Those executed for treason, particularly if by crucifixion, were more likely to be denied basic burials and funeral rites.[67] While officials might show clemency by granting bodies to the family of the deceased,[68] this was probably exceptional.[69] It should be remembered that women as well as men, particularly slavewomen and women of the lower classes, could be summarily arrested, and even executed by means of impalement, crucifixion, beheading, or simply slaughtered in times of political upheaval and war. Even if some ancient descriptions of the torments inflicted upon women are exaggerated, their execution was hardly unimaginable.[70] Although not remarked upon,[71] the family tomb from first century Palestine excavated at Giv'at ha-Mivtar contains evidence that other members of the family besides the crucified man named Yehohanan met with death by violence: they included a strong 50–60 year old woman who died from a blow to the head, a 24–26 year old woman who had burned to death, a 3–4 year old child who died from an arrow wound, and several children who died of starvation.[72] Violence, warfare, and political unrest during ancient times could have fatal consequences for an entire family, not just the men. This family succeeded in providing at least final burial in an ossuary for one who had been crucified in the provinces, presumably for anti-Roman activities.[73]

The Role of Women in Jewish Burial Customs

As in Greek and Roman culture, women played a central role in Jewish funerary practices. Both men and women are described washing bodies for burial and expressing grief for the dead, but again women are stereotypically associated with these roles.[74] Although we have little early evidence for Jewish burial preparation, in later sources men are allowed to prepare only men for burial, but women may prepare corpses of either sex.[75] The usual period between death and burial is unknown, although it is probable that burials took place on the same day as death. Deuteronomy 21:22–23 required that the bodies of executed criminals be taken down and buried before dusk, and it may be safe to assume that all burials proceeded quickly due to the climate.[76] The period of mourning also varied, although in later Judaism seven days, thirty days and one year are often specified.[77] Cremation was rare, except for the worst of criminals;[78] inhumation was the most common form of burial. For a person to go unburied was a great misfortune, and even ordinary criminals were buried.[79] Large Israelite family tombs from various periods have been discovered in natural caves, or cut into soft rock. In early times bodies were placed on vertical ledges, and later in narrow niches cut into the stone. After the remains had decomposed, skeletons were given a second burial, either in special cavities or pits, and later, in ossuaries.[80] Families who could not afford expensive tombs simply buried their dead in the ground, or in common trenches. Foreigners or criminals could also be buried in common pits.[81] Later sources mention charitable societies which helped to care for the dead and comfort the bereaved.[82]

Mourning practices of Israel, particularly the practices of weeping or keening and the singing of formal laments, were similar to those of her neighbors.[83] To have one's death go unsung or unmourned was unfortunate.[84] Other mourning customs included fasting, scattering dust, the tearing of garments, the wearing of sack-cloth, ritual dancing, and funeral feasts (including feeding the dead) at tombs.[85] In later Judaism, mourners were not allowed to work, but this did not include housecleaning, making the bed, or dishwashing.[86] Although both men and women are described in expressions of grief, and although both men and women could be professional mourners, in the ancient Near East as elsewhere, mourning and lamenting the dead were so commonly women's roles that they were stereotypical of women's behavior, not men's.[87] Jeremiah uses the image of a weeping woman to lament the exile of the northern tribes. Rachel weeps (בכה) over the loss of Israel:

> Thus says the Lord: A voice is heard in Ramah,
> lamentation and bitter weeping.
> Rachel is weeping for her children;
> she refuses to be comforted for her children
> because they are not (Jer 31:15; RSV).

Jeremiah also assumes that professional mourners would be women, and that women would teach the skill of lamenting to their daughters (Jer 17:21). This imagery continues in later Jewish texts, as in 2 Esdr 9:26–10:54, where a weeping woman represents Zion in a vision.[88] In laments the dead themselves are usually addressed (2 Sam 1:26; 3:34; Ezek 32:2) although as in Greek lament tradition, the mourners could also call to one another to join in their song.[89] De Ward suggests that the formal lament tradition arose from the popular tradition of women's laments.[90] Later formal rabbinic laments, however, are often characterized by praise of the dead rather than mourning and loss, and may be a genre that developed similarly to the Greek eulogy.[91]

Although mourning was considered a necessary part of concern for the dead, limitations on mourning rites can also be found. Lacerating the flesh is condemned in Deut 14:1; [92] although not described in 1 and 2 Samuel, it was practiced by the prophets of Jezebel (1 Kgs 18:28). There were also attempts to curtail the Canaanite cult of the dead and the custom of leaving food in tombs (1 Sam 28:3–9; Deut 26:14).[93] In Ezek 9:14, the weeping of women for Tammuz in the temple is called an "abomination."[94] In the ancient Near East, and in other parts of the Mediterranean world, the folk religion which focused on the veneration of ancestors was especially practiced by women. Thus, limitations to these and other graveside rituals served to limit women's participation more than men's, both in early Israel and in later Hellenistic times.[95] Excavations of tombs in Palestine from the Late Hellenistic period suggest that certain so-called "pagan" customs persisted among Jews. For example, pre-Maccabean tombs betray the extent of Hellenization within Jewish society.[96] To be sure, later Second Temple tombs show a restraint in artistic representation and amount of grave goods;[97] nevertheless, coins (for the ferryman Charon?),[98] perfume bottles,[99] signs of the anointing of remains,[100] as well as cooking pots[101] found in Jewish tombs reflect the persistence of certain gravesite customs and the continued influence of popular or even Hellenistic burial rites.[102] "Jason's Tomb" near Jerusalem contains a lament over the death of Jason inscribed in Aramaic. The inscription calls visitors to the tomb to grieve for Jason's death and attests to the writer's personal grief over his brother's death.[103] This kind of evidence would imply the continuation of laments and women's rituals of mourning and visits to tombs and burial grounds during the first century.[104]

Later funerary restrictions in rabbinic sources show a more detailed interest in the control of both the expenses of funerals and the women's mourning rituals comparable to that of Greek and Roman legislation.[105] Unlike Greek and Roman practice, however, weeping for the dead is obligatory for both men and women, and verbal expressions of grief are encouraged. Within limits, even extreme expressions of grief honored the dead.[106] Certain common customs, like throwing grave goods on the coffin, were not forbidden, as long as the practice did not become overly wasteful.[107] The third day visit persists, and is given the purpose of confirming the death.[108] Still, Both the *Mishnah* and the later tractate *Semahot* restrict women's behavior at funerals. The *Mishnah* prohibits setting funeral biers down in the open street, proscribes mourning by women at certain yearly festivals, and forbids their mourning the dead after the corpse has been buried.[109] The *Mishnah* also declares that criminals executed by the religious court may not be buried in a family tomb, but should be interred in a place designated by the court for this purpose.[110] The *Semahot* prohibits certain mourning gestures for those not next of kin,[111] and denies funeral rites to suicides[112] as well as those executed by the (religious) court. Such a condemned person may be buried, but is not to be mourned.[113] Nonetheless, all mourning rites are to be observed for those executed by the (presumably Roman) state, but the family is discouraged from trying to steal the body.[114] More research is needed to determine why Jewish mourning rituals, particularly those performed by women, needed additional limitation in the centuries following the Jewish wars.[115] It is reasonable to assume that women continued various mourning rituals particular to their own religious experience (as both Christian and other Hellenistic women did during these same centuries). In light of the functions of lament suggested for ancient Greek cultural contexts,[116] the lack of restrictions on mourning following state executions betrays an awareness on the part of certain rabbis of the potential for national protest through the vehicle of family mourning (especially that of women) following a state (presumably Roman) execution. The banning of mourning following executions, and the burial of executed criminals in court-controlled burial grounds shows a similar awareness of the potential opposition to religious court decisions that could be expressed by women lamenting at the graves of their dead.[117]

It is difficult to determine the applicability of these later regulations to first century Palestine. We have only the remains of one crucified individual from Roman Palestine, in spite of the thousands who were put to death during Roman occupation.[118] However, it seems reasonable to conclude that at least executed criminals were buried in common plots due to the application of Deut 21:22–23. A pesher from Qumran (4QpNah) and a passage from the Temple Scroll (11QTemple 64:6–13) illustrate a pre-Christian association of death by "hanging on a tree" (Deut 21:22–23) with crucifixion by certain Jews in first century B.C.E. or C.E. Palestine.[119] Furthermore, comments by Josephus suggest that although Roman officials might refuse to comply, Jews generally attempted to provide proper burial not only for social and religious outcasts, but criminals executed by Roman authorities.[120] The story of Tobit's burial of executed Jews encourages Jewish readers that an ideal of Jewish piety can prevail even under the forces of hostile occupation (Tob 1:18–20; 2:3–10). And the burial of Yehohanan in an ossuary shows that it was possible for a family with good connections to recover the remains of a family member for an honorable second burial.[121] On the basis of this instance it seems reasonable to assume that some families did recover the corpses of their loved ones. That the only known remains of a crucified person come from Palestine, rather than elsewhere in the Roman world, may well indicate the ancient Jewish predilection for burial, even in the case of criminals. Primary (and honorable) burials in family plots, however, were probably very rare exceptions, limited to wealthier families like Yehohanan's.[122] The possibility of a family recovering a body at any time would depend on the temperament of the Roman authority in question.[123] At any rate, it seems unlikely, that family members would be allowed to gather in close proximity to the crucifixion site itself.[124] Given human fascination with pubic spectacle, onlookers might gather at a distance, but it is also possible that crucifixions were so commonplace and gruesome that some would not find them all that interesting. After all, executions were intended to provide a public display of Roman force to serve as a deterrent to dissent, and the proceedings were hardly intended to facilitate public mourning and normal burial practices. In view of the inherant potential for disruption posed by women's emotional lamentation of the dead, this is not surprising. This would particularly be the case in occupied Roman Palestine.[125] However, women and families no doubt strained for a glimpse of arrested relatives, attempted to secure the remains of their loved ones, mourned their death and visited their gravesites if known.

Women in the Context of Heroic and Noble Deaths

It is widely accepted that New Testament portrayals of Jesus reflect certain literary motifs or themes commonly found in stories about heroes, immortals, so-called "divine men," great philosophers and the like.[126] Such themes were no doubt widely employed in both popular folklore and artistic representations as well as in literature.[127] Given the tendency of popular folklore traditions to create and recreate heroes in a Hellenistic mode, one need not posit an exact literary model or type of a "divine man."[128] Yet, if one can demonstrate a similar function (rather than simple anecdotal correspondence) between gospel narratives and descriptions of Hellenistic "divine men" or heroes, such a comparison can be informative.[129] Most discussions have focused on miracle traditions in the gospels and the relationship of Jesus to other Hellenistic wonder workers.[130] The gospel of Mark in particular has been shown to have an interest in affirming the miraculous nature of Jesus' ministry, while at the same time demonstrating that Jesus is no mere thaumaturge.[131] The Passion narrative is usually juxtaposed with traditions of the miraculous in Mark and John, to make the point that Christian understandings of Jesus' death served as a critique of primitive divine man theologies.[132] However, John's Passion account serves John's interests in the glorification of Jesus, not just through the many signs he performs, but through his death on the cross.[133] The power of Jesus as a great thaumaturge is also no doubt the point of Mark's portrayal of Jesus' last cry, which forcefully rends the temple curtain and elicits the declaration of the centurion, "Truly this man was the Son of God."[134] Furthermore, the desertion of Jesus' disciples during the Passion week follows a common aretalogical theme.[135] Finally, once Hellenistic Jewish martyrological literature is understood (properly) to be the genre behind Mark's Passion account[136] then Mark's description of Jesus' death must also be analyzed in light of the Hellenistic concepts of the noble and heroic deaths which these martyrologies presuppose.[137] This has in fact already been done,[138] but what has not been done is an analysis of the function of gender in the Markan Passion and subsequent Passion accounts.[139] Stereotypes of men's and women's appropriate expressions of grief and emotion are reflected in ancient literary portrayals of deaths, particularly deaths of notable individuals, known in Latin as *exitus illustrium virorum*.[140] Attention to the gender of the characters in each gospel story and their expressions of grief (or lack thereof) clarifies how these stories of Jesus' death fit into the larger theological interests of each evangelist.

Negative Views of Grief and Mourning

Objections to women's religious rituals of grief and the marginalization of women's customs evolved into social stereotypes which raised the marginalization process to an ideological level, and resulted in images which reflect ideals of behavior during the Hellenistic period. One way to control human behavior is through criticism. Labeling and the setting up of categories of ideal and proscribed behaviors is a powerful form of social control. In antiquity preferred gender roles were reinforced through catalogues of virtues (how men and women were supposed to behave) and vices (how men and women often behaved, but weren't supposed to). Stereotypical gendered categories of ideal behavior appear in epitaphs and pervade Greek, Roman, Jewish, and Christian literature of the Hellenistic period.[141] Such ideal categories include cultural stereotypes about male and female grief. Laments and expressions of grief are associated with femininity, moderation of grief with masculinity. Plutarch writes in his *Letter to Apollonius*:

> Yes, mourning is truly feminine, and ignoble, since women are more given to it than men, and barbarians more than Greeks, and inferior men more than better men.[142]

If expressed at all, according to Plutarch, grief and emotion (πάθος) should be expressed in moderation, particularly by men.[143] In *Consolation to His Wife*, he praises her moderate behavior following the death of their daughter, Timoxena. He is pleased that she did not allow behavior he considers excessive at their daughter's funeral, which was conducted in silence (σιωπῇ) with only close family members present.[144] Conversely, in his discussion of Solon's funerary legislation, Plutarch remarks that women breaking the new restrictions would be punished by a board of censors of women for unmanly (ἀνάνδρος) and effeminate (γυναικώδης) behavior.[145] Cicero expresses similar sentiments. Such displays of grief lead to "womanish superstition" (*superstitio muliebris*).[146] Ideal masculine behavior is stoic and controlled, as in that of the noble philosopher Pythagoras who was said to show neither gaiety (χαρά) nor grief (λύπη).[147] Hellenistic Jewish texts also reflect ideals of masculine behavior. The Alexandrian *Sentences of Pseudo-Phocylides,* written roughly between 30 B.C.E. and 40 C.E., recommends "Be moderate in your grief; for moderation is the best."[148] Similarly, the Wisdom of Ben Sira, written in Jerusalem around 180 B.C.E. recommends mourning for a day or two, but more than that does the dead no good.[149] Josephus' description of Herod's funeral instructions, which include the slaughter of one person in every household in the country to insure protracted grief throughout the land, is no doubt meant to portray Herod as crass.[150] Thus, concurrent with a variety of actual burial customs and mourning practices, a particular demeanor is recommended in Hellenistic literature, one that is culturally coded as masculine rather than feminine. These stereotypes influence literary portrayals of deaths, particularly deaths of notable men and women.

Generally, in most "noble death" stories women play a minor, supporting role, gathering about the hero or martyr to cry, weep and wail. A man, usually the martyr or hero, then gets annoyed, and either tells them to be quiet or asks them to leave. The classic case is the death of Socrates, from which many later scenes are no doubt derived. Socrates' wife is not even present for the death scene; she has been taken weeping from the room much earlier.[151] His children are presented to him, the other women of the family gather round him, he says his good-byes, and then the women are dismissed.[152] Only his male disciples and a servant are present for the death scene proper. Some of the men start to weep (*δακρύω*) and Socrates tells them to stop. Eventually they all break down weeping (*κατακλαίω*). Socrates, annoyed with them says:

> 'What conduct is this, you strange men! I sent the women away chiefly for this reason, that they might not behave in this absurd way; for I have heard that it is best to die in silence. Keep quiet and be brave.' Then we were ashamed and controlled our tears.[153]

In ancient literature many death scenes follow this basic model. Family, friends, or disciples gather, the women weep, are told to be quiet, and are then asked to leave, or are escorted stage left. The hero is ringed by his close male friends or attendants, but not mothers, wives or daughters. While a certain amount of restrained grief is a sign that the onlooking friends and family honor the dead and dying, if the men start to carry on, they too are told to stop weeping–and be *men*.[154] Grief, when restrained, is a sign of true friendship and discipleship, but too much grief is "womanish" and "irrational."[155] In order to show true courage (*ἀνδρεία*), men must exhibit characteristics culturally defined as feminine and then overcome them.[156] Yet in one scene a woman's death is "noble." In Euripides' *Iphegenia at Aulis*, the heroine's death is noble, because it is voluntary and on behalf of the state.[157]

In depictions of the death of Hercules, only men or his mother have prominent roles. The scene in Seneca's *Hercules Oetaeus* is a good example. Mourning among the crowd is led by Hercules' mother, who beats her breasts (stripped naked to the waist) filling the air with "womanish bewailings" (*voce feminea*). Hercules tells her to stop weeping. When she is at last quiet the narrator declares her "well nigh equal to her son." Still, when the funeral pyre is lit,

Hercules declares: "Now you are parent true of Hercules; thus it is proper that you should stand, my mother, beside the pyre, and thus it is proper that Hercules be mourned." The crowd, however, is speechless. After his death, Hercules appears to his mother.[158] The version of the story most often compared with Jesus,' that found in Diodorus of Sicily, death does not feature his mother Heracles' companions build the pyre. One friend, Iolaüs, after doing what Hercules asks, withdraws (*ἀποβαίνω*) from the pyre to watch. Another, Philoctetes, lights the fire. Afterwards, Iolaüs and his friends come to retrieve Hercules' remains, but no bones can be found.[159] Lucian blends the death Socrates and that of Hercules in his parody *The Passing of Peregrinus*:

> The Cynics stood about the fire, not weeping to be sure, but silently evincing a certain amount of grief as they gazed into the fire . . . I said, 'Let us go away, you simpletons. It is not an agreeable spectacle to look at an old man who has been roasted, getting our nostrils filled with a villainous reek. Or are you waiting for a painter to come and picture you as the companions of Socrates in prison are portrayed beside him?'[160]

Thus in the majority of death scenes only male disciples or friends are present for the death, the women often having been dismissed. The men show some grief, and then cease weeping, usually after being reprimanded by the teacher/hero. The exception is certain stories of the death of Hercules, where his mother is present.

It is no surprise that Hellenistic Jewish death scenes follow along similar lines. Josephus' death of Moses follows this model. The crowd weeps, the women weep and beat their breasts, Moses tells them to be quiet, steps away from them to put their weeping in the distance, and then Eleazar and Joshua escort him up the mountain, where he disappears.[161] Very few such stories feature women. Although not a death scene, 2 Esdras 9:26–10:54 portrays Zion as a weeping woman. She so annoys the prophet that she is zapped into a vision of a resplendent city to shut her up.[162] And Susanna is a paragon of righteous suffering, surrounded by weeping family and friends at her trial, but she does not die.[163] The most interesting development in Jewish martyrological literature, however, is the story of the woman and her seven sons in 2 and 4 Maccabees.[164] Here a woman dies a truly noble death, and encourages each of her children to do so as well.[165] Of special interest are the two speeches in 4 Macc.

16. The first is indicates how the mother would have behaved if she were fainthearted. She would have wept and mourned for the death of her children (16:5–11). The narrator says that she of course did not give this speech, but rather the one in 16:16–23! Barbara Miller has identified elements in the first speech that coincide with women's ancient and modern formal laments.[166] Although a scribal appropriation of a woman's lament, it still contains essential elements common to other Greek and Hebrew laments. The formal address and reproach to the dead remains (16:6–11).[167] The mother's second speech, which the narrator assures us she really spoke, encourages the sons to die on behalf of their people. Elements of this speech coincide more with the masculine eulogy in praise of men who die on behalf of the state.[168] For this speech the mother is called "manly" : she is a "soldier of God" who is "more powerful than a man" (*ἀνήρ*) (4 Macc 16:14; RSV). These Jewish stories follow a set pattern, so that the person suffering is portrayed as "righteous," as well as "noble." This genre of the suffering righteous one has been defined and analyzed by George Nickelsburg.[169] It should be noted that while Nickelsburg's model for the Markan Passion fails to take them into account, the Psalms also imply the presence of family and friend as onlookers, if only from a distance.[170] Thus, there is good precedent in Jewish Hellenistic tradition for the martyrological themes in the Passion narratives. The presence of family and friends is expected, and expressed grief is a prerequisite for the scene. Whereas men should restrain their grief in the face of death, women are expected to weep. If a woman does not mourn, if she overcomes her grief, she demonstrates nobility; she can even be described as a "man."

Stereotypes of Women's Rituals: Tomb Visitation and Magic

Besides being stereotyped as overly emotional, women's tomb visitation and lamentation also came to have necromantic overtones to a greater degree than men's, even though magical practices and conjuring the dead at tombs are sometimes ascribed to men. First, there is a strong tradition in Greek and Roman literature featuring laments which links the lamentation of women (and sometimes men) to conjuring up the dead, especially in the context of visits to the tomb. The shades or spirits of the dead (called by the Greeks δαίμων, or εἴδωλον, or collectively *lemures* or *manes* by the Romans) were thought to remain near the place of burial where they could be visited, as well as fed. That was therefore the most likely place for an appearance of a departed spirit, the tomb being its "house," as it were.[171] The shades of the dead were considered powerful, able to inflict illness or distress if neglected, but able to bring good fortune or aid in healing if propitiated.[172] Magical texts were therefore often folded neatly and placed in graves, requesting help in various cricumstances as well as calling for curses or revenge.[173] In one Coptic Christian example from 7th century Egypt, a widow tucks her ritual spell into the bindings of a mummy, and invokes the spirit of the dead to bring her vengeance in a judicial matter:

> The mummy [on] which this [papyrus for] vengeance is placed must appeal night and day [to the lord (?)], from its [bed] to the ground in which it is buried with the other mummies lying around this grave, all of them calling out, together, what is in this papyrus, until god hears and [brings] judgment on our behalf, quickly! Amen.[174]

The late date demonstrates the persistence of these graveside customs.

The spirits of those who had died untimely or violent deaths (those murdered or executed) were considered especially powerful, and to have possession of the body was to have control over the power of the dead person's spirit;[175] indeed many magical texts include a piece of such a corpse in the list of ingredients. The spirits of those untimely or violently killed were condemned to wander the earth, and it was these spirits which were thought particularly open to invocation by workers of necromancy.[176] This potential traffic in corpses in part explains the formulas found in funerary inscriptions which lay curses on any who would disturb the resting place of the deceased.[177] Cynics, Epicureans and Stoic philosophers considered such beliefs superstitious, and were fond of quoting the words of Theodore the Atheist to Lysimachus, who was threatening him with death without burial: "What matters it if I rot on the earth or under it?"[178] Socrates, of course, was also notable for his lack of concern for his own burial. When asked how he would like to be buried, he replied, "However you please, if you can catch me."[179] Other philosophers, especially Cynics, expressed a similar lack of concern for the disposal of their remains.[180] Still, for many ancient people, the common beliefs and religious practices connected to gravesites were no doubt simply a part of everyday religious life. What is labeled "magic" is often indistinguishable from other practices labeled and thus legitimized as "religion." Magical texts from antiquity attest to the pervasive interest of many ancient people in rituals which would provide healing, help in childbirth, assure faithfulness in marriage, help bring success in legal, business and financial matters, as well as afford protection from evil people or demonic powers.[181] Performers of such religious rituals could be of either sex; in a number of extant spells the ritualist is a man, not a woman.

In literary portrayals, however, women enacting such rituals are defined negatively as witches, and often are compared with male necromancers or magicians. Male ritualists tend to be labeled wonder workers or prophets, and are given positive appeal. A good example of this is found in Apuleius' *Metamorphoses*, written in Roman Africa in the early to mid-second century C.E. The character Thelyphron is hired to watch the remains of a man the night before the funeral, lest his corpse be mutilated by witches. He hesitates:

> I greatly fear the blind and inevitable hits of witchcraft, for they say that not even the graves of the dead are safe, but the bones and slices of such are slain to be digged up from tombs and pyres to afflict and torment such as live: and the old witches (*cantatrices anus*) as soon as they hear of the death of any person do forthwith go and uncover the hearse and spoil the corpse before it ever be buried.[182]

What will these old hags do? They are planning to take bites out of the corpses' faces to use in their magical arts (*artis magicae supplementa*).[183] The next morning, as the body is being carried through the streets, the widow is accused of poisoning him. An Egyptian prophet "of the first rank" (*Aegyptius propheta primarius*) steps forth to settle the matter by raising the man from the dead by means of herbs and incantations.[184] The raised man declares that he was indeed murdered by his wife. Notice that the man involved in such ritual arts is a "prophet" but the women are "witches," even though both are practicing what would be called "magic" or "necromancy." There are similar stories linking women to the raising of the dead by means of religious rituals at gravesites and tombs. Lucan, writing in Rome around 50 C.E., writes of women who frequent funerals and graveyards in order to steal pieces of corpses, especially from those left unburied. Even the vultures are scared away by these women, who take the place of carrion birds by their scooping out eye-balls from the dead or gnawing at fingers or noses in the most grisly manner. One poor corpse is stolen, raised, and used by a woman to speak oracles about the future.[185]

Since lamentation was done by the gravesite, dirges became associated with the raising of the dead at tombs by women, and thereby with necromancy and magical arts. Since the chief mourner was considered to be in direct communication with the dead, the role of the mourner is thought to be the model for the later magician (*γόης*).[186] The word for "magician" (*γόης*) is derived from the word "lament" (*γόος*).[187] A formal funerary lament is also called *θρῆνος* and follows a formal structure: 1) address of the dead 2) narrative 3) renewed address. Formal laments are more regular, but in many ways are parallel to folk laments still sung by women in modern rural Greece.[188] Laments are characterized by antiphonal structure and antithetical thought; one singer leads the lament and calls to the rest of the women to follow her in song. This basic antiphonal structure still survives in formal laments in modern rural Greece.[189] These dirges serve as a form of communication with the dead, and attest to a tradition of interpretation of death and suffering by women.[190]

As a form of communication with the dead, however, lamentation can also be described in literature as a form of necromancy. In Aeschylus' *The Persians*, for example, Darius' widow Atossa brings offerings to her husband's tomb. A chorus of lamenters come with her (in this case men). Their joint task? To summon the dead king from Hades. When Darius rises and speaks, it is on account of the force of their wailing lament. He declares:

> As I behold my consort hard by my tomb I feel alarm, and I accept her libations in kindly mood; while you (pl.), standing near my tomb, make lament (*θρηνειτ'*) and with shrilling cries (*γόοις*) that summon the spirits of the dead, invoke me piteously. Not easy is the path from out of the tomb.[191]

At the end of the play it is Xerxes who leads a staged lament, calling to the chorus to respond: "Lift up your voice in the lamentation (γόοις)!" The antiphonal shouts this precipitates probably reflect what would have been a female lament in ancient Greek funerary practice.[192] A similar scene is found in Aeschylus' *The Libation Bearers,* where Electra brings offerings to her father Agamemnon's tomb, accompanied by a chorus (all women). She pours libations on the grave and laments. As wails of the chorus urge her on, she cries out to Hermes as a mediator of the spirits of the dead to return her brother Orestes from exile to help her avenge her father's death. Upon his return, both brother and sister (accompanied by the chorus) pour libations on their father's tomb together, invoking his spirit to empower them to avenge his murder and the mutilation of his corpse.[193] Thus, laments function in these stories as a powerful form of magic, stirring up the dead, especially to exact vengeance.[194] As such they are meant to invoke fear in the audience (primarily male) and serve as a powerful vehicle for cultural catharsis.[195] This literary motif linking women, laments, tombs, and communication with the dead is a prominent theme in Greek tragedy[196] which carries over into literature of the Roman period as well. For example, in Seneca's Hercules Oeateus Hercules appears to his mother Alcmena following her lamentation. She witnesses his death, lamenting it both before and after. He then appears to her and tells her to be quiet.[197] Elsewhere mourning wives are translated into the air to be with their dead husbands and immediately their husbands tell them to stop crying.[198] The woman's lament in Fourth Maccabees 16:5–11 retains this element of the address of the dead.

Even in Jewish religion women continued to be associated with tomb visitation, lamentation and communication with the dead. Necromancy also flourished in spite of laws and pronouncements to the contrary. Both men and women perform these kinds of religious rituals in the Hebrew Bible as well as in ancient Near Eastern texts.[199] The bones of the prophet Elisha, for example, were thought to be powerful enough to raise the dead (2 Kgs 13:20–21).[200] According to Leviticus 20:27, both men and women could conjur spirits from the grave; both men and women could be put to death by stoning for doing so.[201] Divinized ancestors could also be invoked in times of trouble and given offerings (so Gen. 28:17–18; 1 Sam 1:11).[202] Such texts attest to the powers that the dead were thought to have in regards to fortelling the future, reviving life, and exacting vengeance.[203] Monotheist reforms such as Josiah's were directed in part against the ongoing cult of the dead practices among Israelites.[204]

The best known story from the Hebrew Bible involving necromancy concerns the so-called Witch of Endor, who raises the spirit of the dead prophet Samuel for Saul.[205] The account in First Samuel appears to be a literary stereotype parodying women's religious rituals in the ancient Near East. Ancient Mesopotamian texts also describe religious rituals performed by women "witches," including the placement of figurines representing individuals into graves with corpses.[206] A woman necromancer was sometimes likened to a harlot (Isa 57:3).[207] In Proverbs, wisdom is said to protect one from this kind of whore who is connected with death cults.[208] Later Jewish writers repeat and discuss the tale of the Witch of Endor. Josephus, for example, has no trouble admitting that Samuel was raised by means of the woman's power,[209] but in spite of maintaining a belief in the possibility of necromancy, the author of *Biblical Antiquities* prefers to add that Samuel appeared by means of God's command, not the woman's.[210] Later rabbis considered necromancy possible, although sinful, but still acknowledge that the woman raised the prophet by magical means.[211]

Women in the Passion Narratives: The Empty Tomb

In light of literary and social historical evidence, the women followers of Jesus in both the Passion and empty tomb accounts are remarkably silent. Generally, they do not lament (*θρηνέω*) they do not cry or weep (*κλαίω*), they do not beat their breasts (*κόπτω*). When they come to the tomb they do anything but lament, coming rather to anoint (*ἀλείφω* Mark 16:1; Luke 24:1), to sit (*κάθημαι*) (Matt 27:61), to watch or see (*θεωρέω* Matt 28:1), or they simply come (*ἔρχομαι* John 20:1). If they do come to lament (Peter 13:55–57), they never get the chance, but are interrupted by angels. In Mark they come to anoint the body, a standard burial custom, but they are much too late.[212] Only in John is Mary Magdalene described as weeping (*κλαίω* John 20:11) but she is alone. In other words, the women do not do the one thing one would expect of women under such circumstances: lament the dead. In light of the

Hellenistic evidence, this is suspicious. If the women are at the cross and the tomb, why do they not weep? Why do the authors not protray this common custom? Susan Heine, Carolyn Osiek, Rick Strelan, and Thomas Longstaff have suggested that mourning can be the only reason for the women in Mark 16:1–8 and Matt 27:61 to have gone to the tomb. Heine clearly connects this with women's obligations to visit the tombs of the dead.[213] Sawicki has also highlighted the mourning that must have been done by early Christian women.[214] Surely, then, these women should weep, but they do not. There must be a reason for this. My proposal is that the association of women with the death and burial of Jesus reflects the creedal tradition that Jesus "was buried" (*θάπτω*) and then "was raised on the third day" (*ἐγήγερται τῇ ἡμέρᾳ τῇ τρίτῃ*) (1 Cor. 15:4),[215] and that tradition in turn derives from the common Hellenistic custom of tomb visitation three days after death.

Even when women's lament rituals are quite orderly, their rites are often considered theologically suspect due to their necromantic associations. This tradition had to be modified, and the empty tomb tradition was the result. The association of followers of Jesus (particularly women) going to a tomb on the third day following Jesus' death to commune with the dead through their mournful cries could too closely associate Jesus with everyday "divine men" or heroes, and his followers with magic. The overall effect of the empty tomb tradition, which featured women in this stereotypical role of tomb visitation, functioned to marginalize women followers of Jesus more than men thus weakening their claim to having seen (*ὁράω*) the risen Christ.

In its Hellenistic context, the empty tomb story can be seen as a modification of a strong literary and cultural connection between women, tomb cults and magic. It should be considered as sort of an anti-deification story which employs a common narrative device of an "empty tomb." This fictional device was common in deification or translation stories in antiquity and is also to be found in Hellenistic romances.[216] Cleomedes leaves behind an "empty chest,"[217] Hercules an "empty pyre,"[218] Romulus an "empty chair,"[219] Aristeas an "empty house,"[220] and when Chaereas goes to mourn the death of his beloved Callirhoe, he finds the tomb empty:

> At the crack of dawn (*περίορθον*) Chaereas turned up at the tomb, ostensibly to offer wreaths and libations, but in fact

> with the intention of doing away with himself . . . When he reached the tomb, he found that the stones had been moved (*εὗρε τοὺς λίθους κεκινημένους*) and the entrance was open (*θανερὰν τὴν εἴσοδον*). He was astonished (*ἐξεπλάγη*) at the sight and overcome with fearful perplexity (*ὑπὸ δεινῆς ἀπορίας*) at what had happened. Rumor – a swift messenger– told the Syracusans this amazing news. They all quickly crowded round the tomb, but no one dared go inside until Hermocrates gave an order to do so . . . It seemed incredible that even the corpse was not lying there. Then Chaereas himself determined to go in, in his desire to see Callirhoe again even dead; but though he hunted through the tomb, he could find nothing (*οὐδὲν εὑρεῖν ἠδύνατο*).

Later, Chaereas finds Callirhoe's grave goods from the tomb on a pirate's ship:

> Ah, Callirhoe! These are yours! This is the wreath I put on your head!
> Your father gave you this, your mother this; this is your bridal dress! . . . But – I can see your things but where are you? The tomb's contents are all there – except the body!

It is eventually learned that poor Callirhoe has been seized by tomb robbers, after being awakened from a deep sleep.[221] Many such "empty tombs" (*κενοτάφιον*) of the special dead were known.[222] The Hellenistic translation tradition is certainly the best literary context in which tounderstand Mark's account of the empty tomb.[223] Logically, such translation stories are more likely to have evolved when the actual gravesite of the special dead was unknown.[224] As it stands, Mark 16:1–8 is a fictional anti-translation or deification story.[225]

However, to say this is not enough. The gender of the characters plays more of a role in the story than previous commentators have allowed. The flight of the women from the tomb should also be understood in light of Mark's interest in denegrating the disciples, also an aretalogical commonplace.[226] First the men flee, then the women. That the women flee from a *tomb* is no doubt due to the common connection of women to such activities. The women go to the tomb to do what women are supposed to do, but they fail miserably. Burton Mack, commenting on the empty tomb account in Mark sees the real implications of Mark's narrative when he writes:

> The story of the empty tomb is a poor appearance story since Jesus does not appear. It is also a poor cultic legend of any kind. The young man explains that the women have come to the wrong place. "He is not here." "Go." (Don't come back.)[227]

Tombs are, after all, where one picks up demons (Mark 5:1–5). This is no doubt why Mary Magdalene picks up a few demons herself (Mark 16:9; Luke 8:2). Despite the current interest of feminist scholars in the empty tomb tradition, the cumulative effect of these stories hardly affirms the significance of women or women's religious rituals in antiquity.[228] Celsus certainly offers a trenchant commentary on the overall effect of these gospel accounts: he says that Jesus' resurrection was confirmed by one hysterical female[229] who no doubt hallucinated[230] and saw a ghost.[231] Origen responds weakly that Jesus appeared to other (women?) too.[232] The negative associations of women with death, burial and mourning fuels Celsus' criticism. However, the continued marginalization of women in death and mourning scenes coincides with a continuing significant role for women in the cult of the dead. Gregory Riley has recently suggested a similar theological function for the Thomas appearance tradition in the Gospel of John. By portraying the physicality of Jesus' resurrection, John intends to counteract notions of non-physical resurrections presupposed in the cult of heroes and the dead.[233] Gerd Lüdemann has suggested that Peter's resurrection experience presupposes an experience of extreme grief.[234] Although Peter's grief following Jesus' death is nowhere narrated in the New Testament, Mary Magdalene's is (John 20:4).[235] Furthermore, dreams, daydreams and visions – especially those experienced by women following a death, were commonly linked to the founding of cults in antiquity.[236] The empty tomb and physical appearance stories in the gospels attempt to disavow visionary experience as a possible origin for Christian belief and practice by replacing it with a resurrection theology. They also function, of course, to discourage any current practice of the cult of the dead.

This tradition certainly did not encourage any kind of tomb cult of the special dead in earliest Christian groups. There little evidence that early Christians had much interest in the location of Jesus' tomb until post-Constantinian times.[237] This strongly suggests that the location of Jesus' tomb was simply unknown. Given the strong ancient traditions associating Jesus with powerful, even magical figures, it seems reasonable to conclude that if his tomb had been known early on it would have been venerated. This explains the vague place references in Mark's empty tomb story: "He is not here. Go!" (Mark 16:6–7).[238] There is ample evidence, however, that pre-Constantinian Christians continued a tradition of the cult of the dead unconnected to a particular location of Jesus' tomb, gathering to meet in communal tombs, much like burial societies.[239] The evidence for this kind of cultic practice is the earliest evidence for Christian worship in antiquity.[240]

There may be other traces of this popular funerary tradition in the gospels. For example, the *Sitz im Leben* of cultic funerary practice and formal lament tradition may solve a vexing problem in the interpretation of the "Children in the Marketplace" parable in Q. I first suggested that the images in the parable are best understood as slaves or servants practicing piping (for banquets) and mourning (for funerals) in the marketplace.[241] In the context of Q redaction this is no doubt the case: the mourners serve as a type of fasting (related to John's activity), the pipers to feasting (Jesus' activity). Both Jesus and John are emissaries (children, *τέκνα*) of Wisdom. However, this has never been completely satisfactory, since the parable likens the activity of the servants/children to "this generation." The antiphonal nature of the piping and mourning of the servants/children as mourners (male and female) may be the key to its original form. The association of servants' activity to Jesus' and John's (feasting vs. fasting) respectively is probably secondary. The lack of response of "this generation" may be better understood in the context of lamentation, in which calling back and forth between mourners was commonplace. Seen in this light, there are two sides to "this generation." They criticize each other for refusing to participate in antiphonal mourning: "we piped to you and you did not dance, we wailed and you did not weep" Q 7:31–32. Thus we may see at work in Q a scribal appropriation of a tradition which reflects an ancient cultic lament context.[242] Such scribal appropriation of women's laments is found in every instance of formal laments we have reviewed: Greek, Roman, and Jewish.[243] The isolation of this parable in a previous form as a lament tradition would further support the view that earliest Christian traditions conform to a locative tradition based in cultic meals with the dead rather than a utopian religious perspective (i.e., they are non-apocalyptic). J. Z. Smith writes on the ritual of eating with the dead:

> The dead remain dead, in a sphere other than the living; but there is contact, there is continuity of relationship, there is memorialization, there is presence.[244]

The mistake of Q scholarship up to this point has been to assume that the apocalyptic and non-apocalyptic elements in Q are necessarily congruent traditions rather than competing traditions. Clearly, streams of tradition develop concurrently, while yet in conflict.[245] However, the transfer of lament traditions into (primarily) masculine scribal endeavors is probably most understandable in a Jewish Christian context, since early Judaism was more accepting of both male and female mourning and developed a genre of formal lament.[246] And, although mourning rituals presuppose a certain degree of separation of the sexes (perhaps to separate tables for the meal for example), in funerary contexts men and women hear each other's laments.[247] My analysis isolates two segments of ancient Christian tradition both of which point to the existence of a similar *Sitz im Leben* of burial lamentation: Q 7:31–32 and 1 Cor 15:4. I believe that Mark 15:40–41 and 16:1–8 both serve to modify the implications of 1 Cor 15:4, by placing the women at the cross and the tomb where they do not mourn. In light of this common background, the variations of women's names in 15:40, 47 and 16:1 suggests that these two stories were linked secondarily.[248] Since both a "suffering dikaios" model and a literary "noble death" theme presuppose the presence of women, this favors including them in any posited pre-Markan account. Thus, although the empty tomb tradition does not contain an oral narrative tradition passed through women's networks[249] it may have arisen in response to a tradition that implied women's religious and ritual experience: "he was buried, he was raised on the third day" (1 Cor 15:4). The role of women described in Mark 15:40–41 must have arisen concurrently with their portrayal in Mark 16:1–8 because the one explains the other. Either Mark wrote both stories, or the traditions circulated together.

Women at the Crucifixion and Burial

In the interests of time, we will now turn to the crucifixion scene in the Gospel of Mark from which notions about Matthew's and Luke's should naturally follow. John S. Kloppenborg has dealt sufficiently with Luke's Passion in this regard.[250] The general report of the women at the cross (Mark 15:40–41) is sometimes considered from a traditional Passion source.[251] Mark's account is generally accepted as early, and some claim it to be the one story from which the rest are derived.[252] A gender analysis of John's version supports this. That John gives us independent accounts of the crucifixion, burial and empty tomb seems unlikely for the following reasons: 1) John's account of the crucifixion, empty tomb, and appearances presuppose the Markan account which places only women at the cross and the tomb. Like the gospels of Luke and Peter, John secondarily inserts male characters into these traditions, especially the "beloved disciple" (John 19:26–27). 2) In the burial scene women's roles are further coopted by male characters in that Nicodemus brings spices, rather than the women (John 19:39–40). 3) In the list of women at the cross, Mary Magdalene is named last, rather than being in her usual primary position. This presupposes the Markan lists in which she is placed first, and serves to weaken her importance (John 19:25; cf. Mark 15:40, 47; 16:1). 4) The women do not weep at the cross in John, which is a Markan theme of feminine failure in the case of Jesus' women disciples (Mark 16:10; cf. John 19:25). John does, however reintroduce feminine weeping at the tomb (John 20:4). John's account of these events thus reflects further developments which distance the women from the narrated burial events and includes a reintroduction of a weeping woman.[253] The nearness of the women to the cross and the emphasis on Jesus' mother are often considered Johannine constructions, theologically motivated and historically implausible (19:25–27).[254] And although the women are near the cross, they do not mourn there, and they are not described as following Joseph and Nicodemus to the tomb (John 19:38–42).

Gender analysis suggests the Gospel of Peter is also late; in fact, when viewed in light of the Hellenistic evidence, its novelistic developments become almost comical.[255] Although the omission of the silent women at the cross and the lack of a reference to Galilee are often taken to be a sign of Petrine independence from Mark,[256] the addition of mourning (*λυπέω*) men immediately following the crucifixion scene (7:26–27) makes this unlikely. In fact, the comment by the women when they go to the tomb, "we could not weep or lament on the day he was crucified" (12.56) suggests knowledge of the Markan account (Mark 15:40–41). This also shows a further development than either Luke and John. Men are not only added, but replace the women in and around the crucifixion. The removal of the women from the crucifixion scene is thus a late development in the tradition, not a sign of independent tradition. The reduction of the number of the women at the tomb to Mary Magdalene and friends (12:50–51), rather than being a sign of primitive tradition,[257] merely shows the author's concerted effort to sort out the competing traditions in the Synoptic records and John. Mary Magdalene is most uniformly identified.[258] The inserted epiphany scene (8:28–10:41) also has late elements.[259] The cross motif (10:39) is a very late development in Christian iconography and tradition.[260] The two shorter characters who sustain the taller one as they exit the tomb (10:39) reflects a Roman processional practice which did not influence church liturgy until post-Constantinian times.[261] The crowds at the tomb (9:34) no doubt reflect a post-Constantinian veneration of Jesus' designated tomb.[262] Furthermore, POxy 2949 (usually identified as a second or third century scrap of the Gospel of Peter) has such substantial variations from the eighth or ninth century Akhmim fragment of Peter that it may not even be a piece of the same text at all, and at the least is a different version of the text. It cannot be used to confirm the narrative of the Akhmim fragment nor does it firmly establish an early date for the Gospel of Peter.[263] Thus, the Gospel of Peter should be considered a late novelistic account of the crucifixion and the empty tomb.

Mark's account of the crucifixion should still be considered the earliest. However, Mark comes not to mourn Jesus, as women eyewitnesses would, but to praise him. His report thus has little in it which reflects the characteristics of women's interpretation of death and suffering found in formal or folk laments. The basic structure of Mark's Passion narrative reflects both the Hellenistic "noble death" tradition, and the suffering and righteous martyrdom tradition which presumes noble death themes.[264] Both of these paradigms include the presence of lamenting women, family and friends. As we have seen, Hellenistic noble death scenes usually portray women and friends present or nearby,[265] and the Psalms offer two possible antecedents for the distance of these family and/or friends from the scene, Ps 38:11 and Ps 88:8.[266] In particular Ps 38:11, "My friends and companions stand aloof from my affliction, and my neighbors stand far off (RSV, LXX *ἀπὸ μακρόθεν*)[267] sounds similar to Mark 15:40–41, which reports that a group of women watch (*θεωρέω*) the crucifixion "from afar," or "at a distance," (*ἀπὸ μακρόθεν*) including

"Mary Magdalene, Mary the mother of James and Joseph, and Salome," as well as "many other women" (*ἄλλαι πολλαί*). It is striking that in Mark the women are silent, both at the cross and at the tomb.

It seems logical to conclude that Mark connected the women both to the cross and the tomb because of the conventional linkage of women to death, burial and tombs, the early tradition that Jesus "was raised on the third day" (1 Cor 15:4), and an oral tradition linking women to these events. Mark 15:47 serves as his narrative link between the two stories.[268] As we have noted, there is reason to doubt Johannine independence for the traditions concerning the women both here and in his empty tomb narrative (John 19:25; 20:1–18).[269] This further weakens the hypothesis of a pre-Markan source either for the crucifixion scene proper or the tale of the empty tomb (16:1–8). Given Markan reluctance to associate Mary Magdalene and the other women with mourning rituals and the cult of the dead, Munro may be correct in her assumption that Mark deliberately postpones reference to these women in order to suppress or obscure their role in the Jesus movement.[270] Since both the "suffering dikaios" genre and other literary models for death scenes require them, Mark may have ample reason to include them without reliance on a source.[271] However, the question of a pre-Markan source in this instance is relatively moot when it comes to determining the historicity of the narrative. Whether included in a pre-Markan source modeled on the motif of a "suffering righteous one" or written by Mark's own hand, this aspect of the Markan narrative has clear antecedents in both the genre of the "suffering *δίκαιος*" and in Hellenistic death scenes. Mark differs from these models only in the silence of the women. If his portrayal relied only on literary models, he could easily have the women lament, wail and leave. But he doesn't. This suggests that a strong oral tradition linked women and lamentation to these events. Mark therefore writes women into both the crucifixion scene and his story of the empty tomb;[272] he keeps them in the story in spite of his obvious discomfort with the tradition, but keeps them silent.

As noted earlier, what is interesting about Mark's placement of the women in the narrative is his clear depiction of them as disciples. Like their masculine counterparts, the women form a three-person subset (Peter, James and John/Mary Magdalene, Mary the mother of James and Joseph, and Salome). Like the men, once they are introduced into the narrative, they subsequently flee the scene, show fear of epiphany and do not do as they are instructed.[273] Viewing Mark 15:40–41 in the context of ancient death scenes strengthens the argument that the women here have the role of disciples. Usually, it is the women who are dismissed from the death scene proper, and the male disciples or companions who remain. In Mark this order is reversed; the men flee before the crucifixion scene, and the women remain to observe the death (Mark 14:50–51; 66–72). Later, the women too will flee, but from the tomb (16:8). Adela Yarbro Collins misses this parallel between the men and the women once the women are introduced. She sees the flight of the men (Mark 14:50–51) as referring to Ps 38:11, i.e., the friends are "far off" in that the men are entirely absent.[274] This ignores the clear parallel to Ps. 38:11, *ἀπὸ μακρόθεν*, which is used to describe the stance of the women (Mark 15:40). Notably, subsequent to the flight of the men, Peter "follows" (*ἀκολουθέω*) Jesus "from a distance" (*ἀπὸ μακρόθεν* Mark 14:54).[275] Mark's portrayal of the women as disciples is clear and deliberate: the motif of "service" (*διακονέω* Mark 15:41) implies the women are present at meals with Jesus even though they are absent from scenes like the Last Supper (cf. 14:3–9; 14:12–25).[276] Mark's negative portrayal of the women should therefore be seen as corresponding to his negative portrayal of the men rather than a positive portrayal that juxtaposes them.[277] The women fit into the larger theme of discipleship in Mark,[278] since failure of disciples is a larger Markan and aretalogical theme.[279] Given the theme of failure in Mark and the later fleeing of the women from the tomb (16:8), it seems unlikely that the silence of the women is here meant to be a sign that the women are noble in the sight of death. Thus, although it seems improbable that the Markan narrative derives from early written or eyewitness accounts, it is notable that in Mark the women fill the role of "disciple" along with the men and he includes them in the crucifixion and burial scenes. Mark takes a long while to mention them, and after he does so he modifies their claim to have seen the risen Jesus, but they are there nonetheless. It seems reasonable to conclude that at least a pre-Markan oral tradition links women followers of Jesus to the crucifixion and burial of Jesus.[280]

Given the concern for women's lamentation in all gospel accounts and the common practice of women's lamentation of the dead in antiquity, the most logical link would be oral lament. Both folk and formal laments contain the element of narrative and follow set oral patterns. Lament traditions are transferred into literary and scribal contexts in Greek, Roman and Jewish literature. Judaism in particular has a long tradition of formal laments that scholars believe originated in popular lamentation.[281] The earliest evidence for Christian liturgical practice is funerary. Oral lament traditions offer a plausible context for the transmission of stories about Jesus' death by early Christian men and women. This modality may also explain the use of lament Psalms (esp. Psalm 22) in the development of a written Passion narrative. The oral narrative traditions themselves, unfortunately, like most traditions associated with women, are lost. Mark contains nothing that reflects lament narrative patterns. There is no antiphonal character to the Passion narrative, no address of the dead. There is narrative, but much of its basic structure comes from scripture, namely the Psalms. Although Mark may know an oral tradition linking women to the crucifixion of Jesus, there is little basis to assume any pre-Markan written source. The Markan Passion narrative was clearly formed on the basis of literary and scriptural traditions fostered by men in scribal schools meant to praise and glorify Jesus and elevate his death according to the Hellenistic model of a "noble" death of a "righteous one." In the Passion narratives Jesus' death is not mourned, but praised.

Is there any historical reminiscence in the Markan account? Is there any basis to assume that the women did in fact witness the crucifixion of Jesus? Given the tenacity of women's lament traditions, as well as the overall interest in family retrieval of executed family members, we can at the least assume that the women, and possibly even some of the men,[282] would have tried to watch the crucifixion proceedings, and would have tried to find Jesus' body after he died in spite of the risks that would entail.[283] It seems probable that Jesus was buried in accordance with Deut 21:22–23, especially since the earliest tradition affirms this (1 Cor 15:4). He was probably buried in a common graveyard by a Jewish official named Joseph (Mark 15:42–46).[284] If Jesus was buried in a family tomb by Joseph (Mark 15:42–45, par.), we have to assume that his social status afforded him political connections,[285] or that his celebrity earned him friends in high places.[286] Regardless, it is doubtful that his gravesite was ever found. "Empty tomb" stories like Mark 16:1–8 most commonly evolve when the location of the remains of a venerated figure is unknown.[287] Further, if Jesus' tomb location had been known, there would be more evidence for the veneration of his burial site before the early fourth century C.E.. It seems probable that his followers, especially his women followers, mourned his death in spite of his injunction "Let the dead bury their own dead!" (Matt 8:22/Luke 9:60). All gospel traditions avoid portraying women's lamentation of Jesus' death in both the crucifixion and empty tomb accounts. However, since women in antiquity had thousands of years of tradition on their side, their rituals associated with the cult of the dead remained sanctioned as traditional features of popular religion. That this is assumed in first century Palestine is suggested by grave goods recovered from Second Temple Palestine. This may be particularly applicable to first century Palestine where mourning those unjustly killed could serve to protest Roman occupation. "He was raised on the third day" (1 Cor 15:4) suggests that women at least went to look for Jesus' body on the third day to fulfill their traditional cultic duties to the deceased. This all but assures us that Jesus' followers, especially women, indeed mourned his death and memorialized his presence, probably with a meal. The empty tomb and physical appearance stories were developed to correct the assumption that Jesus' resurrection "on the third day" was the simple matter of women (or other family members) going to the gravesite to commune with the spirit of the deceased as women had done for thousands of years in observance of Greek, Roman and Jewish popular religious ritual.

Even if the story of Jesus' death began as a lament in the *Sitz im Leben* of early Christian burial cults, its contours may be lost to us.[288] Still, since these models do not require that women fill the role of disciples, it seems reasonable to conclude that Mark knew that some of Jesus' disciples were women and that these women (especially Mary Magdalene) were associated with the lamenting of his death and burial. The tradition of the women at the cross and the tomb persists in spite of the obvious attempts by every gospel writer to contain it.

Conclusion

For decades scholars have assumed that the struggle over the place of women among early Christian groups was a specifically Christian one, fostered by the inclusive and egalitarian vision of Jesus himself which reversed an earlier more restrictive Jewish perspective. Eventually, this Christian respect for the rights of women was erased by the growing influence of Hellenistic patriarchalism in the Christian church; an early egalitarian community was transformed into the Catholic church controlled by male hierarchies. This book challenges this reconstruction of the purpose and message of Jesus and labels it a foundational myth for Christian feminism. Although it is the case that women numbered among Jesus' followers or disciples and received the slanderous label of "whores," a careful analysis of Jesus' authentic sayings suggests no interest in women as women or the inequality between the sexes. Although Jesus' teaching contains a critique of class distinctions and slavery in his culture, that critique is not extended to gender distinctions or sex discrimination.

Recent research on women in Hellenistic Judaism and Palestine supports this contention. Jewish women, both in the Diaspora and Palestine lived in freer circumstances than has previously been supposed. Some Jewish women enjoyed certain legal freedoms, joined men for communal meals and became leaders and patronesses of their synagogues. Jewish women's lives thus probably differed little from those of their Hellenistic and Roman sisters living in similar economic and social circumstances during the Roman period. Thus, neither the presence of women among Jesus' disciples, nor the inclusion of women among his table companions necessarily differentiates Jesus from a Greco-Roman or Palestinian environment.

This larger presence of women in other Greco-Roman and Jewish contexts, however, makes it less likely that the presence of women among Jesus' associates reflects an egalitarian aspect of his teaching or proclamation of the Kingdom of God. An analysis of Jesus' teachings commonly considered authentic makes this clear. The bulk of Jesus' teaching shows attention to other matters, particularly in its concern for the poor and the enslaved: the issue of gender can be seen as secondary to other interests: social and economic justice, the true Fatherhood of God and a reform of class and rank structures. And although Jesus attempted to defend the presence of women in his group, he did so by repeating a gender stereotype that labeled them "whores." Indeed, the presence of women in the Jesus movement is clearly demonstrated on the basis of Q, in which these women participants are similarly labeled "whores," but which evinces little interest in defending that presence. Rather, even the potential for gender segregation at meals is preferred, at least at the eschaton (Q 17:34–35). This insulting language leveled against the Jesus Movement is repeated in Q, but is never directly challenged.

Nonetheless, women remain central to the later events of the gospel stories – as witnesses to the crucifixion and empty tomb. It is probable that women witnessed the crucifixion and lamented the death of Jesus. Women's ritual experience in the cult of the dead is reflected in the early Christian creed that Jesus was "buried" then "raised on the third day"(1 Cor 15:4). This suggests the customary association of women with tomb visitation and funeral lamentation on the third day after death or burial in antiquity. However, the memory of the witness of the women to these events remained culturally dangerous, since the association of women with funerary rituals included conjuring the dead at tombs. This led to a distinction between "Galilean" appearances unconnected to Jesus' burial place (to men) and "Jerusalem" experiences near Jesus' tomb (featuring women). Instead of being witnesses to the resurrection, the women in Mark are driven away from the tomb. The empty tomb tradition in Mark serves to distance the women from any resurrection appearances in the vicinity of a tomb and discourages participation in women's rituals in the cult of the dead. Although it is inaccurate to suggest that the women's witness was rejected due to Jewish legal sensibilities, it is quite likely that the witness of Mary Magdalene and other women was rejected due to the cultural stereotypes of women's religious expression connected to the ritual lamentation of the dead at tombs.

Several insights may be gained from this study. First, it is more than ever clear that women were participants within Jesus' own movement and within early Christian groups. At early layers of gospel tradition Jesus is slandered for his association with "tax collectors," "sinners" and "prostitutes" or "whores" and himself repeats the slander. Such caricatures reflect typical calumnies leveled especially against those known for associating with more socially progressive, or "liberated" women. This could also be disparagement of Jesus for associating with women of the lower classes, who were often assumed to be sexually promiscuous. Women like Mary Magdalene, probably a fisherwoman, and Salome, possibly a servant of some kind, could have been characterized as "whores" due to their low social status. Further, a woman like Joanna, probably of higher social standing, could have been slandered as a "prostitute" for her participation in a mixed group including both men and women, and members of the lower social classes. The evidence therefore makes it unlikely that the women in Jesus' movement were by vocation actual prostitutes. Other philosophical and religious groups were similarly stigmatized for having in their company women who could be called "whores" merely for their participation in a mostly male group, or for their participation in gender-mixed dining, a common though controversial aspect of Hellenistic culture generally.

Thus, the group around Jesus cannot be characterized as a "discipleship of equals," since probably only a few women were members of the predominantly male group. The limited participation of women does not suggest a group focused on equality or equal representation, but rather reflects the growing participation of women within other male dominated groups throughout the Greco-Roman world. However, the slander leveled against the women who did participate suggests that they were among the more socially progressive women of their culture. Liberated women were often accused of being libertine.

Second, the evidence suggests that further controversy within these communities over the role of women did not arise until after Jesus' death. It does not seem that Jesus himself engaged directly in discussions concerning the role of women among his followers or within Jewish or Greco-Roman society. Thus, the theory of

Elisabeth Schüssler Fiorenza, that Jesus' teaching contained a "critical feminist impulse," and John Dominic Crossan's conclusion that Jesus' "radical egalitarianism" extended to women, need nuancing. Although it is the case that women numbered among his followers, and was concerned with matters of Greco-Roman rank and poverty, his egalitarianism did not include the concerns for gender inequity specifically. The extension of a gendered inclusivity may have occurred later for early Christians were baptized with the formula "in Christ there is neither Jew nor Greek, neither slave nor free, neither male nor female" (Gal 3:28). However, the evidence suggests that it was not Jesus who extended the principle. The women seem to be around Jesus more as a matter of course than as a result of a gender-equal vision of the Kingdom of God. In fact, given the predominance of a number of women in social, religious and philosophical contexts across the Mediterranean world, and their common presence at gender-inclusive meals, it would be surprising if Jesus' company had not included at least a few women. This aspect of Jesus' movement is therefore notable, but not unique, and certainly not revolutionary.

Third, this study highlights certain aspects of the teachings of Jesus that need further attention. One is his rejection of traditional burial customs and tombsite or gravesite rituals. This is a clearly Hebraic aspect to Jesus' teaching. But since women featured prominently in funerary rites, the cult of the dead, and the rituals surrounding tomb veneration, like Jewish prophets before him, Jesus was rejecting a major location of women's participation in so-called popular religion. In spite of Jesus' rejection of these customs, it seems that the women disciples of Jesus ignored his preferences in this regard and lamented his death anyway, and carried out the common rituals for their special dead. The women who followed Jesus were probably no different from women all over the Mediterranean who similarly ignored attempts to limit their funerary customs and rituals. This suggests that these women carried out a particular pattern of resistance against a male authority in their midst – even though that man was Jesus. This means that the women in the Jesus movement attributed no special authority to this particular aspect of Jesus' teaching. Men often questioned those customs central to women's religious lives, and women usually ignored them. Given that the slander leveled against these women suggests that they were socially progressive, or "liberated" for their day, this willingness on their part to reject an aspect of Jesus' teaching suggests their relative independence from male authority, at least when it came to this one important aspect of their religious lives. This locates a kind of "feminist impulse," or at least a resistant impulse, in the women around Jesus, rather than in Jesus himself.

Further, it is significant that Jesus' teaching can be shown to have a critique of ancient customs of slavery, and that his group included members of the servant class. Here this study can confirm some aspects of previous reconstructions of the Historical Jesus, particularly the reconstruction by John Dominic Crossan. Jesus' teaching clearly involved critique of rank and class, but it included no recognition of sexism in his culture. Thus, that Jesus made a critique of the general forces of what Schüssler Fiorenza has called "kyriarchy" is also confirmed. Such an observation is pertinent for those seeking to discover in the New Testament a challenge to unjust institutions like slavery. As slavery still exists in many parts of the world, such a message still needs hearing.

Finally, illustrating that Jesus was not alone in this acceptance of women within his group demonstrates that it is not necessary to devalue Palestinian Judaism, or the rest of the Greco-Roman world, for that matter, in order to appreciate the inclusivity of Jesus' own movement. Here Schüssler Fiorenza' assumption of a more open Palestinian Judaism is confirmed, making it more likely that the presence of women within Jesus' movement reflects changing social patterns affecting both Hellenistic Judaism and Greco-Roman society generally. Both the impulse toward the inclusion of women within such religious groups and the impulse towards criticizing such inclusion can be charted throughout the ancient Mediterranean. Hellenistic Judaism, the Jesus Movement, and early Christianity were all equally affected by the changing social currents of the age. However, this observation does little to solve the problem of a basic anti-Judaic tendency in Christian exegesis which elevates Jesus and early Christianity over ancient Judaism. As my research locates the impetus for gender inclusivity within a Greco-Roman cultural context that affected Palestinian Judaism, Jesus, and the early church generally, the grounds for a continued criticism ancient Judaism are still present. The gender inclusivity of Jesus' movement, especially in its meals, has Greco-Roman rather than Hebraic roots, at least in the first century. The results of this study, therefore, remain to that degree problematic. Although this study reveals other Hebraic elements of Jesus' teaching, such as his critique of the attention to gravesites and tombsites, in regards to the presence of women in his movement, Jesus appears more influenced by Greco-Roman culture than classic Hebraic culture. The problem of locating a potential for gender inclusivity within pre-Hellenistic Judaism still remains. The results of my study reveal a Jesus who, while deeply Hebraic in his defense of monotheism, was also strongly affected by the currents of Greco-Roman culture. This culture pervaded his everyday practice at a basic level, his meals.

As is the case with most studies of the gospels and Jesus, the study of the Historical Jesus leads to the study of Christian origins and the development of early Christian groups. This study easily places Jesus and the development of the groups that followed his death within a Greco-Roman environment. This cultural context may reflect the more general atmosphere of the first centuries of the common era, during which time new social arrangements including women arose, caused controversy and were defended. That women played a role in Jesus' movement, in the development of gospel and liturgical traditions, and vied for authority in the aftermath of Jesus' death, firmly places Jesus and the Jesus movements within both Jewish Palestinian and larger Greco-Roman contexts that were far more open to women's involvement in religion and society than has previously been supposed.

Some may be disappointed with the conclusions of this study. In the midst of a changing social world, many women and men look to Jesus as a potential model for equality between the sexes. However, the impulse towards equality stands on its own without needing to appeal to an ancient man, however influential he may still be. That women numbered among Jesus' disciples is still noteworthy, as not all religious, philosophical and social institutions in antiquity included them, although many did. That Jesus did challenge ancient assumptions about social rank is also still important, as few in his time made a similar critique of ancient culture. Finally, this study contributes to the overall project of recovering and reconstructing women's history and the role of women in ancient societies, and thus contributes to the re-writing of history from a different perspective. This is a worthy, and even a feminist goal.

Notes

Chapter 1

1. See especially, Goitein, "Women as Creators," 1–33; and also J. Dewey, "From Storytelling to Written Text," 71–78; MacDonald, *The Legend and the Apostle*; Schüssler Fiorenza, *Jesus: Miriam's Child*, 131–62.

2. See D'Angelo, "Re-membering Jesus," 199–218, esp. 207; Grant, *White Woman's Christ, Black Woman's Jesus*, 184; Moltmann-Wendel, *The Women Around Jesus*, 3; Schaberg, "Feminist Experience," 283–84.

3. Borg, *Jesus: a New Vision*, 133–35; idem, *Meeting Jesus Again for the First Time*, 57–58; Crossan, *The Historical Jesus*, 261–264; Funk, *Honest to Jesus*, 194; 196; 200; Gnilka, *Jesus of Nazareth*, 179–180; Horsley, *Jesus and the Spiral of Violence*, 209–45; Theissen and Merz, *The Historical Jesus*, 219–25.

4. Funk and Hoover, eds. *The Five Gospels*.

5. Schüssler Fiorenza, *In Memory of Her*. It is not the case that all historical Jesus scholars have ignored Schüssler Fiorenza's work as Schaberg suggests "(The) A Feminist (Contribution to) Experience of Historical Jesus Scholarship," 266–85, esp. 267. See in particular the most recent discussion of Schüssler Fiorenza's work in Borg, *Jesus in Contemporary Scholarship*, 23-26 (unavailable to Schaberg). Borg fully incorporates feminist insights into his discussion on 105–7.

6.Corley, "Feminist Myths of Christian Origins," 49–65.

7. This phrase was first coined by Elizabeth Castelli in our conversation over Burton Mack's Festschrift, *Reimagining Christian Origins*, which led to the title of my article in that volume. I am grateful to her for sharing her unpublished work on this topic with me: Elizabeth A. Castelli, "Rethinking the Feminist Myth of Christian Origins," (Presentation made at Candler School of Theology, Emory University, February 15, 1994, unpublished manuscript, used by permission). Castelli questions the entire focus on origins within feminist discourse on theology and biblical interpretation.

8. Plaskow was the first to use the term "myth" in reference to early reconstructions of "Jesus the Feminist." See "Blaming Jews for Inventing Patriarchy," 11–12 and more recently, *idem*, "Anti-Judaism in Christian Feminist Interpretation," 117–129. See discussions also by Grant, *White Women's Christ, Black Women's Jesus*, 182–85, and Heschel, "Anti-Judaism in Christian Feminist Theology," 25–28; 95–97.

9. For a complete overview of this discussion among Jewish and Christian feminists, see von Kellenbach, *Anti-Judaism in Feminist Writings*. See also a review of the literature in Levine, "Lilies of the Field," 332–35.

10. This view of women in Judaism was first popularized by Leonard Swidler in the early 1970s, but was also articulated by Jeremias, *Jerusalem in the Time of Jesus*, 359–76; Swidler, "Jesus Was A Feminist," 177–83; *idem*, *Biblical Affirmations of Women*; *idem*, *Women in Judaism*; *idem*, *Yeshua: a Modern for Moderns*, 75–110. Other writers following this trend would include (but are by no means limited to) Stagg and Stagg, *Woman in the World of Jesus*; Tetlow, *Women and Ministry in the New Testament*; Moltmann-Wendel, *Liberty, Equality, Sisterhood*, 9–21; Kee, "The Changing Role of Women," 225–38; Wink, *Engaging the Powers*, 109–37; Witherington, *Women in the Ministry of Jesus*. All major Christian Bible Encyclopedias (which span the past 3 decades) contain this reconstruction of the place of women in Judaism: Scroggs, "Woman in the New Testament," 966–68; Edwards, "Woman," 1089–97; Witherington, "Women (NT)," 957–61. The one exception is Scholer, "Women," 880–87. Apart from Scholer, all the works mentioned in this note follow the basic reconstruction of Jesus and his Jewish context which follows. Archer also reflects this basic understanding of Judaism in *Her Price is Beyond Rubies*. See the critique of this reconstruction in Kraemer, "Jewish Women and Christian Origins," 35–46.

11. *t. Ber.* 7.18; *y. Ber.* 9.2; 13b; *b. Men.* 43b.

12. "Leonard Swidler's Response to A. J. Levine's Review," 717–19. See also however, Osiek, *What Are They Saying About the Social Setting of the New Testament?*, 15–20.

13. Swidler, "Jesus Was a Feminist" and in *Yeshua*, 78.

14. Kee, "Changing Role of Women," 237; 230 (on the subsequent declaration that "in Christ there is neither male nor female"); Moltmann-Wendel, *Liberty*, 30, 32.

15. Kee, "Changing Role of Women," (on the subsequent declaration that "in Christ there is neither male nor female"), 230; Moltmann-Wendel, *Liberty*, 19; Swidler, *Yeshua*, 95; Tetlow, *Women and Ministry*, 46, 93; Wink, *Engaging the Powers*, 134; Ben Witherington, "Women," 959; *idem*, *Women in the Ministry of Jesus*, 52.

16. Tetlow, *Women and Ministry*, 46; Wink, *Engaging the Powers*, 129.

17. Witherington, *Women in the Ministry of Jesus*, 52.

18. Jeremias, *Jerusalem*, 376; Wink, *Engaging the Powers*, 131.

19. Moltmann-Wendel, *Liberty*, 14; Witherington, "Women," 958–59; idem, *Women in the Ministry of Jesus*, 50–52; 129.

20. Edwards, "Woman," 1095, 1097; Moltmann-Wendel, *Liberty*, 37.

21. Kee, "Changing Roles of Women," 237; Scroggs, "Woman," 968; Moltmann-Wendel, *Liberty*, 35, 38–39.

22. Edwards, "Woman," 1097; Scroggs, "Woman," 968; Moltmann-Wendel, *Liberty*, 34.

23. Kee, "Changing Roles of Women," 237; Moltmann-Wendel, *Liberty*, 34–36; Stagg and Stagg, *Woman in the World of Jesus*, 258; Witherington, "Women," 960.

24. Moltmann-Wendel, *Liberty*, 35.

25. Kee, "Changing Roles of Women," 237.

26. Wink, *Engaging the Powers*, 133.

27. Stagg and Stagg, *Woman in the World of Jesus*, 255–58.

28. Edwards, "Woman," 1097; Tetlow, *Women and Ministry*, 78–79.

29. J. Z. Smith, *Drudgery Divine*, esp. 9–14.

30. J. Z. Smith, *Drudgery*, 34.

31. J. Z. Smith, *Drudgery*, 38–9. See also Mack, *A Myth of Innocence*, 4.

32. J. Z. Smith, *Drudgery*, 38–9.

33. Greeley "Domestic Violence: One Strike and You're Out," D4.

34. J. Z. Smith, *Drudgery*, 83.

35. von Kellenbach, *Anti-Judaism*, 57–74.

36. J. Z. Smith, *Drudgery*, 79.

37. J. Z. Smith, *Drudgery*, 81.

38. Richard Horsley now argues that Galilee should be considered culturally and religiously distinct from Judea, with no particular allegiance to the Temple or Temple cult. See *Galilee: History, Politics, People*, esp. 128–57. This sets the stage for a Jesus who is "Galilean" not "Jewish" or "Judean." This is actually an old distinction. See brief mention of the work of Walter Bauer and Walter Grundmann in Freyne, *Galilee, Jesus and the Gospels*, 2.

39. Hence Jacob Neusner's use of the term"Judaisms." See most recently Chilton and Neusner, *Judaism in the New Testament*, esp. 1–41. See also Porton, "Diversity in Postbiblical Judaism," 57–80.

40. Charlesworth, "Greek, Persian, Roman, Syrian, and Egyptian Influences in Early Jewish Theology," 219–43; Flusser, "Paganism in Palestine," 1065–1100; M. S. Smith, *The Early History of God*; Morton Smith, "Palestinian Judaism in the First Century,"67–81.

41. L. Feldman, "How Much Hellenism in Jewish Palestine?" 101–2; Hoenig, "Oil and Pagan Defilement," 63–75.

42. Hachlili, *Ancient Jewish Art and Archaeology of Israel*, 285–87; Goodenough, *Jewish Symbols*, vol. 1, 79–84.

43. Reed, "Population Numbers, Urbanization, and Economics," 203–19.

44. R. Horsley, "The Historical Jesus and Archaeology of the Galilee," 91–135.

45. Fitzmyer, "Did Jesus Speak Greek?" 58–63; 76–77; Funk, *Parables and Presence*, 19–28; R. H. Gundry, "The Language of First Century Palestine," 404–8; Mussies, "Greek in Palestine and the Diaspora," 1040–1064; Porter, "Jesus and the Use of Greek in Galilee," 123–54; M. Silva, "Bilingualism and the Character of Palestinian Greek," 205–26; van der Horst, "Jewish Funerary Inscriptions," 46–57. See also comments by Freyne, *Galilee, Jesus and the Gospels*, 167–75; *idem*, "Urban-Rural Relations in First-Century Galilee," 75–91; and D. Edwards, "The Socio-Economic and Cultural Ethos of the Lower Galilee in the First Century," 53–73. Gundry ("The Language of First Century Palestine") and now John P. Meier suggest Jesus was trilingual, speaking Greek, Aramaic and Hebrew. J. P. Meier, *A Marginal Jew*, vol. 1, 260–68.

46. Boyarin, *Carnal Israel, passim;* Daube, "Rabbinic Methods of Interpretation and Hellenistic Rhetoric," 239–64; Treu, "Die Bedeutung des Griechischen für die Juden im römischen Reich," 132–34; Lieberman, *Greek in Jewish Palestine*.

47. See von Kellenbach's review of research done by Bernadette Brooten, Ross Kraemer, and others (*Anti-Judaism*, 57–74); A. J. Levine, "Review: L. Swidler, *Yeshua: A Modern for Moderns*," 535–36; *idem*, "Response by Levine," 720–21; *idem*, "Introduction," "*Women Like This*"; idem, "Second Temple Judaism," 8–33; See also Kraemer, "Jewish Women and Christian Origins," and "Jewish Women and Women's Judaism(s) at the Beginning of Christianity."

48. Thistlethwaite, *Sex, Race and God*, 94–97.

49. Many books on women and Jesus or the New Testament follow the basic reconstruction I have outlined above. See Faxon, *Women and Jesus*; P. K. Jewett, *Man as Male and Female*; MacHaffie, *Her Story*; Nunnally-Cox, *Foremothers*; Torjesen

Malcolm, *Women at the Crossroads*; Massey, *Woman and the New Testament* ; Mollenkott, *Women, Men and the Bible* ; Scanzoni and Hardesty, *All We're Meant to Be*; Sergio, *Jesus and Woman*; Stephens, *A New Testament View of Women.*

50. For recent treatments see Kam, *Their Stories, Our Stories*, 181; 187–93; 212; Jacobs-Malina, *Beyond Patriarchy*, 11; 19; 27–28; 70; G. Osborne, "Women in Jesus' Ministry," 259–91; Ricci, *Mary Magdalene and Many Others*, 23; W. Robins, "Woman's Place," 85–8 and comments by Gnilka, *Jesus of Nazareth*, 179–80; Schnackenburg, *Jesus in the Gospels*, 198–209.

51. Alexandre, "Early Christian Women," 410; 419–21; B. S. Anderson and Zinsser, *A History of Their Own*, 67–70.

52. Alexandre, "Early Christian Women," 419–21.

53. Anderson and Zinsser, *History of Their Own*, 67–68

54. Pantel, *A History of Women*, 337.

55. Amy-Jill Levine has questioned the egalitarian nature of the teachings of Jesus in Q and the egalitarian nature of the Q community. See "Who's Catering the Q Affair?, 145–62 and *idem*, "Second Temple Judaism, Jesus and Women," 8–33. E. P. Sanders doubts that Jesus travelled with women. See *The Historical Figure of Jesus*, 109–10. See also comments by Grant, *White Women's Christ, Black Women's Jesus*, 184. Most Christian feminist and womanist scholars assume the egalitarian nature of Jesus' movement. See D'Angelo, "Re-membering Jesus," 199–218, esp. 207; Grant, *White Woman's Christ, Black Woman's Jesus*, 184; Moltmann-Wendel, *The Women Around Jesus*, 3; Schaberg, "Feminist Experience," 283–84. A recent discussion by G. Jackson looks at the use of the story of the hemorraging woman in Christian exegesis ("Jesus as First Century Feminist: Christian Anti-Judaism?").

56. Womanist scholars also ground their theology "in history with Jesus' ministry as that is recorded in the gospels" (K. Douglas, *Black Christ*, 113). Douglas still juxtaposes Jesus with Judaism (*Black Christ*, 91). See also Grant, *White Women's Christ, Black Women's Jesus*, 185; 212–14. Womanist scholars, however, are less interested in "Jesus the feminist" and more interested in expanding the focus of the discussion so that Jesus' critique of oppression is not theologically limited to the concerns of white women, who are primarily concerned about patriarchalism and sex discrimination. See K. Douglas, *Black Christ*, 95, 97–117; and Grant, *White Woman's Christ, Black Woman's Jesus*, 195–222, esp. 215–20.

57. This is in spite of the fact that both Alexandre, "Early Christian Women," and Anderson and Zinsser, *A History of Their Own* presuppose the work of at least Schüssler Fiorenza and Rosemary Radford Ruether (Anderson and Zinsser) as well as that of Ross Kraemer, Bernadette Brooten and others (Alexandre).

58. See below.

59. See for example, Borg, *Jesus: a New Vision*, 133–35; *idem*, *Meeting Jesus Again for the First Time*, 57–8; Moltmann-Wendel, *Women Around Jesus*, 2–9; Mott, "Jesus as Social Critic and Anti-Semitism," 37; Newsom and Ringe, eds., *The Woman's Bible Commentary*; Schüssler Fiorenza, ed. *Searching the Scriptures, vol. 2*; Osborne, "Women in Jesus' Ministry;" Schottroff, *Let the Oppressed Go Free*, 73–74; 142–47; *idem*, *Lydia's Impatient Sisters*, 11–6.

60. Carr, *Transforming Grace*, 158–179; Grant, *White Women's Christ, Black Women's Jesus*, 182–85; 215–22; E. A. Johnson, *Consider Jesus*, 49–65; 97–113; Schüssler Fiorenza, *Miriam's Child*, 67–96; Thistlethwaite, *Sex, Race and God*, 94–7.

61. For scholars debating the import of Rabbinic literature for understanding first century women's lives, see Ilan, *Jewish Women*, 27; 32–36; Kraemer, *Her Share of the Blessings*, 93–105; Satlow, "Reconsidering the Rabbinic *ketubah* Payment,"

133–51; and Wegner, "Philo's Portrait of Women," in "*Women Like This.*" On the limits of Rabbinic literature for the historical reconstruction first century Jewish sects, see Ilan, *Jewish Women in Greco-Roman Palestine*, 34; Saldarini, *Pharisees, Scribes and Sadducees*; Stemberger, *Jewish Contemporaries of Jesus*. For a general critique of the uncritical use of Rabbinic literature by Christian scholars in the interpretation of the New Testament and the reconstruction of first century Judaism, see Neusner, *Rabbinic Literature and the New Testament*.

62. The positive remarks about women as well as the history behind differences of opinion on the role of women in Rabbinic texts are often ignored. See Boyarin, *Carnal Israel,* 167–96; Bronner, *From Eve to Esther*; Ilan, *Jewish Women*, 32–36; 226–29; Kraemer, *Her Share of the Blessings*, 93–105; Wegner, "Philo's Portrayal of Women," 43; *idem*, *Chattel or Person*.

63. Originally noted by Kraemer, "Review: In Memory of Her," 1–9. See now also Ilan, *Jewish Women*, 12.

64. Castelli, "Rethinking the Feminist Myth of Christian Origins," 5.

65. Against Schüssler Fiorenza's comments in *In Memory of Her*, "Introduction to the 10th Anniversary Edition," xxxiv.

66. Schüssler Fiorenza, *In Memory of Her*, ch. 4. See also remarks in "Introduction to the 10th Anniversary Edition," *In Memory of Her*, xxxiii.

67. Schüssler Fiorenza, *In Memory of Her*, 107.

68. Schüssler Fiorenza, *In Memory of Her*, 115.

69. See A. J. Levine, "Sacrifice and Salvation, 17–30.

70. *In Memory of Her*, 120–121. See also 118–22. See her critique of my reading in *Jesus and the Politics of Interpretation*, 132. I do not misread her. Schüssler Fiorenza clearly states that Jesus rejected Jewish purity observations thereby stressing "wholeness" in contrast to "holiness."

71. *In Memory of Her*, chs. 5, 6.

72. See below, ch. 3.

73. *In Memory of Her*, chs. 7, 8. This remains the case for Rosemary Radford Ruether's reconstruction as well. See *Sexism and God-Talk*, 33–37. For the use of "Rabbinic" influences as a foil, see Wegner, "Philo's Portrayal of Women," 43–44.

74. See A. Cameron, "Redrawing the Map," 266–71; Corley, *Private Women, Public Meals*, 58–59; 77; *idem*, "Feminist Myths of Christian Origins," 59. The institutionalization of the church is not the only explanation for these cultural shifts, as Alexandre also concludes ("Early Christian Women," 423–24).

75. "Introduction to the 10th Anniversary Edition," *In Memory of Her*, xxxi,

76. "Introduction ot the 10th Anniversary Edition," *In Memory of Her*, xxxiv.

77. "Introduction to the 10th Anniversary Edition," *In Memory of Her*, xxiv.

78. *In Memory of Her*, ch. 4; See critique by Ilan, *Jewish Women*, 12; 26; See also comments by Ross Kraemer in an interview with Murphy, "Women and the Bible," 58.

79. *Jesus, Miriam's Child*, 82.

80. *Jesus, Miriam's Child*, 74; 92–94.

81. "Introduction to the 10th Anniversary Edition," *In Memory of Her*, xxv; *Jesus, Miriam's Child*, 88.

82. *Jesus, Miriam's Child*, 85–88. See also "Introduction to the Tenth Anniversary Edition," *In Memory of Her*, xiii–xlii; *idem*, *Jesus, Miriam's Child*, 82–8; *idem*, "Text and Reality ," 19–34; *idem*, *But She Said*, 80–101.

83. *Jesus, Miriam's Child*, ch. 1.

84. *But She Said*, 31–33; 40–41; *Jesus, Miriam's Child*, 5.

85. *But She Said*, 80–88; *Jesus, Miriam's Child*, 7, 13. See Elizabeth Castelli, "Review: *But She Said*," 296–300. See also The Bible and Culture Collective, *The Postmodern Bible*, 260–7.

86. The Bible and Cultural Collective, *The Post Modern Bible*, 263. See also Castelli, "Review," 298–300.

87. J. W. Scott, "Women's History," 42–66; esp. 55–61. See also *Postmodern Bible*, 264–5.

88. *Jesus and the Politics of Interpretation*, 135.

89. *Sharing Her Word*, 19.

90. *Jesus and the Politics of Interpretation*, 135.

91. Against Schüssler Fiorenza's contention to the contrary *in Jesus and the Politics of Interpretation*, 135.

92. *Jesus and the Politics of Interpretation*, 143.

93. Kloppenborg, *The Formation of Q.*

94. *Jesus, Miriam's Child*, ch. 5.

95. *Jesus, Miriam's Child*, 143–4.

96. Schottroff, "The Sayings Source Q," 529–30.

97. *Jesus, Miriam's Child*, 140.

98. *Jesus, Miriam's Child*, 124–27.

99. *Jesus, Miriam's Child*, 72; *Jesus and the Politics of Interpretation*, ch. 4.

100. *Jesus, Miriam's Child*, 29. This is in reference to Amy-Jill Levine's work on Q, and in fact misrepresents Levine's views, in that Levine clearly states that women were members of the Q community. See A. J. Levine, "Who's Catering the Q Affair?," 156.

101. Corley, "Egalitarian Jesus," passim; Kraemer, "Review: *In Memory of Her*," 1–9.

102. Here she engages an earlier version of this chapter, titled, "The Egalitarian Jesus: A Christian Myth of Origins." Schüssler Fiorenza has never addressed the basic thesis of either *Private Women, Public Meals* or "Egalitarian Jesus" nor my reconstruction of the real reasons behind the struggle over women's participation in early Christianity.

103. *Jesus and the Politics of Interpretation*, 52–53. See also discussion in "Rhetorics and Politics in Jesus Research," 271–72.

104. Against Schüssler Fiorenza, *Jesus and the Politics of Interpretation*, 131.

105. See below, ch. 3.

106. Schüssler Fiorenza, *In Memory of Her*, 107. Her claims in *In Memory of Her* were far greater than what she now asserts in *Jesus and the Politics of Interpretation*, 133. "Egalitarian elements" that challenge ""kyriarchal structures" now will suffice to prove her thesis of a "feminist impulse" in Jesus' message and ministry.

107. Crossan, *Historical Jesus*, 263.

108. See articles in *The Jewish Family in Antiquity*, ed. by Shaye D. Cohen; Ilan, *Jewish Women*, 205–11.

109. Corley, *Private Women, Public Meals*, 66–75.

110. Corley, *Private Women, Public Meals*, 68; Lee Klosinski, "Meals in Mark," 92–3; D. E. Smith,"Social Obligation in the Context of Communal Meals," 178–9.

111. Brooten, "Konnten Frauen," 66–80. See discussion in von Kellenbach, *Anti-Judaism*, 61–2.

112. Brooten, *Women Leaders*. See also H. Safrai, "Women and the Ancient Synagogue," 41–42.

113. Kraemer, "Monastic Jewish Women," 342–70.

114. Ilan, *Jewish Women*, 190–204. There was a debate among Rabbinic teachers concerning the appropriateness of teaching daughters Torah. See also Brooten, "Jewish Women's History," 26; Kraemer, "Monastic Jewish Women," 367ff; Lieberman, *Greek in Jewish Palestine*, 23–24. Ilan notes, however, that even animals and inanimate objects quote scripture in Rabbinic sources (*Jewish Women*, 197). She suggests that Genesis would be the most likely book for women to have studied (*Jewish Women*, 204).

115. Ilan, *Jewish Women*, 192, esp. n. 28; Lieberman, *Greek in Jewish Palestine*, 23–24.

116. See in particular the articles in "*Women Like This*," A. J. Levine, ed. and Kraemer, *Her Share of the Blessings*, 106–27.

117. *t. Ber.* 7.18; *y. Ber.* 9.2; 13b; *b. Men.* 43b. This is variously attributed to Thales, Socrates and Plato. See Diogenes Laertius I.33. Witherington, "Rite and Rights for Women," 593–594 and Tetlow, *Women and Ministry*, 12.

118. Brooten, *Women Leaders*; Kraemer, *Her Share of the Blessings*, 126; *idem*, "Jewish Women and Women's Judaism(s)," 63–65; H. Safrai, "Women and the Synagogue," 41; 45.

119. Grossman, "Women and the Jerusalem Temple,"19; Jewett, *Man as Male and Female*, 90; Kraemer, "Jewish Women and Women's Judaism(s)," 62–63.

120. Grossman, "Women and the Jerusalem Temple," 22–27; Kraemer, *Her Share of the Blessings*, 95; Kraemer, "Jewish Women and Women's Judaism(s)," 62–63.

121. Grossman, "Women and the Jerusalem Temple," 19; Jewett, *Man as Male and Female*, 90.

122. Grossman, "Women and the Jerusalem Temple," 20–27; Ilan, *Jewish Women*, 179–181; 184; Kraemer, "Jewish Women and Women's Judaism(s)," 62–63. See also S. Safrai, "Pilgrimage to Jerusalem," 12–21.

123. Ilan, *Jewish Women*, 100–5.

124. Kraemer, *Her Share of the Blessings*, 102–4; idem, "Jewish Women and Jewish Women's Judaism(s)," 65–66.

125. As long as the ritually impure stayed away from the temple precincts, most Jewish people were not concerned about their impurity. Cohen, "Menstruants and the Sacred in Judaism and Christianity," 278–79.

126. B. Wright, "Jewish Ritual Baths," 190–214. The debate over the identification of these so-called "ritual baths" is a heated one. See also Reich,"The Great Mikveh Debate," 52–53; *idem*, "The Hot Bath-House," 102–7; *idem*, "More on Miqva'ot," 59–60. For an opposing view see La Sor, "Discovering What Jewish Miqva'ot Can Tell us about Christian Baptism," 52–9 as well as Small, "Late Hellenistic Baths in Palestine," 59–74.

127. Cohen, "Menstruants and the Sacred;" M. Douglas, *Purity and Danger*. See also Fredriksen, "Did Jesus Oppose the Purity Laws?" 19–25; 42–47.

128. Fredriksen, *Jesus of Nazareth*, 201

129. Kraemer, *Her Share of the Blessings*, 103–4. But see Ilan's comments on the availability and allowance of birth control and even sterilization among Jews (*Jewish Women*, 67; 108; 113–14; 120). Women in antiquity did know of ways to end their pregnancies. See Riddle, et al., "Ever Since Eve," 29–35.

130. Hengel, *Judaism and Hellenism*. See also Brooten, "Early Christian Women," 70–71; Schüssler Fiorenza, *In Memory of Her*, 100; 109–18; Osiek, *What Are They Saying*, 16–20; J. Z. Smith, *Drudgery*, 81.

131. Crossan, *The Historical Jesus,* 17–19; Mack, *Myth of Innocence*, 65–6; *idem*, *The Lost Gospel*, 51–68.

132. Porter, "Jesus and the Use of Greek in Galilee."

133. Osiek, *What Are They Saying*, 18–20; Peskowitz, "'Family/ies' in Antiquity," 15–16.

134. Crossan, *Historical Jesus*, 18.

135. See Lenski, *Power and Privilege*, *passim.*

136. Corley, "Jesus' Table Practice," 453.

137. Innkeeping implies travel. See Ilan, *Jewish Women*, 128–31; 186–8. Since material remains from Roman Ostia and Pompeii are often compared with Palestinian evidence, it is notable that artistic depictions from Roman Ostia show women chatting at marketplaces, selling poultry, rabbits and other produce as well as selling drinks in a tavern. One woman is depicted as a traveling merchant. In scenes from Pompeii, women and men sell pots, food, and clothing in the open air market. On Roman Ostia, see Kampen, *Image and Status*, 31; 52–86. On Pompeii see Kampen, *Image and Status*, 101; 104; D'Avino, *The Women of Pompeii*, 15–21.

138. Against R. Horsley, "The Historical Jesus and Archaeology of the Galilee," 91–135.

139. For further on the cultural connections between Galilee and Judea to the South, see E. M. Meyers, "The Cultural Setting of Galilee," 693. For an opposing view, see Fredricksen, *Jesus of Nazareth*, 160–65.

140. Brooten, "Early Christian Women," 70; Schüssler Fiorenza, *In Memory of Her*, 100; 109–10.

141. Josephus, *AJ* 15. 260. See J. Collins, "Marriage, Divorce and Family in Second Temple Judaism," 104–162, esp. 120; Ilan, *Jewish Women*, 146.

142. *Nahal Se'elim* 13. See J. Collins, "Marriage, Divorce and Family," 120–21; Ilan, *Integrating Women*, 253–62. Debate over the reading of this document has continued. It is described as either a receipt for a divorce bill or a divorce bill. The first scholar to ague that the document referred to a *get* sent by a woman was J. T. Milik, "Le travail d'éditions des manuscrits du Désert de Juda," esp. 21. For recent discussions reflecting Milik's original view, see Ilan, "Notes and Observations on a Newly Published Divorce Bill from the Judean Desert," 95–202; Ilan, *Jewish Women*, 146–47; as well as Brooten, "Konnten Frauen," 71–2. For the veiw that the document refers to a divorce bill sent by a man, see A. Yardeni, *Nahal Se'elim Documents*; Yardeni and Greenfield, "A Receipt for a Ketubba," 197–208 (English summary, 147–48). At any rate, the existence of such a receipt is a powerful attestation of her legal rights in that situation.

143. Brooten, "Konnten Frauen," 68–70; J. Collins, "Marriage, Divorce and Family," 119–20; Lipinski, "The Wife's Right to Divorce," 26. Both Brooten and Lipinski consider the Babatha contract to reflect the same Semitic legal tradition as the Aramaic contracts from Elephantine. See also "Satlow, "Reconsidering the Rabbinic *ketubah* Payment," 137–41; Kraemer, "Jewish Mothers and Daughters," 99–101; and Isaac, "The Babatha Archive," 71–3; Yadin, et al., "Babatha's *Ketubah*," 75–99. For more on Babatha, see Kraemer, "Jewish Women and Women's Judaism(s)," 54–60.

144. Josephus, *BJ* 4:9.3–8 (503–44), esp. 505. I am grateful to the late Winsome Munro for these references from her unpublished manuscript, "The Honor of 'Shameless' Biblical Women," 24.

145. Goodman, *The Ruling Class of Judaea*, 206.

146. Josephus, *BJ*, 4.508. See Goodman, *Ruling Class*, 204; 207.

147. Goodman, *Ruling Class*, 205. Goodman considers the presence of the women in Gioras' group to be a sign of its "unbrigand-like" character. However, Josephus' lack of comment on the matter makes this less likely. Simon bar Gioras' group may be indicative of a larger presence of women among Zealots and brigands than Goodman allows.

148. Josephus *AJ* 13. 15. 5 - 16.12 (401–15); 17. 2. 4 (41–45). See Ilan, "The Attraction of Aristocratic Jewish Women to Pharisaic Judaism;" idem., *Integrating Women*, 11–37; Kraemer, "Jewish Women and Women's Judaism(s)," 66–67; Stemberger, *Jewish Contemporaries of Jesus*, 9; 12; 14; 19; 116. See also P. Oxy 840 which contains a "woe" of Jesus against the Pharisees for consorting with "prostitutes" (*πόρναι*) and "flute-girls" (*αὐλητρίδες*). This is certainly the language of caricature and insult, but it does serve to connect the Pharisees with women.

149. Josephus, *BJ* 6.5. 2 (283).

150. Matt 21:32. See Corley, *Private Women, Public Meals*, 154–58; Jeremias, *Jerusalem*, 376. The *Gospel of the Nazoreans* records that Jesus' mother was among these women (Jerome, *Dial. adv. Pelag.* 3, 2). Against Kraemer, "Jewish Women and Women's Judaism(s)," 71.

151. For Herod's fortress, see Schwank, "Neue Funde," 429–35, esp. 434.

152. Corley, *Private Women, Public Meals*, 69.

153. Sir 9:9; Corley, *Private Women, Public Meals*, 69–70.

154. Josephus, *AJ* 14.10.3–8 (196–215); 14.10.24 (260). See Theissen, "Review: Kathleen E Corley, *Private Women, Public Meals*," 632.

155. Josephus, *AJ* 17.11.2 (304–9); *BJ* 1.25.6 (511). See Freyne, "The Geography, Politics and Economics of Galilee," 102–3.

156. 3 Macc 5:48–50; 6:30–32; *T. Job* 10:1–7. See Theissen, "Review: Kathleen E. Corley, *Private Women, Public Meals*," 633.

157. Corley, *Private Women, Public Meals*, 69–70.

158. *m. Pesahim* 10; *b. Pesahim* 108a. See Bahr, "The Seder of Passover," 181; G. R. H. Horsley, "Reclining at the Passover Meal," 75; S. Stein, "The Influence of Symposia Literature," 13–44; D. Smith, "Social Obligation," 178.

159. Horsley, "Reclining," 75.

160. Roman style funerary busts with inscriptions found in Palestine date from around the time of the first Jewish War to the third century C.E. 74 of 178 busts catalogued represent women. Although most come from urban centers like Skythopolis, Gadara and Beth Shean and were no doubt costly, names with Semitic roots do occur in certain bust inscriptions, including women's. See Skupinska-Lovset, *Funerary Potraiture of Roman Palestine*, 118–119 on Semitic women's names.

161. Archer, for example, does not even mention Qumran in her book on Jewish women in Roman Palestine (*Her Price is Beyond Rubies*). Ilan describes the role of women in Qumran sect as "limited" (*Jewish Women*, 216). But see her more positive remarks in "In the Footsteps of Jesus," 127; idem, "Attraction of Aristocratic Women to Pharisaism," 28–33; idem., *Integrating Women*, 38–42. She too is now convinced by the burial evidence.

162. Elder, "The Woman Question," 220–34, esp. 223–24; Kraemer, "Jewish Women and Women's Judaism(s)" 67–69; Ilan, "Attraction of Aristocratic Women to Pharasaism," 29.

163. 1QSa I.4–11 (the Rule of the Congregation) and 4Q502. See Baumgarten, "4Q502, Marriage or Golden Age Ritual?" 125–35; *idem*, "The Qumran-Essene Restraints on Marriage," 13–14; Elder, "The Woman Question," 225–32; Ilan, *Jewish Women*, 41; Qimron, "Celibacy in the Dead Sea Scrolls," 289;

E. Schuller, "Women in the Dead Sea Scrolls," 123–24 on 1QSa. The Damascus Document also contains references to women in the community. See Schuller, "Women in the Dead Sea Scrolls," 118–23.

164. Baumgarten, "Qumran-Essene Restraints on Marriage;" Elder, "Woman Question," 228–29; Qimron, "Celibacy in the Dead Sea Scrolls;" Schiffman, "Laws Pertaining to Women in the Temple Scroll," 210–28; Schuller, "Women in the Dead Sea Scrolls," 118–22; Vermes, "Sectarian Matrimonial Halakhah in the Damascus Rule," 50–56.

165. 1QSa I.4–11. The clear reference to women's obligation to give witness in judicial hearings in the community has so confounded many interpreters that 1QSa I.11 is often emended to refer to a man (*yqbl*) "he will be accepted/received" in spite of clear feminine (*tqbl*) "she will be accepted/received" in the text itself. Baumgarten began this trend of emendation in "On the Testimony of Women in 1QSa," 266–69. However, many Qumran scholars now argue against the need for emendation in this instance. For an early acknowledgement of the clear reference to women's testimony in 1QSa I.11, see Richardson, "Some Notes on 1QSa," 119 as well as Elder, "The Woman Question,"228; Ilan, *Jewish Women*, 41; 163–66; *idem*, "The Attraction of Aristocratic Women to Pharisaism," 30–31; E. Schuller, "Women in the Dead Sea Scrolls," 123–124.

166. 4Q365 6 ii (known as the Revised Pentateuch). See Brooke, "Power to the Powerless," 62–65; E. Schuller, "Women in the Dead Sea Scrolls," 125.

167. Genesis Apocryphon 20:2–8a. See E. Schuller, "Women in the Dead Sea Scrolls," 125.

168. Philo, *Vit. Cont.* 80; So Brooke, "Power to the Powerless." See also Kraemer, "Monastic Jewish Women," 347ff.

169. So E. Schuller, "Women in the Dead Sea Scrolls."

170. This is a matter of greater dispute, but see Crown and Cansdale, "Qumran: Was it an Essene Settlement?" 31; 76, nn. 16 and 19; Meeks, "Images of the Androgyne," 177–78, n. 70.

171. So Ross Kraemer in private correspondence dated June 2, 1996.

172. Corley, *Private Women, Public Meals*, 68; Klosinski, "Meals in Mark," 92–93; D. Smith, "Social Obligation," 178–79.

173. Brooke, "Power to the Powerless;" Elder, "The Woman Question."

174. Corley, *Private Women, Public Meals*, 70–1; Kraemer, "Monastic Jewish Women," *passim*.

175. See Corley, *Private Women, Public Meals*, 185–86. Averil Cameron was the first to suggest that the mixed nature of early Christian groups may have had more to do with the society and class of its constituency than with any particular aspect of its theology. See A. Cameron, "Neither Male Nor Female," 60–68; *idem*, "Redrawing the Map," 266–71. For further on the lack of slave/free/distinctions among the lower classes, see Kampen, *Image and Status*, 31.

176. Several recent reconstructions of Jesus have been criticized in this manner, including those of Mack, Crossan, and the corporate views of the Jesus Seminar. See Chilton, "Jesus Within Judaism," 262–84. For his critique of Crossan, see "Jesus Within Judaism," 278–80. A. J. Levine has also criticised Crossan in this regard ("Yeast of Eden," *passim*).

177. E. P. Sanders, *Jesus and Judaism*; *idem*, *Jewish Law from Jesus to the Mishnah*; Vermes, *Jesus the Jew, idem, Changing Faces of Jesus*. See also Charlesworth, ed. *Jesus' Jewishness*; Chilton, "Jesus Within Judaism;" *idem, Pure Kingdom*; Fredriksen, *From Jesus to Christ*; *idem., Jesus of Nazareth*; Hagner, *The Jewish Reclamation of Jesus*; Young, *Jesus the Jewish Theologian*.

Chapter 2

1. See for example E. P. Sanders, who doubts women travelled with Jesus, and if they did, it was only rarely; women played primarily supporting roles in the movement. Further, Sanders distinguishes between disciples and followers (*Historical Figure of Jesus*, 110). Fredriksen sees the women as being in supportive householder roles – i.e., they supported the male itinerants, or came to hear Jesus' teachings and solicit cures. Thus they are "followers" of Jesus in a general sense and are to be distinguished from the all male Twelve. See *Jesus of Nazareth*, 214. Vermes also sees the women as part of the larger entourage of Jesus. See *Changing Faces of Jesus*, 175. On the probable role of women as true disciples of Jesus see Funk and the Jesus Seminar, *Acts of Jesus*, 157–58; 293.

2. Q 7:34; see ch. 4.

3. Corley, *Private Women, Public Meals*, 93; see below.

4. Here I refer to Gerhard E. Lenski's categories of social classes in pre-industrial agrarian societies that have become popular in discussions of antiquity and the Historical Jesus. John Dominic Crossan uses these categories in his class analysis of Palestine (*The Historical Jesus*, xxiv). According to Lenski's model there are four lower classes and four upper classes. The lower classes are 1) expendables (5–10% of the population), 2) unclean and degraded classes (5%), 3) artisan class (5–7%), 4) peasant class (60–70%). Upper and privileged classes are 1) merchant class (3–4%), 2) retainer class combined with 3) priestly class (7–8%) and 4) governing class (1–2%). See Lenski, *Power and Privilege*, 210–84.

5. Corley, *Private Women, Public Meals*, 84–6. I am in part dependent upon my previous discussion for the following remarks.

6. Winsome Munro argued that Mark portrays these women as disciples, although he evades mentioning them to the end of his story. See "Women Disciples in Mark?" 225–41. Other scholars have argued that Mark positions the women at the end of the story as positive foils to the unbelieving male disciples. See Beavis, "Women as Models of Faith," 3–9; J. Dewey, *Disciples on the Way*, 123–37; *idem*, "The Gospel of Mark," 506; Grassi, "The Secret Heroine," 10–15; Kopas, "Jesus and Women," 912–20: Malbon, "Fallible Followers," 29–48; *idem*, *Narrative Space*, 35–7; Schierling, "Women as Leaders," 250–56; Schmitt, "Women in Mark's Gospel,"228–33; Selvidge, "And Those Who Followed Feared," 396–400. Other scholars have concurred with this general appraisal of Mark 15:40–41, including Witherington, Moltmann-Wendel, Stagg, Swider, and Schüssler Fiorenza. The scholarly consensus had been that the women in Mark 15:40–41 were not disciples, but present only for menial purposes. See for example, Kee, *Community of the New Age*, 152–53. For further discussion, see Kinukawa, *Women and Jesus in Mark*, 90–106; *idem*, "Women Disciples of Jesus;" Meier, *Marginal Jew*, vol 3, 73–80; Phillips, "Full Disclosure;" Swartley, 'The Role of Women in Mark's Gospel."

7. In his commentary on the Gospel of John, R. Bultmann remarks that here Mark agrees with John in mentioning the women witnesses to the crucifixion; it is early tradition (*Gospel of John*, 666–7). In his *History of the Synoptic Tradition*, he remarks that the reference to the women is patently unhistorical, both here and in Mark 15:47. The women are only mentioned because the men are not available (274–75). Some scholars argue that the reference to the women is traditional, in a pre-Markan Passion account, and/or historical. See Barrett, *John*, 551; Brown, *The Death of the Messiah*, 2.1194–1196; Dauer, *Passionsgeschichte*, 194–95; Lüdemann, *Resurrection of Jesus*, 160.

8. Olrik, "Epic Laws," 133–34.

9. For a convenient list of scholar's views, see Brown, *Death of the Messiah*,

2.1516–17; J. Green, *Death of Jesus*, 295. See also A. Collins, "Composition of the Markan Passion Narrative," 76; *idem*, *Beginning of the Gospel*, 116–117; Crossan, *The Cross that Spoke*, 281–90; *idem*, *Who Killed Jesus*, 171; Matera, *Kingship of Jesus*, 52. See also Matera, *Kingship of Jesus*, 50–51

10. Olrik, "Epic Laws," 133–34.

11. See below, ch. 5.

12. Malbon, "Fallible Followers," *passim*. So also Catchpole, "The Fearful Silence of the Women at the Tomb," 3–10; Grassi, "Secret Heroine," 14; Kinukawa, *Women and Jesus*, 95; Munro, "Women Disciples," 230–311; Schrottroff, *Let the Oppressed Go Free*, 101; Selvidge, "Those Who Followed Feared," *passim*; Tannehill, "Disciples," 152; Tolbert, "Mark," 273.

13. Dewey, *Disciples on the Way*, 123–25.; Malbon, "Fallible Followers," 40ff.; Munro, "Women Disciples," 230–33. So also Kopas, "Jesus and Women in Mark's Gospel," 912ff.; Schmitt, "Women in Mark's Gospel," 231–32; and Schierling, "Women as Leaders," 252–54.

14. Schweizer argues that Matthew limits even the three named women's travel to the final journey to Jerusalem. See Schweizer, *Matthew*, 518. Gundry argues that Matthew's use of ἀπό (the women travel with Jesus "from" Galilee, not ἐν ["in"] Galilee (cf. Mark 15:41b; Matt 27:55) does not limit their travel to the final journey, but emphasizes their role in accompanying Jesus to the cross. See Gundry, *Matthew*, 578. So also Wainwright, *Towards a Feminist Reading*, 297; Corley, *Private Women, Public Meals*, 172. On women travelling to Passover celebrations, see above, ch. 1; so also Witherington, *Women in the Ministry*, 121–22.

15. Against Ilan, "In the Footsteps of Jesus," 121; Kinukawa, *Women and Jesus*, 94.

16. Wainwright, *Towards a Feminist Reading*, 297.

17. Gundry, *Matthew*, 578; see also Wainwright, *Towards a Feminist Reading*, 294.

18. See below, ch. 5.

19. See below, ch. 5.

20. See Atwood, *Mary Magdalene*, 60–61; Barrett, *John*, 551–52; Benoit, *Passion and Resurrection*, 189; Brown, *Death of the Messiah*, 2.1014–15; 1018–19; Lindars, *John*, 579; Witherington, *Women in the Ministry*, 120.

21. See below, ch. 5.

22. My remarks here are dependent on my previous discussion in *Private Women, Public Meals*, 110–19. See also Jane Schaberg, "Luke," 286; Seim, *The Double Message*, 25–28; *idem*, "The Gospel of Luke," 734,

23. Corley, *Private Women, Public Meals*, 111; 114.

24. Grassi, *Hidden Heroes*, 85–87.

25. So also Seim, *Double Message*, 28.

26. The plural is well supported by the Alexandrian, Western and Caesarean text types. The singular (αὐτῷ) may reflect the influence of Matt 13:4 and Mark 4:4 and a Christocentric correction by Marcion. The editors of both the UBS and NA editions prefer the plural reading, and the editors of the UBS rate their decision with a {B}. See Metzger, *A Textual Commentary*, 144; Corley, *Private Women, Public Meals*, 110, esp. n. 7; Schaberg, "Luke," 287; Seim, *Double Message*, 62–64; idem, "The Gospel of Luke," 739; Witherington, *Women in the Ministry*, 119.

27. Corley, *Private Women, Public Meals*, 116–19; and now also see Seim, *Double Message*, 85–8.

28. Corley, "Jesus' Table Practice," 452; 457. For Lenksi's class categories, see *Power and Privilege*, 210–84.

29. On slavery in antiquity and the mixture of slaves and free among the classes most often represented in the New Testament, see Corley, *Private Women, Public Meals*, 32–33, n. 46. For slave stewards, see *Private Women, Public Meals*, 48–49, n. 128; for slave stewards/overseers in Palestine, see Hamel, *Poverty and Charity*, 152; See also especially A. Cameron, "Neither Male Nor Female."

30. See below on Mark 15:40–41.

31. Josephus records that slaves and freedmen were common in the households of the Herods. On slaves in the court of Herod, see Josephus, *BJ* 1.33.9 (673); Urbach, "Laws Regarding Slavery," 31.

32. See Buchanan, "Jesus and the Upper Class," 195–209; J. Green, "Good News to Whom?" 59–74; Judge, "The Early Christians as a Scholastic Community," 9–11.

33. See Pervo, *Profit with Delight*, 40, 77–81.; 106. See also Fitzmyer, *Luke*, 1.698; Ricci, *Mary Magdalene and Many Others*, 155; Schaberg, "Luke," 287; Schottroff, *Let the Oppressed Go Free*, 65; 92; 131–36; Schüssler Fiorenza, *In Memory of Her*, 140; Seim, *Double Message*, 38; *idem*, "Gospel of Luke," 735; 741–42; Witheringon, "On the Road with Mary Magdalene, Joanna, and Other Disciples," 246. Witherington still considers this pericope to have historical value in spite of its Lukan compositional characteristics. See *Women in the Ministry*, 116. So also Luise Schottroff now in *Lydia's Impatient Sister* who argues that the women gave not only of their financial resources (which may have been limited), but of their love and physical labor (210).

34. Corley, *Private Women, Public Meals*, 121–30.

35. Schaberg, "Luke," 287; Seim, *Double Message*, 38–39. See also Schottroff, "Women as Followers of Jesus in New Testament Times," 420. Against Witherington, *Women In the Ministry*, 117.

36. See below.

37. See below, ch. 4.

38. Corley, *Private Women, Public Meals*, 116–17; Schaberg, "Luke," 287; For further on the issue of the demonic possession of Mary Magdalene, see below.

39. So Schaberg, "Luke," 286; see also Seim, *Double Message*, 32; *idem* "The Gospel of Luke," 734–35.

40. Seim, *Double Message*, 28.

41. Ilan, "Notes on the Distribution of Jewish Women's Names," 195; *idem, Jewish Women*, 53–55; Mayer, *Die jüdische Frau in der hellenistisch-römischen Antike*, 103–4.

42. Ilan, "Notes on the Distribution of Jewish Women's Names, 199; Mayer, *Die jüdische Frau*, 110. In particular the name Susanna is highly unlikely to have come from a Palestinian source as Witherington suggests (*Women in the Ministry*, 117).

43. Against Ilan, "In the Footsteps of Jesus," 123.

44. For a convenient chart, see Brown, *Death of the Messiah*, 2.1016.

45. Atwood, *Mary Magdalene in the New Testament*, 60–1; Barrett, *John*, 551–2; Benoit, *Passsion and Resurrection*, 189; Brown, *Death of the Messiah*, 2.1014–15; 1018–19; Lindars, *The Gospel of John*, 579.

46. For cautionary remarks, see George R. Beasley-Murray, *John* (WBC; Waco, TX: Word Books, 1987), 349; Schnackenburg, *John*, v. 3, 276–77.

47. The high incidence of these two names throughout all of our sources, including Josephus, the New Testament, Rabbinic literature and inscriptions makes the chances of error in this statistic slim. See Ilan, "Notes on the Distribution of Women's Names," 191–92.

48. Ilan,"Notes on the Distribution of Women's Names," 192.

49. See Haskins, *Mary Magdalene*, 3–57; King, "The Gospel of Mary Magdalene," 617–620.

50. Finegan, *Archaeology*, 81–82.

51. So Seim, *Double Message*, 34–35.

52. Tarichea comes from the Greek τάριχος. Josephus' description of Magdala as having forty-thousand inhabitants and a fleet of hundreds of fishing boats is probably an exaggeration, but does indicate that Magdala was well known as a fishing town. See *BJ* 2.21.3–4 (595–609); 3.10.1 (462–70); Finegan, *Archaeology*, 81–82; Ricci, *Mary Magdalene and Many Others*, 130.

53. So also now Schottroff, *Lydia's Impatient Sisters*, 84. Sawicki sees her as prominent in the fishing industry (i.e. a businesswoman) and therefore still considers her of a higher status, following Luke. See "Magdalenes and Tiberiennes," 191–93.

54. See Corley, *Private Women, Public Meals*, 14, esp. n. 55. For the many occupations of working women in Palestine, see Ilan, *Jewish Women*, 184–90. See also remarks by Schottroff, "Women Followers of Jesus," 420–21; *Let the Oppressed Go Free*, 88–90; Schüssler Fiorenza, *In Memory of Her*, 127–28. For additional references to fisherwomen in antiquity, see Schottroff, *Lydia's Impatient Sisters*, 83.

55. Pomeroy, *Goddesses Whores, Wives and Slaves*, 199–202; Schottroff, *Lydia's Impatient Sisters*, 93–97; Yamaguchi, "Re-Visioning Martha and Mary, 85.

56. On debt slavery, see below.

57. Schottroff, Lydia's *Impatient Sisters*, 79–84; Yamaguchi, "Re-Visioning Mary and Martha," 83.

58. Corley, *Private Women, Public Meals*, 48–52.

59. Corley, *Private Women, Public Meals*, 89–93. On the interpetation of "sinners" as members of lower class service occupations, see Abrahams, "Publicans and Sinners," 55; Schüssler Fiorenza, *In Memory of Her*, 128; Jeremias, *Jerusalem*, ch. 14.

60. So now also Schottroff, *Lydia's Impatient Sisters*, 84.

61. Schaberg, "Luke," 286.

62. See discussion of Ubieta, "Mary Magdalene and the Seven Demons," 220–21.

63. See below, ch. 5.

64. On tomb visitation and women see below, ch. 5.

65. E. R. Dodds, *Greeks and the Irrational*, 64–101; Jamison, *Touched With Fire*, 50–2.

66. See below, ch. 5 on women and necromancy. See also Ilan, "In the Footsteps of Jesus," 134–35.

67. For further on Mary Magdalene's status as a prophet, see Ilan, "In the Footsteps of Jesus," 134–35; King, "Prophetic Power and Women's Authority," 21–41. For her possible status as a teacher, see D'Angelo, "Reconstructing 'Real' Women," 123. For her possible status as a deacon, see D"Angelo, *ibid.*, 115; 122.

68. See E. P. Sanders on Jesus' probable erratic behavior, *Historical Figure*, 151.

69. Against Ilan, "In the Footsteps of Jesus," 122.

70. See Crossan, "Mark and the Relatives of Jesus," 105–10; Kinukawa, *Women and Jesus*, 92; Munro, "Women Disciples; Secret Mark," 57. Against Robert Gundry, *Mark*, 977; Witherington, *Women in the Ministry*, 92.

71. *Acts of Pilate*, 116–17; Coptic *Assumption of the Virgin*, 196–97; *Book of the Resurrection of Christ* by Bartholomew the Apostle, 151, See Munro, "Women

Disciples: Secret Mark," 57, esp. n. 33; Witherington, *Women in the Ministry*, 121.

72. All major uncials and good early versions read "Is this not the carpenter, the son of Mary?" (ὁ τέκτων ὁ υἱός). Several witnesses such as p45 show the influence of Matt 13:55 and read "Is not this the son of a carpenter, the son of Mary?" (τοῦ τέκτονος υἱός or τοῦ τέκτων ὁ υἱός). The Palestinian Syriac simply omits ὁ τέκτων. The UBS edition rates their decision with an {A}. This may reflect early concern about Jesus' humble vocation. (Metzger, *Textual Commentary*, 88), but the early reading in p45 remains problematic. See Witherington, *Women in the Ministry*, 88.

73. There is no evidence that Joseph is dead. For this view, see Brown, et al. *Mary in the New Testament*, 64.

74. This tradition is recorded about 570 C.E. by the Pilgrim Piacenze in his *Travels*. See Batey, *Jesus and the Forgotten City*, 20.

75. Corley, *Private Women, Public Meals*, 32–33, n. 46; 48–49; 59, n. 208. See especially A. Cameron, "Neither Male Nor Female."

76. See further on Lenski below.

77. See esp. Ilan, "'Man Born of Woman...' Job 14:1," 23–45; but also Brown, *Mary in the New Testament*, 63–64; McArthur, "Son of Mary," 38–58. So also A.J. Levine, "Matthew," 253; *idem*, *The Social and Ethnic Dimensions of Matthean Salvation History*, 63–88, esp. 87. Against Schaberg, *The Illegitimacy of Jesus*, 160–164; Funk, *Honest to Jesus*, follows Schaberg (288); see also Dewey, "Gospel of Mark," 482; Witherington, *Women in the Ministry*, 88.

78. Matthew's infancy story is clearly concerned about Mary's reputation. See Corley, *Private Women, Public Meals*, 147–52; Schaberg, *Illegitimacy*, 36–41; 145–94. Dewey reads "son of Mary" as an insult to Jesus and his mother ("Gospel of Mark," 482).

79. On the infancy gospels *Proto-James* and *Pseudo-Matthew*, see Cullmann, "Infancy Gospels: The Protevangelium of James," 421–69; Hock, *The Infancy Gospels of James and Thomas*; Schaberg, "The Infancy of Mary of Nazareth," 718.

80. Frag. 2 (III. 16). See Munro, "Women Disciples: Secret Mark," 47–64.

81. Thomas 61; see Corley, "Salome and Jesus."

82. Clement of Alexandria, *Strom.* iii. 45, 64, 66, 68, 91ff. 97, *Excerpta ex Theodoti* 67.

83. Manichaean Psalms 191:21ff. and 194:19–22 in Allberry, *A Manichaean Psalmbook*. See Bauckman, "Salome the Sister of Jesus," 263; Corley, "Salome," 286.

84. Infancy James 20. Bauckman, "Salome," 249–53; Corley, "Salome," 286; Cullman, "Infancy Gospels," 434–35; Schaberg, "Infancy of Mary of Nazareth," 726; See also Trautman, "Salomé l'incrédule: récits d'une conversion," 61–72.

85. See Crossan, "Mark and the Relatives of Jesus;" Munro, "Women Disciples: Secret Mark," 56–58; Tolbert, "Mark," 271.

86. So Munro, "Women Disciples;" Women Disciples: Secret Mark," 58.

87. I am dependent on *Private Women, Public Meals*, 85–86 for the following discussion. Material used with permission of Hendrickson Publishers.

88. Kittel, "*Akoloutheo, ktl*," *TDNT*, 2.210.

89. Philostratus, *Life of Apollonius of Tyana*, 1.20. Translation by F. C. Conybeare (LCL).

90. So Gundry, *Mark*, 979; Against Schottroff, *Lydia's Impatient Sisters*, 214.

91. Corley, *Private Women, Public Meals*, 93–95.

92. Jones, "Slavery in the Ancient World," 1. For similar rabbinic statistics for typical Jewish households, see Urbach, "The Laws Regarding Slavery," 32. See

also below, on "Children in the Marketplace," ch. 4; Corley, *Private Women, Public Meals*, 48–49. Against Seim, *Double Message*, 61.

93. See for example Seneca, *On Anger* (*de Ira*) 3.27.3; Bradley, *Slaves and Masters in the Roman Empire*, 113–37. For a slave contract insuring the right of the new master to the physical punishment of the 10 year old slavegirl named Abaskantis, see Llewelyn and Kearsley, "The Sale of a Slave Girl," 50.

94. Corley, *Private Women, Public Meals*, 48–52.

95. Casson, *Travel in the Ancient World*, 76.

96. Corley, *Private Women, Public Meals*, 15; Pomeroy, *Goddesses*, 191–92; Schottroff, *Let the Oppressed Go Free*, 89; Yamaguchi, "Re-Visioning Martha and Mary," 86. Yamaguchi notes Judith's appointment of a woman slave to management of her real estate (Judith 8:10).

97. Corley, *Private Women, Public Meals*, 48–52; Pomeroy, *Goddesses*, 191–2; Schottroff, *Let the Oppressed Go Free*, 89; Yamaguchi, "Re-visioning Martha and Mary," 85–86.

98. Corley, *Private Women, Public Meals*, 48–52.

99. Crossan, *Historical Jesus*, 293–95; Daube, *Roman Law*, 92–94; Horsley, *Jesus and the Spiral of Violence*, 232–33; Goodman, "The First Jewish Revolt," 417–27; Kloppenborg, "Alms, Debt and Divorce," 192–93; See also Mendelsohn, *Slavery in the Ancient Near East*, 5–19; Patterson, *Slavery and Social Death*, 124–26; Schottroff, "Women as Followers," 423; *idem*, *Let the Oppressed Go Free*, 97. See also Veyne, "Slavery,"55; Westermann, *Slave Systems*, 120–39.

100. Martin, "Slavery and the Ancient Jewish Family," 113–29; Ilan, *Jewish Women*, 205–11. Corley, *Private Women, Public Meals*, 58–59; Solodukho, "Slavery in the Hebrew Society," 1–9. Orlando Patterson has demonstrated that manumission rates of slaves in antiquity were unaffected by developments in philosophy or religious perspective. See Orlando Patterson, *Slavery and Social Death*, 273–93.

101. The standard discussion is Urbach, "The Laws Regarding Slavery," 1–94; see also Paul Flesher, *Oxen, Women or Citizens?*; Goodman, "First Jewish Revolt," 423, esp. n. 40; Lemche, "The Manumission of Slaves," 38–59; Solodukho, "Slavery in the Hebrew Society;" Zeitlin, "Slavery During the Second Commonwealth," 225–69; Van der Ploeg, "Slavery in the Old Testament," 72–87. See also Heichelheim, *An Economic Survey of Ancient Rome: Roman Syria*; Mendelsohn, *Slavery in the Ancient Near East*, *passim* and Osiek, "Slavery in the Second Testament World," 174–79. In opposition to the views expressed by Urbach, see Heinemann, "The Status of the Jewish Labourer," 268–9.

102. Goodman, "First Jewish Revolt," 421, esp. n. 29.

103. Heichelheim, *Economic Survey of Ancient Rome*, 164–65; Goodman, "First Jewish Revolt," 425; Westermann, *Slave Systems*, 124.

104. On the distinctions in clothing between slave and free in Palestine, see Hamel, *Poverty and Charity*, 77; 86–88; on the duties of wives that could be transferred to their women slaves, see Hamel, *Poverty and Charity*, 112. See also Paul Veyne, "Slavery," 55.

105. Westermann, *Slave Systems*, 125; Urbach, "Laws Regarding Slavery," 55.

106. Urbach, "Laws Regarding Slavery," 47. Orlando Patterson has documented a similar trend in the fluctuations in the Roman slave market of the same time period. See Patterson, *Slavery and Social Death*, 247. For a further discussion of these manumission trends in the Augustan age, see Corley, *Private Women, Public Meals*, 58–59. Late second century Jewish manumission documents from the

Diaspora in Lower Russia in fact mirror Delphic manumissions. See Westermann, *Slave Systems,* 125.

107. Hamel, *Poverty and Charity,* 152. See also Veyne, "Slavery," 55

108. See below ch. 3. Of the parables voted red or pink by the Jesus Seminar, eight out of twenty-one, or nearly half of them refer to slaves, day laborers, or other household and agricultural servants. Of the parables voted grey, two out of six do. See Funk, et al, *The Parables of Jesus.* Hamel makes a similar point on the basis of these and other parables (*Charity and Poverty,* 163, n. 91). So also Osiek, "Slavery in the Second Testament World," 177.

109. Gibbs and Feldman, "Josephus' Vocabulary for Slavery," 293.

110. Other pertinent Hebrew biblical texts on slavery are Exod 23:10–11; Deut 15:1–18; Lev 25; Jer 32:6–15; 34:8–20; Neh 5:1–13; 2 Kgs 4:1; Numbers 34. See Goodman, "First Jewish Revolt," 423, esp. n. 49; Lemche, "Manumission," *passim.*

111. At times of impoverishment, the regulations of biblical texts fell into regular dissuse. See Urbach, "Laws Regarding Slavery," 11–17; Baltzer, "Liberation for Debt Slavery After the Exile," 481.

112. Exod 22:1. See Josephus, *AJ* 3.12.3 (282) and discussion by Urbach, "Laws Regarding Slavery," 18–19.

113. Goodman, "First Jewish Revolt," 423; Zeitlin, "Slavery," 193–97.

114. Goodman, "First Jewish Revolt," 423, esp. 40. On the solutions for cancellation of debts in Roman Palestine, including debt slavery, see also Hamel, *Poverty and Charity,* 159–63; Horsley, *Jesus and the Spiral of Violence,* 232–33; on the sale of children the poor and indigent see Veyne, "Slavery," 55; on the sale of children by slavewomen for the purposes of earning manumission, see Corley, *Private Women, Public Meals,* 50–51. For close documentary evidence for the existence of debt slavery in this geographical area, see Heichelheim, *Roman Syria,* 165; Rostovtzeff and Welles, ""A Parchment Contract of Loan from Dura-Europus," 67.

115. See discussion by Zeitlin, "Slavery," 196. So also Osiek, "Slavery in the Second Testament," 177.

116. On the "slave-wife" (*amah*) see Avigad, "Epitaph of a Royal Steward," 146, n. 18; *idem,* "A Seal of a Slave-Wife (Amah)," 125–32; Epstein, *Marriage Laws in the Bible and the Talmud,* 34–76; Ilan, *Jewish Women,* 205; Jepson, "Amah und Schiphchah," 293–297; Mendelsohn, *Slavery in the Ancient Near East,* 50–55; *idem,* "The Conditional Sale into Slavery of Free-born Daughters," 190–95; Van der Ploeg, "Slavery in the Old Testament," 75. On the distinctions between Exod 21:7–11 and Deut 15:12–18, see Lemche, "Manumission," 44 and i*dem,* "The 'Hebrew Slave,'" 139; 143; and also Japhet "The Laws of Manumission of Slaves," 200.

117. Goodman, "First Jewish Revolt," 423, esp. n. 40.

118. Horsley, *Jesus and the Spiral of Violence,* 232–33; Ilan, *Jewish Women,* 206. On the duties of wives that could be transferred to a woman's slaves, see *m. Ketub.* 55; *t. Ketub.* 5.4; *y. Ketub.* 30a; Hamel, *Poverty and Charity,* 112; Yamaguchi, "Re-visioning Martha and Mary," 85–86.

119. Ilan, *Jewish Women,* 203–11.

120. See arguments by Ilan, *Jewish Women,* 207–11.

121. Judith is described as freeing a slavewoman upon her death (Judith 16:23). See Ilan, *Jewish Women,* 205.

122. For further discussion, see Corley, *Private Women, Public Meals,* 50–51; and now also Llewelyn and Kearsley, "Manumission in Thessaly and at Delphi,"

76–81. Late second century Jewish manumission documents from the Diaspora in lower Russia in fact mirror the manumission trends found in the Delphic manumissions. See Westermann, *Slavery Systems*, 125.

123. See Ilan, *Jewish Women*, 205–11. Horsley, *Jesus and the Spiral of Violence*, 232–33.

124. Josephus, *BJ* 4. 508. See Goodman, *Ruling Class*, 204; 207; and above, ch. 1.

125. In Lucian's *Fugitivi*, a female Cynic leaves her husband and runs away with two slaves. See Corley, *Private Women, Public Meals*, 63, n. 230. See also a Greek slave sale contract (P. Turner 22, 142 C.E., Pamphylia) that insures the buyer that the ten year old slavegirl named Abaskantis will not run away: Llewelyn and Kearsley, "The Sale of a Slave Girl: The New Testament Attitude to Slavery," 48. For a Syriac sale contract (Dura Pg. 20, May 243 C.E., Edessa) making the potential loss from the flight of a twenty-eight year old slavewomen named Amath-Sin the problem of the new owner, see Heichelheim, *Roman Syria*, 166–7.

126. Horsley, *Jesus and the Spiral of Violence*, 232–33; Ilan, *Jewish Women*, 206. On the real problem of peasant indebtedness as a background for Jesus' interest in debts, see also Kloppenborg, "Alms, Debt and Divorce," esp. 192–3; Oakman, *Jesus and the Economic Questions of His Day*, 72–80

127. Urbach, "Laws Regarding Slavery," 17.

128. The flight of slaves was not uncommon in antiquity. The classic case is of course Onesimus in the New Testament. Lucian's *Fugitivi* also describes a wealthy woman running away with her two slaves. See Corley, *Private Women, Public Meals*, 63, n. 230.

129. Frag. 2 (III. 16).

130. On Mark 2:17, see below. On Q 7:29 see ch. 4.

131. D. Smith, "Table Fellowship and the Historical Jesus," 160–61.

132. Lenski, *Power and Privilege*, 278.

133. The political endorsements by artisans at Pompeii come to mind. I am indebted to David Seeley for this remark. See also Veyne, "The Household and Its Freed Slaves," 82–83; *idem*, "Slavery," 53–57.

134. Hamel, *Poverty and Charity*, 195; 169–70.

135. For ample bibliography, see, Corley, *Private Women, Public Meals*, 32–33, esp. n. 46.

136. For ample bibliography, see Corley, *Private Women, Public Meals*, 32–33, esp. n. 46; 48–49, esp. n. 128. On slavewomen household managers, see Yamaguchi, "Re-visioning Martha and Mary," 86.

137. Goodman, "First Jewish Revolt," 425, esp. n. 46.

138. Goodman, *Ruling Class*, 8.

139. Urbach, "Laws Regarding Slavery," 66–67.

140. On the prejudice against manumission in later Jewish sources, see Solodukho, "Slavery in the Hebrew Society," 7; Westermann, *Slave Systems*, 125; Urbrach, "Laws Regarding Slavery," 55.

141. See comments by Veyne, "Slavery," 52; also Matt 18:23–35.

142. So Buchanan, "Jesus and the Upper Class," *passim*; and esp. Judge, "Early Christianity as a Scholastic Movement," 9–11.

143. See also Downing, "A Bas Les Aristos," 221–30 who demonstrates the cultural interaction between "elite" and "popular" culture in antiquity.

144. It is not impossible that Jesus simply left home. Eusebius quotes Hegesippus' account of the two grandsons of Jude in *Hist. eccl.* 3.19.1–3.20.7.

145. This comment by Paul is usually considered mythic, but the context in no way requires this interpretation, given that Paul is clearly discussing the actual social status and poverty of the Corinthian church. The hymnic structure and ascent/descent pattern of Christ hymns such as Phil. 2: 6–11 is not clearly evident in 2 Cor. 8:9. See also T. Schmidt, *Hostility to Wealth*, 119–22.

146. Origin, *Contra Celsum* 1.28. See Hamel, *Poverty and Charity*, 194.

147. So also in the early Christian community according to Acts 4:32–37. See also remarks by Gerd Theissen concerning the comparable social backgrounds of the Jesus movement and the community of Qumran, which included those from priestly and wealthy backgrounds, as well as artisans such as bricklayers, leather-workers, smiths, bakers and the like. Theissen, *Social Reality and the Early Christians*, 75–6. The Qumran community also included women (see above, ch. 1).

148. Matt 21:23–43/Luke 20:9–18/Thomas 65; Luke 12:16–21/Thom 63:1; Matt 25:14–30/Luke 19:12–27; Luke 16:1–9; Matt 20:1–15.

149. Hamel, *Poverty and Charity*, 151.

150. See below, ch. 4.

151. Corley, "Were the Women Around Jesus Really Prostitutes?" 521; *Private Women, Public Meals*, 48–52. I am in essential agreement with Horsley, *Jesus and the Spiral of Violence*, 223. Against Schottroff, *Let the Oppressed Go Free*, 97; Luise Schottroff and Wolfgang Stegemann, *Jesus and the Hope of the Poor*, trans. Matthew J. O'Connell (Maryknoll, NY: Orbis Books, 1986), 15–16.; Schüssler Fiorenza, *In Memory of Her*, 121–22; *Miriam's Child*, 93–94.

152. See Corley, *Private Women, Public Meals*, 147–52; Levine, "Matthew,"253; *idem*, *Social and Ethnic Dimensions*, 87–88; Schaberg, *Illegitimacy of Jesus*, 20–36.

153. Corley, *Private Women, Public Meals*, 86.

154. See below, ch. 5.

155. See ch. 5 below.

156. Corley, *Private Women, Public Meals*, 48–49; Seim, *Double Message*, 61. On the role of children in household service, see Golden, πaῖs, 'Child' and 'Slave,'" 98–99. For the use of διακονέω as the household work of women and slaves, see Schottroff, *Lydia's Impatient Sisters*, 83, but also cautionary remarks on 206.

157. Corley, *Private Women, Public Meals*, 48–49; on poor women, see n. 128.

158. See Corley, *Private Women, Public Meals*, 48–49; 106–7, n. 117. D'Arms, "Slaves at Roman Convivia," 171–83.

159. Marvin Meyer has suggested that another model male disciple may have been present in an earlier version of Mark, that being the νεανίσκος, "young man" seen at the garden and the tomb (Mark 14:51–52; 16:5–6). Meyer suggests that should the fragments of the Secret Gospel of Mark which feature this young man be considered as part of the original version of Mark's gospel, then Mark would be depicting an ideal male disciple throughout his story similar to the "Beloved Disciple" in the Gospel of John. See Meyer, "The Youth in the Secret Gospel of Mark," 129–53; *idem*, "The Youth in Secret Mark and the Beloved Disciple in John," 94–105. Meyer observes that like the νεανίσκος, the women disciples also fall short, since they flee the scene and tell no one about the resurrection ("The Youth in the Secret Gospel," 147). This observation was made to me by Winsome Munro. See Munro, "Women Disciples: Secret Mark," 51. Since young men could be used to serve meals, the νεανίσκος could also be likened to the ideal διάκονος who serves others in Mark 10:43–45. See *Private Women, Public Meals*, 106–7, n. 117.

160. Corley, *Private Women, Public Meals*, 86.

161. See below.

162. Corley, *Private Women, Public Meals*, 84–86. So also Schottroff, *Lydia's Impatient Sisters*, 214.

163. See Corley, *Private Women, Public Meals*, 24–79. For the Syrian provenance of Mark, see Koester, *Ancient Christian Gospels*, 288–92.

164. Casson, *Travel*, 75–77; 82; 128, pl. 6; 147; 160; 176–7. On runaway slavegirls in both ancient novels and documents, see Corley, *Private Women, Public Meals*, 63, n. 230; Heichelheim, *Roman Syria*, 167.

165. Ilan, *Jewish Women*, 128–29; 132–34; 176–84; Ilan corrects the assumption that Egyptian Jewish Hellenistic sources are necessarily applicable to Palestine in response to Jeremias, *Jerusalem*, 361–62. For secluded wealthy women and virgins see 3 Macc 1:18–20; 2 Macc 3:19; Pseudo-Phocylides 215; *Sir* 26:10; 42:11–12. For Ilan's critique of Jeremias, see *Jewish Women*, 132–3. See also remarks by Schottroff, "Women Followers of Jesus," 420–21; *idem, Let the Oppressed Go Free*, 88–90; Schüssler Fiorenza, *In Memory of Her*, 127–28.

166. Ilan, *Jewish Women*, 132–34.

167. Women could marry as late as their 20's. See Ilan, *Jewish Women*, 67–69.

168. Horsley, *Jesus and the Spiral of Violence*, 246–49. But see the conclusions of S. R. Llewelyn and R. A. Kearsley that P. Ups. Frid. 7 is a document granting a slavewoman her freedom of movement. This would imply that she would not automatically have such freedom. The interpretation of this text is disputed. See Llewelyn and Kearsley, "He gives authority to his slaves, to each his work," 62.

169. This also implies that prostitutes could be expected to meet these higher fares. See Casson, *Travel*, 154.

170. Casson, *Travel*, 76.

171. Casson, *Travel*, 85.

172. Casson, *Travel*, 142–44. For ample ancient references, see 346.

173. Levine, "Yeast of Eden," 18.

174. On women missionaries in the Hellenistic churches, see D'Angelo, "Women Partners" *passim*; Schottroff, "Women as Followers of Jesus," 424–26; Schüssler Fiorenza, *In Memory of Her*, 168–75.

175. See above ch. 1.

176. Josephus, *BJ*, 4.9.3–8 (503–44, esp. 505). See above, ch. 1.

177. Ilan, *Jewish Women*, 64; Kraemer, *Her Share of the Blessings*, 133–34; 144; Schottroff, "Women as Followers of Jesus," 421. So also Sim, "The Women Followers of Jesus," 60.

178. The marriage of a former slavewoman to her master would mirror the practices of other Greco-Roman people. See Corley, *Private Women, Public Meals*, 49–50. On Jewish slavewomen, see Ilan, *Jewish Women*, 206; Urbach, "Laws Regarding Slavery,"47–49.

179. Ilan, *Jewish Women*, 64.

180. See above.

181. For this common Roman Catholic view, see Brown, et al. *Mary in the New Testament*, 64

182. See Sim, "What About the Wives and Children of the Disciples?" 373–90.

183. See discussion by Ilan, *Jewish Women*, 62–65; see also Kraemer, *Her Share of the Blessings*, 133–34; so also D'Angelo, "Remembering Jesus," 215–16.

184. See for example, Dewey, "Gospel of Mark," 478–9; Horsley, *Jesus and the Spiral of Violence*, 232–44; Schüssler-Fiorenza, *In Memory of Her*, 145–47.

185. Nor Jesus'. See ch. 3 below. So D'Angelo, "Abba and Father," 629–30; "Theology in Mark and Q," 162. Against Borg, *Meeting Jesus*, 57; Crossan, *Historical Jesus*, 301–2; Kloppenborg, "Alms, Debt and Divorce," *passim*; Schottroff, *Let the Oppressed Go Free*, 95–97; Schüssler Fiorenza, *In Memory of Her*, 143–45.

186. So D'Angelo, "Abba and Father," 629–30; "Theology in Mark and Q," 162.

187. Corley, *Private Women, Public Meals*, 146, n. 195; Pervo, *Profit with Delight*, 181, n. 79; 24–25; 127–30; Seim, *Double Message*, 185–248.

188. For a recent discussion of the relationship between Jesus and John the Baptist, see Tatum, *John the Baptist and Jesus*.

189. Ilan, *Jewish Women*, 64; Schottroff, "Women as Followers of Jesus," 418–27.

190. Note Gundry's remarks on Mark 15:40–41: Mark is trying to make up for a "culturally embarrassing tradition" (*Mark*, 978).

191. Munro, "Women Disciples."

192. E. P. Sanders' reasons for denying the historicity of the gospel descriptions of women traveling with Jesus must therefore be rejected. According to Sanders, this tradition is unlikely to be historical because the gospels show no echoes of a criticism of Jesus' scandalous behavior. Both Mark 15:40–41 and the "tax-collectors and sinners/prostitutes" traditions in Mark and Q, however, show clear signs of "echoes of scandalous behavior." See E. P. Sanders, *The Historical Figure*, 110. Here I am drawing back from my analysis of Mark in *Private Women, Public Meals*. I now think that Mark is more uncomfortable with the tradition in Mark 15:40–41 than I had previously assumed. See below on the crucifixion and resurrection, ch. 5.

193. See Corley, *Private Women, Public Meals* 89–93 for many of the following remarks. Permission to repeat this material given by Hendrickson Publishers.

194. Mack, *Myth of Innocence*,183. Burton Mack and Vernon Robbins have argued that behind the composition of gospel narratives is a practice of "chreia elaboration." This was a literary process learned by schoolboys, whereby short pithy statements were elaborated into larger narratives. See Mack and Robbins, *Patterns of Persuasion in the Gospels*. Markan composition of this section was noticed long ago. See Bultmann, *History of the Synoptic Tradition*, 47–48; Wm. O. Walker, "Jesus and the Tax-Collectors," 221–38; D. Smith, "Jesus at Table," 475–76.

195. Bultmann, *History of the Synoptic Tradition*, 47–48; D. Smith, "Jesus at Table," 476.

196. The addition of καὶ πίνει (and drink) to Mark 2:16 probably reflects the influence of Luke 5:30. The editors of the UBS rate their decision to omit καὶ πίνει with a {B}. See Metzger, *Textual Commentary*, 78.

197. Corley, *Private Women, Public Meals*, 89–93. See now also Freyne, "Jesus the Wine-drinker," 174.

198. So D. Smith, "Jesus at Table," 476.

199. Corley, *Private Women, Public Meals*, 108–46.

200. See ch. 4 below.

201. Corley, *Private Women, Public Meals*, 147–79.

202. Cohen, "Menstruants and the Sacred," 278–79; E. P. Sanders, "Jesus and the Sinners," 13.

203. Fredriksen, "Did Jesus Oppose the Purity Laws? 23; *idem, Jesus of Nazareth*, 67; Sanders, "Jesus and the Sinners," 13.

204. Saldarini, *Pharisees, Scribes and Sadducees*, 216–20; E. P. Sanders, "Jesus

and the Sinners," esp. 14–15; *Jesus and Judaism*, 176–99; Stemberger, *Jewish Contemporaries* of *Jesus*, 41; 47–48; 75–82; 83–84. Jacob Neusner holds that the New Testament portrayal of the Pharisees as being concerned with ritual purity, tithes and sabbath observance accurately reflects the Pharisaic program of the first century. See *From Politics to Piety*; *idem*, *The Pharisees*; *idem*, "Two Pictures of the Pharisees," 525–38.

205. Against Freyne, "Jesus the Wine-drinker," 175.

206. See above on Mark 15:40–41 and ch. 5 (Q 7:34).

207. Saldarini, "The Social Class of the Pharisees in Mark," 71; *idem*, "Political and Social Roles of the Pharisees and Scribes in Galilee," 200–9.

208. D. Smith, "Table Fellowship and the Historical Jesus," 160–61. See also below ch. 3.

209. I.e., concerns over purity may not have mediated the concerns over class. Marcus Borg connects purity issues to class issues. See *Jesus a New Vision*, 157–60, and especially *Meeting Jesus for the First Time*, 46–68. Crossan also connects Jesus' open commensality to a rejection of social boundaries created by Jewish purity regulations (*Historical Jesus*, 322–24).

210. Purity does not correspond to social class. See Fredriksen, "Did Jesus Oppose the Purity Laws?" 23; idem., *Jesus of Nazareth*, 201. Against Freyne, "Jesus the Wine-Drinker, " 175; Hamel, *Poverty and Charity*, 82–93. Increased distinctions between the *haberim* (who were men of leisure) and ordinary people is best understood as a later development in rabbinic literature. See above remarks on the *haberim*.

211. And there is no evidence that Jesus did not observe basic purity regulations in regards to the temple or food. See Fredriksen, "Did Jesus Oppose the Purity Laws?" 42–43. Against Borg, *Meeting Jesus*, 46–68; Crossan *Historical Jesus*, 355; Freyne, "Jesus the Wine-Drinker," 175.

212. See J. Scott, *Domination and the Arts of Resistance*; *idem*, *Weapons of the Weak*.

213. So also Schüssler Fiorenza, *In Memory of Her*, 122–25; 127–28; 135–6.

214. Voted grey by the Jesus Seminar. See Funk, *Parables of Jesus*, 62. See discussion below, ch. 3.

215. Corley, *Private Women, Public Meals*, 100, esp. n. 82. On manumission of slaves *per mansam*, see Wiedemann, *Greek and Roman Slavery*, 233–36. The most popular form of manumission was by will, when the slave was freed upon the death of his or her master. See Duff, *Freedmen*, 21–25.

216. See Seneca, *Ep*. 47 and discussion in Corley, *Private Women, Public Meals*, 100, n. 82; see also Ps. Heraclitus 9.5. I am indebted to David Seeley for this second reference.

217. See Cameron, "Neither Male Nor Female;" Corley, *Private Women, Public Meals*, 31–33, esp. n. 46; Fiorenza, *In Memory of Her*, 179–82.

218. So Crossan, *Historical Jesus*, 261–64; 335. See also Corley, "Jesus' Table Practice;" Schüssler Fiorenza, *Jesus, Miriam's Child*, 93–94.

219. So Crossan, *Historical Jesus*, 263; and Schottroff, *Let the Oppressed Go Free*, 93–94; 104.

220. See above.

221. Hamel, *Poverty and Charity*, 215.

222. See above ch. 1.

223. Funk and the Jesus Seminar, *Acts of Jesus*, 66–67. Fredriksen says this indicates that Jesus was not ascetic like John. *Jesus of Nazareth*,192–93.

224. D. Smith, "Historical Jesus at Table," 480–86; *idem*, "Table Fellowship and the Historical Jesus," 143–48; 161–62; see also *idem*, "Table Fellowship as a Literary Motif," 636–38.

225. See ch. 6.

226. Corley, *Private Women, Public Meals*, 132–33.

227. See below, ch. 3.

228. Freyne, "Jesus the Wine-drinker," 176.

229. Here the instincts of Renita Weems are confirmed. See *Just a Sister Away,* 86. Jesus called poor men and poor *women*. See now also Stegemann and Stegemann, *Jesus Movement*, 384.

230. See Corley, *Private Women, Public Meals, passim.*

Chapter 3

1. Schüssler Fiorenza, *In Memory of Her*, 107.

2. Borg, *Jesus: A New Vision*, 133–5; *idem*, *Meeting Jesus*, 57–58; Crossan, *Historical Jesus*, 261–64.

3. Crossan, *In Parables;* C. H. Dodd, *The Parables of the Kingdom*; Funk, *Parables and Presence*; Hedrick: *Parables as Poetic Fictions*; Herzog, *Parables as Subversive Speech*; Jeremias, *The Parables of Jesus*; Linnemann, *Parables of Jesus*; Perrin, *Rediscovering*; B. Scott, *Hear Then the Parable.*

4. Funk, *Parables and Presence*, 19–28; Hedrick, *Parables as Poetic Fictions*, part 2; Scott, *Hear Then the Parable*, 41–42.

5. See A.-J. Levine, "Yeast of Eden," 23–24.

6. Arnal, "Gendered Couplets in Q," 75–94.

7. Rogers, "Female Forms of Power," 727–56; idem, "A Woman's Place," 148.

8. Durber, 'The Female Reader," 59–78; A.-J. Levine, "Yeast of Eden," 25–6; Schottroff, *Lydia's Impatient Sisters*, 79–118; Waller, "The Parable of the Leaven," 99–109.

9. Slee, "Parables and Women's Experience," 20–31. See also Durber, "Female Reader," 69.

10. Jesus Seminar vote: red. The Jesus Seminar has a simple system of votes for the authenticity of Jesus traditions. Red means authentic, Pink is likely authentic, grey is probably not authentic, but contains elements of Jesus' authentic teaching, and black is definitely not authentic.

11. Funk, *Parables of Jesus*, 29; against Waller, "Parable of the Leaven," 102.

12. Jeremias, *Parables*, 146–19; Perrin, *Rediscovering*, 157–58.

13. Crossan, *In Parables*, 38.

14. B. Scott, *Hear Then the Parable*, 321–29; Funk, *Parables*, 29.

15. Dodd, *Parables*, 154–55.

16. Schottroff, *Lydia's Impatient Sisters*, 79–90; Waller, "Parable of the Leaven," 107.

17. Funk, *Parables of Jesus*, 29

18. So A.-J. Levine, "Yeast of Eden," 25. Against Schottroff, *Lydia's Impatient Sisters*, 79–90; Waller, "Parable of the Leaven," 107.

19. B. Scott, *Hear Then*, 321–29.

20. Jesus Seminar vote: pink

21. Crossan, *In Parables*, 38.

22. Schottroff, *Lydia's Impatient Sisters*, 92; B. Scott, *Hear Then the Parable*, 311.

23. Schottroff, *Lydia's Impatient Sisters*, 94

24. Popularized by Jeremias, *Parables*, 134; rejected by Schottroff, *Lydia's Impatient Sisters*, 95–96; B. Scott, *Hear Then*, 311.

25. Crossan, *In Parables*, 38.

26. Schottroff, *Lydia's Impatient Sisters*, 100; see also discussion in Durber, "Female Reader," 71.

27. But probably not with the unclean. Against B. Scott, *Hear Then*, 313; See also remarks on the Prodigal Son by Crossan, *In Parables*, 72.

28. The Jesus Seminar voted this parable pink. This means there is a high probability that the parable goes back to Jesus.

29. Text and Translation by M. Meyer, *The Gospel of Thomas*, 61.

30. Against B. Scott, "The Empty Jar," 78.

31. So B. Scott, "Empty Jar," 77–78; A.-J. Levine, "Yeast of Eden," 25.

32. A parallel identified both by B. Scott, "Empty Jar," 78–79 and Waller, ""Parable of the Leaven," 103.

33. B. Scott, *Hear Then*, 79.

34. Jesus Seminar vote: pink.

35. So Schottroff, who titles this parable the Stubborn Widow (*Lydia's Impatient Sisters*, 101). I follow Hedrick, *Parables*, 187–207.

36. B. Scott, *Hear Then*, 180–81.

37. Ps 68:5; 146:9; Deut 10:18.

38. See Deut 24:17–18; Exod 22:21–24; ; Ezek 22:7; cf. Zech 7:10; Ps 94:6; Isa 1:23; 10:1–2; Jer 5:28.

39. Jeremias, *Parables*, 156.

40. Linnemann, *Parables*, 187; Hedrick, *Parables*, 190; Herzog, *Parables*, 218; B. Scott, *Hear Then*, 177.

41. See B. Scott, *Hear Then the Parable*, 186–87.

42. Against B. Scott, *Hear Then the Parable*, 187; see instead Herzog, *Parables*, 215–32; Schottroff, *Lydia's Impatient Sisters*, 101–118.

43. Borg, *Jesus: A New Vision*, 133–15; *idem*, *Meeting Jesus*, 57–8; Crossan, *Historical Jesus*, 261–64; Schüssler Fiorenza, *In Memory of Her*, 118–22; idem, *Miriam's Child*, 93–94.

44. Borg, *Jesus: A New Vision*, 133–35; *idem*, *Meeting Jesus*, 57–58; Schüssler Fiorenza, *In Memory of Her*, 118–22. In *Jesus, Miriam's Child* Fiorenza does not mention purity (93–94).

45. Crossan, *Historical Jesus*, 261–64; Schottroff, *Let the Oppressed Go Free*, 93–94; 104.

46. See above, ch. 1 and comments by Fredriksen, *From Jesus to Christ*, 105–6.

47. On Mark, see above, ch. 2; on Q below, ch. 4; Corley, *Private Women, Public Meals*, 89–95;Corley, "Jesus' Table Practice, *passim*.

48. D. Smith, "Table Fellowship and the Historical Jesus," 160–61.

49. D. Smith, "Table Fellowship and the Historical Jesus," 161.

50. See above, ch. 2.

51. See below, ch. 4.

52. I thank Jack Kugelmass for his comments on the function of humor. Jack Kuglemass, "Undser Shtik: The Meaning of Humor for American Jews," Institute for Research in the Humanities Seminar, University of Wisconsin-Madison, Spring 1996.

53. See discussion of the function of "tax collectors and sinners" in chapters 2 (on Mark) and 4 (on Q). See also Funk, *Honest to Jesus*, 194.

54. On Jesus and humor see Funk, *Honest to Jesus*, 158–62; Mack, *A Myth of*

Innocence, 61–62 on Jesus probable "playful mode of response;" and Sandifer, "The Humor of the Absurd," 287–97.

55. Of the parables voted red or pink by the Jesus Seminar, eight out of twenty-one, or nearly half of them refer to slaves, day laborers, or other household and agricultural servants. Of the parables voted grey, two out of six do. See Funk, et al., *The Parables of Jesus*. Hamel makes a similar point on the basis of these and other parables (*Charity and Poverty*, 163, n. 91). So also Osiek, "Slavery in the Second Testament World," 177.

56. Gibbs and Feldman, "Josephus' Vocabulary for Slavery," 293.

57. See above, ch. 2 and remarks by Solodukho, "Slavery in the Hebrew Society of Iraq and Syria," esp. 8.

58. See esp. Beavis, "Ancient Slavery," 37–54.

59. Crossan, *In Parables*, 96–120; see also *idem*, "The Servant Parables," 17–62.

60. Luke 16:1–8, Jesus Seminar vote: red. Matt. 18:23–24, Jesus Seminar vote: pink.

61. Crossan, *In Parables*, 107; Fitzmyer, 'The Story of the Dishonest Manager," 166–67; Herzog, *Parables*, 234–35; Kloppenborg, "The Dishonored Manager," 476; B. Scott, *Hear Then*, 256–60.

62. C. H. Dodd, *Parables*, 30.

63. C. H. Dodd, *Parables*, 17; Jeremias, *Parables* 182; Perrin, *Rediscovering*, 114–15.

64. Kloppenborg, "Dishonored Manager," 479; Crossan, "Servant Parables," 46.

65. Beavis, "Slavery," 48–52; Kloppenborg, "Dishonest Manager;" Herzog, *Parables*, 223–58.

66. Beavis, "Slavery," 45. Against Herzog, *Parables*, 241; Kloppenborg's sources imply the steward might have been a freedman, but he does not point this out ("Dishonored Manager)," 492.

67. Beavis, "Slavery." For a translation of the *Life of Aesop*, see Daly, *Aesop Without Morals*.

68. Beavis, "Slavery," 48. Thus it is not necessary to posit that the initial misconduct of the steward was the mishandling of loans. Against Fitzmyer, "Dishonest Manager," 161–84.

69. Thus the story still hinges on the escapades of the steward, not the honor of the master. Against Kloppenborg, "Dishonored Master."

70. Beavis, "Slavery," 53; Herzog, *Parables*, 233–58.

71. Herzog, *Parables*, 131–3; Jeremias, *Parables*, 97; Linnemann, *Parables*, 105–8; B. Scott, *Hear Then*, 268–69.

72. Herzog, Parables, 131–49; B. Scott, *Hear Then*, 270.

73. Herzog, *Parables*, 147.

74. Jeremias, *Parables*, 97; 213.

75. See above, ch. 2 and Goodman, "The First Jewish Revolt: Social Conflict and the Problem of Debt," 423 and *passim*; Kloppenborg, "Alms, Debt and Divorce, 192–193; Oakman, "Jesus and Agrarian Palestine, 57–73; *idem*, *Jesus and the Economic Questions of His Day*, 72–7.

76. Jesus Seminar vote: grey.

77. Jesus Seminar vote: black.

78. Jesus Seminar vote: black.

79. Jesus Seminar vote: black.

80.Mark 10:14b, Jesus Seminar vote: pink; Mark 10:15, Jesus Seminar vote: grey.

81. See J. Bailey, "Experiencing the Kingdom as a Little Child," 58–67; Best, "Mark 10:13–16," 119–34; Derrett, "Why Jesus Blessed the Children," 1–18; Fowl, "Receiving the Kingdom of God as a Child," 153–158; Nkwoka, "Mark 10:13–16," 100–10; Patte, ed., *Kingdom and Children*; Weber, *Jesus and the Children.*

82. Golden, "Chasing Change in Roman Childhood," 92. Golden critiques Thomas Wiedemann, *Adults and Children in the Roman Empire.*

83. Jesus Seminar vote: grey.

84. Jesus Seminar vote: grey.

85. LSJ, 1289; Josephus, *BJ*, 8.314; 18:192–93; Philo, *Vit. Cont., 50–51.* See also Spicq, "Le vocabulaire de l'esclavage," 220–4; Westermann, *Slave Systems*, 121. See also discussion on use of term "children" in the so-called "children of the marketplace" pericope in Q (ch. 4 below).

86. MM, 474.

87. Beavis, "Slavery," 53.

88. Jesus Seminar vote: pink.

89. For a discussion of the usual interpretation of the Eunuch saying, see Brant James Pitre, "Marginal Elites: Matthew 19:12 and the Social and Political Dimensions of Becoming Eunuchs for the Sake of the Kingdom." Paper presented at the Annual Meeting of the national SBL. Boston, Mass. November 21, 1999. Pitre argues, as do I, that eunuchs were not celibate. Rather, the saying is about recommending childlessness due to a heightened sense of the coming eschaton. See also now *idem*, "Blessing the Barren and Warning the Fecund."

90. Funk and Hoover, *The Five Gospels*, 220,

91. Spencer, "The Ethoipian Eunuch and His Bible," 156–57.

92. 1 Clement 55. Text and translation by Kirsopp Lake (LCL)

93. Jesus Seminar vote: pink.

94. Jesus Seminar vote: red.

95. Jesus Seminar vote: red. On these sayings see Wink, "Neither Passivity Nor Violence," 5–28.

96. Jesus Seminar vote: grey.

97. Jesus Seminar vote: pink.

98. Jesus Seminar vote: grey.

99. Jesus Seminar vote: grey.

100. Hamel, *Poverty and Charity*, 215.

101. According to the Stoics humans were made free by God (Epictetus 4.17.16), slaves were to be treated as fully human (Seneca, *Ep* 47.18), there should be no distinction between barbarians, slaves and freemen, and the slave is able to be friends with the free (Seneca, *De Beneficiis* 3.18.2; *Ep* 31. 11). See discussion in Gibbs and Feldman, "Josephus' Vocabularly for Slavery," 281, n. 2; Manning, "Stoicism and Slavery in the Roman Empire," 1518–43; Seeley, "Rulership and Service," 234–249.

102. See above ch. 1 and Freyne, *Galilee, Jesus and the Gospels, passim.*

103. Jesus Seminar vote: pink.

104. Jesus Seminar vote: pink.

105. Jesus Seminar vote: pink.

106. See for example Schüssler Fiorenza, *In Memory of Her*, 145–46.

107. Susan Carol Rogers, "Female Forms of Power;" *idem*, "A Woman's Place," 148–49.

108. Jesus Seminar vote: black.

109. Jesus Seminar vote: pink.

110. So Koester, *Ancient Christian Gospels,* 94. See also discussion in Jacobsen, "Divided Familes," esp. 363–4.

111. Danforth, *Death Rituals*, 120.

112. I. Ellis, "Jesus and the Subversive Family," 176; Funk and Hoover, *Five Gospels*, 343.

113. Jacobsen, "Divided Families," 363; following Schüssler Fiorenza, *In Memory of Her*, 145–46.

114. See Sim, "What About the Wives and Children of the Disciples?" 373–90; Rogers, "Female Forms of Power," *passim*; *idem*, "A Woman's Place," 148–9.

115. Jesus Seminar vote: Mark 10:5–10, grey; Matt 19:3–8, grey, 19:9, black; Luke 16:18, grey; Matt 5:32, black.

116. Funk and Hoover, *Five Gospels*, 143; 219–20; R. Gundry, *Matthew*, 90; 381.

117. Against D'Angelo, "Re-Membering Jesus," 214–16. D'Angelo attributes the divorce prohibition to early Christian women prophets.

118. Luck, *Divorce and Remarriage*, 133–34; Rabello, "Divorce of Jews," 92–93.

119. Gen 1:27; 5:2. See 11QTemple 57:17–19; CD 2:14–6:1. See Fitzmyer, "Divorce Among First-Century Palestinian Jews," 103–10; *idem*, "The Matthean Divorce Texts," 197–226; Mueller, "The Temple Scroll and the Gospel Divorce Texts," 247–56.

120. See J. Collins, "Marriage, Divorce and Family," 149.

121. See chapter 1.

122. See Musonius Rufus 14; Dio Chrysostom 3.122; Lucian, *Demonax*, 9; Seneca, *Ep.* 94.26. For a discussion of Hellenistic philosophical views on marriage, see Balch, "1 Cor 7:32–35," 429–39; Downing, *Christ and the Cynics* , 139–40.

123. Jesus Seminar vote: red. See also comments by Betz, *The Sermon on the Mount*, 372.

124. Jeremias, *Abba*, 15–67; ET: *The Prayers of Jesus*, 11–65.

125. Hammerton-Kelly, *God the Father*; *idem*, "God the Father in the Bible and in the Experience of Jesus: The State of the Question," 95–102.

126. Schüssler Fiorenza, *In Memory of Her*, 145–51; Ruether, *Sexism and God-Talk*, 64–68: Schneiders, *Women and the Word*, 48–9.

127. D' Angelo, "Theology in Mark and Q," 149–74; *idem*, "*Abba* and 'Father,'" 611–30. See also critique of Jeremias by Charlesworth, "A Caveat on Textual Transmission," 1–14.

128. The use of God as Father in Jewish prayer is more common than has previously been supposed. See 4Q372 1; 3 Macc 6:3; Apoc. Ezek. frag. 3; Wis 14:3; Sir 23:1. On the biblical and Jewish precedents to the appelation of God as "father," see Charlesworth, "Caveat," 5–10; D'Angelo, "Theology in Mark and Q," 152–156; *idem*, "Abba and Father," 618–19; Deissler, "The Spirit of the Lord's Prayer," 5–6; Hammerton-Kelly, *God the Father*, 20–51; Jeremias, *Prayers of Jesus*, 11–29; McCasland, "Abba, Father," 83–84; Oesterrecher, "Abba, Father," 130–33; Eileen Schuller, *Post-Exilic Prophets*, 70–9. On 4Q372 1 and "father" in Jewish prayer, see Schuller, "4Q372 1: A Text About Joseph," 355, 362–63; *idem*, "The Psalm of 4Q372 1," 68, 71. Honi the Circle-Drawer also prayed "Father, Father, give us rain." See Charlesworth, "Caveat," 9; Vermes, *Jesus the Jew*, 211.

129. D'Angelo, "Theology in Mark and Q," 151; *idem*, "Abba and Father,"

614. See Barr, "Abba Isn't 'Daddy,'" 28–47; idem, "'Abba, Father,'" 173–79; Charlesworth, "Caveat," 5–10.

130. D'Angelo, "Theology in Mark and Q," 173–174; *idem*, "Abba and Father," 623–30.

131. D'Angelo, "Theology in Mark and Q," 174;

132. So D'Angelo, "Abba and Father," 630.

133. So D'Angelo, "Theology in Mark and Q,"159. Against Jeremias, *Prayers of Jesus*, 55–56; Oesterreicher, "Abba, Father," 121–22.

134. D"Angelo, "Abba and Father," 615.

135. D'Angelo, 'Theology in Mark and Q," 167–73; see also Kloppenborg, *The Formation of Q*, 197–203.

136. Betz, *Sermon on the Mount*, 374–75.

137. D'Angelo,"Theology in Mark and Q," 174.

138. See Corley, *Lament and Gospel.*

139. De Ward, "Mourning Customs II," 165–166; De Vaux, *Ancient Israel*, 59. For the cutting of flesh and hair, see also Job 1:20; Isa 22:21; Ezek 7:18; Amos 8:10; Jer 16:6; 41:5; 48:37.

140. 1 Sam 28:39; Deut 26:14; Hos 9:4; Amos 6:10; Jer 16:7; Ezek 24:17; Ps 106:28; 22; see also Cant 2:4; 5:1. See De Ward, "Mourning Customs II," 166; De Vaux, *Ancient Israel*, 59–60. Later Hellenistic sources probably reflect Greek tendencies (Tob 4:17; 2 Macc 12:38–46), although these customs are also native to the ancient Near East as well. See Pope, "Love and Death," *passim*; M.S. Smith, *Early History of God*, 128–29.

141. Isa 8:19; 19:3; 28:15-18; 29:4; 57:9; 65:4.

142. Jer 16:1–13; Ezek 24:15–18. Priests are directed to go only to funerals of those next of kin. See Lev 21:1–3.

143.See Corley, *Lament and Gospel*; McCane, "Let the Dead Bury Their Own Dead, 32–34.

144.Greenhut, "Burial Cave of the Caiaphas Family," 29–36; 76.

145.Ilan, *Jewish Women*, 53.

146.Jeremias, *Heiligengräber in Jesu Umwelt*, 114. Jeremias discusses over 40 cult sites in Palestine and the surrounding areas, which he views as precursors to the later Christian cult of the martyrs (5). Peter Brown also finds a similar precursor to the cult of the saints in Jewish veneration of martyrs and prophets (The *Cult of the Saints*. 3; 10; 33). See also Halliday, "Cenotaphs and Sacred Localities," 188–89; E. Meyers, *Jewish Ossuaries*, 54, n. 31; Paton, *Spiritism and the Cult of the Dead*, 238. See also ch. 4.

147. Jeremias, *Heiligengräber*, 126–41.

148. It was the purpose of Jeremias' study to confirm the historical background to the "woe" attributed to Jesus against the Pharisees for building and beautifying the tombs of the prophets and the righteous (*Heiligengräber*, 5). On Q and Jesus, see below, ch. 4.

149. See Finegan, *The Archaeology of the New Testament*, 305–10.

150. Finegan, *Archaeology*, 38–39; Jeremias, *Heiligengräber*, pl. 4.

151. L. Y. Rahmani, "Jerusalem's Tomb Monuments," *passim.*

152. Pseudo-Philo, *Bib. Ant.* 33:5. Trans. D. J. Harrington.

153. 2 Bar 85:1; 12.

154. RSV. Jesus Seminar vote on the saying "Let the dead bury their own dead": pink.

155. RSV. Jesus Seminar vote: grey.

156. Jesus Seminar vote: pink.

157. RSV. Jesus Seminar vote: black.

158. NRSV. Jesus Seminar vote: black.

159. RSV. Jesus Seminar vote: grey.

160. See overview in McCane, "Let the Dead," 38–39. He notes one exception, Robert Gundry, *Matthew*, 153–54. See also discussion in Basser, "Let the Dead Bury Their Dead," 84–85; V. Robbins, "Foxes, Birds, Burials and Furrows," 72–73.

161. McCane, "Let the Dead," 38–39.

162. Philip Sellew came to this conclusion independently of myself. See Sellew, "Death, Body, and the World," 530–34. On ancient epitaphs see Lattimore, *Themes in Greek and Latin Epitaphs*.

163. See Aristotle, *History of Animals* 7.592b; 11.615a; 30.618b–619b; Prov 30:17. On the authenticity of this saying, see Guenther, "When 'Eagles' Draw Together," 140–150.

164. Cumont, *After Life In Roman Paganism*, 65. Unfortunately this citation is made by Cumont without sources.

165. Plato, *Phaedo*, 115C.

166. See Diog. Laer., 4.52; 4.79; *Cynic Epistles*, 25; Cicero, *Tusc.* 1.104 (quoting Diogenes); Lucian, *Demon.*, 35; 66. I would like to thank David Seeley for these references.

167. See below ch. 4.

168. See below, ch. 4. I would like to thank John Kloppenborg for his remarks in this regard in a personal correspondence dated June 7, 1996.

169. See Steck, *Israel und das gewaltsame Geschick der Propheten*. See David Seeley, "Jesus' Death in Q," 223; *idem*, "Blessings and Boundaries," 135. See also Knowles, *Jeremiah in Matthew's Gospel*, 96–109; on Q see 116–17; Jacobsen, *The First Gospel*, 72–76; Kloppenborg, *Formation*, ch. 4; R. Miller, "The Rejection of the Prophets in Q," 226–33.

170. For a discussion of the Matthean emphasis on the heavenly father, see now Sheffield, "The Father in the Gospel of Matthew."

171. For Jesus as a prophet, see Mark 8:28/Matt 16:14/Luke 9:19; Matt 21:11; 21:46; Mark 6:14–15/Matt 14:1–2/Luke 9:7–9; Luke 7:16; 7:39–50; 13:33; John 4:19; 7:52; 9:17. See discussion in N.T. Wright, *Jesus and the Victory of God*, 164–65.

172. Mack, *Myth of Innocence*, 53–77.

173. The "days of Noah" warning in Q does not disparge patriarchal marriage as Luise Schottroff has suggested but reflects the ordinariness and therefore unexpected nature of the time of judgment. See Schottroff, "Itinerant Prophetesses," 349.

174. Jacobsen, "Divided Families," 361–63.

175. So A.-J. Levine, "Yeast of Eden" and in private correspondence.

Chapter 4

1. See above, ch. 3.

2. Recent articles include Batten, "More Queries for Q," 44–51; A.J. Levine, "Who's Catering the Q Affair?," 145–62; *idem*, "Yeast of Eden," 30–33; idem, "Women and the Q Communit(ies); Schottroff, "Itinerant Prophetesses: A Feminist Analysis of the Sayings Source Q," (I cite the IAC version); *idem*, "The Sayings Source Q," 510–34; Tuckett, "Feminine Wisdom in Q?", 112–28. See also recent

discussions in Schüssler Fiorenza, *Jesus, Miriam's Child* ch. 5 and Schottroff, *Let the Oppressed Go Free,* ch. 4.

3. First detailed by Schüssler Fiorenza, *In Memory of Her*, and now again in *Jesus, Miriam's Child*, 88–96. See also Borg, *Jesus a New Vision*, 133–35; *idem, Meeting Jesus* , 56; 66–67, n. 36; Corley, "Jesus' Table Practice," 444–59; Crossan, *The Historical Jesus,* 261–64; 334–35.

4. A. J. Levine, "Who's Catering;" *idem*, "Yeast of Eden;" Tuckett, "Feminine Widsom in Q?.

5. See esp. the work of E. Johnson, "Jesus, the Wisdom of God," 261–94; idem, "Redeeming the Name of Christ," 115–37; *idem*, "Wisdom Was Made Flesh," 95–117; as well as Cady, et al., *Sophia* and more recently Schüssler Fiorenza, *Jesus, Miriam's Child,* 131–62. Here she builds on her earlier work in *In Memory of Her*, 130–40. Schottroff disagrees that the character of Sophia from the Wisdom school is useful for feminist theological constructions, due to the androcentric nature of the wisdom school itself, and the problematic dichotomy created by the joint images of "Lady Folly"/"Lady Wisdom" from Prov. 1–9. Schottroff does not consider Wisdom tradition the best background for Q, but favors the prophetic tradition ("Sayings Source Q," 528–531). See discussion below.

6. Batten, "More Queries for Q," 47–48; Schottroff, "Itinerant Prophetesses," 5–8; *idem*, "Sayings Source Q," 52–54. See also Arnal, "Gendered Couplets in Q, 75–94.

7. Batten, "More Queries for Q," 49; Schottroff, "Itinerant Prophetesses," 9–10.

8. Schottroff, "Itinerant Prophetesses," 10; *idem*, "Sayings Source Q," 514.

9. Schottroff, "Itinerant Prophetesses;" "Sayings Source Q," 512–15; Schüssler Fiorenza, *Jesus, Miriam's Child*, 140–43; Wire, "Gender Roles in a Scribal Community," 119, n. 82. See also Blasi, *Early Christianity as a Social Movement*, 122–23. This assumption has been challenged, however, by Levine, "Who's Catering," 151–53; "Yeast of Eden," 27, n. 55. The reconstruction of the earliest Palestinian Jesus movement as an itinerant group of wandering charisimatics supported by local community sympathizers was suggested by Theissen, "Itinerant Radicalism," 84–93; idem, *The Sociology of Early Palestinian Christianity*. Theissen found an analogy for the early Jesus movement in the wandering philosophers of Greco-Roman Cynicism. For a critique of Theissen's reconstruction, see R. Horsley, *Sociology and the Jesus Movement*, 43–64.

10. Batten, "More Queries for Q," 47; Kloppenborg, "Literary Convention," 89–90, *idem*, "The Sayings Gospel Q," 17–18; 22. See also A. J. Levine, "Who's Catering," 147–49 and "Yeast of Eden," 26.

11. See Sim, "What About the Wives and Children," 373–90.

12. A.J. Levine, "Who's Catering," 151–53; "Yeast of Eden," 27, n. 55; "Women in the Q Communit(ies)," 157.

13. For a full discussion of the possible configurations of early missionary pairs, see D'Angelo, "Women Partners," 65–86. Jewish Christians like Priscilla and Aquila probably did not begin their itinerant life for missionary purposes, but were forced to leave Rome due to the Edict of Claudius (Acts 18:2–3). See A. J. Levine, "Yeast of Eden," 18.

14. Particularly if Q comes from Galilee. I am indebted to A.J. Levine for this remark.

15. See also ch. 5 on Mark 15:40–41. For the mobility of peasant women, see Ayrout, *The Egyptian Peasant*, 78–79, 82–83; 108; 21–22; N. Brown, *Peasant*

Politics in Modern Egypt, 34–5; Deere, *Household and Class Relations*, 109–10; 208–9; 284; Wolf, *Peasants*, 46–47. The greater mobility of lower class women also accounts for their presence in street riots during times of peasant protest. See Arouyt, *The Egyptian Peasant*, 111; Beames, *Peasants and Power*, 59; Bercé, *Revolt and Revolution*, 81–84; 107–9; Brown, *Peasant Politics*, 116–17; Frader, *Peasants and Protest*, 123; 154–57. This in fact occurred in first century Palestine. See Josephus, *AJ* 18.263, 269; *BJ* 2.192–93; Philo, *Leg.* 222–25. For a fuller discussion of the lives of peasant women, see Corley, "Jesus' Table Practice," 452–56.

16. I am indebted to conversations with A.-J. Levine for these remarks. See also Mack, "The Kingdom that Didn't Come," 623; *idem*, *The Lost Gospel*, 130. See approving remarks by Kloppenborg, "Sayings Gospel Q," 22 and the characterization of these trips as "morning walks."

17. Following the work of Kloppenborg, *The Formation of Q*, most Q scholars assume the stratigraphy of Q into at least two layers. On the connection of Q with a lower level of retainer class scribes, see also Kloppenborg, "Sayings Gospel Q," 24–28.

18. Kloppenborg's organization of Q into two distinct layers has not received wide support outside of the IAC International Q Project and in certain circles of American scholarship, although many scholars acknowledge that Q shows signs of redaction and literary organization. See Kloppenborg, "Sayings Gospel Q," 9–12. For a recent discussion of the history of scholarship on the composition of Q, see Jacobson, *The First Gospel*, ch. 3. See also Kloppenborg, *Excavating Q*, 112–65.

19. See A.J. Levine, "Who's Catering," 148–49. On scholarly disagreement on whether or not the poverty implied in Q 10 was voluntary or involuntary, see Kloppenborg, "Sayings Gospel Q," 16–18. Furthermore, as Anthony Blasi notes, the many Q sayings encouraging its audience to rely on God for sustenance are unlikely to have been fostered by the desperately poor (*Early Christianity*, 131).

20. Kloppenborg, *Formation of Q*; *idem*, "Sayings Gospel Q," 25–28. Although Kloppenborg cautions drawing naive conclusions from literary analyses ("Sayings Gospel Q," 17), he suggests that the conflicts in Q between the Jesus Movement and their opponents is "already part of an elaborated *scribal* argument," and is thus a "scribal resistance to a southern, hierarchically defined vision of Israel" (27). Horsley has challenged the separation of Q into two layers of tradition (sapiential and apocalyptic), since both genres are products of Jewish scribalism. See R. Horsley, "Wisdom Justified by All Her Children," 733–51. See also J. Z. Smith, "Wisdom and Apocalyptic," 67–87.

21. Wire, "Gender Roles in A Scribal Community," 89–94.

22. A. J. Levine, "Yeast of Eden," 20–33. The men fare no better, however. See Batten, "Queries for Q," 48.

23. Arnal, "Gendered Couplets," *passim*.

24. Arnal, "Gendered Couplets," 92.

25. Apart, that is, from the identification of wisdom with Jesus. The imagery and reflective moves, however, are similar. Rather than locating wisdom in the temple or in Torah, wisdom is located in a line of prophets, and in Jesus. Kloppenborg, "Wisdom Christology in Q," 129–37; Tuckett, "Feminine Wisdom." Here I am in basic disagreement with Schüssler Fiorenza, *Jesus, Miriam's Child*, 139–45.

26. Jacobson, *First Gospel*, 149–150; Kloppenborg, "Wisdom Christology,"143–44; *idem*, *Formation of Q*, 198–99. Schottroff's denials of the clear presence of wisdom motifs in this passage and throughout Q are not convincing. Having rejected them as wisdom motifs, she then defines them as prophetic motifs

in order to make the Q material more useful for feminist theology and reconstruction as possible prophetic traditions spoken and developed by women prophets ("Sayings Source Q," 525–26; 532).

27. Jacobson, *First Gospel*, 149–50; Kloppenborg, "Wisdom Christology," 143; *idem*, *Formation of Q*, 198–99; A.J. Levine, "Yeast of Eden," 32; Schottroff, "Sayings Source Q," 525–27.

28. Schottroff, "Sayings Source Q," 525–7. See also Wire, "Gender Roles in a Scribal Community," 89–94.

29. Schottroff, "Itinerant Prophetesses," 1–5.

30. Corley, *Private Women, Public Meals*. The "open table fellowship" of the Jesus movement is therefore not necessarily grounded in a special practice or vision of Jesus (as is suggested by Borg, *Jesus a New Vision*, Crossan, *Historical Jesus*, 261–64; Schüssler Fiorenza, *In Memory of Her*, 118–21), but may be indicative of a Greco-Roman social trend or Jewish social convention.

31. See Funk and the Jesus Seminar, *Acts of Jesus*, 66–67. For an overview of this discussion, see D. Smith, "The Historical Jesus at Table," 466–86; *idem*, "Table Fellowship and the Historical Jesus," 135–62. D. Smith argues that the association of Jesus at meals is a literary motif and presupposes enough of a social formation to render it inauthentic. See above ch. 2 on Mark 2:16. Here I follow closely my discussions in Corley, *Private Women, Public Meals*, 89–93; 130–33; 152–58. Material reused here is with the permission of Hendrickson Publishers.

32. Abrahams, "Publicans and Sinners," 54–61; Donahue, "Tax Collectors and Sinners," 39–60; Dunn, "Pharisees, Sinners and Jesus," 264–89; Farmer, "Who Are the 'Tax collectors and Sinners,'" 167–74; Gibson, "*Hoi Telonai kai hai Pornai*," 429–33; Jeremias, *Jerusalem*, ch. 14; *idem*, *New Testament Theology*, 108–12; Osborne, "Women: Sinners and Prostitutes;" Perrin, *Rediscovering*, 102–8; E. P. Sanders, *Jesus and Judaism*, 182–99; D. Smith, "The Historical Jesus at Table," 466–86; *idem*, "Table Fellowship and the Historical Jesus." See *Private Women, Public Meals*, 89–93 and D. Smith, "Historical Jesus at Table," 474–84.

33. Donahue, "Tax Collectors and Sinners," 59–61. So also R. Horsley, *Jesus and the Spiral of Violence*, 212. F. Herrenbrück has suggested that the "tax collectors" were Hellenistic tax farmers rather than Roman *publicani* or part of the Roman tax gathering system. See Herrenbrück, "Wer waren die 'Zöllner'?" 178–94.

34. Abrahams, "Publicans and Sinners;" Farmer, "Who Are the 'Tax Collectors and Sinners;'" Gibson, "*Hoi Telonai*," 430. This thesis is disputed by Herrenbrück, "Zum Vorwurf der Kollaboration des Zöllners mit Rom," 186–99. Herrenbruck suggests that the phrase "sinful tax-collectors" was coined by the Pharisees who were the social and political rivals of tax collectors.

35. Abrahams, "Publicans and Sinners," 54; Donahue, "Tax Collectors and Sinners," 52; Jeremias, *New Testament Theology*, 110–11.

36. Horsley, *Jesus and the Spiral of Violence*, 213.

37. Farmer, "Who are the Tax Collectors and Sinners," 168; Perrin, *Rediscovering*, 103. Horsley doubts that either tax or toll collectors were regarded as "sinners" or Gentiles, i.e., outside of the Jewish community (*Jesus and the Spiral of Violence*, 213–14).

38. Donahue, "Tax Collectors and Sinners."

39. Jeremias, *New Testament Theology*, 109–13. See Sanders *Jesus and Judaism*, 182–99.

40. Sanders, *Jesus and Judaism*, 177.

41. Meier, *Marginal Jew*, vol 3, 28.

42. Abrahams, "Publicans and Sinners," 55; Schüssler Fiorenza, *In Memory of Her*, 128.

43. Borg, *Jesus: A New Vision*, 129–35; *idem*, *Meeting Jesus*, 55–56; Corley, "Jesus' Table Practice"; Crossan, *Historical Jesus*, 335; Schüssler Fiorenza, *In Memory of Her*, 118–130; *Jesus, Miriam's Child*, 93–94 (she cites Alan F. Segal).

44. See esp. Fredriksen, "Did Jesus Oppose the Purity Laws?" 23; *idem*, *Jesus of Nazareth*, 67; E. P. Sanders, *Jesus and Judaism*, 182–85.

45. See above, ch. 1. This is the basis of the reconstruction presented by Schüssler Fiorenza in *In Memory of Her*, where she juxtaposes Jesus' open table praxis with "sinners" (characterized by "wholeness") to that of the Pharisee's table practice of cultic purity (characterized by "holiness") (118–22). Her discussion of Jesus' meals in *Jesus, Miriam's Child*, however, is devoid of this distinction (93–94). Borg's reconstruction mirrors Schüssler Fiorenza's original premise in his *Jesus: A New Vision*, 129–35; see also *Meeting Jesus*, 55–56 where he places Jesus within a diverse Judaism but offering "compassion" as opposed to "purity" and "holiness." This common distinction between Jesus and Judaism follows a Lutheran historiographical pattern, "Law" vs. "Grace," and uses Judaism as a negative foil (J. Z. Smith, *Drudgery*, 79–81).

46. Josephus, *AJ* 17.11.2 (304–9); *BJ* 1.25. 6 (511). See Freyne, "Geography, Politics, and Economics of Galilee," 102–3.

47. The accusation is assumed to be false. See R. Horsley, *Jesus and the Spiral of Violence*, 215–21; D. Smith, "Historical Jesus at Table," 482, 484.

48. D. Smith, "Jesus at Table," 477–79., *idem*, "Table Fellowship as a Literary Motif," 634.

49. Aeschines, *In Tim.* 117–20; Cicero, *Verr.* II.1.39.101; Dio Chrysostom, *Or.* 4.97–98; *Or.* 14.14; Lucian, *Men.* 11; Plutarch, *Mor.* 236B-C; Theophrastus, *Char.* 6.5–6; F. Hauck and S. Schultz, "*Porne, ktl*" TDNT, 6.579–95; esp. 582; Licht, *Sexual Life in Ancient Greece*, 334; V. and B. Bullough, *Prostitution*, 48; Corley, *Private Women, Public Meals*, 40–1.

50. Suetonius, *Tib.* 35; Bullough and Bullough, *Prostitution*, 48; 52–53; Corley, *Private Women, Public Meals*, 40–1, 64–65

51. See Dio Chrysostom, where these two trades are "unseemly" or "base" (*Or.* 14.14); In Lucian tax collectors are linked to pimps, adulterers, and other despised individuals (*Men.* 11). In Theophrastus, a character called "Willful Disreputableness" looks for various kinds of jobs, including innkeeping, brothel-keeping, and tax collecting (*Char.* 6). For this association in Palestine, see Gibson, "*Hoi Telonai*," 431–33.

52. *Mor.* 236C.

53. *Or.* 4.98. See Corley, *Private Women, Public Meals*, 40–1; 89–93.

54. For one examples Cicero, *Verr.* II.1.39.101; for further discussion, see Corley, *Private Women, Public Meals*, 38–48.

55. Hock, "The Will of God and Sexual Morality," 35; K. H. Rengstorf, "*Hamartolos, ktl*," 317–18. The use of *hamartolos* in inscriptions is probably not pertinent (Rengstorf, 318). For a contrary view, see Deismann, *Light From the Ancient Near East*, 113–15.

56. Rengstorf, 317. It may also have been a insulting designation for slaves (Rengstorf, 318).

57. Deismann, *Light*, 113–15.

58. *Mor. 25C,* Rengstorf, 319.

59. For full discussion, see Corley, *Private Women, Public Meals*, 121–30.

60. Dunn, "Pharisees, Sinners and Jesus," 276–80; followed by D. Smith, "Jesus at Table," 482–84. See also L. Johnson, "The New Testament's Anti-Jewish Slander," 438–39.

61. D. Smith, "Jesus at Table," 482–84; Corley, *Private Women, Public Meals*, 63–66.

62. See Charlesworth, "The Foreground of Christian Origins," 68–9; Jacob Neusner's critique of Shaye Cohen's *Judaism from the Maccabees to the Mishnah* in *Wrong Ways and Right Ways in the Study of Formative Judaism*, 141–50; and more recently Anthony Saldarini's discussion of Matthew's group (not "community") in *Matthew's Christian-Jewish Community*, 13–18; 84–123.

63. Saldarini, *Matthew*, 17.

64. Corley, *Private Women, Public Meals*, 93; Johnson, "Anti-Jewish Slander," 441; D. Smith, "Historical Jesus at Table," 486. See also Robinson, "The Jesus of Q as Liberation Theologian," 268. Thus it is highly unlikely that this tradition can be used to identify real prostitutes, sinners or tax collectors among Jesus' followers as is commonly assumed by Borg, *Jesus: A New Vision*, 130–35; *Meeting Jesus*, 55–58; Schüssler Fiorenza, *In Memory of Her*, 118–30; *Jesus, Miriam's Child*, 93–94.

65. Corley, *Private Women, Public Meals*, 40–1.

66. *Verr.* II.3.68.159–60; II.5.12.30–13.31; II.5.13.34; II.5.32.83; II.5.36.94; Corley, *Private Women, Public Meals*, 36–38; 42–53.

67. See Plummer, 'The Woman That Was a Sinner," 42–43, and Luke 15:11–32, where the Prodigal Son is similarly an example of a "sinner" who wastes his money on "loose living," which includes prostitutes. Thus Walker's suggestion that what we have here is an image of "sporter," "pimps" or "playboys" is not far from the truth, although his positing of a mispelled word to make this conclusion is unnecessary ("Jesus and the Tax Collectors," 237).

68. Vaage, *Galilean Upstarts*, 88. Ivan Havener sees this as a label given to Jesus by his opponents. See *Q: The Sayings of Jesus*, 66. Cotter and Vaage also assume this accusation reflects Jesus' actual conduct. See Cotter, "Yes, I Tell You," 147; Vaage, "More Than a Prophet," 190. Funk calls Jesus an "urban partygoer" (*Honest to Jesus*, 192).

69. D. Smith, "Historical Jesus at Table."

70. Deut 21:18–21; Prov 23:19–25; 28:7; 29:1–3. C. Brown, "The Parable of the Rebellious Son (s)," (unpublished manuscript used by permission). See also Funk, *Honest to Jesus*, 193.

71. Johnson, "Anti-Jewish Slander," 441. D. Smith, suggests that the most it might suggest is that Jesus is not ascetic ("Jesus at Table," 486). See also comments by Horsley, *Jesus and the Spiral of Violence*, 215; Hartin, "Yet Wisdom is Justified by her Children," 154.

72. Vaage sees this accusation of demon possession against John as similar to insults leveled by philosophers against other philosophers, but does not consider a similar origin for the insult against Jesus. See Vaage, "More Than a Prophet," 191.

73. Kloppenborg, *Formation of Q*, 111; Robinson critiques Vaage in a similar manner ("Jesus of Q a Liberation Theologian," 268–69). See also Horsley, *Jesus and the Spiral of Violence*, 215.

74. Corley, *Private Women, Public Meals*, 24–77.

75. Johnson, "Anti-Jewish Slander," 431–32; Corley, *Private Women, Public Meals*, 63–65.

76. See the Cynic Epistles, esp. the Letters of Crates addressed to Hipparchia. In Lucian's *Fugitivi*, a woman Cynic leaves her husband and runs away

with two of her slaves. See Downing, *Jesus and the Threat of Freedom*, 115–21, *idem*, *Christ and the Cynics*, 1–5.

77. Meeks, "The Images of the Androgyne," 172.

78. Catherine J. Castner, "Epicurean Hetairai," 51–57; D. Smith, "Social Obligation," 57.

79. William Klassen, "Musonius Rufus, Jesus and Paul," 185–206. See also Motto, "Seneca on Women's Liberation," 155–57 for Seneca's encouragement of women to follow Stoic discipline, and comments by Wicker, "Mulierum Virtutes," 114.

80. Johnson, Anti-Jewish Slander," 431; Corley, *Private Women, Public Meals*, 63–66.

81. Balch, *Let Wives Be Submissive*, chs. 5–6. See also Corley, *Private Women, Public Meals*, 64–65.

82. Corley, *Private Women, Public Meals*, 64–65.

83. Even in this instance, however, the problems with neat stratification of Q are evident. For example, in spite of the fact that most Q scholars would place this passage from Q in "Q2," Leif Vaage puts it in Q1 because it can be construed to fit his thesis about the Cynic nature of the formative layer of Q (Vaage, *Galilean Upstarts*, 87–90). On the usual assignment of 7:34 to the second redactional layer of Q, see Kloppenborg, *Formation of Q*, 110–12; Jacobson, *The First Gospel*, 120–23.

84. Kloppenborg, "The Sayings Gospel Q," 27–28.

85. And also at the time of Jesus. See ch. 3 on Jesus' repetition of the slander that he consorted with "tax collectors and prostitutes." For this reason Dennis Smith considers this tradition unhistorical and not useful for reconstructions of the "Historical Jesus." Corley, *Private Women, Public Meals*, 64–65; 89–93; Dunn, "Pharisees, Sinners and Jesus," 276–80; D. Smith, "Jesus at Table," 482, 484. For D. Smith's views, see above, ch. 2 on Mark 2:16.

86. Jerome, *Dial. Adv. Pelag.* 3, 2. See Jeremias, *Jerusalem*, 375–76; Levine, "Yeast of Eden," 18.

87. See survey Kloppenborg in *Q Parallels*, 58–59. In discussions of the International Q Project, William Arnal has defended the inclusion of some form of Lk 7:29–30 in Q, including the reference to πορναι ("Reconstruction of Q 7:29–30." Arnal came to this decision independently of my comments in *Private Women, Public Meals*, 130–133; 152–158. He rates his decision with a {C}. Five initial reponses have been given to Arnal's thesis: Hartin, "First Response: Q 7:29–30" (Q included some form of 7:29–30, rating {C}; that it included a reference to "prostitutes," undecided); S.R. Johnson, "Second Response: Q 7:29–30" (Q included some form of 7:29–30, rating {C}, including a reference to "prostitutes," rating {B}); Robinson, "Q 7:29–30: Third Response" (Q included some form of 7:29–30, including reference to "prostitutes," rating {C}); Hoffmann, "Q 7:29–30: Fourth Response" (Q did not include any form of 7:29–30, rating {C}); Robinson, "Luke 7:29–30/Matt 21:31b–32" (Q did not include any form of 7:29–30, rating {C}–following Hoffmann). Robinson later reversed his position following Arnal at the November 1996 meeting of the IQP. The published *Critical Edition of Q* prints Q 7:29–30, but omits the reference to πόρναι and indicates the uncertainty of its inclusion. Hoffmann still registers his view that Q 7:29–30 was not part of Q. Robinson, et al., *Critical Edition of Q*, 138–39. All papers of the International Q Project are used with permission.

88. The International Q Project voted against Arnal's reconstruction of Q 7:29–30 in May 1994. The vote was revised in November 1996, but the question of

the inclusion of πόρναι in Q 7 was not readdressed. Inclusion of 7:29–30 was rated a {D}. The question of presence of πόρναι in the periocope was not addressed. See also Cameron, "What Have You Come Out to See?," 35–69, esp. 40–41; Gundry, *Matthew*, 422–23; Kloppenborg does not include this pericope in Q 7 (*Formation of Q*); but see remarks by Bultmann, *History of the Synoptic Tradition*, 177. Until Arnal pushed the question of including "prostitutes" in Q 7 (along with the "tax collectors" in opposition to John the Baptist), it had been assumed from the first draft of "Pap Q" (prepared by Jon Daniels in 1986) that 7:29–30 contained minimal Q, particularly a reference to John the Baptist and "tax collectors." This was assumed in all subsequent preliminary drafts of critical texts of Q prepared by the International Q Project until May 1994.

89. Gundry, *Matthew*, 211; Schweizer, *Matthew*, 410.

90. Both James M. Robinson and Paul Hoffmann in their initial responses to Arnal's reconstruction of Q 7:29–30 show their inattention to the function of images of gender and class in these texts, not only in Q 7 but in ancient literature overall. Once the gendered nature of ἁμαρτολοί and παιδία are recognised, then the obvious thematic correspondences between Lk 7:29/Mt 21:31–32 become clear. This accusation against Jesus hinges on negative images involving sexuality and gender, not purity (as Hoffmann assumes, "Q 7:29–30: Fourth Response," 6).

91. So Hoffmann, "Q 7:29–30: Fourth Response," esp. 5–8.

92. See below, against Hoffmann, "Q 7:29–30: Fourth Response," 3.

93. Thus Hoffmann's misses the point that the issue here in Q 7 is also John's lifestyle, not just his preaching ("Q 7:29–30: Fourth Response," 3).

94. Kloppenborg, "Social History of the Q People," 100–1; *idem*, "Sayings Gospel Q," 17, 27.

95. Proverbs 1–9. See Schottroff, "Sayings Source Q," 528–31.

96. Text and translation found in Kloppenborg, *Q Parallels*, 109.

97. Crossan, *Historical Jesus*, 261–64; 335; see also Corley,"Were the Women Around Jesus Really Prostitutes?" 466–86; *idem*, "Jesus' Table Practice," *passim*.

98. See Barbara Ehrenreich's discussion of the term "bitch," in "A Term of Honor," 64. The use of the title *Lilith* for the Jewish feminist journal serves a similar function, implying that the Jewish women writing for this journal want to be associated with the figure of Lilith (Adam's first wife in midrashic tradition who left him because he wouldn't treat her like an equal and who is subsequently turned into a demon and cast into the abyss).

99. Here I will follow the basic arguments presented in Arnal, "Reconstruction of Q 7:29–30."

100. So Hoffmann, "Q 7:29–30: Fourth Response," 4, 7–8.

101. Fully admitted by Arnal, "Reconstruction of Q 7:29–30," 11. Hoffmann (Q 7:29–30: Fourth Response") argues that the redactional work of the evangelists more than accounts for much of Luke 7:29/Matt 21:31–32. The rest he argues comes from a common "oral topos" in the Jesus tradition. See below.

102. For distinctions among prostitutes in antiquity, see Corley, *Private Women, Public Meals*, 46–47. For the many euphemisms for "whore" see Licht, *Sexual Life in Ancient Greece* , 330–32. Licht considers *porne* the most coarse.

103. I.e., "the most difficult reading." If not in Q, Matt 21:31–32 certainly contains a most ancient tradition. Hoffmann, "Q 7:29–30: Fourth Response," 4; Schottroff, *Let the Oppressed Go Free*, 97.

104. The similar story elements between Luke's version of the anointing (Lk 7:36–50) and Mark's (Mk 14:3–9) are too numerous. That Luke is dependent on

Mark is the best explanation for the many unlikely coincidences between them. See Gundry, *Mark*, 810 and Mack, "The Anointing of Jesus," 90; Corley, "The Anointing of Jesus in the Synoptic Tradition," 2–3.

105. Corley, *Private Women, Public Meals*, 121–33.

106. Corley, *Private Women, Public Meals*, 124; for the many colorful euphemisms for prostitute in antquity, see Licht, *Sexual Life in Ancient Greece*, 330–32.

107. Hoffmann, "Q 7:29–31: Fourth Response," 8; Robinson, "Luke 7:29–30//Matt 21:31b–32," 3.

108. Hoffmann, "Q 7:29–30: Fourth Response," 8.

109. Corley, *Private Women, Public Meals*, 108–46.

110. See full discussion in Corley, *Private Women, Public Meals*, 121–30.

111. Robinson misses the difference between the accusation of Lk 5:30 and the narrative portrayal in Lk 5:29 ("Q 7:29–30: Third Response," 5). See Corley *Private Women, Public Meals*, 131. Thus, the term "sinners" appears only in the dialogue between Jesus and the scribes and Pharisees (5:30, 32) and not in the narrative as in Mark 2:15.

112. Corley, *Private Women, Public Meals*, 108–46.

113. In Mark there is no hint that the woman is not respectable. Luke brings these tensions out, but Mark seems unaware of them. See Corley, *Private Women, Public Meals*, 102–6.

114. Hoffmann, "Q 7:29–30: Fourth Response," 8; Robinson, "Lk 7:29–30//Matt 21:31b–32," 3.

115. Corley, *Private Women, Public Meals*, 125–26.

116. Hoffmann, "Q 7:29–30: Fourth Response," 7–8.

117. The reading of Luke as the "gospel to the poor and the marginalized" is primarily a modern scholarly construction. See Buchanan, "Jesus and the Upper Class," 195–209. J. Green, "Good News to Whom?," 59–74; Judge, "The Early Christians as a Scholastic Community," 4–15.

118. Corley, *Private Women, Public Meals*, 127–30.

119. Q 7:32: "we wailed (θρηνέω) and you did not weep (κλαίω).

120. Corley, *Private Women, Public Meals*, 131–132; 156–157.

121. Acknowledged by Hoffmann, "Q 7:29–30: Fourth Response," 5. Here some attention to issues of gender in Matthew could support Hoffmann's argument. On the women in Matthew's genealogy (including "Rahab the Harlot") see Corley, *Private Women, Public Meals*, 147–52.

122. Hoffmann,"Q 7:29–30: Fourth Response," 4, 6. So also Schüssler Fiorenza, *In Memory of Her*, 127.

123. Even Matt 25:1–13 (the parable of the "Ten Virgins") may be another version of the parable of the "Closed Door" (Luke 13:22–28). Even if the "Ten Virgins" parable is special Matthew, virgins are not whores. On Luke's interest in women, see Corley, *Private Women, Public Meals*, 108–9. On the women in Matthew's genealogy, see *Private Women, Public Meals*, 147–52.

124. For example, Luke 6:24–26; 11:5–8; 11:27–28; 12:35–38; 15:8–10; 17:20–21.

125. As does Hoffmann, "Q 7:29–30: Fourth Response," 4.

126. Gundry, *Matthew*, 423–24; Schweizer, *Matthew*, 410.

127. ὁδῷ (cf. Q 7:27) and ἦλθεν γάρ Ἰωάννης (cf. Q 7:33). Arnal, "Reconstruction of Q 7:29–30," 12.

128. Robinson, "Luke 7:29–30/Matt 21:31–32," 2.

129. *Ibid.*

130. Hoffmann, "Q 7:29–30: Fourth Response," 4. If Matt 21:31 originated in Q, then the Q redactor would have ample "motivation" to develop Luke 7:29/Matt 21:32. Such a vulgar epithet on the lips of Jesus would merit explanation (against Hoffmann, "Q 7:29–30: Fourth Response," 4).

131. Matt 21:28–31a is only superficially linked to Matt 21:31b–32; see Hoffmann, "Q 7:29–30: Fourth Response," 5 (citing Wellhausen).

132. Arnal also notes that the use of the term *τέκνα* in Matt 21:28–31a may also be a "Matthean reminiscence" of the original Q association in the "Children of the Marketplace" pericope preserved in Luke (cf. Luke 7:35/Matt 11:19) ("Reconstruction of Q 7:29–30," 5).

133. Luke lists the positive reaction to the Baptist first in Luke 7:29 (see Hoffmann, "Q 7:29–30: Fourth Response," 2). The seemingly fixed order of responses in Matt 21:32 weakens this discrepancy as an argument against placing this pericope in Q.

134. Corley, *Private Women, Public Meals*, 153–55.

135. This is of course the most obvious in Matthew, since he retains the term *πόρνη* in Matt 21:31–32. See Corley, *Private Women, Public Meals*, 152–58.

136. Robinson, "The Q Trajectory," 173–94.

137. This would also reinforce Ron Cameron's suggestion that Jesus and John are characterized as Cynics in Q 7, in that Cynics were known to have women, particularly so-called "prostitutes" in their circles ("Characterizations," 60). For women and Greco-Roman Cynicism, see Corley, *Private Women, Public Meals*, 63–65, esp. 63, n. 230.

138. Corley, *Private Women, Public Meals*, 160–64.

139. So Hoffmann, "Q 7:29–30: Fourth Response," esp. 4–5.

140. Jacobson, *The First Gospel*, 72–76; Kloppenborg, *Formation of Q*, ch. 4; idem., *Excavating Q*, 121.

141. Seeley, "Blessings and Boundaries," 139–41.

142. Deut 21:18–21; Prov 23:19–25; 28:7; 29:1–3. C. Brown, "The Parable of the Rebellious Son (s)," (unpublished manuscript used by permission).

143. See section entitled "The Deuteronomistic History," by Laffey, *An Introduction to the Old Testament*, 71–143; as well as chapters on Deuteronomy (by Tikva Frymer-Kensky), Joshua and Judges (by Danna Nolan Fewell), 1 and 2 Samuel (by Jo Ann Hackett) and 1 and 2 Kings (by Claudia V. Camp) in the *Woman's Bible Commentary*.

144. Camp, *Wise, Strange, and Holy*, 308–10; Fewell, "Joshua," 66; Laffey, *Introduction*, 85–89.

145. Camp, "1 and 2 Kings," 102. Camp notes that in Kings the Queen of Sheba is a representative of Lady Wisdom cast in narrative form. See also Camp, *Wise, Strange and Holy*, 148.

146. Camp, "1 and 2 Kings," 109; Laffey, *Introduction*, 139–42.

147. Other sexually suspect women were also admired for their roles in the history of Israel. See especially A. T. Hanson, "Rahab the Harlot in Early Christian Tradition," 53–60; as well as Amaru, "Portraits of Biblical Women in Josephus' Antiquities," 143–70; Bird, "The Harlot as Heroine," 119–39; Bronner, *From Eve to Esther*, 142–62; For further discussion of the sexually suspect women of Jewish tradition found in Matthew's genealogy, see Corley, *Private Women, Public Meals*, 147–52.

148. Lassner, *Demonizing the Queen of Sheba*; Silberman, "The Queen of Sheba

in Judaic Tradition," and Watson, "The Queen of Sheba in Christian Tradition," both in Pritchard, ed. *Solomon and Sheba*, 65–84; 115–51. On the historical Queen Sheba (Makeda) of Ethiopia, see L. Williams and Finch, "The Great Queens of Ethiopia," in *Black Women in Antiquity*, 16–20. See also Schüssler Fiorenza, *But She Said*, 196, 250, n. 3.

149. The first designation found in Patristic literature is of course based on the gospels, namely Q. See Watson, "Queen of Sheba in Christian Tradition," 116–17.

150. Corley, *Private Women, Public Meals*, 147–52.

151. See also 1 Clement 12 who extols Rahab the Harlot for her faith and hospitality.

152. Thomas 105. See translation and notes by M. Meyer, *The Gospel of Thomas*, 106.

153. See n. 98.

154. For ample examples of this stereotype outside of Jewish literature in Greco-Roman antiquity, see Corley, *Private Women, Public Meals*, 3–79. The prostitute and unfaithful wife is the classic example from prophetic literature (Hosea). "Dame Folly" is of course the anti-type to "Dame Wisdom" in Proverbs 1–9. Other Wisdom writers repeat these stereotypes. See for example, Trenchard's discussion of views of women in Ben Sira, which include "Women as Good Wife," "Mother and Widow," on the one hand and "Women as Bad Wife," "Adulteress and Prostitute" on the other *Ben Sira's View of Women*. For a discussion of this theme in elsewhere in Hellenistic Judaism, particularly Philo, see Corley, *Private Women, Public Meals*, 66–75. It is for this very reason that Schottroff objects to finding Wisdom traditions in Q and rejects the image of "Lady Wisdom" as beneficial for feminist theological constructions ("Saying Source Q," 525–27).

155. Torjesen, *When Women Were Priests*, 142

156. See above, ch. 1.

157. So A. -J. Levine, "Yeast of Eden," 29–32. On the notion that the divorce prohibition of Jesus was anti-patriarchal ethic assuming the notion of "equal partnership," see Schüssler Fiorenza, *In Memory of Her*, 143–45. For scholars who place this prohibition of divorce against a negative Jewish framework, see Borg, *Meeting Jesus*, 57; Crossan, *Historical Jesus*, 301–2. Kloppenborg also assumes the denial of women's divorce rights in "Alms, Debt and Divorce," 182–200.

158. See helpful remarks by Kloppenborg, "Alms, Debt and Divorce," 193–94.

159. See for example, my discussion of Philo's description and defense of the mixed dining among the Therapeutae in Corley, *Private Women, Public Meals*, 70–72 and other remarks by Torjesen, *When Women Were Priests*, 143–44.

160. So A. -J. Levine writes, "Q may represent a community externally reviled and internally confused . . . This group needed order. And it found this order within its own ranks. The Q community defined and maintained itself by controlling the one group within its power, women" ("Yeast of Eden," 32).

161. Kloppenborg was the first to correct this misunderstanding of the "two on a bed." See "Symbolic Eschatology and the Apocalypticism of Q," 302, n. 57. I was unaware of this reference when I wrote *Private Women, Public Meals* (117–18). That this saying refers to a dining couch, and not a bed has long been understood by scholars of the Gospel of Thomas, since it occurs there in Saying 61 where Salome and Jesus recline on a couch for a meal. See Patterson, *The Gospel of Thomas and Jesus*, 46–47; M. Meyer, *Gospel of Thomas*, 93–94 and Ron Cameron's forthcom-

ing Hermeneia commentary on the Gospel of Thomas. The International Q Project has voted the Lukan version of this saying as Q (cf. Matt 24:40–42 which has two men in a field). See Asgeirsson and Robinson, "The International Q Project: Work Sessions 12–14 July 22, November 1991," 508. See also critique of Q 17:34–35 by A. J. Levine, "Yeast of Eden," 23–24. The Lukan version probably preserves Q. See Jefford, "The Dangers of Lying in Bed," 106–10.

162. Crossan has suggested that the Feast parable challenges both rank and gender: Crossan, *Historical Jesus*, 261–64; 335. But see critique of Crossan by A. J. Levine, "Yeast of Eden," 22–26. Levine argues that if Jesus denied all forms of Jewish dietary rituals and roles for women, he here coopts women's roles and "strips women of a point of honor." See above on Mark 15:40–41, ch. 2. I argue that Jesus coopts the role of the slave, which could include women, but would not be restricted to women (as food servers, preparers, etc.).

163. Schüssler Fiorenza, *In Memory of Her*, 119; Kloppenborg, *Formation of Q*, 111; Robinson, "The Jesus of Q as Liberation Theologian," 268–69, esp. n. 61.

164. Jacobson admits that this correspondence is somewhat clumsy. Another interpretation is that the "piping" and "mourning" activities do not correspond to Jesus and John's, but to those of "this generation." See Jacobson, *The First Gospel*, 123, esp. n. 183 as well as Kloppenborg, *Formation of Q*, 111. Cotter argues that it is "this generation" that does the calling in "Parable of the Children in the Marketplace," 295.

165. Matthew's *ἔργα* "deeds" (Matt 11:19) is undoubtedly secondary. See Kloppenborg, *Formation of Q*, 110; idem. *Excavating Q*, 123; 126; Jacobson, *The First Gospel*, 124.

166. Hartin, "Yet Wisdom is Justified by Her Children," 155; Jacobson, *The First Gospel*, 123–25; Kloppenborg, *Formation of Q*, 111; Cotter also argues that Jesus and John are the "children of Wisdom" ("Parable of the Children," 303; idem. "Yes, I Tell You," 146).

167. Corley, *Private Women, Public Meals*, 121–30.

168. Cotter, "Parable of the Children." Cotter focuses on the possible connotations of the phrase *τοῖς ἐν ἀγορᾷ καθεμένοις* and argues that these children (who are equated with "this generation") are sitting in judgment of their peers (as if they were adults), but their youth exposes the self-righteousness of their behavior ("Parable of the Children," 299–302). See also Cotter, "Yes, I Tell you," 146–47.

169. See above, ch. 4; Corley, *Private Women, Public Meals*, 48–49; 128–30; 153, esp. n. 26. Even poorer families hired at least two flute players and one woman mourner for funerals. See Matt 9:23; *b. Ketub.* 46b; Gundry, *Matthew*, 175; Lachs, *A Rabbinic Commentary on the New Testament*, 172.

170. Meltzer, *Slavery*, 72–75; Garlan, *Slavery in Ancient Greece*, 62, 68, 70; Ingram, *A History of Slavery and Serfdom*, 21. See discussion in Corley, *Private Women, Public Meals*, 48–49.

171. Found in Tomb II at Marissa. See Finegan, *Archaeology*, 301–5; Goodenough, *Jewish Symbols*, vol. 3, pl. 14.

172. For further discussion see Golden, "*Pais*, 'Child' and 'Slave,'" 91–104; G. H. R. Horsley, "paidarion," 87.

173. Men were also fluteplayers and musicians, but women more often fulfilled this role. Corley, *Private Women, Public Meals*, 26–28; 48–49.

174. See below, ch. 5. For mourners in the gospels, see for example Matt 9:23 (fluteplayers) and Lk 23:27 (the "daughters of Jerusalem" who mourn the death of Jesus).

175. Corley, *Private Women, Public Meals*, 26–28; 48–49; Starr, "An Evening with the Flute-girls," 401–10; on the connection between flute-players and the term πόρνη see also BAGD, 700.

176. Corley, *Private Women, Public Meals*, 48–49, 128–30; 153, n. 26; see discussion above.

177. Corley, *Private Women, Public Meals*, 26–27; 48–49; 153, n. 26

178. This Widsom saying therefore may have circulated independently, and was attached to this cluster at some compositional stage of Q. Kloppenborg, *Formation of Q*, 110–11. Jacobson argues the opposite (*The First Gospel*, 124). However, the possibility that the term τέκνα (v. 34) interprets παιδίοις (v. 32) in a way inconsistent with the sense of the parable itself is an argument in favor of Kloppenborg's position.

179. A. -J. Levine ignores the possibility that some of the "children" could be girls ("Yeast of Eden," 27, n. 54). A. -J. Levine cites Arthur Dewey to support the notion that the distinction between male and female slaves in other Q passages is Lukan (Dewey, "A Prophetic Pronouncement," 100). However, that both men and women are portrayed as slaves in various household contexts and service capacities can hardly be attribited merely to Luke. See LSJ, 1287. It must be admitted that children could be assigned household roles similar to those as slaves, both in fields and at meals (Golden, "*Pais*, 'Child' and 'Slave," 98–99) but this does not seem to have included participation in musical entertainment.

180. Earlier scholars suggested the contrast was weddings and funerals. See Linton, "Parable of the Children's Game," 174.

181. See below. There is therefore no "tension" between John and "tax collectors" in Q as Hoffmann suggests (juxtaposing Q7:27 to Q 7:33–35, "Q 7:29–30: Fourth Response," 3–4). "Tax Collectors" along with the "children of wisdom" are among the "envoys of Wisdom," and are not to be equated with "this generation."

182. Kloppenborg, *Formation of Q*, 107. See also Linton, "The Parable of the Children's Game," 171–175 for comments on earlier discussions.

183. Jacobsen, *The First Gospel*, 122–23. Jacobson admits that this correspondence is somewhat clumsy. Another interpretation is that the "piping" and "mourning" activities do not correspond to Jesus and John's, but to those of "this generation." See Jacobson, *The First Gospel*, 123, esp. n. 183 as well as Kloppenborg, *Formation of Q*, 111. Cotter argues that it is "this generation" that does the calling ("Parable of the Children," 295).

184. See Olof Linton, "Parable of the Children's Game," 162; 173.

185. See discussion of past scholarship in Linton, "Parable of the Children's Game," 162.

186. The occurrence of a similar theme in Neh 9:26 makes it impossible to rule out Jesus' knowledge of the notion of the "killing of the prophets." See above, ch. 3.

187. O. H. Steck has argued that by the first century C.E. two views came together in prophetic thought: 1) the Deuteronomic view of history which assumed that God's judgment was precipitated by Israel's disobedience to God's law and 2) the notion that prophets were habitually killed by Israel (c. Neh 9:26). See O. H. Steck, *Israel und das gewaltsame Geschick der Propheten*. See also Seeley, "Jesus' Death in Q," 223; *idem*, "Blessings and Boundaries," 135. See also Knowles, *Jeremiah in Matthew's Gospel*, 96–109; on Q see 116–17; Jacobsen, *The First Gospel*, 72–76; Kloppenborg, *Formation*, ch. 4; R. Miller, "The Rejection of the Prophets in Q," 226–33.

188. Kloppenborg, *Formation*, 141–42; Seeley, "Blessings and Boundaries," 141. R. Miller comments that the logic of Q breaks down at this point ("The Rejection of the Prophets," 230).

189. Jeremias, *Heiligengräber*, 114. Jeremias discusses over 40 cult sites in Palestine and the surrounding areas, which he views as precursors to the later Christian cult of the martyrs (5). Peter Brown also finds a similar precursor to the cult of the saints in Jewish veneration of martyrs and prophets (*Cult of the Saints*, 3; 10; 33). See also Halliday, "Cenotaphs," 188–89; Meyers, *Jewish Ossuaries*, 54, n. 31; Paton, *Spiritism*, 238.

190. Jeremias, *Heiligengräber*, 126–41.

191. It was the purpose of Jeremias' study to confirm the historical background to the "woe" attributed to Jesus against the Pharisees for building and beautifying the tombs of the prophets and the righteous (*Heiligengräber*, 5). On Q and Jesus, see below.

192. See Finegan, *The Archaeology of the New Testament*, 305–10.

193. Finegan, *Archaeology*, 38–39; Jeremias, *Heiligengräber*, pl. 4.

194. Sered, *Women as Ritual Experts*, 114–20.

195. Rahmani, "Jerusalem's Tomb Monuments."

196. 2 Macc 12:43–45; 15:12–16. Jeremias discusses Jewish belief in intercessory prayers of the dead, *Heiligengräber*, 126–29. See also the prayers to the "fathers" at the graves of the Patriarchs in *b. Sotah* 34b and translation of Enoch to the dwelling place of the ancestors in 1 Enoch 70:4.

197. 2 Bar 85:1, 12.

198. See above ch. 3.

199. J. Z. Smith, *Drudgery Divine*, 142–43.

200. See below, ch.5.

201. For the identification of God as Father in Q, see D' Angelo, "Theology in Mark and Q," 162–173; *idem*, "Abba and "Father," 628–30. For further on Jesus' address to God as "Father," see above, ch. 3.

202. See above ch. 3. I would like to thank John Kloppenborg for his remarks in this regard in a personal correspondence dated June 7, 1996. Steck's research also shows the ready availability of this motif in Palestinian Judaism between 200 BCE and 100 CE. See Steck, *Israel*, 189. For a summary of Steck's conclusions, see Knowles, *Jeremiah in Matthew's Gospel*, 101–102.

203. See below, ch.5.

204. Fiorenza, *In Memory of Her*, 119; Kloppenborg, *Formation of Q*, 111; Robinson, "The Jesus of Q as Liberation Theologian," 268–69, esp. n. 61.

205. Mark 5:21–43; Luke 8:40–56; Matt 9:18–26; Luke 7:11–17; John 11:17.

206. The dismissal of women mourners from death scenes, however, is a common literary motif in portrayals of "noble deaths" of heros and philosophers. See below, ch. 5.

207. Probably at ordinary funerals of other Jewish Christians. See below, ch. 5.

208. Fitzmyer, *Luke*, 2. 1033–35; Jacobsen, *First Gospel*, 209–13; Kloppenborg, *Formation*, 227–29; Schüssler Fiorenza, *Miriam's Child*, 140–41.

209. So Knowles, *Jeremiah in Matthew's Gospel*," 143; Miller, "Rejection," 234; Steck, *Israel*, 227–28.

210. See below, ch. 5.

211. D. Jacobs-Malina notices the similarities of the "Lament of Jersualem"

to women's laments, but attributes this lament to Jesus himself. For Jacob-Malina, Jesus is using a woman's oral genre in his proclamation (D. Jacobs-Malina, *Beyond Patriarchy*, 56–57; see also 43–44.

212. Ps 117:26 LXX. Jacobsen, *First Gospel*, 209–13; Kloppenborg, *Formation*, 227–9; Miller, "Rejection of the Prophets," 234–35.

213. Dobbs-Allsopp, *Weep, O Daughter of Zion*. Dobbs-Allsopp compares the City-Lament genre to other Greek lament antecedents. See esp. 10–29; 157–63. For other biblical precendents, see Psalm 137 and Lam 1:22; 4:21–22; Jeremiah 50–51.

214. See Jer 9:16–19; Ezek 32:16; and Goitein, "Women as Creators," 24–26.

215. On the basis of Psalm 137, Lam 1:22; 4:21–22; Jeremiah 50–51. Dobbs-Allsopp, *Weep, O Daughter of Zion*, 162: Goitein makes similar observations, "Women as Creators," 26–27. For other reapplication's of Deuteronomic motifs of God's retaliation against Israel and Judah by means of the destruction of Jerusalem, see discussions of Second Temple Jewish texts and Rabbinic literature by Knowles, *Jeremiah in Matthew's Gospel*, 96–109.

216. See above, ch. 1 and Ilan, *Jewish Women*, 190–204. Jacobs-Malina suggests the similarities between the "woes" of the Pharisees and women's lamentation and assumes that Jesus himself is using a women's oral genre in his teaching (*Beyond Patriarchy*, 43–44; 56–57).

217. Fitzmyer, *Luke*, 2.1037; Str.-B. 1.850.

218. Steck, *Israel*, 219. See summary of Steck's work by Knowles, *Jeremiah in Matthew's Gospel*, 109.

219. See above, ch. 3.

220. See below, ch. 5.

221. Theissen, "Itinerant Radicals;" *Sociology of Early Palestinian Christianity*. See also Goitein, "Women as Creators," 2; 29–30.

222. See ch. 3. So also Burton Mack, *Who Wrote the New Testament?* 40. Matthew's rendition of this section from Q makes the prophetic identification even clearer (Matt 23:1–36). Seeley has already suggested a similar shift in the redaction of Q 7:31–35 from a Cynic ethic to a prophetic theme ("Blessings and Boundaries," 145). Seeley has also argued that Q 14:27 reflects a Cynic-Stoic understanding of Jesus' death in Q ("Jesus' Death in Q," 224–34).

223. See above, ch. 3.

224. See above, ch. 3.

225. The Jesus Seminar voted the "Marketplace" parable grey, but consider it confirming Jesus' practice of "wine bibbing and gluttony" as it does in Q. See *Five Gospels*, 302–3.

226. See Corley, *Private Women, Public Meals*.

Chapter 5

1. Young, *Anthology*, xxi.

2. Alexiou, *Ritual Lament in Greek Tradition*; Holst-Warhaft, *Dangerous Voices*; Garland, *The Greek Way of Death*.

3. Alexiou, *Ritual Lament*, 4–7; 27; Garland, *Greek Way*, 23–24

4. Garland, *Greek Way*, 30.

5. Garland, *Greek Way*, 30.

6. Garland, *Greek Way*, 30.

7. Alexiou, *Ritual Lament*, 4–7; 10–14; 29–31; Holst-Warhaft, *Dangerous Voices*, 105–14; Garland, *Greek Way*, 25–37.

8. Alexiou, *Ritual Lament,* 7–10; 32–33; Garland, *Greek Way*, 104–20. The internment could also be done on the third day following a death (Rush, *Death and Burial in Christian Antiquity* , 150–1).

9. Holst-Warhaft, *Dangerous Voices* 103–14.

10. Holst-Warhaft, *Dangerous Voices, ibid.* See also Loraux, *The Experiences of Tiresias.* Thus, in Homer, in order to show true manliness or courage (*andreia*) a warrior must exhibit characteristics culturally coded as feminine, and then transcend them. "Or to put it another way, fear can be transcended, but without fear there is no epic" (Loraux, 75). In Plato's ideal state, however, stories of men's grief are to be attributed to women and poets should not be allowed to portray the gods as weeping or lamenting (*Republic* 387B–388C).

11. Garland, *Greek Way*, 29.

12. Garland, *Greek Way*, 33.

13. As we have seen, these professionals were also often slaves, as owners sent their domestic servants out into the marketplace to look for work on off days. Slave women could also be fluteplayers, but male fluteplayers are often shown in funeral contexts as well. Slaves and professionals hired for banquets would come from the same social class. Corley, *Private Women, Public Meals*, 48–9, 129–30, 153. Matthew mentions a group of fluteplayers (*τοὺς αὐλετάς*) in 9:23, but in Greek the masculine plural does not exclude the possibility that the group of professional mourners was mixed (correction to *Private Women, Public Meals*, 153; see Barbara Butler Miller, "Women, Death, and Mourning in the Ancient Eastern Mediterranean," (Ph.D. Diss., Univ. of Michigan, Ann Arbor, 1994), 61–62.

14. Alexiou, *Ritual Lament,* 108–109; *Dangerous Voices*, 131–33.

15. Garland, *Greek Way*, 110–15.

16. See J. Z. Smith, *Drudgery Divine*, 132: "The dead remain dead, in a sphere other than the living; but there is contact, there is continuity of relationship, there is memorialization, there is presence."

17. Garland, *Greek Way*, 34–35. Ian Morris suggests that inhumation may also have been practiced concurrently with cremation. Cremation has generally been considered a "Greek custom," and was so labeled in antiquity. See Morris, *Death Ritual and Social Structure in Classical Antiquity*, 52–69.

18. Although the best evidence comes from Athens, funerary legislation was also enacted in Ioulis on the island of Keos, at Delphi and Sparta, Nisyrus in the Sporades, Gortyn in Crete, Gambreion and Myltilene in Asia Minor, Cyrene in Libya, and Catana and Syracuse in Sicily. For a complete discussion of all of the pertinent legislation, see Robert Garland, "The Well-Ordered Corpse: An Investigation Into the Motives Behind Greek Funerary Legislation," *Bulletin for the Institute for Classical Studies* 36 (1989) 1–15. See also Alexiou, *Ritual Lament,* 14–23; Holst-Warhaft, *Dangerous Voices,* 114; Garland, *Greek Way*, 29–30.

19. Alexiou, *Ritual Lament,* 21; Holst-Warhaft, *Dangerous Voices,* 114–15; Garland, "Well-Ordered Corpse," 4.

20. Demothenes, *Against Macartatus*, 62–66; Plutarch, *Solon*, 21; Cicero, *Laws*, 2.24.61–64. Garland, "Well Ordered Corpse," 3–5.

21. Alexiou, *Ritual Lament,* 14–23; Holst-Warhaft, *Dangerous Voices,* 114–15; Garland, "Well Ordered Corpse," 8–9.

22. Thus the right to inherit was related to the right to mourn. To secure these rights, several men could appear to take responsibility for the funeral expenses. Alexiou, *Ritual Lament,* 17–22; Holst-Warhaft, *Dangerous Voices,* 115–17.

23. Alexiou, *Ritual Lament,* 21. Holst-Warhaft *Dangerous Voices,* reinforces

this argument by an analysis of the function of women's laments in 20th century Greece in similar contexts of blood feud and war. Garland follows Alexiou's discussion as well ("Well-Ordered Corpse," 4–5). He comments "There can be no doubt that in Greece, as commonly throughout the Mediterranean to this day, the task of mourning the dead fell chiefly to the women, whose displays of grief, unless checked, might amount to a social nuisance" (5). Holst-Warhaft, however, has demonstrated that expressions of women's grief amounted to more than a simple "nuisance."

24. Alexiou, *Ritual Lament,* 104–11; Holst-Warhaft, *Dangerous Voices,* 119–26; Garland, "Well-Ordered Corpse," 15. See also Loraux, *The Invention of Athens.*

25. Cross-cultural studies show that women's lamenting is quite orderly and controlled. Men are much less likely to channel their grief into organized mourning than women (Holst-Wahrhoft, *Dangerous Voices,* 122).

26. Holst-Warhaft, *Dangerous Voices,* 123–4.

27. See for example Thucydides, *Hist.*, II. 46, where Pericles tells the women to mourn quickly and leave. Even the "Oration of Aspasia," supposedly by a woman, encourages moderation among women in their mourning and declares that the dead are better praised than mourned (Plato, *Men.*, 246D–249D). For the dismissal of mourning women from death scenes, see below.

28. Garland, *Greek Way*, 29, 33–4; 110–13. Archaeological excavations of tombs and funerary art belie the assumption that such legislative measures had great effect on the actual behavior of women.

29. Holst-Warhaft, *Dangerous Voices,* 127–170. See also Caraveli, "The Bitter Wounding," 169–194; Caraveli-Chavez, "Bridge Between Worlds," 129–57. There are dissenters to this view that women's laments could function to disrupt society. Women's lamentation also has a therapeutic and communal function that reinforces women's roles by helping women adjust to their suffering and oppression. See Mernissi, "Women, Saints and Sanctuaries," 101–12. This reading of women's ritual does not account for continued societal interest in their control.

30. Garland, *Greek Way*, 94–95. This was particularly true in the case of Solon's ban on taking offerings to the dead at tombs: "Solon's ban was widely disregarded" (Garland, *Greek Way*, 113).

31. Toynbee, *Death and Burial in the Roman World* , 6–17.

32. Toynbee, *Death and Burial,* 43.

33. Rush, *Death and Burial,* 101–5; Toynbee, *Death and Burial,* 43–44.

34. Cicero, *Verr.* 5.45.118; Rush, *Death and Burial,* 101.

35. Rush, *Death and Burial,* 106.

36. This may be an over-generalization. Morris notes that only 66 of 644 graves exhumed from the fourth century B.C.E. in Olynthus had a coin in them; none were found in the North Cemetery near Corinth. Some graves have more coins than others (*Death-Ritual,* 105–6). See also Rush, *Death and Burial,* 92–99; Toynbee, *Death and Burial,* 44.

37. Rush, *Death and Burial,* 113–14; 117–25; Toynbee, *Death and Burial,* 44.

38. Rush, *Death and Burial,* 133–37.

39. Rush, *Death and Burial,* 117–25.

40. Rush, *Death and Burial,* 108–9

41. Rush, *Death and Burial,* 110–11. This role was taken up by young men in the early church, or clerics. See Acts 5:6, 10; 8:2.

42. Toynbee, *Death and Burial,* 44–7. See especially plates 9 and 11.

43. Rush, *Death and Burial,* 109.

44. Rush, *Death and Burial,* 163.

45. Rush, *Death and Burial,* 168–70; 181–82; 228–31; Toynbee, *Death and Burial,* 44–47.

46. Rush, *Death and Burial,* 168–69; 188–91. Corley, *Private Women, Public Meals,* 48–49; Plutarch mentions a man named Xenophantus as a renowned flute player who played at the funeral of Demetrius (Plutarch, *Demetrius,* 53.2).

47. Women were also eulogized. Rush, 258–73. In the early church this time of oration was used for the preaching of doctrine to the Christian community rather than being a speech in praise of the dead (Rush, *Death and Burial,* 262–73).

48. Rush, *Death and Burial,* 236–53; Toynbee, *Death and Burial,* 49–50. See also A. D. Nock, "Cremation and Burial in the Roman Empire," 278–307.

49. Nock sees this as a mere shift in fashion, rather than due to the influence of the mysteries ("Cremation and Burial," 306–7). For a full discussion of this shift in Roman practices in light of archaeological evidence and cross-cultural anthropological perspectives, see Morris, *Death Ritual.* Although generally in agreement with Nock, Morris still finds it significant that Roman burial practices became homogenized at the same time as "economic and political regionalism was increasing" (*Death Ritual,* 203).

50. Rush, *Death and Burial,* 238.

51. Toynbee, *Death and Burial,* 54–55. See also G.R. H. Horsley, "Funerary Practice in Hellenistic and Roman Rhodes," *New Documents Illustrating Early Christianity,* 2 (Macquarie University: Ancient History Documentary Research Center, 1982), 48–52, esp. 49–50.

52. Toynbee, *Death and Burial,* 50.

53. The time between wake and burial is difficult to determine during Roman times (Rush, *Death and Burial,* 150–1). Wakes in the home could last for up to seven days before a burial (Rush, *Death and Burial,* 153–54). Poorer people probably buried their dead more quickly, especially since they would not have been able to afford ointments and preservatives (Rush, *Death and Burial,* 153).

54. Toynbee, *Death and Burial,* 50–52; 61–64.

55. Toynbee, *Death and Burial,* 51, 136.

56. Cicero, *Laws,* 2.25.64. Garland, "Well-Ordered Corpse," 3.

57. Cicero, *Laws,* 2.26.65–66.

58. A point emphasized by Daube, *Roman Law: Linguistic, Social and Philosophical Aspects* , 117–30. Curbing expenditure was also in the interests of close relatives and the upper classes as more property was left over to pass on the next generation. On Roman funerary legislation, see also Rush, *Death and Burial,* 176–86; Toynbee, *Death and Burial,* 54–55.

59. Zanker, *The Power of Images in the Age of Augustus,* 291–95. See also Morris, *Death Ritual,* passim, and 149–55.

60. Zanker, *Power of Images,* 338.

61. Lucian, *On Funerals,* esp. 12, 19, 20.

62. Lucian, *On Funerals,* 19. Translation and text by A. E. Harmon (LCL).

63. Rush, *Death and Burial,* 174–86. See also 108–9. Certain orders of nuns were even instructed to keep complete silence at funerals while the chanting of Psalms was done by monks (Rush, *Death and Burial,* 183) and the nuns in funeral processions were limited to a few old women (Rush, *Death and Burial,* 204–5).

64. The theme of the theft of executed criminals became proverbial. See Hengel, *Crucifixion,* 47–48; Rush, *Death and Burial,* 123, 194.

65. Rush, *Death and Burial,* 101–2, 123. See above on the patience of mothers in hopes of giving the last kiss to their condemned children.

66. R. Brown, *The Death of the Messiah*, 2. 1207–9; Crossan, *The Historical Jesus*, 391–4; *idem*, *Who Killed Jesus?*, 160–68; Hengel, *Crucifixion*, 22–32.

67. Brown, *Death of the Messiah*, 2. 1207–8; Hengel, *Crucifixion*, 39–45.

68. Brown, *Death of the Messiah*, 2.1207–9.

69. Crossan, *Historical Jesus*, 391–4; *Who Killed Jesus?*, 160–3.

70. For the execution of women and children, especially in the presence of husbands or parents,, see Plato, *Gorgias*, 473C; Herodotus, 9.120; Plutarch, *Agis and Cleomenes*, 19.7; Josephus, *AJ*, 8.380; *BJ*, 1.97–98. On the crucifixion of women, see Hengel, *Crucifixion*, 81–82; comments by Opocenská, "Women at the Cross," 43 and Schottroff, *Let the Oppressed Go Free* ,172. Schottroff cites Josephus, *BJ*, 2.307 (196) to which I would add Xenophon, *An Ephesian Tale*, 4.4 (free woman crucified) and 4.6 (the crucifixion of the heroine Anthia is considered). In the New Testament, Paul meets Junia in prison (Rom 16: 7) and Sapphira is executed (albeit by divine intervention) shortly after her husband (Acts 5:7–10). See also Loraux, *Tragic Ways of Killing a Woman*. See also Ford, "The Crucifixion of Women in Antiquity."

71. Except by Crossan, *Who Killed Jesus?*, 167–68.

72. N. Haas, "Anthropological Observations of the Skeletal Remains from Giv'at ha-Mivtar," 38–59.

73. For further discussion of the remains of the crucified man from Giv'hat ha Mivtar, see J. Navneh, "The Ossuary Inscriptions from Giv'at ha-Matar," 33–37; V. Tzaferis, "Crucifixion: The Archaeological Evidence," 44–53; *idem*, "Jewish Tombs at and near Giv'at ha-Mivtar," 18–32; Y. Yadin, "Epigraphy and Crucifixion," 18–22; J. Zias and E. Sekeles, "The Crucified Man From Giv'at ha-Mivtar: A Reappraisal," 22–28.

74. Washing of corpses is not mentioned in the Hebrew Bible, but rather in later Jewish sources. The most complete discussion of later customs of Jewish mourning can be found in the tractate "Mourning," or *Semahot*. See translation and commentary by D. Zlotnick. The date of this source is a matter of debate, and suggestions range from the third to the eighth centuries C.E.. Many scholars would still argue that this source contains very ancient traditions (Zlotnick, 4–5). For general discussions of Jewish burial and mourning practices, see De Vaux, *Ancient Israel: Its Life and Institutions* , 56–61; Eileen F. De Ward, "Mourning Customs in 1, 2 Samuel," 1–27; *idem*, "Mourning Customs in 1,2 Samuel II," 145–66; Feldman, *Biblical and Post-Biblical Defilement and Mourning: Law as Theology*,; S. Safrai, "Home and Family," in *The Jewish People in the First Century*, v. 2, 728–92, esp. 773–87.

75. Sem. 12:10. The Mishnah requires that the corpse be washed *(m. Shabbath* 23:5). In Acts 9:36–37 women prepare the body of Tabitha in Joppa by washing it.

76. De Vaux, *Ancient Israel,* 57; De Ward, "Mourning Customs I," 2–3; Safrai, "Home and Family," 774.

77. De Ward, "Mourning Customs I," 3. For further references to Mishnaic sources and the tractate *Semahot*, see Safrai, "Home and Family," 774.

78. The cremation of Saul and his sons is considered an exception (1 Sam 31:12). See also Gen 38:24; Lev 20:14; 21:9; De Vaux, *Ancient Israel,* 57; De Ward, "Mourning Customs II," 146. Annanias and Sapphira are also buried quickly in Acts 5:6–10; Safrai, "Home and Family," 774. Later sources require burial on the same day as death (For further references see Safrai, "Home and Family," 774).

79. De Ward, "Mourning Customs II," 146–47; see Deut 21:22–23; Ezek. 32:18–32 and 1 Sam. 31:12.

80. On Jewish burial practices and tombs, see L. Y. Rahmani, "Ancient Jerusalem's Funerary Customs and Tombs," 171–77 (Part 1); 44:4 (1981) 229–35 (Part 2); 45:1 (1981) 43–53 (Part 3); 45:2 (1982) 109–19 (Part 4); and Erwin R. Goodenough, "Jewish Tombs of Palestine" in *Jewish Symbols in the Greco-Roman Period,* 61–84. See also De Vaux, *Ancient Israel,* 57, De Ward, "Mourning Customs II," 145–46.

81. Jer. 26:23; 2 Kgs 23:6; De Vaux, *Ancient Israel,* 57–58

82. Safrai, "Home and Family," 775.

83. De Ward, "Mourning Customs II," 155.

84. Job 27:15; Ps 78:64; De Ward, "Mourning Customs II," 153.

85. De Ward, "Mourning Customs I and II," De Vaux, *Ancient Israel,* 59–60.

86. *Semahot* 11.9.

87. De Vaux, *Ancient Israel,* 59–61; De Ward, "Mourning Customs II," 154–59; Safrai, "Home and Family," 775. For Ancient Near Eastern images of weeping women, see Samuel Noah Kramer, "The Weeping Goddess: Sumerian Prototypes of the *Mater Dolorosa,*" 69–80; *idem*, "BM 98396: A Sumerian Prototype of the *Mater-Dolorosa,*" 141–46; T. Dothan, "A Female Mourner Figure from the Lachish Region," 43–47 (Hebrew); Miller, "Women, Death and Mourning," passim; Karel Van der Toorn, *From Her Cradle to Her Grave,* 119–21. For a further discussion of women's roles in mourning, including later Judaism, see Archer, *Her Price is Beyond Rubies,* 280–90.

88. On Rachel's lament and the debate over the presence of professional mourners in ancient Israel, see De Ward, "Mourning Customs II," 159; Miller, "Women, Death and Mourning," 83–84; 135–38. Professional mourners are explicitly mentioned only in later texts. In the tannaitic literature only women mourners/keeners are mentioned (Safrai, "Home and Family," 775, esp. nts. 1, 4). Safrai cites *m. Ket.* 4:4; *Sem.* 14:7; *m. Moed Katan* 3:9 and other texts.

89. De Ward, "Mourning Customs II," 157. See also discussion of ancient Near Eastern women's laments by Van der Toorn, 119.

90. DeWard, "Mourning Customs II," 159.

91. See the contrast of a "woman's" lament and a "noble" or "manly" lament in 4 Macc 16 discussed by Miller, "Women, Death and Mourning," 149–57. Miller has demonstrated that the first lament (which the narrator denies the mother spoke) (16:5–12) contains elements typical of women's lament traditions. There is also a later rabbinic tradition of stylized laments, which praise the dead for their nobility (Feldman, *Biblical and Post Biblical Defilement,* 110–19, esp. 125–29). The few women's laments attributed to professional women mourners in rabbinic sources are in Aramaic (Feldman, *Biblical and Post Biblical Defilement,* 129–32). Both women and men could receive funeral eulogies (Safrai, "Home and Family," 779).

92. De Ward, "Mourning Customs II," 165–66; De Vaux, *Ancient Israel,* 59. For the cutting of flesh and hair, see also Job 1:20; Is 22:21; Ezek. 7:18; Amos 8:10; Jer. 16:6; 41:5; 48:37.

93. See De Ward, "Mourning Customs II," 166; De Vaux, *Ancient Israel,* 59–60. Later Hellenistic sources probably reflect Greek rather than Canaanite tendencies (Tob 4:17; 2 Macc 12:38–46).

94. Van der Toorn, *From Her Cradle to Her Grave,* 120

95. Van der Toorn, *From Her Cradle to Her Grave,* 119.

96. Goodenough, "Jewish Tombs," 63–78

97. Goodenough, "Jewish Tombs," 79–83.

98. Evidence that coins were placed in the mouths of the deceased has been found in Second Temple Jewish tombs in both Jerusalem and Jericho, including the one found in the skull of an adult woman placed in an ossuary inscribed "Miriam, daughter of Simon" from the family tomb of the High Priest Caiphas. Although their significance is a matter of heated debate, I am in agreement with Zvi Greenhut, "Burial Cave of the Caiphas Family," 29–36, 79; that many coins found in Second Temple Jewish tombs reflect this Greek custom. For a further discussion of coins, see R. Hachlili, "Ancient Burial Customs Preserved in Jericho Hills," 28–35, esp. 34–34; L. Y. Rahmani, "Jason's Tomb," 61–100, esp. 92–93. Morris' cautions on making immediate generalizations about the significance of all coins found in graves are germane here. Although two skeletons have one or two coins in the skull, in other graves coins are not in the general vicinity of human remains. In "Jason's Tomb," 42 coins from 30/31 CE were found in a single *kokh* (Rahmani, "Jason's Tomb," 92–3). See Morris, *Death-Ritual*, 105–6.

99. Rahmani, "Jason's Tomb," 81–85; James F. Strange, "Late Hellenistic and Herodian Ossuary Tombs at French Hill Jerusalem," 39–67, esp. 60–1 on alabastra found in tombs.

100. Haas, "Anthropological Observations," 39–40.

101. Hachlili, "Ancient Burial Customs," 34; Rahmani, "Jason's Tomb," 85–7; Strange, "Late Hellenistic," 49–58.

102. So Greenhut, "Burial Cave," 35–36.

103. N. Avigad, "Aramaic Inscriptions in the Tomb of Jason" 101–11. Avigad suggests that the lament follows a Hellenistic formula (105–6). Most Jewish funerary inscriptions are in Greek, although many are bilingual (Greek and Aramaic). See Pieter W. Van der Horst, "Jewish Funerary Inscriptions: Most Are in Greek," 46–57; R.A. Kearsley, "The Goliath Family at Jericho, 162–4. For a further discussion of Jason's Tomb, see Rahmani, "Jason's Tomb."

104. The interpretation of burial remains is a vexing problem, but it is still possible to detect some patterns of rituals from burial remains. See Morris, *Death-Ritual*, 12–15. I agree that the complete abandonment of all evidence is not helpful.

105. Again, most scholars focus on the concern for the reduction of expenses. See Safrai, "Home and Family," 777. See also D. Zlotnick, *Semahot*, 22–6.

106. Zlotnick, *Semahot*, 23–4.

107. Zlotnick, *Semahot,* 25.

108. *Sem.* 8.1. Certain manuscripts read "thirty." The reading "three" is supported by many medieval commentators and corresponds more to the purpose of the visit suggested. See Zlotnick, *Semahot*, 135. Visits to the tomb on both the third day and the thirtieth day were common in antiquity (Garland, *Greek Way*, 104).

109. *Moed Katan* 3.8–9.

110. *m. Sanh.* 6:5.

111. *Semahot* 9, *passim.*

112. *Semahot* 2. 1–3

113. *Semahot* 2.6.

114. Which of course implies that the family might try to steal it. *Semahot* 2.9.

115. Additional attention to the major shift in Jewish burial practice (to the use of ossuaries) before the wars is also called for. As ossuaries fell out of use immediately following the period of the Jewish Wars, the decline in ossuary usage would then coincide with changes (or attempts at changes) in other funerary customs. The

common view that ossuary usage corresponds to developments in theological ideas such as "resurrection from the dead" is implausible (E. Meyers, *Jewish Ossuaries.*) Similar theories concerning the significance of the shift from cremation to inhumation among Romans have been questioned for sometime. See Morris, *Death Ritual*, 31–34; Nock, "Cremation and Burial," 285–93.

116. See above.

117. Byron R. McKane's discussion of these later rabbinic regulations assumes that all in the community would have agreed with decisions by the religious court, and would therefore have meekly followed such restrictions. However, this seems to be an unreasonable assumption, given apparent ineffectiveness of most funerary restrictions in antiquity. See "Where No One Had Yet Been Laid: The Shame of Jesus' Burial," 473–84, esp. 478–79.

118. Crossan, *Who Killed Jesus?*, 168.

119. Baumgarten "Hanging and Treason in Qumran and Roman Law," 7–16; Fitzmyer, "Crucifixion in Ancient Palestine, Qumran Literature, and the New Testament," 493–513. See also Hengel, *Crucifixion*, 85.

120. Josephus, *BJ*, 3.8.5 (377); 4.5.2 (317); *AJ*. 4.8.24 (264–65). See also Philo, *Against Flaccus*, 83; Brown, *Death of the Messiah*, 2.1209–11; Crossan, *Who Killed Jesus?*, 167.

121. Brown, *Death of the Messiah*, 2.1210; Crossan, *Who Killed Jesus?*, 167.

122. And they, of course, may not even have accomplished that. What we have evidence for is secondary burial in the family tomb, not primary burial. Crossan, *Who Killed Jesus?*, 168.

123. Philo, *Against Flaccus*, 83; Brown, *Death of the Messiah*, 2.1209–10; Crossan, *Historical Jesus*, 391–94; *Who Killed Jesus?*, 167.

124. C.K. Barrett is certainly correct in this instance. The rabbinic sources cited by Strack-Billerbeck and others which are commonly marshaled to support such a contention either deal with such hypothetical situations that they are hardly germane or describe religious, not state executions. See Barrett *John*, 551; Str.-B. 2.580. Commonly cited as evidence are *y. Gittin* 7:1 (330) or *Baba Metzia* 83b. For example, *Baba Metzia* 83b describes R. Eleazar weeping under the gallows of a man hanged for violating religious law (rape of an engaged woman); *y. Gittin* 7:1 describes a wildly hypothetical situation involving divorce.

125. Here Holst-Warhaft's discussion of the function of women's lament in times of political change and unrest in antiquity as well as in modern times seems most applicable (*Dangerous Voices, passim*).

126. The literature on this topic is immense, but see Moses Hadas and Morton. Smith, *Heroes and Gods: Spiritual Biographies in Antiquity*; Erwin Rohde, *Psyche: The Cult of Souls and Belief in Immortality among the Greeks*, 115–209; 525–80; Morton Smith, "Prolegomena to a Discussion of Aretalogies: Divine Men, The Gospels and Jesus," 174–99; Kee, "Aretalogy and Gospel," 402–22; Toynbee, *A Study of History*, v. 4, 376–559; on the relationship of Jesus to Hercules, see most recently Aune, "Heracles and Christ, 3–19. The original one-to-one literary relationships suggested by F. Pfister, "Herakles und Christus," *ARW* 34 (1937) 42–60 (unavailable to me) were critiqued early on. See H. J. Rose, "Heracles and the Gospels," 113–42; Toynbee, *Study of History*, v. 4, 376–77; W. L. Knox, "The 'Divine Hero' Christology in the New Testament," 229–49; Marcel Simon, *Heracle et le Christianisme* , esp. critique of Pfister, 51–55. On Socrates and Jesus, see Oscar Cullmann, "Immortality of the Soul or Resurrection of the Dead?" 9–53, esp. 12–20; Toynbee, *Study of History*, 486–508. On Moses, see Gager, *Moses in Greco-Roman Paganism* , esp. 134–66.

127. On the oral transmission of myth and folklore, see Toynbee, *Study of History*, v. 4, 500–8; on the visual transmission of myth and folklore through art, see Toynbee, *Study of History*, v. 4, 508–34; Nock, "Cremation and Burial," 290–91 mentions the popularity of visual representations of Hercules, but knows of only one mural picturing his death. See also Simon, *Hercule*, 62; Zanker, *Power of Images*, 336–37. The magical papyri give ample attestation to the attribution of special power to many figures. For popular spells calling on the name of Jesus or Christ: PGM 4.3007–86; 4.1227–64; 100.1–7; 128.1–11; Herakles: PGM 7.1–148 (based on Homer); 12.401–44; 5.370–446; Solomon: PGM 4.850–929; Moses: PGM 3.424–66; 5.96–172; 7.619–27; 13.1–34; 313.646–734; 13.734–1077; Socrates: PGM 12.201–69; Apollonius of Tyana: PGM 11.a.1–40; Homeric verses used: PGM 4.2145–2240; 4.470–74, 821–24; spirits of dead heroes and gladiators invoked: PGM 4.1390–1495. See Betz, *The Greek Magical Papyri in Translation.*

128. Aune, "Heracles and Christ," 19; Gallagher, *Divine Man or Magician?*. See also Lord Raglan, "The Hero of Tradition," 140–57; Toynbee, *Study of History*, v. 4, 444–57, esp. 454 on the "jetsam of 'folklore'" and Simon, *Hercule*, 62.

129. Gallagher, *Divine Man, passim*, J.Z. Smith, "Good News is No News: Aretalogy and Gospel," 21–38.

130. Again, the literature is immense, but see Achtemeier, "Gospel Miracle Traditions and the Divine Man," 174–97; Betz, "Jesus as Divine Man," 114–31; Kingsbury, *The Christology of Mark's Gospel*, 25–45; Koester, "One Jesus and Four Primitive Gospels," 203–47, esp. 230–36; Weeden, *Mark – Traditions in Conflict.* For a review of literature, see Barry Blackburn, *Theios Aner and the Markan Miracle Traditions* . According to Gallagher (*Divine Man or Magician*, 10–14), L. Bieler's, *Theios Aner: das Bild des "göttlichen Menchen" im Späntike und Frühchristentum* has never been given a fair hearing. Bieler focused only on parallels that had similar meanings, rather than incidental ones.

131. Betz, "Jesus as Divine Man," 124–25; Koester, "One Jesus," 232–33; Weeden, *Mark: Traditions in Conflict.*

132. Betz, Koester, Weeden, *ibid.* See also Hans Conzelmann, "History and Theology in the Passion Narratives," *Int* 2 (1979) 178–97, esp. 183–84.

133. Fortna, "Christology in the Fourth Gospel," 489–504.

134. Jackson, "The Death of Jesus in Mark and the Miracle from the Cross," 16–37.

135. J. Z. Smith, "Good News is No News."

136. Nickelsburg, "The Genre and Function of the Markan Passion Narrative," 153–84 and *idem*, *Resurrection, Immortality, and Eternal Life in Intertestamental Judaism*, 48–111.

137. Sherman E. Johnson, "Greek and Jewish Heroes: Fourth Maccabees and the Gospel of Mark," 155–75; Seeley, *The Noble Death*, esp. 84–141; Droge and Tabor, *A Noble Death.* See also Toynbee, *Study of History*, v. 4, 444–45 and Nickelsburg, *Resurrection*, 48–111.

138. A. Collins, "From Noble Death to Crucified Messiah," 481–503; *idem*, "Genre of the Passion Narrative;" *idem*, *The Beginning of the Gospel: Probings of Mark in Context* , 92–118. See also Pilch, "Death with Honor," 65–70. On Luke's Passion account, see Kloppenborg, "*Exitus clari viri.*"

139. For example, since A. Collins doesn't see the parallel between the men and the women in the Passion narrative, she mistakenly applies the use of Psalm 38:11, "My friends and companions stand aloof from my affliction, and my neighbors stand far off" (NRSV) only to the fleeing of Peter and the disciples, but not to

the women ("Genre of the Passion," 14). Nickelsburg's discussion of the Passion Narrative does not mention the women near the cross. Kloppenborg, however, does notice the motif of mourning women in Luke's addition of the weeping "Daughters of Jerusalem" ("*Exitus clari viri*," 113–115).

140. Pliny, *Letters*, 8.12. For more on this genre see A. Collins, "The Genre of the Passion Narrative," 3–28, esp. 6, 13, 23, n. 22 and Kloppenborg, "*Exitus clari viri*: 106–20, esp. 106–8.

141. See Corley, *Private Women, Public Meals*, esp. 59–62; Torjesen, *When Women Were Priests*, esp. 111–32; 135–52.

142. *Mor.* 113A. Translation by F. C. Babbitt (LCL). According to Plutarch, women's quarters are also full of λύπη (grieving) *(Mor.* 465D). The cries of prisoners being led off to slavery is called "womanish" (Polybius, *Hist.* 1.56.7–9; Xenophon, *Hell.* 2.2.3). Grief and emotion (πάθος) are therefore irrational (Diogenes Laertius, *Lives* (Zeno), 7.110–11.

143. Plutarch, *Mor.* 449D–E.

144. Plutarch, *Mor.* 608F.

145. Plutarch, *Solon*, 21.5. For a further discussion of Plutarch's views on grief, see Hubert Martin, Jr., and Jane E. Phillips, "*Consolatio ad Uxorem* (*Moralia* 608A–612B)," 394–441.

146. Cicero, *Tusc.*, 3.26.63–3.30.73, esp. 3.29.72. Trans. by J. E. King (LCL).

147. Porphyry, *Life of Pythagoras*, 35. Text by E. Des Places, *Porphyre* (Paris, 1982).

148. *Sentences*, 98. This can also be translated, "set limits to (the grief) of your family (and friends)." The text is uncertain. See text and translation by P. W. Vander Horst, *The Sentences of Pseudo-Phocylides*, 95, 180.

149. Sir 38:16–23. Sir 22:12 suggests mourning for seven days. Only a fool would weep any longer.

150. *AJ*, 17. 174–78; *BJ*, 1.666.

151. Plato, *Phaedo*, 60A.

152. *Phaedo*, 116B–C.

153. *Phaedo*, 117C–E. Text and translation by H. N. Fowler (LCL).

154. Death of Aratus, companions present: Plutarch, *Aratus* 52–53; Caius Gracchus, followers keep watch the night before, sleeping on and off, wife enters crying, forbidden to mourn further, Caius leaves her, his friends follow: Plutarch, *Tiberius and Caius Gracchus*, 14–15. See also death of Seneca: Tacitus, 15.61–64; death of Thraesea: Tacitus, 16.34–35; death of Otho: Plutarch, *Otho*, 16–18; death of Socrates: Xenophon, *Apology*, 27–28. See also death of Oedipus, Sophocles, *Oedipus at Colonus*, 1570–1770 (mourning daughters asked to leave, Oedipus disappears and he has no tomb); burial of Achilles, *Odyssey*, 24.35–75 (mother present, daughters of the sea wail, but only warriors surround the funeral pyre).

155. Kloppenborg, *Exitus clari viri*, 111–12.

156. Loraux, *Experience of Tiresias*, 116–39; 150–58. See also Loraux, "Herakles: The Supemale and the Feminine," 21–52.

157. *Iphegenia at Aulis*, 1368ff.

158. Seneca, *Hercules Oetaeus*, 1620–1970, esp. 1667–90, 1738–59. Trans. F. J. Miller (LCL).

159. Diodorus of Sicily, 4.38.4–5. This basic story is repeated in Apollodorus, 2.7.7. See also Sophocles, *The Women of Trachis*, 1065–1275, where Hercules weeps himself, then calls weeping "womanish," and tells his son not to cry but "be a man."

160. Lucian, *Passing of Peregrinus*, 37. Trans. by A. M. Harmon (LCL).

161. *AJ*, 4.320–26.

162. See Miller, "Women, Death and Mourning," 168–70. See also Bar. 4:23.

163. Susanna, 31–33.

164. 2 Macc. 7; 4 Maccabees, passim.

165. Seeley, *Noble Death*, 113–41. See also Plutarch, *Agis and Cleomenes*, where a woman is executed after her son (but she weeps) (19.6ff.). In other accounts men watch their wives and/or children executed before they die. See Herodotus, 9.120; Plato, *Gorgias*, 473C; Josephus, *BJ*, 1.97 and of course the death of Eleazar in 2 Macc. 6:18–31.

166. Miller "Women, Death and Mourning," 150–2.

167. Miller, "Women, Death and Mourning," 151.

168. See above.

169. Nickelsburg, *Resurrection, Immortality, and Eternal Life in Intertestamental Literature* , 48–111; idem, "The Genre and Function of the Markan Passion Narrative."

170. Psalm 38:11; 88:8. See below.

171.Cumont, *After Life*, 45–56. On the tomb as the house of the dead, see J. H. M. Strubbe "Cursed Be He that Moves My Bones," esp. 40.

172. Cumont, *After Life*, 60–1.

173. For and introduction to ancient magic and translations of various magical texts, see Betz, *The Greek Magical Papyri;* Luck, *Arcana*; Meyer and R. Smith, *Ancient Christian Magic.*

174. Munich Coptic Papyrus 5. Text by W. Henstenberg, "Koptische Papyri." In *Beiträge zur Forschung: Studien und Mitteilungen aus dem Antiquariat Jacques Rosenthal, München*, vol. 1 (= "erste Folge"), 95–100, 8–11. Trans. by Marvin Meyer, in Meyer and R. Smith, *Ancient Christian Magic*, 188–190, esp. 190.

175. See PGM 4.1875–2240; A. Delatte, *La catoptromancie grecque et ses dérivés* 94; 106–107, 141; Luck, *Arcana Mundi*, 26; 166–68; 176–80; 184–85; 192–204; 212–17; 222–25.

176. Cumont, *After Life*, 64–69; Rohde, *Psyche*, 210–11, nts. 144–48; 593–95; 603–5

177. See Lattimore, *Themes in Greek and Latin Epitaphs* ; Strubbe, "Cursed Be He," 33–59;

178. Cumont, *After Life*, 65. This citation is made by Cumont unfortunately without sources.

179. Plato, *Phd.* 115C.

180. See Diog. Laert. 4.52; 4.79; *Cynic Epistles*, 25; Cicero, *Tusc.* 1.104 (quoting Diogenes); Lucian, *Demon.* 35; 66. I would like to thank David Seeley for these references.

181. See discussion by Meyer and R. Smith of the definitions of "magic" vs. "religion," *Ancient Christian Magic*, 1–9.

182. Apuleius, *Met.* 2. 20, text and translation W. Adlington (LCL).

183. Apuleius, *Met.* 2.21.

184. Apuleius, *Met.* 2.28.

185. Lucan, *Pharasalia*, 6.415–830. See also Heliodorus, *Aeth.* 6.14–15; Ovid., *Met.* 7. 235–294. For another example of a man raising the spirit of the dead in a similar manner, see Seneca, *Oedipus*, 548–650.

186. Vermeule, *Aspects of Death*, 17; 215, n. 31.

187. Thompson with Headlam, v. 2, *The Oresteia of Aeschylus* , 189.

188. Alexiou, *Ritual Lament*, 13; Holst-Warhaft, *Dangerous Voices*, 112.

189. Alexiou, *Ritual Lament*, 131–205; Holst-Warhaft, *Dangerous Voices*, 111–12.

190. Holst-Warhaft, *Dangerous Voices*, 127–28.

191. Aeschylus, *Pers.* 683–8; trans. by H. Weir Smythe (LCL); Holst-Warhaft, *Dangerous Voices*, 132.

192. Aeschylus, *Pers.* 1050–56; trans. by Holst-Warhaft, *Dangerous Voices*, 132–33. Text by H. Weir Smythe (LCL).

193. Aeschylus, *Cho.* 429–584; Holst-Warhaft, *Dangerous Voices*, 143–44, 151.

194. Holst-Warhaft, *Dangerous Voices*, 144–49. On necromancy and Aeschylus see H. D. Broadhead, *The Persae of Aeschylus*, 302–9; S. Eitrem, "The Necromany in the Persai of Aischylos," 1–16; W. Headlam, "Ghost Raising, Magic and the Underworld," 52–61; de Romilly, *Magic and Rhetoric in Ancient Greece*, 16–19; H. J. Rose, "Ghost Ritual in Aeschylus," 257–80. A negative response to Headlam may be found in J. C. Lawson, "The Evocation of Darius," 79–89.

195. Holst-Warhaft, *Dangerous Voices*, 129, 133–34.

196. Holst-Warhaft, *Dangerous Voices, passim.*

197. Seneca, *Hercules Oeateus*, esp. 1863–1970.

198. Ovid, *Met.* 829–851; Ovid, *Fasti*, 459–516.

199. For concern about necromancy in biblical texts, see Deut 18:9–11; Lev 19:31; 1 Sam 28:6–25; 2 Kgs 21:6; Isa 8:19; 19:3; 29:4. On the prevalence of necromancy among Israelites, see Avishur, "Ghost-Expelling Incantation from Ugarit," 22–23; Beuken, "1 Samuel 28: The Prophet as Hammer of Witches," 3–17; Burns, "Necromancy and the Spirits of the Dead in the Old Testament," 1–14; Kennedy, "Cult of the Dead," 106; Lewis, *Cults of the Dead*, 111–17; 126–27; 132; 137; Paton, *Spritism*, 237; Brenner, *The Israelite Woman*, 67–77; M.S. Smith, *Early History of God*, 127–29.

200. See also Sir 48:13–14; M.S. Smith, *Early History of God*, 131.

201. See also Deut 18:10–11.

202. For further discussion, see Bloch-Smith, *Judahite Burial Practices*, 122–125.

203. Bloch-Smith, *Judahite Burial Practices*, 121–22.

204. Bloch-Smith, *Judahite Burial Practices*, 130–1.

205. 1 Sam 28:6–25. See also 1 Chr 10:13–14. Beuken, "The Prophet as the Hammer of Witches;" Bloch-Smith, *Judahite Burial Practices*, 121–22; Brenner, *Israelite Woman*, 34–35; 72–74; Lewis, *Cults of the Dead*, 111–17; Goitein, "Women as Creators," 14–15; K. A. D. Smelik, "The Witch of Endor: 1 Samuel in Rabbinic and Christian Exegesis Till 800 A. D." 160–179; M.S. Smith, *Early History of God*, 127.

206. Rollin, "Women and Witchcraft in Ancient Assyria (900–600 BC)," 41.

207. See also Lev 20:6; Ezek 43:7–9. See discussion by Lewis, *Cults of the Dead*, 146–47; 152; 157–58; 162–63.

208. Prov 2:16–18; Lewis, *Cults of the Dead*, 158.

209. Josephus, *AJ.* 6.327–42.

210. Pseudo-Philo, *Bib. Ant.* 64.1–3. See Smelik, "The Witch of Endor," 162. For Josephus and Pseudo-Philo's discussions of the "Witch of Endor," see also C. Brown, *No Longer Silent*, 181–211.

211. See Smelik, "Witch of Endor," 162–63 for numerous references to rabbinic discussions of the "Witch of Endor" and 1 Sam. 28.

212. Osiek, "The Women at the Tomb: What Are They Doing There?" 97–107, esp. 98.

213. Osiek, "Women at the Tomb," 100–101; Heine, "Eine Person von Rang und Namen: Historische Konturen der Magdalenerin," 179–94, esp. 185; Longstaff,

"What Are Those Women Doing at the Tomb of Jesus?" 199–203; Strelan, "To Sit Is To Mourn," passim. See now also Myllykoski, "What Happened to the Body of Jesus?" 65.

214. Sawicki, *Seeing the Lord*, 164–64; 255–58.

215. A facsimile of this has been suggested before. See John Dominic Crossan's review of literature in "Empty Tomb and Absent Lord (Mark 16:1–8)," in the *Passion in Mark: Studies on Mark 14–16*, 135–52, esp. 137–38. However, no adequate antecedent, scriptural or otherwise has ever been suggested for the "raised (ἐγείρω) on the third day" tradition. Any connection with Hosea 6:2 is quite doubtful, even a "loose connection," given the parallelism between "three days" and "two days" (Gundry, *Mark*), 447–48. There is little evidence that the story of Jonah (see Jonah 1:17) was ever interpreted in pre-Constantinian Christianity to be about "resurrection from the dead." See Snyder, *Ante Pacem*, 45–49.

216. Rohde, *Psyche*, 42–3. This was of course first mentioned by Celsus (Origen, *Contra Celsum*, 3.33. Celsus also compared the gospel stories to the translations of Aristeas (3.26), Heracles and others (2.55). See Simon, *Hercule*, 67–71. Justin Martyr also contended with the similarities of Jesus to heroes like Hercules (*Apology*, 1.21; *Dialogue with Trypho*, 69). On Origen and Justin Martyr, see Simon, *Hercule*, 67–71. See also A. Collins, "The Empty Tomb in the Gospel According to Mark," 107–40, esp. 123–18; *idem*, *Beginning of the Gospel*, 138–48; R. Pesch, *Das Markusevangelium*, 2.522–25; 536–38.

217. Pausanias, 2.9.7.

218. Diodorus of Sicily, 4.38.5.

219. Livy, 1.16.2–3.

220. Herodotus, 4.14.

221. A la Juliet. *Chariton, Chaereas and Callirhoe*, 3.3. Translation by B. P. Reardon, in *Collected Ancient Greek Novels*. Text by G. Molinié, *Chariton. Le roman de Chairéas et Callirhoé.*

222. Achilles Tatius, 5.14.4. Text and translation by S. Gaselee (LCL).

223. A. Collins, "Empty Tomb," and *idem, Beginning of the Gospel*, 119–48; See also Toynbee, *Study of History*, v. 4, 474–75.

224. Rohde, *Psyche*, 144, n. 43.

225. This of course has been suggested before. See A. Collins, "Empty Tomb," and *idem, Beginning of the Gospel*, 119–48; See also Toynbee, *Study of History*, v. 4, 474–75. Collins thinks that Mark wrote his empty tomb account under the influence of these stories, but she stops short of saying Mark 16:1–8 is an example of one: "In his composing the story of the empty tomb, the author of Mark interpreted the proclamation that Jesus had been risen" (*Beginning of the Gospel*, 145). See also Funk and the Jesus Seminar, *Acts of Jesus*, 465–67.

226. J. Z. Smith, "Good News is No News."

227. *Myth of Innocence*, 308. John Dominic Crossan's instincts on this matter are certainly correct. See "Empty Tomb and Absent Lord (Mark 16:1–8)," 135–152.

228. Osiek, "Women at the Tomb," 104–5; Schaberg, "The Feminist Contribution to Experience of Historical Jesus Scholarship," 266–85, esp. 284; Schüssler Fiorenza, *Jesus, Miriam's Prophet, Sophia's Child*, 90.

229. *Contra Celsum*, 2.55, 59.

230. *Contra Celsum*, 2.60.

231. *Contra Celsum*, 3.22.

232. *Contra Celsum*, 3.59. Celsus has surely read John. Translation by H. Chadwick.

233. Riley, *Resurrection Reconsidered.*

234. Lüdemann, *The Resurrection of Jesus*, 84–114.

235. In light of the Hellenistic evidence for the role of women in mourning rituals at the gravesite and the cultic context of "feeding the dead" in earliest Christian groups, the documentation of visions of deceased love ones in the context of natural grieving can therefore not be so easily dismissed as pertinent to this discussion. See Stacy Davids, MD, "Appearances of the Resurrected Jesus and the Experience of Grief," paper presented to the Jesus Seminar, Spring 1995; *idem*, "What is the Truth About the Resurrection of Jesus? The Testimony of Mary Magdalene," (unpublished paper, used by permission).

236. E. R. Dodds, *The Greeks and the Irrational*, 108–11; 117; 118–19; 127, n. 52.

237. Mack, *Myth of Innocence*, 308; Nock, "Cremation and Burial," 303–4; J. Z. Smith, *Drudgery Divine*, 142, esp. n. 43; *idem*, *To Take Place*, 74–95. See also Perkins, *Resurrection*, 93–94; Funk and the Jesus Seminar, *Acts of Jesus*, 467.

238. Usually taken to be a sign of Mark's shift away from a source. See A. Collins, "Composition of the Passion Narrative, 64; *idem*, *Beginning of the Gospel*, 117.

239. J. Z. Smith, *Drudgery Divine*, 131–33.

240. On early Christian "feeding the dead" and catacomb art, see J. Z. Smith, *ibid.*; see also Graydon Snyder, *Ante Pacem*, passim.

241. Corley, *Private Women, Public Meals*, 128–33; 152–58.

242. See ch. 4 for more detailed discussion of the "Children of the Marketplace" pericope.

243. See above.

244. *Drudgery Divine*, 132.

245. For this reason the identification of layers of Q on the basis of wisdom vs. apocalyptic may not be the most helpful designation of divergent traditions. Apocalyptic and Wisdom speculation are trajectories worked out by the same scribal class. See Horsley, "Wisdom is Justified by All Her Children," 733–51.

246. See above.

247. The fact that Solon's legislation required the separation of men and women as they left the gravesite indicates that for parts of the ritual they were in close proximity. See Garland, *Greek Way*, 37.

248. So Bultmann, *History of the Synoptic Tradition*, 280.

249. As Osiek has suggested, "Women at the Tomb," 103–4.

250. Kloppenborg, "*Exitus clari viri*."

251.On a possible pre-Markan source, see below. On a pre-Johannine source for the women, see Brown, *Death of the Messiah*, 2.1019; Dauer, *Passionsgeschichte*, 195–96; Green, *Death of Jesus*, 309–310 ; Fortna, *John and His Predecessor*, 177, 185. For a chart listing elements of a possible pre-gospel passion narrative and commentators views, see also Brown, *Death of Jesus*, 2.1502–17; Green, *Death of Jesus*, 294.

252. See below.

253. Luke 23:27–31. See Kloppenborg, *Exitus clari viri*, 111–13; Jerome H. Neyrey, "Jesus' Address to the Women of Jerusalem," 74–86. See also *Acts of Pilate* 284–5.

254. Barrett, *John*, 551; Brown, *Death of the Messiah*, 2.1019; 1028–29, *idem*, "Roles of Women in the Fourth Gospel," 688–99, esp. 698; Dauer, *Passionsgeschichte*, 192–193; Fortna, *The Fourth Gospel and Its Predecessor*, 177; 181. Schnackenburg, *The Gospel According to John*, v. 3, 277, 279–82; Even Joel B. Green notes that John moves this tradition forward so that Jesus' family and friends are not pictured as aloof (*The*

Death of Jesus, 310). See also Turid Karlsen Seim, "Roles of Women in the Gospel of John," 56–73, esp. 61. For more caution in regards to the symbolism of the scene, see Haenchen, *John*, v. 2, 193; Beasley-Murray, *John*, 350–51. For the argument that John's account is independent, see Jeremias, *The Eucharistic Words of Jesus*, 89–96.

255. Women are not present for the crucifixion. The men continually mourn before and after the empty tomb scene (*GPet* 7:26–27; 14:58–59). Crowds, Jewish authorities, soldiers and angels all witness the empty tomb before the women (8:28–33; 9:34–39). Although the women go to the tomb to mourn, they never get the chance, but are interrupted by angels (15:55–57). There is reason to suspect that Jesus' appearance to the men occurs in the context of their mourning. It is unfortunate that the story breaks off at that point. Translation by C. Mauer (NTA), text by Mara, *Évangile de Pierre*.

256. B. Johnson, "Empty Tomb Tradition in the Gospel of Peter," 34. See also Crossan, *The Cross that Spoke* which argues throughout for early traditions in the *Gospel of Peter*.

257. Johnson, "Empty Tomb Tradition," 32.

258. See below.

259. Against Koester, *Ancient Christian Gospels*, 233.

260. Snyder, *Ante Pacem*, 26–9.

261. Josef Jungmann even cites the *Gospel of Peter* as an example of this influence. See Josef A. Jungmann, *The Early Liturgy to the Time of Gregory the Great*, 131–33. Now acknowledged by Crossan, *Who Killed Jesus*, 196.

262. J. Z. Smith, *Drudgery Divine*, 142, 43; *To Take Place*, 74–95.

263. Treat, "The Two Manuscript Witnesses to the Gospel of Peter," 191–9. See also P. Oxy. 2949 in G. M. Browne, et al., *The Oxyrhynchus Papyri*, v. 49.

264. Collins, "From Noble Death to Crucified Messiah;" Nickelsburg, "Genre of the Markan Passion Narrative."

265. Toynbee, *Study of History*, v. 4, 403–4, 524–25, and discussion above.

266. Collins, "Genre of the Passion," 14; *Beginning of the Gospel* does not include this reference; Munro, "Women Disciples in Mark?" 225–41, esp. 226; Toynbee, *Study of History*, v. 4, 421;

267. Luke reinforces this connection with Psalm 38:11 by the addition of *oi gnostoi* (friends) (Lk 24:49).

268. Bultmann, *History of the Synoptic Tradition*, 276; Matera, *Kingship of Jesus*, 51.

269. See above, ch. 2.

270. Munro, "Women Disciples?"

271. Positing a pre-Markan written source is difficult, in spite of the valiant attempts of many scholars to do so. Lack of agreement among scholars in this endeavor may be a sign of hopelessness of the task. For a review of scholarship, see Mack, *Myth of Innocence*, 249–68; Telford, "The Pre-Markan Tradition in Recent Research," in *The Four Gospels: Festschrift for Frans Neirynck*, v. 2, F. van Segbroeck, et al. eds., 693–723. Many elements of the Passion narrative can be accounted for on the basis of the "suffering *dikaios*" model, the "noble death" model and references to lament Psalms. See Mack, *Myth of Innocence*, 269–312 and the collection of articles in Werner H. Kelber, *Studies on Mark 14–16*. Crossan's thesis (*Cross that Spoke*) that the Gospel of Peter contains early elements is not convincing due to the late manuscript evidence, the novelistic developments in the story, and its lack of clear independence from the Markan account (see above).

272. So Crossan, "Empty Tomb," and *Cross that Spoke*, 281–90.

273. Malbon, "Fallible Followers," *passim*; Munro, "Women Disciples," 230–31; Selvidge, "And Those Who Followed Feared," *passim*. See also Catchpole, "The Fearful Silence of the Women at the Tomb," 3–10; Corley, *Private Women, Public Meals*, 84–85; Kinukawa, *Women and Jesus*, 95–96.

274. Collins, "Genre of the Passion Narrative," 14. Again, this association is nowhere found in *Beginning of the Gospel*.

275. Malbon, "Fallible Followers, 43; Munro, "Women Disciples," 235; Kinukawa, *Women and Jesus*, 95.

276. Corley, *Private Women, Public Meals*, 85–6.

277. Some commentators juxtapose the women over against the men as positive role models of faith. See Schmidt, "The Women in Mark's Gospel," 228–33.

278. Weeden, *Mark–Traditions in Conflict*. See also Best, *Following Jesus: Discipleship in the Gospel of Mark* ; Corley, *Private Women, Public Meals*, 84–85; Crossan, *Who Killed Jesus*, 182–84; Dewey, *Disciples on the Way*, 123–37; Kinukawa, *Women and Jesus*, 105–6; Malbon, "Fallible Followers."

279. J. Z. Smith, "No News is Good News."

280. It seems reasonable to conclude hat Mark is the author of both crucifixion and empty tomb narratives (so Crossan), but that does not mean he has no oral traditions at his disposal (see below).

281. De Ward, "Mourning Customs II," 159.

282. If the desertion of a teacher by his followers is an aretalogical theme, there is no reason not to consider the possibility that a few men mingled with a crowd to watch the crucifixion.

283. See now Funk and the Jesus Seminar, *Acts of Jesus*, 157–58.

284. It is highly unlikely that Joseph was a friend or disciple of Jesus. See Brown, *Death of the Messiah*, 2.1239–41. I doubt that Joseph is a completely fictional character as Crossan argues (*Who Killed Jesus?*, 172–73). See critique of Crossan by Gerald O'Collins and Daniel Kendall, "Did Joseph of Arimathea Exist?" 235–41.

285. Like the family of Yehohanan. One ossuary from Giv'at ha-Mivtar is inscribed "Simon," "a builder of the Temple." This confirms that a certain level of artisan, like temple builders, masons or engineers could afford large tombs and expensive ossuaries. See J. Naveh, "The Ossuary Inscriptions from Giv'at ha-Mivtar," 33–37.

286. E. A. Judge, "The Early Christians as a Scholastic Community," 4–15, esp. 9–11.

287. Rohde, *Psyche*, 144, n. 38.

288. For a complete discussion of the role of women in the creation of the Passion narrative, see *Lament and Gospel: Women's Voices in Passion Tradition* (New York: Oxford, forthcoming). Others see the lamenting of women as central to the development of Passion traditions. See Marianne Sawicki, *Seeing the Lord*, 165; Also now John Dominic Crossan, following Sawicki and myself in *The Birth of Christianity*, ch. 26.

Bibliography

Ancient Authors

Achilles Tatius. Text and trans. S. Gaselee. *Achilles Tatius*. LCL. London: William Heinemann; New York: G. P. Putnam's Sons, 1917.

Aeschylus. *The Persians*. Text and trans. Herbert Weir Smythe. *Aeschylus*, vol. 1. LCL. Cambridge, MA: Harvard University Press; William Heinemann, 1956.

Chariton. *Chaereas and Callirhoe*. Text by G. Molinié. *Chariton. Le roman de Chairéas et Callirhoé*. Paris: Collection des universités de France, 1979. Trans. B. P Reardon, "Chaereas and Callirhoe." In *Collected Ancient Novels*, 17–124 Ed. B. P. Reardon. Berkeley and Los Angeles: University of California Press, 1989.

Cicero. *Tusculan Disputations*. Text and trans. J. E. King. *Cicero. Tusculan Disputations*. LCL. Cambridge, MA: Harvard University Press; London: William Heinemann, 1945.

First Letter of Clement. Text and trans. Kirsopp Lake. *The Apostolic Fathers*, vol. 1. LCL. London: William Heinemann, 1962.

Gospel of Peter. Text by Mara, M. Grazia, ed. *Évangile de Pierre*. SC 201. Paris: Éditions du Cerf., 1973. Trans. Christian Maurer, "The Gospel of Peter." In *New Testament Apocrypha*, vol. 1, 223–227. Ed. Wilhelm Schneemelcher. Louisville, KY: Westminster/John Knox, 1991.

Gospel of Thomas. Text and trans. Bentley Layton, *Nag Hammadi Codex II, 2–7*, vol. 1, 38–128. Leiden: Brill, 1989. Text and trans. Marvin Meyer. *The Gospel of Thomas: The Hidden Sayings of Jesus*. San Francisco: HarperSan Francisco, 1992.

Lucian. *On Funerals*. Text and trans. A. M. Harmon. *Lucian*, vol. 4. LCL. London: William Heinemann; Cambridge, MA: Harvard University Press, 1969.

The Mishnah. Trans. Herbert Danby. Oxford: Oxford University Press, 1992.

Munich Coptic Papyrus 5. Text by W. Henstenberg, "Koptische Papyri." In *Beiträge zur Forschung: Studien und Mitteilungen aus dem Antiquariat Jacques Rosenthal, München*, vol 1 (= "erste Folge"), 95–100, 8–11. Ed. Jacques Roenthal. Münich: Verlag von Jacques Rosenthal, 1915. Translation by Marvin Meyer in Marvin Meyer and Richard Smith. *Ancient Christian Magic: Coptic Texts of Ritual Power*. San Francisco: HarperSan Francisco, 1994, 188–190.

Origen. *Contra Celsum*. Translation by Henry Chadwick. *Origen: Contra Celsum*. Cambridge: Cambridge University Press, 1953.

Philostratus. *Life of Apollonius of Tyana*. Text and trans. F. C. Conybeare. *Philostratus: Life of Apollonius of Tyana*. LCL. Cambridge: Harvard University Press; London: William Heinemann, 1960.

Plato. *Phaedo*. Text and trans, Harold North Fowler. *Plato*, vol. 1. LCL. London: William Heinemann; Cambridge, MA: Harvard University Press, 1971.

Plutarch. *Moralia*. Text and trans. F. C. Babbitt, et al. *Plutarch's Moralia*. LCL.Cambridge, MA: Harvard University Press; London: William Heinemann, 1927–1969.

Porphyry. *Life of Pythagoras*. Text by Édouard des Places. *Porphyre. Vie de Pythagore, Lettre a Marcella*. Paris: Collection des universités des France, 1982.

Pseudo-Philo. *Biblical Antiquities*. Text by Daniel J. Harrington, *Pseudo- Philon*, vol. 1. Source chrétiennes 229. Paris: Editions du cerf, 1976. Trans. D. J. Harrington, *Old Testament Pseudepigrapha*, vol. 2, 297–377. Ed. James H. Charlesworth. Garden City, New York: Doubleday, 1985.

Pseudo-Phocylides. *Sentences*. Text and trans. by P. W. Van der Horst. *The Sentences of Pseudo-Phocylides*. Leiden: Brill, 1978.

Seneca. *Hercules Oetaeus*. Text and trans. Frank Justus Miller. *Seneca. Tragedies*, vol. 2. LCL. Cambridge, MA: Harvard University Press; London: William Heinemann, 1968.

Septuaginta. Stuttgart: Deutsche Bibelgesellschaft, 1979.

Zlotnick, Dov. *The Tractate "Mourning" (Semahot)*. New Haven: Yale University Press, 1966.

Modern Authors

Abrahams, I. "Publicans amd Sinners." In *Studies in Pharisaism and the Gospels*, 54–61. New York: KTAV Publishing House, 1967.

Achtemeier, Paul J. "The Disciples in Mark." In *Mark*. Proclamation Commentaries. Philadelphia: Fortress Press, 1986.

____. "Gospel Miracle Traditions and the Divine Man." *Interpretation* 26 (1972) 174–197.

Alexandre, Monique. "Early Christian Women." In *A History of Women I: From Ancient Goddesses to Christian Saints*, 409–444. Ed. Pauline Schmitt Pantel. Cambridge, MA: Harvard University Press, 1992.

Alexiou, Margaret. *The Ritual Lament in Greek Tradition*. Cambridge: Cambridge University Press, 1974.

Allberry, C. R. C., ed. *A Manichaean Psalmbook*, II. Stuttgart: W. Kohhammer, 1938.

Amaru, Betsy Halpern. "Portraits of Biblical Women in Josephus' Antiquities." *Journal of Jewish Studies* 39 (1988) 143–170.

Anderson, Bonnie S. and Judith P. Zinsser. *A History of Their Own: Women from Pre-history to the Present*, vol. 1. New York: Harper and Row, 1988.

Archer, Léonie J. *Her Price is Beyond Rubies: The Jewish Woman in Greco-Roman Palestine*. Sheffield: JSOT Press, 1990.

Arnal, William E. "Gendered Couplets in Q and Legal Formulations: From Rhetoric to Social History." *Journal of Biblical Literature* 116 (1997) 75–94.

____ . "Reconstruction of Q 7:29–30." Paper presented to the International Q Project. Claremont, CA, May 1994.

Asgeirsson, Jon Ma. and James M. Robinson. "The International Q Project: Work Sessions 12–14 July, 22 November 1991." *Journal of Biblical Literature* 111 (1992) 500–508.

Atwood, Richard. *Mary Magdalene in the New Testament and Early Tradition*. New York: Peter Lang, 1993.

Aune, David E. "Heracles and Christ: Heracles Imagery in the Christology of Early Christianity." In *Greeks, Romans and Christians: Essays in Honor of Abraham Malherbe*. Minneapolis: Fortress Press, 1990.

Avigad, N. "Aramaic Inscriptions in the Tomb of Jason." *Israel Exploration Journal* 17 (1967) 101–111.

____. "The Epitaph of a Royal Steward from aSiloam Village." *Israel Exploration Journal* 3 (1953) 137–152.

____ . A Seal of a Slave-Wife (Amah)." *Palestine Exploration Quarterly* 78 (1946) 125–132.

Avisur, Y. "A Ghost-Expelling Incantation from Ugarit." *Ugarit-Forschungen* 13 (1981) 13–25.

Ayrout, Henry Habib. *The Egyptian Peasant*. Boston: Beacon Press, 1963.

Bahr, Gordon J. "The Seder of Passover and Eucharistic Words." *Novum Testamentum* 12 (1970) 181–202.

Bailey, James L. "Experiencing the Kingdom as a Little Child: A Rereading of Mark 10:13–16." *Word and World* 15 (1995) 58–67.

Balch, David L. "1 Cor 7:32–35 and Stoic Debates about Marriage, Anxiety and Distraction." *Journal of Biblical Literature* 102 (1983) 429–439.

____ . *Let Wives Be Submissive: The Domestic Code in 1 Peter*. Chico, CA: Scholars Press, 1981.

Baltzer, Klaus. "Liberation from Debt Slavery After the Exile in Second Isaiah and Nehemiah." In *Ancient Israelite Religion: Essays in Honor of Frank Moore Cross*, 477–484. Eds. Patrick D. Miller, et al. Philadelphia: Fortress Press, 1987.

Barr, James. "'Abba, Father' and the Familiarity of Jesus' Speech." *Theology* 91 (1988) 173–179.

____ . "Abba Isn't Daddy." *Journal of Theological Studies* 39 (1988) 28–47.

Barrett, C. K. *The Gospel According to St. John*. London: SPCK, 1978.

Basser, Herbert W. "Let the Dead Bury Their Dead: Rhetorical Features of Rabbinic and New Testament Literature. In *Approaches to Ancient Judaism*, vol. 5, 79–95. Eds. Herbert W. Basser and Simcha Fishbane. New Series. Atlanta, GA: Scholars Press, 1993.

Batey, Richard A. *Jesus and the Forgotten City: New Light on Sepphoris and the Urban World of Jesus*. Grand Rapids, MI: Baker Book House, 1991.

Batten, Alicia. "More Queries for Q: Women and Christian Origins." *Biblical Theology Bulletin* 24 (1994) 44–51.

Bauckman, Richard. "Salome the Sister of Jesus, Salome the Disciple of Jesus and the Secret Gospel of Mark." *Novum Testamentum* 33 (1991) 245–275.

Baumgarten, Joseph M. "4Q502: Marriage or Golden Age Ritual?" *Journal of Jewish Studies* 34 (1983) 125–135.

____. "Hanging and Treason in Qumran and Roman Law." *Eretz-Israel* 16 (1982) 7–16.

____. "On the Testimony of Women in 1QSa." *Journal of Biblical Literature* 26 (1957) 108–122.

____. "The Qumran-Essene Restraints on Marriage." In *Archaeology and History in the Dead Sea Scrolls*, 13–24. Ed. Lawrence Schiffman. Sheffield: JSOT Press, 1990.

Beames, Michael. *Peasants and Power. The Whiteboy Movements and Their Control in Pre-Famine Ireland.* Sussex: Harvester Press; New York: St. Martin's Press, 1983.

Beasley-Murray, George. *John.* Waco, TX: Word Books, 1987.

Beavis, Mary Ann. "Ancient Slavery as an Interpretive Context for the New Testament Servant Parables With Special Reference to the Unjust Steward." *Journal of Biblical Literature* 111 (1992) 37–54.

____. "Women as Models of Faith in Mark." *Biblical Theology Bulletin* 18 (1988) 3–9.

Benoit, P. *The Passion and Resurrection of Jesus Christ.* New York: Herder and Herder, 1969.

Bercé, Yves-Marie. *Revolt and Revolution in Early Modern Europe.* New York: St. Martin's Press, 1987.

Best, Ernst. *Disciples and Discipleship. Studies in the Gospel According to Mark.* Edinburgh: T and T Clark, 1986.

____. *Following Jesus: Discipleship in the Gospel of Mark.* Sheffield: JSOT Press, 1981.

____. "Mark 10:13–16: The Child as Model Recipient." In *Biblical Studies: Essays in Honor of William Barclay*, 119–134. Eds. Johnston R. McKay and James F. Miller. Philadelphia: Westminster Press, 1976.

____. "The Role of the Disciples in Mark." *New Testament Studies* 23 (1977) 377–401.

Betz, Hans Dieter. *The Greek Magical Papyri in Translation.* Chicago: University of Chicago Press, 2nd edition, 1992.

____. "Jesus as Divine Man." In *Jesus the Historian*, 114–131. Edited by F. T. Trotter. Philadelphia: Westminster Press, 1968.

____. *The Sermon on the Mount.* Minneapolis: Fortress Press, 1995.

Beuken, W. A. M. "1 Samuel 28: The Prophet as Hammer of Witches" *Journal for the Study of the Old Testament* 6 (1978) 3–17.

The Bible and Culture Collective. *The Postmodern Bible.* New Haven and London: Yale University Press, 1995.

Bieler, L. *Theios Aner: das Bild des "göttlichen Menchen" im Späntike und Frühchristentum.* Darmstadt: Wissenschaftliche Buchgessellschaft, 1976.

Bird, Phyllis A. "The Harlot as Heroine: Narrative Art and Presupposition in Three Old Testament Texts." *Semeia* 46 (1989) 119–139.

Blackburn, Barry. *Theios Aner and the Markan Miracle Traditions.* Tübingen: J.C.B. Mohr, 1991.

Blasi, Anthony J. *Early Christianity as a Social Movement.* Toronto Studies in Religion 5. New York: Peter Lang, 1988.

Bloch-Smith, Elizabeth. *Judahite Burial Practice and Beliefs About the Dead.* Sheffield: Sheffield Press, 1992.

Booth, Alan, "The Age of Reclining and Its Attendant Perils." In *Dining in a Classical Context,* 105–120. Ed. William J. Slater. Ann Arbor: University of Michigan Press, 1991.

Borg, Marcus J. *Jesus, A New Vision: Spirit, Culture, and the Life of Discipleship.* San Francisco: Harper San Francisco, 1987.

____ . *Jesus in Contemprary Scholarship.* Valley Forge, PA: Trinity Press International 1994.

____ . *Meeting Jesus Again for the First Time: The Historical Jesus and the Heart of Contemporary Faith.* San Francisco: HarperSan Francisco, 1994.

Boyarin, Daniel. *Carnal Israel: Reading Sex in Talmudic Culture.* Berkeley: University of California Press, 1993.

Bradley, K. R. *Slaves and Masters in the Roman Empire: A Study in Social Control.* New York and Oxford: Oxford University Press, 1984.

Brenner, Athalya. *The Israelite Woman: Social and Literary Type in Biblical Narrative.* Sheffield: JSOT Press, 1985.

Broadhead, H.D. *The Persae of Aeschylus.* Cambridge: Cambridge University Press, 1960.

Bronner, Leila Leah. *From Eve to Esther: Rabbinic Reconstructions of Biblical Women.* Louisville, KY: Westminster/John Knox, 1994.

Brooke, George J. "Power to the Powerless: A Long-lost Song of Miriam." *Biblical Archaeology Review* 20 (May/June 1994) 62–65.

____ . ed. *Women in the Biblical Tradition.* Lewiston; Queenston; Lampeter: Edwin Mellen Press, 1992.

Brooten, Bernadette. "Early Christian Women and Their Cultural Context: Issues in Method and Historical Reconstruction." In *Feminist Perspectives on Biblical Scholarship*, 65–91. Ed. Adela Yarbro Collins. Chico, CA: Scholars Press, 1985.

____ . "Jewish Women's History in the Roman Period: A Task for Christian Theology." *Harvard Theological Review* 79 (1986) 22–30.

____ . "Konnten Frauen im alten Judentum die Scheidung betreiben?" *Evangelische Theologie* 42 (1982) 66–80.

____ . *Women Leaders in the Ancient Synagogue.* Chico, CA: Scholars Press, 1982.

Brown, Carole Anne. *No Longer Silent: First Century Jewish Portraits of Biblical Women.* Louisville, KY: Westminster/John Knox Press, 1992.

Brown, Colin. "The Parable of the Rebellious Son (s)." Unpublished manuscript. Used with perimission.

Brown, G. M. et al., eds. *The Oxyrhynchus Papyri*, v. 41. London: Egypt Exploration Society, 1972.

Brown, Nathan J. *Peasant Politics in Modern Egypt: The Struggle Against the State.* New Haven and London: Yale University Press, 1990.

Brown, Peter. *The Cult of the Saints: Its Rise and Function in Latin Christianity.* Chicago: University of Chicago Press, 1981.

Brown, Raymond E. *The Death of the Messiah. A Commentary on the Passion Narratives in the Four Gospels.* 2 vols. New York; Doubleday, 1994.

____ , et al. *Mary in the New Testament.* New York; Mahwah: Fortress Press, 1978.

Browne, G. M. *The Oxyrhynchus Papyri*, vol. 41. London: Egypt Exploration Society, 1972.

Buchanan, George Wesley. "Jesus and the Upper Class." *Novum Testamentum* 7 (1964–65) 195–209.

Bullough, Vern and Bonnie. *Prostitution: An Illustrated Social History*. New York: Crown Publishers, 1978.

Bultmann, Rudolf. *Gospel of John: A Commentary*. Philadelphia: Westminister Press, 1971.

____ . *History of the Synoptic Tradition.* Translated by John Marsh. New York: Harper Collins, 1963.

Burns, John Barclay. "Necromancy and the Spirits of the Dead in the Old Testament." *Transactions of the Glaskow University Historical Society* 26 (1976) 1–14.

Cady, Susan, et al. *Sophia: The Future of Feminist Spirituality*. San Francisco: Harper and Row, 1986.

Cameron, Averil. "Neither Male Nor Female." *Greece and Rome* 27 (1980) 60–68.

____ . "Redrawing the Map: Early Christian Territory After Foucault." *Journal of Roman Studies* 76 (1986) 266–71.

Cameron, Ron. "What Have You Come Out to See? Characterizations of John and Jesus in the Gospels." *Semeia* 49 (1990) 35–69.

Camp, Claudia V. "First and Second Kings." In *The Woman's Bible Commentary*, 96–109. Eds. Carol A. Newsom and Sharon H. Ringe. Louisville, KY: Westminster/John Knox, 1992.

____. *Wise, Strange and Holy: The Strange Woman and the Making of the Bible.* Sheffield: Sheffield Academic Press, 2000.

Caravelli, Anna. "The Bitter Wounding: The Lament as Social Protest in Rural Greece." In *Gender and Power in Rural Greece*, 169–184. Edited by Jill Dubisch. Princton, NJ: Princeton University Press, 1986.

Caravelli-Chavez, Anna. "Bridge Between Worlds: The Greek Lament as Communicative Event." *Journal of American Folklore* 93 (1980) 129–157.

Carr, Anne E. *Transforming Grace: Christian Tradition and Women's Experience.* San Francisco: HarperSan Francisco, 1988.

Casson, Lionel. *Travel in the Ancient World.* Baltimore and London: Johns Hopkins University Press, 1994.

Castelli, Elizabeth. "Rethinking the Feminist Myth of Christian Origins." Paper presented at Candler School of Theology, Emory Univerisity. February 15, 1994.

____ . "Review: Elisabeth Schüssler Fiorenza, *But She Said* and *Jesus: Miriam's Child and Sophia's Prophet.*" *Religious Studies Review* 22 (1996) 296–300.

____ , and Hal Taussig, eds. *Reimagining Christian Origins: A Colloquium Honoring Burton L. Mack.* Valley Forge, PA: Trinity Press International, 1996.

Castner, Catherine J. "Epicurean Hetairai as Dedicants to Healing Deities?" *Greek, Roman and Byzantine Studies* 23 (1982) 51–57.

Catchpole, David. "The Fearful Silence of the Women at the Tomb: A Study in

Markan Theology." *Journal of Theology for Southern Africa* 18 (1977) 3–10.
Charlesworth, James H. "A Caveat on Textual Transmission and the Meaning of the Lord's Prayer." In *The Lord's Prayer and Other Prayer Texts from the Greco-Roman Era*, 1–14. Ed. James H. Charlesworth, et al. Valley Forge, PA: Trinity Press International, 1994.
____ . "The Foreground of Christian Origins and the Commencement of Jesus Research." In *Jesus' Jewishness: Exploring the Place of Jesus Within Early Judaism*, 63–83. New York: Crossroad, 1991.
____ . "Greek, Persian, Roman, Syrian and Egyptian Influences in Early Jewish Theology." In *Hellenica et Judaica: Hommage á Valentin Nikiprowetzky*, 219–243. Ed. A. Caquot, et al. Leuven and Paris: Peeters, 1986.
____ , ed. *Jesus' Jewishness: Exploring the Place of Jesus Within Early Judaism*. New York: Crossroad, 1991.
Chilton, Bruce. "Jesus Within Judaism." In *Judaism and Late Antiquity*, vol. 2, 278–280. Ed. Jacob Neusner. Leiden: Brill, 1995.
____ . *Pure Kingdom: Jesus' Vision of God*. Grand Rapids, MI: Eerdmans, 1996.
Chilton, Bruce and Jacob Neusner. *Judaism in the New Testament: Practices and Beliefs*. New York and London: Routledge, 1995.
Cohen, Shaye J. D., ed. *The Jewish Family in Antiquity*. Atlanta, GA: Scholars Press, 1993.
____ . "Menstruants and the Sacred in Judaism and Christianity." In *Women's History and Ancient History*, 273–299. Ed. S. B. Pomeroy, Chapel Hill and London: University of North Carolina Press, 1991.
Collins, Adela Yarbro. *The Beginning of the Gospel: Probings of Mark in Context*. Minneapolis: Fortress Press, 1992.
____ . "The Composition of the Markan Passion Narrative." *Sewanee Theological Review* 36 (1992) 57–77.
____ . "The Empty Tomb in the Gospel According to Mark." In *Hermes and Athena: Biblical Exegesis and Philosophical Theology*, 107–140. Edited by E. Stump and T. P. Flint. Notre Dame, IN: University of Notre Dame Press, 1993.
____ . "From Noble Death to Crucified Messiah." *New Testament Studies* 40 (1994) 481–503.
____ . "The Genre of the Passion Narrative." *Studia Theologica* 47 (1993) 3–28.
Collins, John J. "Marriage, Divorce and Family in Second Temple Judaism." In *Familes in Ancient Israel*, 104–162. Eds. Leo Perdue, et al. Louisville, KY: Westminster/John Knox, 1997.
Conzelmann, Hans. "History and Theology in the Passion Narratives." *Interpretation* 2 (1979) 178–197.
Corley, Kathleen E. "The Anointing of Jesus in the Synoptic Tradition." *Journal for the Study of the Historical Jesus*, forthcoming.
____. "The Egalitarian Jesus: A Christian Myth of Origins." *Forum* NS 1, 2 (1990) 291–325.
____ . "Feminist Myths of Christian Origins." In *Reimagining Christian Origins: A Colloquium Honoring Burton L. Mack*, 49–65. Eds. Elizabeth A. Castelli and Hal Taussig. Valley Forge, PA: Trinity Press International, 1996.

____ . *Private Women, Public Meals: Social Conflict in the Synoptic Tradition.* Peabody, MA: Hendrickson, 1993.

____ . "Jesus' Table Practice: Dining With 'Tax Collectors and Prostitutes,' Including Women." In *Society of Biblical Literature 1993 Seminar Papers*, 444–459. Ed. Eugene H. Lovering. Atlanta, GA: Scholars Press, 1993.

____ . *Lament and Gospel: Women's Voices in Passion Tradition* (Oxford University Press, forthcoming).

____ . "Salome." *International Standard Bible Encyclopedia*, vol. 4, 286. Grand Rapids, MI: Eerdmans, 1988.

____. "Salome and Jesus at Table in the Gospel of Thomas." *Semeia* 86 (2001) 85–97.

____ . "Were the Women Around Jesus Really Prostitutes? Women in the Context of Greco-Roman Meals." *Society of Biblical Literature 1989 Seminar Papers*, 487–521. Ed. David J. Lull. Atlanta, GA: Scholars Press, 1989.

Cotter, Wendy. "Parable of the Children in the Marketplace [Q [Lk]] 7:31–35]: An Examination of the Parable's Image and Significance." *Novum Testamentum* 29 (1987) 289–304.

____ . "'Yes, I Tell You, and More Than a Prophet:' The Function of John in Q." In *Conflict and Invention: Literary, Rhetorical, and Social Studies on the Sayings Gospel Q*, 135–150. Ed. John S. Kloppenborg. Valley Forge, PA: Trinity Press International, 1995.

Crossan, John Dominic. *The Birth of Christianity.* San Francisco: HarperSan Francisco, 1998.

____. *The Cross that Spoke: The Origins of the Passion Narrative.* San Francisco: Harper Collins, 1988.

____ . "Empty Tomb and Absent Lord (Mark 16:1–8)." In *The Passion in Mark: Studies on Mark 14–16*, 135–152. Edited by W. H. Kelber. Philadelphia: Fortress Press, 1976.

____ . *The Historical Jesus: The Life of a Mediterranean Jewish Peasant.* San Francisco: HarperCollins, 1991.

____ . *In Parables: The Challenge of the Historical Jesus.* Sonoma, CA: Polebridge Press, 1992.

____ . "Mark and the Relatives of Jesus." *Novum Testamentum* 15 (1973) 81–113.

____ . "The Servant Parables of Jesus." *Semeia* 1 (1974) 17–62.

____ . *Who Killed Jesus? Exposing the Roots of Anti-Semitism in the Gospel Story of the Death of Jesus.* San Francisco: HarperSan Francisco, 1995.

Crown Alan D. and Lena Cansdale. "Qumran: Was It an Essene Settlement?" *Biblical Archaeology Review* (Sept/Oct 1994) 24–35.

Cullmann, Oscar. "Immortality of the Soul or Resurrection of the Dead?" In *Immortality and Resurrection*, 9–53. Edited by K. Stendahl. New York: Macmillan, 1965.

Cumont, Franz. *Afterlife in Roman Paganism.* New Haven: Yale University Press, 1922.

Daly, Lloyd W. *Aesop Without Morals.* New York and London: Thomas Yoseloff, 1961.

Danforth, Loring M. *The Death Rituals of Rural Greece.* New Jersey: Princeton University Press, 1982.

D' Angelo, Mary Rose. "'*Abba*' and 'Father': Imperial Theology and the Jesus Traditions." *Journal of Biblical Literature* 111 (1992) 611–630.

____. "Reconstructing "Real" Women From Gospel Literature." In *Women and Christian Origins*, 105–128. Eds. Ross S. Kraemer and Mary Rose D'Angelo. New York: Oxford University Press, 1999.

____ . "Re-membering Jesus: Women, Prophecy and Resistance in the Memory of the Early Churches." *Horizon* 19 (1992) 199–218.

____ . "Theology in Mark and Q: '*Abba*' and 'Father' in Context." *Harvard Theological Review* 85 (1992) 149–74.

____ . "Women Partners in the New Testament." *Journal of Feminist Studies in Religion* 6 (1990) 65–86.

D'Arms, John H. "Slaves at Roman Convivia." In *Dining in a Classical Context*, 171–183. Ed. William Slater. Ann Arbor: University of Michigan Press, 1991.

Daube, David. "Rabbinic Methods of Interpretation and Hellenistic Rhetoric." *Hebrew Union College Annual* 22 (1949) 239–264.

____ . *Roman Law: Linguistic, Social and Philosophical Aspects*. Edinburgh: University Press, 1969.

Dauer, Anton. *Die Passionsgeschichte im Johannesevangelium*. Munich: Kösel-Verlag, 1972.

Davids, Stacy. "Appearances of the Resurrected Jesus and the Experience of Grief." Paper presented to the Jesus Seminar. Spring 1995.

____ . "What is the Truth About the Resurrection of Jesus? The Testimony of Mary Magdalene." Unpublished paper. Used with permission.

D'Avino, Michele. *The Women of Pompeii*. Trans. Monica Hope Jones and Luigi Nusco. Napoli: Loffredo, 1967.

Deere, Carmen Diana. *Household and Class Relations: Peasants and Landlords in Northern Peru*. Berkeley; Los Angeles; Oxford: University of California Press, 1990.

Deissler, Alfons. "The Spirit of the Lord's Prayer in the Faith and Worship of the Old Testament." In *The Lord's Prayer and Jewish Liturgy*, 3–17. Ed. Jakob J. Petuchowski and Michael Brocke. New York: Seabury Press, 1978.

Deissmann, Adolf. *Light from the Ancient Near East*. Trans. L. R. M. Strachan. London: Hodder and Stoughton, 1927.

Delatte, A. *La catoptromancie grecque et ses dérivés*. Liege and Paris: l'Université de Liége, 1932.

Derrett, J. Duncan M. "Why Jesus Blessed the Children (Mark 10:13–16, Par.)." *Novum Testamentum* 15 (1983) 1–18.

De Romilly, Jacqueline. *Magic and Rhetoric in Ancient Greece*. Cambridge: MA: Harvard University Press, 1975.

De Vaux, Roland. *Ancient Israel: Its Life and Institutions*. London: Darton, Longman and Todd, 1961.

De Ward, Eileen F. "Mourning Customs in 1, 2 Samuel." *Journal of Jewish Studies* 23 (1972) 1–27.

____ . "Mourning Customs in 1, 2 Samuel II." *Journal of Jewish Studies* 23 (1972) 145–166.

Dewey, Arthur. "A Prophetic Pronoucement: Q 12:42–46." *Forum* 5.2 (1989) 99–108.

Dewey, Joanna. *Disciples on the Way: Mark on Discipleship*. UMC: Women's Division, Board of Global Ministries, 1976.

____. "From Storytelling to Written Text: The Loss of Early Christian Voices." *Biblical Theology Bulletin* 26 (1996) 71–78.

____. "The Gospel of Mark." In *Searching the Scriptures*, vol. 2, 470–509. Ed. Elisabeth Schüssler Fiorenza. New York, Crossroad, 1994.

Dibelius, Martin. *From Tradition to Gospel.* Greenwood, SC: Attic Press, 1982.

Dobbs-Allsopp, F. W. *Weep, O Daughter of Zion: A Study of the City-Lament Genre in the Hebrew Bible.* Rome: Pontificio Istituto Biblico, 1993.

Dodd, C. H. The Parables of the Kingdom. New York: Charles Scribner's Sons, 1961.

Dodds, E. R. *The Greeks and the Irrational.* Berkeley: University of California Press, 1968.

Donahue, John R. "Tax Collectors and Sinners: An Attempt at Identification." *Catholic Biblical Quarterly* 33 (1971) 39–60.

Dothan, T. "A Female Mourner Figure from the Lachish Region." *Eretz-Israel* 9 (1966) 43–47.

Douglas, Kelly Brown. *The Black Christ.* Maryknoll, NY: Orbis, 1994.

Douglas, Mary. *Purity and Danger: An Analysis of the Concepts of Pollution and Taboo.* London: Routledge, 1966.

Downing, F. Gerald. "*A Bas Les Aristos*: The Relevance of Higher Literature for the Understanding of Earliest Christian Writings." *Novum Testamentum* 30 (1988) 212–230.

____. *Christ and the Cynics.* Sheffield: Sheffield Academic Press, 1988.

____. *Jesus and the Threat of Freedom.* London: SCM Press, 1987.

Droge, Arthur J. and James D. Tabor. *A Noble Death: Suicide and Martyrdom among Christians and Jews in Antiquity.* San Francisco: HarperCollins, 1992.

Duff, A. M. *Freedmen in the Early Roman Empire.* NY: Barnes and Noble, 1958.

Dunn, James D. G. "Pharisees, Sinners and Jesus." In *The Social World of Formative Christianity and Judaism: Essays in Tribute to Howard Clark Kee*, 264–289. Ed. Jacob Neusner, et al. Philadelphia: Fortress Press, 1988.

Durber, Susan. "The Female Reader of the Parables of the Lost." *Journal for the Study of the New Testament* 45 (1992) 59–78.

Edwards, R. B. "Woman." *International Standard Bible Encyclopedia*, vol. 4, 1089–1097. Grand Rapids, MI: Eerdmans, 1988.

Edwards, Douglas. "The Socio-Economic and Cultural Ethos of the Lower Galilee in the First Century: Implications for the Nascent Jesus Movement." In *The Galilee in Late Antiquity*, 53–73. Ed. Lee I. Levine. New York and Jerusalam: Jewish Theological Seminary of America; Cambridge: Harvard University Press, 1992.

Ehrenreich, Barbara. "A Term of Honor." *Time* (23 Jan 1995) 64.

Eitrem, S. "The Necromancy of the Persai of Aischylos." *Symbolae Osloenses* 6 (1928) 1–16.

Elder, Linda Bennett. "The Woman Question and Female Ascetics Among Essenes." *Biblical Archaeologist* 57:4 (1994) 220–234.

Ellis, Ieuan. "Jesus and the Subversive Family." *Scottish Journal of Theology* 38 (1985) 173–188.

Epstein, Louis M. *Marriage Laws in the Bible and the Talmud.* Cambridge, MA: Harvard University Press, 1942.

Farmer, William R. "Who Are the 'Tax collectors and Sinners' in the Synoptic

Tradition?" In *From Faith to Faith. Essays in Honor of Donald G. Miller on His 70th Birthday*, 167–174. Ed. D. Y. Hadidan. Pittsburgh: Pickwick Press, 1979.

Faxon, Alicia Craig. *Women and Jesus*. Philadelphia: United Church Press, 1973.

Feldman, Emanuel. *Biblical and Post-Biblical Defilement and Mourning: Law as Theology*. New York: Yeshiva University Press, KTAV, 1977.

Feldman, Louis H. "How Much Hellenism in Palestine?" *Hebrew Union College Annual* 57 (1986) 83–111.

Fewell, Dann Nolan. "Joshua." In *The Woman's Bible Commentary*, 63–66. Eds. Carol A. Newsom and Sharon H. Ringe. Louisville, KY: Westminster/John Knox, 1992.

____ . "Judges." In *The Woman's Bible Commentary*, 67–77. Eds. Carol A. Newsom and Sharon H. Ringe. Louisville, KY: Westminster/John Knox, 1992.

Finegan, Jack. *The Archaeology of the New Testament*. Princeton, NJ: Princeton University Press, 1992.

Fitzmyer, Joseph A. "Crucifixion in Ancient Palestine, Qumran Literature, and the New Testament." *Catholic Biblical Quarterly* 40 (1978) 493–513.

____ . "Did Jesus Speak Greek?" *Biblical Archaeology Review* 18.5 (1992) 58–63; 76–77.

____ . "Divorce Among First-Century Palestinian Jews." *Eretz-Israel* 14 (1978) 103–110.

____ . *The Gospel According to Luke*. 2 vols. Garden City, NY: Doubleday, 1981–85.

____ . "The Matthean Divorce Texts and Some New Palestinian Evidence." *Theological Studies* 37 (1976) 197–226.

____ . "The Story of the Dishonest Manager (Luke 16:1–3)." In *Essays on the Semitic Background of the New Testament*, 161–184. Missoula, MT: Scholars Press, 1974.

Flesher, Paul Virgil McCracken. *Oxen, Women, or Citizens? Slaves in the System of the Mishnah*. Atlanta, GA: Scholars Press, 1988.

Flusser, D. "Paganism in Palestine," In *The Jewish People of the First Century*, vol. 2, 1065–1100. Ed. S. Safrai, et al. Assen/Maastricht: Van Gorcum; Philadelphia: Fortress Press, 1987.

Ford, J. Massingbaerde. "The Crucifixion of Women in Antiquity." *Journal of Higher Criticism* 3 (1996) 291–309.

Fortna, Robert T. "Chistology in the Fourth Gospel: Redaction-Critical Perspectives." *New Testament Studies* (1975) 489–504.

____ . *The Fourth Gospel and Its Predecessor*. Minneapolis: Fortress Press, 1988.

Fowl, Stephen. "Receiving the Kingdom of God as a Child: Children and Riches in Luke 18:15ff." *New Testament Studies* 39 (1993) 153–158.

Frader, Laura Levine. *Peasant Protest: Agricultural Workers, Politics and Unions in the Aude, 1850–1914*. Berkeley; Los Angeles; Oxford: University of California Press, 1991.

Fredriksen, Paula. "Did Jesus Oppose the Purity Laws?" *Bible Review* 11:3 (June 1995) 18–25; 42–45.

____ . *From Jesus to Christ: The Origins of the New Testament Images of Jesus*. New Haven and London: Yale University Press, 1988.

____. *Jesus of Nazareth, King of the Jews: A Jewish Life and the Emergence of Christianity*. New York: Alfred A. Knopf, 2000.

Freyne, Seán. *Galilee, Jesus and the Gospels: Literary Approaches and Historical Investigations*. Philadelphia: Fortress Press, 1988.

____ . "The Geography, Politics, and Economics of Galilee and the Quest for the Historical Jesus." In *Studying the Historical Jesus: Evaluations of the State of Current Research*, 75–121. Eds. Bruce Chilton and Craig Evans. Leiden and New York: Brill, 1994.

____. "Jesus the Wine-drinker: A Friend of Women." In *Transformative Encounters: Jesus and Women Re-viewed*, 162–180. Ingrid Rosa Kitzberger, Ed. Leiden: Brill, 2000.

____ . "Urban-Rural Relations in First-Century Galilee: Some Suggestions from the Literary Sources." In *The Galilee in Late Antiquity*, 75–91. Ed. Lee I. Levine. New York and Jerusalem: Jewish Theological Seminary of America; Cambridge: Harvard University Press, 1992.

Frymer-Kensky, Tikva. "Deuteronomy." In *The Woman's Bible Commentary*, 52–62. Eds. Carol A. Newsom and Sharon H. Ringe. Louisville, KY: Westminster/John Knox, 1992.

Funk, Robert W. *Honest to Jesus: Jesus for a New Millennium*. San Francisco: HarperSan Francisco, 1996.

____. *Parables and Presence: Forms of the New Testament Tradition*. Philadelphia: Fortress Press, 1982.

____ , et al. *The Parables of Jesus: Red Letter Edition*. Sonoma, CA: Polebridge Press, 1988.

Funk, Robert W. and The Jesus Seminar. *The Acts of Jesus: What Did Jesus Really Do*? San Francisco: HarperSan Francisco, 1998.

Funk, Robert, Roy Hoover, and the Jesus Seminar. *The Five Gospels: The Search for the Authentic Words of Jesus*. New York: Macmillan Publishing Co., 1993.

Gager, John G. *Moses in Greco-Roman Paganism*. New York: Abingdon, 1972.

Gallagher, Eugene V. *Divine Man or Magician? Celsus and Origen on Jesus*. Chico, CA: Scholars Press, 1982.

Garlan, Yvon. *Slavery in Ancient Greece*. Trans. Janet Lloyd. Ithaca and London: Cornell University Press, 1988.

Garland, Robert. *The Greek Way of Death*. Ithaca, NY: Cornell University Press, 1985.

____ . "The Well-Ordered Corpse: An Investigation Into the Motives Behind Greek Funerary Legislation." *Bulletin of the Institute for Classical Studies* 36 (1989) 1–15.

Gibbs, John G. and Louis H. Feldman, "Josephus' Vocabulary for Slavery." *Jewish Quarterly Review* 76 (1986) 281–310.

Gibson, J. "*Hoi Telonai kai hai Pornai.*" *Journal of Theological Studies* 32 (1981) 429–433.

Gnilka, Joachim. *Jesus of Nazareth: Message and History*. Peabody, MA: Hendrickson, 1997.

Goitein, S. D. "Women as Creators of Biblical Genres." *Prooftexts* 8 (1988) 1–33.

Golden, Mark. "Chasing Change in Roman Childhood." *Ancient History Bulletin* 4 (1990) 90–94.

____ . "*Pais*, 'Child' and 'Slave.'" *L' antique classique* 54 (1985) 91–104.

Goodenough, Erwin R. *Jewish Symbols in the Greco-Roman Period*. 13 Volumes. New York: Pantheon Books, 1953.

Goodman, Martin. "The First Jewish Revolt: Social Conflict and the Problem of Debt." *Journal of Jewish Studies* 33 (1982) 417–427.

____ . *The Ruling Class of Judea: The Origins of the Jewish Revolt Against Rome A.D. 66–70*. Cambridge: Cambridge University Press, 1987.

Grant, Jacquelyn. *White Woman's Christ, Black Woman's Jesus: Feminist Christology and Womanist Responses*. Atlanta, GA: Scholars Press, 1989.

Grassi, Joseph A. *Hidden Heroes of the Gospels: Female Counterparts of Jesus*. Collegeville, MN: Liturgical Press, 1989.

____ . "The Secret Heroine of Mark's Drama." *Biblical Theology Bulletin* 18 (1988) 10–15.

Greeley. Andrew M. "Domestic Violence: One Strike and You're Out." *The Press Democrat*. 9 July 1994, D4.

Green, Joel B. *The Death of Jesus: Tradition and Interpretation in the Passion Narrative*. Tübingen: J. C. B. Mohr, 1988.

____ . "Good News to Whom? Jesus and the 'Poor' in the Gospel of Luke." In *Jesus of Nazareth: Lord and Christ*, 54–74. Ed J. B. Green and M. Turner. Grand Rapids, MI: Eerdmans, 1994.

Greenhut, Zvi. "Burial Cave of the Caiaphas Family." *Biblical Archaeology Review* 18.5 (1992) 29–36.

Grossman, Susan. "Women and the Jerusalem Temple." In *Daughters of the King: Women and the Synagogue*, 15–37. Ed. Susan Grossman and Rivka Hunt. Philadelphia; New York; Jerusalem: Jewish Publication Society, 1992.

Guenther, Heinz, O. "When 'Eagles' Draw Together." *Forum* 5 (1989) 140–50.

Gundry, Robert H. "The Language of First Century Palestine: Its Bearing on the Authenticity of the Gospel Tradition." *Journal of Biblical Literature* 83 (1964) 404–408.

____ . *Mark: A Commentary on His Apology for the Cross*. Grand Rapids, MI: Eerdmans, 1993.

____ . *Matthew: A Commentary on His Literary and Theological Art*. Grand Rapids, MI: Eerdmans, 1982.

Haas, N. "Anthropological Observations of the Skeletal Remains from Giv'at ha-Mivtar." *Israel Exploration Journal* 20 (1970) 38–59.

Hachlili, R. "Ancient Burial Customs Preserved in the Jericho Hills." *Biblical Archaeology Review* 5.4 (1979) 28–35.

____ . *Ancient Jewish Art and Archaeology of Israel*. Leiden: Brill, 1988.

Hadas, Moses and Morton Smith. *Heroes and Gods: Spiritual Biographies in Antiquity*. New York: Harper and Row, 1965.

Haenchen, Ernst. *John*. 2 Volumes. Philadelphia: Fortress Press, 1984.

Hagner, Donald. *The Jewish Reclamation of Jesus: An Analysis and Critique of the Modern Jewish Study of Jesus*. Grand Rapids, MI: Zondervan, 1984.

Halliday, W. R. "Cenotaphs and Sacred Localities." *Annual of the British School at Athens* 17 (1910–11) 182–192.

Hamel, Gilda. *Poverty and Charity in Roman Palestine, First Three Centuries C.E.* Berkeley; Los Angeles; Oxford: University of California Press, 1990.

Hammerton-Kelly, Robert. "God the Father in the Bible and in the Experience of Jesus: The State of the Question." In *God as Father?* 95–102. Eds. Johannes-Baptist Metz and Edward Schillebeeckx. Edinburgh: T and T Clark; New York: Seabury Press, 1981.

____ . *God the Father: Theology and Patriarchy in the Teaching of Jesus*. Philadelphia: Fortress Press, 1979.

Hanson, A. T. "Rahab the Harlot in Early Christian Tradition." *Journal for the Study of the New Testament* 1 (1978) 53–60.

Hartin, Patrick J. "First Response: Q 7:29–30." Paper presented to the International Q Project. Claremont, CA, May, 1994.

____ . "'Yet Wisdom is Justified By Her Children' (Q 7:35): A Rhetorical and Compositional Analysis of Divine Sophia in Q." In *Conflict and Invention: Literary, Rhetorical, and Social Studies on the Sayings Gospel Q*, 151–164. Ed. John S. Kloppenborg. Valley Forge, PA: Trinity Press International, 1995.

Haskins, Susan. *Mary Magdalene: Myth and Metaphor*. New York; San Diego; London: Harcourt Brace, 1993.

Hauck, F. and S. Schulz. "*porne, ktl.*" *Theological Dictionary of the New Testament*, Vol. 6, 579–95. Ed. G. Kittel. Grand Rapids, MI: Eerdmans, 1968.

Havener, Ivan. *Q: The Sayings of Jesus*. Wilmington, Delaware: Michaal Glazier, 1987.

Headlam, W. "Ghost Raising, Magic and the Underworld." *Classical Review* 16 (1902) 52–61.

Hedrick, Charles W. *Parables as Poetic Fictions: The Creative Voice of Jesus*. Peabody, MA: Hendrickson, 1994.

Heichelheim, F. M. *An Economic Survey of Ancient Rome: Roman Syria*. Baltimore: John Hopkins Press, 1938.

Heine, Susan. "Eine Person von Rang und Namen: historische Konturen der Magdalenerin." In *Jesu Rede von Gott und ihre Nachgeschichte im frühen Christentum: Beiträge zur Verkündigung Jesu und zum Kerygma der Kirche. Festschrift für Willi Marxen zum 70. Geburtstag,* 179–194. Edited by D.-A. Koch, et al. Gütersloh: Gütersloher Verlagshaus Gerd Mohn, 1989.

Heinemann, Joseph. "The Status of the Labourer in Jewish Law and Society in the Tannaitic Period." *Hebrew Union College Annual* 25 (1954) 263–325.

Hengel, Martin. *Crucifixion*. Philadelphia: Fortress Press, 1977.

____ . *Judaism and Hellenism*. Philadelphia: Fortress Press, 1974.

Herrenbrück, F. "Wer waren die 'Zöllner'?" *Zeitschrift für die neutestamentliche Wissenschaft* 72 (1981) 178–194.

____ . "Zum Vorwurf der Kollaboration des Zöllners mit Rom." *Zeitschrift für die neutestamentliche Wissenschaft* 78 (1987) 186–199.

Herzog, William R. *Parables as Subversive Speech: Jesus as Pedagogue of the Oppressed*. Louisville, KY: Westminster/John Knox 1994.

Heschel, Susannah. "Anti-Judaism in Christian Feminist Theology." *Tikkun* 5 (1990) 25–28; 95–97.

Hock, Ronald F. *The Infancy Gospels of James and Thomas*. Santa Rosa, CA: Polebridge Press, 1995.

____ . "The Will of God and Sexual Morality: I Thess. 4:3–8 in Its Social and Intellectual Context." Paper presented at the Society of Biblical Literature Annual Meeting. New York, 1982.

Hoenig, Sidney B. "Oil and Pagan Defilement." *Jewish Quarterly Review* 61 (1970/71) 63–75.

Hoffman, Paul. "Q 7:29–30: Fourth Response." Paper presented to the International Q Project. Claremont, CA, May 1994.

Holst-Warhaft, Gail. *Dangerous Voices: Women's Laments in Greek Literature.* London: Routledge, 1992.

Horsley, G. R. H. "Funerary Practice in Hellenistic and Roman Rhodes." In *New Documents Illustrating Early Christianity*, v. 2, 48–52. Ed. G. R. H. Horsley. Macquarie University: Ancient History Documentary Research Centre, 1982.

____ . "*Paidarion.*" In *New Documents Illustrating Early Christianity*, vol. 1, 87. Ed. G. R. H. Horsley. Macquarie University: Ancient History Documentary Research Centre, 1981.

____ . "Reclining at the Passover Meal." In *New Documents Illustrating Early Christianity*, vol. 2, 75. Ed. G. R. H. Horsley. Macquarie University: Ancient History Documentary Research Centre, 1982.

Horsley, Richard A. *Galilee: History, Politics, People.* Valley Forge, PA: Trinity Press International, 1995.

____ . "The Historical Jesus and Arhcaeology of the Galilee: Questions from Historical Research to Archaeologists." *Society of Biblical Literature 1994 Seminar Papers*, 91–135. Ed. E. H. Lovering. Atlanta, GA: Scholars Press, 1994.

____ . *Jesus and the Spiral of Violence: Popular Jewish Resistance in Roman Palestine.* Minneapolis: Fortress Press, 1987.

____ . *Sociology and the Jesus Movement.* New York: Continuum, 1994.

____ . "Wisdom is Justified by All Her Children: Examining Allegedly Disparate Traditions in Q." In *Society of Biblical Literature 1994 Seminar Papers*, 733–751. Ed. E. H. Lovering. Atlanta, GA:
1994.

Ilan, Tal. "The Attraction of Aristocratic Jewish Women to Pharisaic Judaism During the Second Temple Period," *Harvard Theological Review* 88 (1995) 1–33.

____. "In the Footsteps of Jesus: Jewish Women in a Jewish Movement." In *Transformative Encounters: Jesus and Women Re-viewed*, 115–136. Ingrid Rosa Kitzberger, Ed. Leiden: Brill, 2000.

____ . *Integrating Women Into Second Temple History.* Peabody, MA: Hendrickson, 2001.

____. *Jewish Women in Greco-Roman Palestine: An Inquiry into Image and Status.* Tübingen: J .C. B. Mohr, 1995; Reprint, Peabody, MA: Hendrickson, 1996.

____ . "'Man Born of Woman...' (Job 14:1): The Phenomenon of Men Bearing Metronymes at the Time of Jesus." *Novum Testamentum* 34 (1992) 23–45.

____ . "Notes and Observations on a Newly Published Divorce Bill From the Judean Desert." *Harvard Theological Review* 89 (1996) 195–202.

____. "Notes on the Distribution of Jewish Women's Names in Palestine in the Second Temple and Mishnaic Periods." *Journal of Jewish Studies* 40 (1989) 186–200.

Ingram, John Kells. *A History of Slavery and Serfdom*. London: Adam and Charles Black, 1895.

Isaac, Benjamin. "The Babatha Archive: A Review Article." *Israel Exploration Journal* 42 (1992) 62–75.

Jackson, Glenna. "Jesus as First-Century Feminist: Christian Anti-Judaism?" *Feminist Theology*, no. 19 (September 1998) 85–98.

Jackson, Howard M. "The Death of Jesus in Mark and the Miracle from the Cross." *New Testament Studies* 33 (1987) 16–37.

Jacobs-Malina, Diane. *Beyond Patriarchy: The Images of Family in Jesus*. New York/Mahwah, NJ: Paulist Press, 1993.

Jacobsen, Arland. "Divided Families and Christian Origins." In *The Gospel Behind the Gospel: Current Studies on Q*, 361–380. Ed. Ronald A. Piper. Leiden: Brill, 1995.

____. *The First Gospel: An Introduction to Q*. Sonoma, CA: Polebridge Press, 1992.

James, M. *The Apocryphal New Testament*. Oxford: Oxford Clarendon Press, 1963.

Jamison, Kay Redfield. *Touched With Fire: Manic Depressive Illness and the Artistic Temperment*. New York: Simon and Schuster, 1993.

Japhet, Sara. "The Laws of Manumission of Slaves and the Question of the Relationship Between Collections of Laws in the Pentateuch." In *Studies in Bible and the Ancient Near East. Presented to Samuel E. Loewenstamm*, vol. 1, 199–200. Ed. Yitschak Avishur and Joshua Blau. Jerusalem: E. Rubinstein's Publishing House, 1978.

Jefford, Clayton N. "The Dangers of Lying in Bed: Luke 17:34–35 and Parallels." *Forum* 5 (1990) 106–110.

Jepson, A. "Amah and Schiphchah." *Vestus Testamentum* 8 (1958) 293–297.

Jeremias, Joachim. *Abba. Studien zur neutestamentlischen Theologie und Zeitgeschichte*. Göttingen: Vandenhoeck and Ruprecht, 1966.

____. *The Eucharistic Words of Jesus*. London: SCM Press, 1966.

____. *Heilingengräber in Jesus Umwelt*. Göttingen: Vandenhoeck and Ruprecht, 1958.

____. *Jerusalem in the Time of Jesus*. Philadelphia: Fortress Press, 1975.

____. *New Testament Theology*. New York: Charles Scribner's Sons, 1971.

____. *The Parables of Jesus*. New York: Charles Scribner's Sons, 1972.

____. *The Prayers of Jesus*. Trans. John Bowden. Naperville, IL: Allec Allenson, 1967.

Jewett, Paul K. *Man as Male and Female*. Grand Rapids, MI: Eerdmans, 1975.

Johnson, Benjamin A. "Empty Tomb Tradition in the Gospel of Peter." Ph. D. Thesis. Harvard University, 1965.

Johnson, Elizabeth A. *Consider Jesus: Waves of Renewal in Christology*. New York: Crossroad, 1995.

____. "Jesus the Wisdom of God: A Biblical Basis for Non-Androcentric Christology." *Ephemerides theologicae lovanienses* 61 (1985) 261–294.

____ . "Redeeming the Name of Christ: Christology." In *Freeing Theology: The Essentials of Theology in Feminist Perspective*, 115–137. Ed. Catherine Mowry Lacugna. San Francisco: HarperSan Francisco, 1993.

____ . "Wisdom Was Made Flesh and Pitched Her Tent Among Us." In *Reconstructing the Christ: Essays in Feminist Christology*, 95–117. Ed. Maryanne Stevens. New York; Mahwah: Paulist Press, 1993.

Johnson, Elizabeth I. "Grieving for the Dead, Grieving for the Living: Funeral Laments of Hakka Women." In *Death Ritual in Late Imperial and Modern China*, 135–163. Eds. James L. Watson and Evelyn S. Rawski. Berkeley; Los Angeles; London: University of California Press, 1988.

Johnson, Luke T. "The New Testament's Anti-Jewish Slander and the Conventions of Ancient Polemic." *Journal of Biblical Literature* 108 (1989) 419–441.

Johnson, Sherman E. "Greek and Jewish Heroes: Fourth Maccabees and the Gospel of Mark." In *Early Christian Literature and the Classical Intellectual Tradition*, 155–175. Edited by W. R. Schoedel and R. L. Wilken. Paris: Éditions Beauchesne, 1979.

Johnson, Steven R. "Second Response: Q 7:29–30." Paper presented to the International Q Project. Claremont, CA, May, 1994.

Jones. A. H. M. "Slavery in the Ancient World." In *Slavery in Classical Antiquity*. Ed. M. I. Finley. Cambridge: W. Heffer and Sons, 1960.

Judge, E. A. "The Early Christians as a Scholastic Community." *Journal of Religious History* 1 (1960) 4–15.

Jungmann, Josef A. *The Early Liturgy to the Time of Gregory the Great*. Trans. F. A. Brunner. Notre Dame, IN: Notre Dame University Press, 1959.

Kam, Rose Sallberg. *Their Stories, Our Stories: Women of the Bible*. New York: Continuum, 1995.

Kampen, Natalie. *Image and Status: Roman Working Women in Ostia*. Berlin: Gebr. Mann, 1981.

Kearsley, R. A. "The Goliath Family at Jericho." *New Documents Illustrating Early Christianity*, vol. 6, 162–164. Ed. S. R. Llewelyn and R. A. Kearsley. Macquarie University: Ancient History Documentary Research Centre, 1992.

Kee, Howard Clark. "Aretalogy and Gospel." *Journal of Biblical Literature* 92 (1972) 402–422.

____ . "The Changing Role of Women in the Early Christian World." *Theology Today* 49 (1992) 225–238.

____ . *Community of the New Age: Studies in Mark's Gospel*. Philadelphia: Westminster Press, 1977.

Kelber, Werner H. *The Passion in Mark: Studies on Mark 14–16*. Philadelphia: Fortress Press, 1976.

Kennedy, Charles A. "Cult of the Dead." *Anchor Bible Dictionary*, vol. 2, 106. New York: Doubleday, 1992.

King, Karen L. "The Gospel of Mary Magdalene." In *Searching the Scriptures*, vol. 2, 601–634. Ed. Elisabeth Schüssler Fiorenza. New York: Crossroad Press, 1994.

____ . "Prophetic Power and Women's Authority: The Case of the Gospel of Mary (Magdalene)." In *Women Preachers and Prophets Through Two Millennia of*

Christianity, 21–41. Eds. Beverly Mayne Kienzle and Pamela J. Walker. Berkeley; Los Angeles; London: University of California Press, 1998.

Kingsbury, Jack D. *The Christology of Mark's Gospel.* Philadelphia: Fortress Press, 1983.

Kinukawa, Hisako. *Women and Jesus in Mark: A Japanese Feminist Perspective.* Maryknoll, NY: Orbis Books, 1994.

____. "Women Disciples of Jesus." *In A Feminist Companion to Mark*, 171–190. Ed. Amy-Jill Levine. Sheffield: Sheffield Academic Press, 2001.

Kitzberger, Ingrid Rosa, Ed. *Transformative Encounters: Jesus and Women Re-viewed.* Leiden: Brill, 2000.

Klassen, William. "Musonius Rufus, Jesus and Paul: Three First Century Feminists?" In *From Jesus to Paul. Studies in Honor of Francis Wright Beare*, 185–206. Ed. P. Richardson and J. Hurd. Ontario: Wilfred Laurier University Press, 1984.

Kloppenborg, John S. "Alms, Debt and Divorce: Jesus' Ethics in Their Mediterranean Context." *Toronto Journal of Theology* 6 (1990) 182–200.

____ , ed. *Conflict and Invention: Literary, Rhetorical, and Social Studies on the Sayings Gospel Q.* Valley Forge, PA: Trinity Press International, 1995.

____ . "The Dishonored Manager." *Biblica* 70 (1989) 474–495.

____. *Excavating Q: The History and Setting of the Sayings Gospel Q.* Minneapolis: Fortress Press, 2000.

____ . "*Exitus clari viri*: The Death of Jesus in Luke." *Toronto Journal of Theology* 8 (1992) 106–120.

____ . *The Formation of Q: Trajectories in Ancient Wisdom Collections.* Philadelphia: Fortress Press, 1987.

____ . "Literary Convention, Self-Evidence and the Social History of the Q People." *Semeia* 55 (1991) 77–102.

____ . *Q Parallels.* Sonoma, CA: Polebridge Press, 1988.

____ . "The Sayings Gospel Q: Recent Opinion on the People Behind the Document." *Currents in Research* 1 (1993) 9–34.

____ . "Symbolic Eschatology and the Apocalypticism of Q." *Harvard Theological Review* 80 (1987) 287–306.

____ . "Wisdom Christology in Q." *Laval théologique et philosophique* 34 (1978) 129–137.

Klosinski, Lee. "Meals in Mark." Ph.D. Dissertation. The Claremont Graduate School, 1988.

Knowles, Michael. *Jeremiah in Matthew's Gospel: The Rejected-Prophet Motif in Matthean Redaction.* Sheffield: JSOT Press, 1993.

Knox, W. L. "The 'Divine Hero' Christology in the New Testament." *Harvard Theological Review* 41 (1948) 229–249.

Koester, Helmut. *Ancient Christian Gospels.* Philadelphia: Trinity Press International; London: SCM Press, 1990.

____. "One Jesus and Four Primitive Gospels," *Harvard Theological Review* 61 (1968) 203–247.

Kopas, Jane. "Jesus and Women in Mark's Gospel." *Review for Religious* 44 (1985) 912–920.

Kraemer, Ross. *Her Share of the Blessings: Women's Religions Among Pagans, Jews and Christians in the Greco-Roman World.* New York and Oxford: Oxford University Press, 1992.

____ . "Jewish Mothers and Daughters in the Greco-Roman World." In *The Jewish Family in Antiquity*, 89–112. Ed. Shaye J. D. Cohen. Atlanta, GA: Scholars Press, 1993.

____. "Jewish Women and Christian Origins: Some Caveats." In *Women and Christian Origins*, 35–49. Eds. Ross S. Kraemer and Mary Rose D'Angelo. New York: Oxford University Press, 1999.

____. "Jewish Women and Women's Judaism(s) at the Beginning of Christianity." In *Women and Christian Origins*, 50–79. Eds. Ross S. Kraemer and Mary Rose D'Angelo. New York: Oxford University Press, 1999.

____ . "Monastic Jewish Women in Graeco-Roman Egypt: Philo Judaeus on the Therapeutrides." *Signs* 14 (1989) 342–70.

____ . "Review: Elisabeth Schüssler Fiorenza, *In Memory of Her*." *Religious Studies Review* 11 (1985) 1–9.

____, and Mary Rose D'Angelo, eds. *Women and Christian Origins*. New York: Oxford University Press, 1999.

Kramer, Samuel Noah. "BM 98396: A Sumerian Prototype of the *Mater-Dolorosa*." *Eretz-Israel* 16 (1982) 141–146.

____ . "The Weeping Goddess: Sumerian Prototypes of the *Mater Dolorosa*." *Biblical Archaeologist* 46 (Spring, 1983) 69–80.

Kugelmass, Jack, "Undser Shtik: The Meaning of Humor for American Jews." Paper presented to the Institute for Research in the Humanities Seminar. University of Wisconsin-Madison, Spring 1996.

Lachs, Samuel Tobias. *A Rabbinic Commentary on the New Testament: The Gospels Matthew, Mark and Luke*. Hoboken, NJ: KTAV Publishing House; New York: Anti-defamation League of B'nai B'rith, 1987.

Laffey, Alice L. *An Introduction to the Old Testament: A Feminist Perspective*. Philadelphia: Fortress Press, 1988.

LaSor, William Sanford. "Discovering What Jewish Miqva'ot Can Tell Us About Christian Baptism." *Biblical Archaeology Review* 13 (January/February 1987) 52–59.

Lassner, Jacob. *Demonizing the Queen of Sheba: Boundaries of Gender and Culture in Postbiblical Judaism and Medieval Islam*. Chicago: University of Chicago Press, 1993.

Lattimore, Richard. *Themes in Greek and Latin Epitaphs*. Urbana: University of Illinois Press, 1942.

Lawson, J. C. "The Evocation of Darius." *Classical Quarterly* 28 (1934) 79–89.

Lemche, N. P. "The 'Hebrew Slave:' Comments on the Slave Law Ex 21:2–11." *Vetus Testamentum* 25 (1975) 129–144.

____ . "The Manumission of Slaves – The Fallow Year – The Sabbatical Year – The Jobel Year." *Vetus Testamentum* 26 (1976) 38–59.

Lenski, Gerhard E. *Power and Privilege. A Theory of Social Stratification*. New York; St. Louis; San Francisco: McGraw-Hill, 1966.

Levine, Amy-Jill., ed. *A Feminist Companion to Mark*. Sheffield: Sheffield Academic Press, 2001.

____, ed. *A Feminist Companion to Matthew*. Sheffield: Sheffield Academic Press, 2001.

____. "Lilies of the Field and Wandering Jews: Biblical Scholarship, Women's Roles, and Social Location." In *Transformative Encounters: Jesus and Women Re-viewed*, 329–352. Ingrid Rosa Kitzberger, Ed. Leiden: Brill, 2000.

____. "Matthew." In *The Woman's Bible Commentary*, 252–262. Ed. Carol A. Newsom and Sharon H. Ringe. Louisville, KY: Westminster/John Knox, 1992.

____ . "Response by Levine to L. Swidler." *Journal of Ecumenical Studies* 26 (1989) 720–21.

____ . "Review: L. Swidler, *Yeshua: A Modern for Moderns*." *Journal of Ecumenical Studies* 26 (1989) 535–36.

____ . "Sacrifice and Salvation: Otherness and Dosmestication in the Book of Judith." In *"No One Spoke Ill of Her:" Essays on Judith*, 17–30. Ed. James C. VanderKam. Atlanta, GA: Scholars Press, 1992.

____ . "Second Temple Judaism, Jesus and Women: Yeast of Eden." *Biblical Interpretation* 2 (1994) 8–33.

____ . *The Social and Ethnic Dimensions of Matthean Salvation History*. Lewiston; Queenston; Lampeter: Edwin Mellen Press, 1988.

____ . "Who's Catering the Q Affair? Feminist Observations on Q Parenesis." *Semeia* 50 (1990) 145–162.

____. "Women in the Q Communit(ies) and Traditions." In *Women and Christian Origins*, 150–170. Eds. Ross S. Kraemer and Mary Rose D'Angelo. New York: Oxford University Press, 1999.

____ , ed. *"Women Like This": New Perspectives on Jewish Women in the Graeco-Roman World.* Atlanta, GA: Scholars Press, 1991.

Lewis, Theodore J. *Cults of the Dead in Ancient Israel and Ugarit.* Atlanta, GA: Scholars Press, 1989.

Licht, Hans. *Sexual Life in Ancient Greece*. New York: Barnes and Noble, 1953.

Liebermann, Saul. *Greek in Jewish Palestine: Studies in the Life and Manners of Jewish Palestine in the II–IV Centuries C.E.* New York: Jewish Theological Seminary of America, 1942.

Lindars, Barnabas. *The Gospel of John*. London: Oliphants, 1972.

Linnemann, Eta. *Parables of Jesus: Introduction and Exposition*. London: SPCK, 1982.

Linton, Olaf. "The Parable of the Children's Game." *New Testament Studies* 22 (1976) 159–179.

Lipinski, E. "The Wife's Right to Divorce in Light of An Ancient Near Eastern Tradition." *Jewish Law Annual* 4 (1981) 9–27.

Llewelyn, S. R. "He Gives Authority to His Slaves to Each His Work..." In *New Documents Illustrating Early Christianity*, vol. 6, 60–63. Ed. S. R. Llewelyn. Macquarie University, Australia: Ancient Documentary Research Centre, 1992.

____ . "Manumission at Delphi and Thessaly." In *New Documents Illustrating Early Christianity*, vol. 6, 76–81. Ed. S. R. Llewelyn. Macquarie University, Australia: Ancient Documentary Research Centre, 1992

____ ."The Sale of a Slave-Girl: The New Testament's Attitude to Slavery." In *New Documents Illustrating Early Christianity*, vol. 6, 48–55. Ed. S. R. Llewelyn. Macquarie University, Australia: Ancient Documentary Research Centre, 1992.

____ . "A Petition Concerning a Runaway: Paul's Letter to Philemon." In *New Documents Illustrating Early Christianity*, vol. 6, 55–60. Ed. S. R. Llewelyn. Macquarie University, Australia: Ancient Documentary Research Centre, 1992.

Longstaff, Thomas R. W. "What Are Those Women Doing at the Tomb of Jesus? Perspectives on Matthew 28:1." In *A Feminist Companion to Matthew*, 196–204. Ed. Am-Jill Levine. Sheffield: Sheffield Academic Press, 2001.

Loraux, Nicole. *The Experience of Tiresias: The Feminine and the Greek Man.* Princeton, NJ: Princeton University Press, 1995.

____. "Herakles: The Supermale and the Feminine." In *Before Sexuality: The Construction of Erotic Experience in the Ancient Greek World*, 21–52. Eds. D. M. Halperin, et al. Princeton, NJ: Princeton University Press, 1990.

____. *The Invention of Athens: The Funeral Oration in the Classical City.* Cambridge: Harvard University Press, 1986.

____. *Tragic Ways of Killing a Woman.* Cambridge, MA: Harvard University Press, 1987.

Luck, Georg. Arcana Mundi*: Magic and the Occult in the Greek and Roman Worlds.* Baltimore and London: Johns Hopkins University Press, 1985.

Luck, William F. *Divorce and Remarriage: Recovering the Biblical View.* San Francisco: Harper and Row, 1987.

Lüdemann, Gerd. *The Resurrection of Jesus: History, Experience, Theology.* Minneapolis: Fortress Press, 1994.

McArthur, Harvey. "Son of Mary." *Novum Testamentum* 15 (1973) 38–58.

McCane, Byron R. "Let the Dead Bury Their Own Dead: Secondary Burial and Matt 8:21–22." *Harvard Theological Review* 83 (1990) 31–43.

____. "Where No One Had Yet Been Laid: The Shame of Jesus' Burial." *Society of Biblical Literature 1993 Seminar Papers*, 473–484. Ed. by E. H. Lovering. Atlanta, GA: Scholars Press, 1993.

McCasland, Vernon S. "Abba, Father." *Journal of Biblical Literature* 72 (1953) 79–91.

MacDonald, Dennis R. *The Legend and the Apostle: The Battle for Paul in Story and Canon.* Philadelpha: Westminster, 1983.

MacHaffie, Barbara J. *Her Story: Women in Christian Tradition.* Philadelphia: Fortress Press, 1986.

Mack, Burton L. "The Anointing of Jesus: Elaboration Within a Chreia." In *Patterns of Persuasion in the Gospels*, 85–106. Burton L. Mack and Vernon K. Robbins. Sonoma, CA: Polebridge Press, 1989.

____. "The Kingdom that Didn't Come: Social History of the Q Tradents." In *Society of Biblical Literature 1988 Seminar Papers*, 608–635. Ed. David Lull. Atlanta, GA: Scholars Press, 1988.

____. *The Lost Gospel: The Book of Q and Christian Origins.* San Francisco: Harper San Francisco, 1993.

____. *A Myth of Innocence: Mark and Christian Origins.* Minneapolis: Fortress Press, 1988.

____. *Who Wrote the New Testament? The Making of the Christian Myth.* San Francisco: Harper San Francisco, 1995.

Mack, Burton and Vernon Robbins. *Patterns of Persuasion in the Gospels.* Sonoma, CA: Polebridge Press, 1989.

Malbon, Elizabeth Struthers. "Fallible Followers: Women and Men in the Gospel of Mark." *Semeia* 28 (1983) 29–48. Reprinted in Elizabeth Struthers Malbon. *In the Company of Jesus.* Louisville, KY: Westminster John Knox, 2000. 41–69.

____. *Narrative Space and Mythic Meaning in Mark.* San Francisco: Harper and Row, 1986.

Malcolm, Kari Torjesen. *Women at the Crossroads.* Downers Grove, IL: Intervarsity Press, 1982.

Manning, C. E. "Stoicism and Slavery in the Roman Empire." *Aufstieg und Niedergang der römischen Welt.* II.36, 1518–43. Ed. W. Haase. Berlin and New York: Walter de Gruyter, 1989.

Martin, Dale B. "Slavery and the Ancient Jewish Family in Antiquity." In *The Jewish Family in Antiquity*, 113–129. Ed. Shaye J. D. Cohen. Atlanta, GA: Scholars Press, 1993.

Martin, Hubert Jr. and Jane E. Phillips. "*Consolatio ad Uxorem* (Moralia 608A–612B)." In *Plutarch's Ethical Writings and Early Christian Literature*, 394–441. Ed. Hans Dieter Betz. Leiden: Brill, 1978.

Massey, Lesly F. *Women and the New Testament.* Jefferson, NC and London: McFarland and Co., 1989.

Matera, Frank J. *The Kingship of Jesus: Composition and Theology in Mark 15.* Chico, CA: Scholars Press, 1982.

Mayer, Günter. *Die jüdische Frau in der hellenistisch-römischen Antike.* Stuttgart; Berlin; Köln; Mainz: W. Kolhammer, 1987.

Meeks, Wayne. "The Image of the Androgyne: Some Uses of a Symbol in Earliest Christianity." *History of Religions* 13 (1974) 165–208.

Meier, John P. *A Marginal Jew: Rethinking the Historical Jesus.* 3 vols. New York: Doubleday, 1991; 1994; 2001.

Meltzer, Milton. *Slavery from the Rise of Western Civilization to the Renaissance.* New York: Cowles Book Co., 1971–72.

Mendelsohn, Isaac. "The Conditional Sale into Slavery of Free-Born Daughters in Nuzi and the Law of Exodus 21:7–11." *Journal of the American Oriental Society* 55 (1935) 190–195.

____. *Slavery in the Ancient Near East.* New York: Oxford University Press, 1949.

Mernisi, Fatima, "Women, Saints and Sanctuaries," *Signs* 3 (1977) 101–112.

Metzger, Bruce M. *A Textual Commentary on the Greek New Testament.* London; New York: United Bible Society, 1975.

Meyer, Marvin. *The Gospel of Thomas: The Hidden Sayings of Jesus.* San Francisco: HarperSan Francisco, 1992.

____. "The Youth in Secret Mark and the Beloved Disciple in John." In *Gospel Origins and Christian Beginnings: In Honor of James M. Robinson*, 94–105. Ed. James E. Goehring, et al. Sonoma, CA: Polebridge Press, 1990.

____. "The Youth in the Secret Gospel of Mark." *Semeia* 49 (1990) 129–53.

Meyer, Marvin and Richard Smith. *Ancient Christian Magic: Coptic Texts of Ritual Power.* San Francisco: HarperSan Francisco, 1994.

Meyers, Eric M. "The Cultural Setting of Galilee: The Case of Regionalism and Early Judaism." *Aufstieg und Niedergang der römischen Welt.* II. 19.1, 686–702. Ed. W. Haase. Berlin and New York: Walter de Gruyter, 1979.

____. *Jewish Ossuaries: Burial and Rebirth.* Rome: Biblical Institute Press, 1971.

Milik, J. T. "Le travail d' éditions des manuscrits du Désert de Juda." *Volume du congres Strasbourg 1956. Supplements to Vetus Testamentum IV*, 17–26. Leiden: Brill, 1956.

Miller, Barbara Butler. "Women, Death and Mourning in the Ancient

Mediterranean." Ph.D. Dissertation. University of Michigan, Ann Arbor, 1994.
Miller, Robert J., ed. *The Complete Gospels: Annotated Scholars Version*. Rev. and expanded ed. Santa Rosa, CA: Polebridge Press, 1994.
____ . "The Rejection of Prophets in Q." *Journal of Biblical Literature* 107 (1988) 225–240.
Mollenkott, Virginia Ramey. *Women, Men and the Bible*. Nashville: Abingdon Press, 1977.
Moltmann-Wendel, Elisabeth. *Liberty, Equality, Sisterhood: On the Emancipation of Women in Church and Society*. Philadelphia: Fortress Press, 1978.
____ . *The Women Around Jesus*. New York: Crossroad, 1988.
Morris, Ian. *Death Ritual and Social Structure in Classical Antiquity*. Cambridge: Cambridge University Press, 1992.
Mott, Stephen Charles. "Jesus as a Social Critic and Anti-Semitism." *Christian Social Action* 3.9 (1990) 37.
Motto, Anna Lydia. "Seneca on Women's Liberation." *Classical World* 65 (1972) 155–157.
Mueller, James R. 'The Temple Scroll and Gospel Divorce Texts." *Revue de Qumran* 38 (1980) 247–256.
Munro, Winsome. "The Honor of 'Shameless' Biblical Women." Unpublished manuscript.
____ . "Women Disciples in Mark?" *Catholic Biblical Quarterly* 44 (1982) 225–241.
____ . "Women Disciples: Light From Secret Mark." *Journal of Feminist Studies in Religion* 9 (1992) 47–64.
Murphy, Cullen. "Women and the Bible." *Atlantic Monthly* 272/2 (August 1993) 39–64.
Mussies, G. "Greek in Palestine and the Diaspora." In *The Jewish People of the First Century*, vol. 2, 1040–1064. Ed. S. Safrai, et al. Assen/Maastrict: Van Gorcum; Philadelphia: Fortress Press, 1987.
Myllykoski, Matti. "What Happened to the Body of Jesus?" *In Fair Play: Diversity and Conflicts in Early Christianity: Essays in Honour of Heikki Räisänen*, 43–82, Eds. Ismo Dunderberg, et al. Leiden; Boston; Köln: Brill, 2002.
Naveh, J. "The Ossuary Inscriptions from Giv'at ha-Mivtar." *Israel Exploration Journal* 20 (1970) 33–37.
Neusner, Jacob. *From Politics to Piety: The Emergence of Pharasaic Judaism*. Englewood Cliffs, NJ: Prentice Hall, 1973.
____. *Judaism in the New Testament: Practices and Beliefs*. New York and London: Routledge, 1995.
____ . *The Pharisees: Rabbinic Perspectives*. Hoboken, NJ: KTAV Publishing House, 1985.
____ . *Rabbinic Litearature and the New Testament: What We Cannot Show We Do Not Know*. Valley Forge, PA: Trinity Press International, 1994.
____ . "Two Pictures of the Pharisees: Philosophical Circle or Eating Club?" *Anglican Theological Review* 64 (1982) 525–538.
____ . *Wrong Ways and Right Ways in the Study of Formative Judaism*. Atlanta, GA: Scholars Press, 1988.

Newsom, Carol A. and Sharon H. Ringe, eds. *The Woman's Bible Commentary*. London: SPCK; Louisville, KY: Westminster/John Knox, 1992.

Neyrey, Jerome H. "Jesus' Address to the Women of Jerusalem (Lk 23:27–31)–A Prophetic Judgment Oracle." *New Testament Studies* 29 (1983) 74–86.

Nickelsburg, George W. E. "Genre and Function of the Markan Passion Narrative." *Harvard Theological Review* 73 (1980) 153–84.

____ . *Resurrection, Immortality, and Eternal Life in Intertestamental Judaism*. Cambridge: Cambridge University Press, 1972.

Nkwoka, A. O. "Mark 10:13–16: Jesus' Attitude to Children and Its Modern Challenges." *Africa Theological Journal* 14 (1985) 100–110.

Nock, Arthur Darby. "Cremation and Burial in the Roman Empire." In *Arthur Darby Nock: Essays on Religion and the Ancient World*, 278–307. Ed. by Z. Stewart. Cambridge, MA : Harvard University Press, 1972.

Nunnally-Cox, Janet. *Foremothers: Women of the Bible*. New York: Seabury Press, 1981.

Oakman, Douglas E. "Jesus and Agrarian Palestine: The Factor of Debt." *Society of Biblical Literature 1985 Seminar Papers*, 57–73. Ed. Kent Richards. Atlanta, GA: Scholars Press, 1985.

____ . *Jesus and the Economic Questions of His Day*. Lewiston and Queenston: Edwin Mellen Press, 1986.

O'Collins, Gerald and Daniel Kendall. "Did Joseph of Arimathea Exist?" *Biblica* 75 (1994) 235–241.

Oesterrecher, John M. "Abba, Father! On the Humanity of Jesus." In *The Lord's Prayer and Jewith Liturgy*, 119–136. Ed. Jacob J. Petuchowski and Michael Brocke. New York: Seabury, 1978.

Olrik, Axel. "Epic Laws of Folk Narrative." In *The Study of Folklore*, 129–141. Edited by Alan Dunde. Engelwood Cliffs, NJ: Prentice-Hall, 1965.

Opocenská, Jana. "Women at the Cross, at Jesus' Burial, and After the Resurrection: Mk 15:40; 16:10." *Reformed World* 47 (1997) 40–48.

Osborne, Delores. "Women: Sinners and Prostitutes." Paper presented at the Society of Biblical Literature Pacific Coast Region. Long Beach, CA, April 1987.

Osborne, Grant R. "Women in Jesus' Ministry." *Westminster Theological Journal* 51 (1989) 259–91.

Osiek, Carolyn. "Slavery in the Second Testament World." *Biblical Theology Bulletin* 22 (1992) 174–179.

____ . *What Are They Saying About the Social Setting of the New Testament?* New York/Mahwah: Paulist Press, 1992.

____ . "The Women at the Tomb: What Are They Doing There?" *Ex Auditu* 9 (1993) 97–107. Reprinted in *A Feminist Companion to Matthew*, 205–220. Ed. Amy Jill Levine. Sheffield: Sheffield Academic Press, 2001.

Paton, Lewis Bayles. *Spiritism and the Cult of the Dead in Antiquity*. New York: Macmillan, 1921.

Patte, Daniel, ed. *Kingdom and Children: Aphorism, Chreia, Structure. Semeia* 29 (1983).

Patterson, Orlando. *Slavery and Social Death: A Comparative Study*. Cambridge, MA: Harvard University Press, 1982.

Patterson, Stephen. *The Gospel of Thomas and Jesus*. Sonoma, CA: Polebridge Press, 1993.

Perkins, Pheme. *Resurrection: New Testament Witness and Contemporary Reflection*. Garden City, NY: Doubleday, 1984.

Perrin Norman. *Rediscovering the Teaching of Jesus*. New York and Evanston: Harper and Row, 1967.

Pervo, Richard. *Profit With Delight: The Literary Genre of the Acts of the Apostles*. Philadelphia: Fortress Press, 1987.

Pesch, R. *Das Markusevangelium*. Freiburg: Herder, 1970.

Peskowitz, Miriam. "Family/ies in Antiquity: Evidence from Tannaitic Literature and Roman Galilean Architecture." In *The Jewish Family in Antiquity*, 9–36. Ed. Shaye J. D. Cohen. Atlanta, GA: Scholars Press, 1993.

Pfister, F. "Herakles und Christus." *Archiv für Religionswissenschaft* 34 (1937) 42–60.

Phillips, Victoria. "Full Disclosure: Towards a Complete Characterization of the Women Who Followed Jesus in the Gospel According to Mark." *In Transformative Encounters: Jesus and Women Re-viewed*, 13–32. Ingrid Rosa Kitzberger, Ed. Leiden: Brill, 2000.

Pilch, John J. "Death with Honor: The Mediterranean Style of the Death of Jesus in Mark." *Biblical Theological Bulletin* 25 (1995) 65–70.

Pitre, Brant James. "Blessing the Barren and Warning the Fecund: Jesus' Message for Women Concerning Pregnancy and Childbirth." *Journal for the Study of the New Testament* 81 (2001) 59–80.

____ ."Marginal Elites: Matthew 19:12 and the Social and Political Dimensions of Becoming Eunuchs for the Sake of the Kingdom." Paper presented at the Annual Meeting of the National SBL. Boston, Mass. November 21, 1999.

Plaskow, Judith. "Anti-Judaism in Christian Feminist Interpretation." In *Searching the Scriptures*, vol. 1, 117–129. Ed. Elisabeth Schüssler Fiorenza. New York: Crossroad, 1993.

____ . "Blaming the Jews for Inventing Patriarchy." *Lilith* 7 (1980) 11–12.

Plummer, Alfred. "The Woman That Was a Sinner." *Expository Times* 27 (1915–19) 42–43.

Pomeroy, Sarah B. *Goddesses, Whores Wives and Slaves: Women in Classical Antiquity*. New York: Schocken Books, 1975.

Pope, Marvin. "Love and Death." In *Song of Songs*, 210–229. Garden City, NY: Doubleday, 1977.

Porter, Stanley E. "Jesus and the Use of Greek in Galilee." In *Studying the Historical Jesus: Evaluations of the State of Current Research*, 123–154. Ed. Bruce Chilton and Craig A. Evans. Leiden: Brill, 1994.

Porton, Gary G. "Diversity in Postbiblical Judaism." In *Early Judaism and Its Interpreters*, 57–80. Ed. Robert A. Kraft and George W. E. Nickelsburg. Philadelphia: Fortress Pres; Atlanta, GA: Scholars Press, 1986.

Qimron, Elisha. "Celibacy in the Dead Sea Scrolls and the Two Kinds of Sectarians." In *The Madrid Congress Proceedings of the International Congress on the Dead Sea Scrolls, Madrid. 18–21 March 1991*, vol. 1, 287–294. Ed. Julio Trebolle Barrea and Luis Vegas Montaner. Leiden; New York; Köln: Brill, 1992.

Rabello, Alfredo Mordechai. "Divorce of Jews in the Roman Empire." *Jewish Law Annual* 4 (1981) 79–102.

Raglan, Lord. "The Hero of Tradition." In *The Study of Folklore*, 140–157. Edited by Alan Dundes. Englewood Cliffs, NJ: Prentice Hall, 1965.

Rahmani, L. Y. "Ancient Jerusalem's Funerary Customs and Tombs," Parts 1–4. *Biblical Archaeologist* 44.3 (1981) 171–177; 44.4 (1981) 229–235 (Part 2); 45.1 (1981) 43–53 (Part 3); 45.2 (1982) 109–119 (Part 4).

____. "Jason's Tomb." *Israel Exploration Journal* 17 (1967) 61–100.

Reardon, B. P. *Collected Greek Novels*. Berkeley, CA: University of California Press, 1989.

Reed, Jonathan L. "Population Numbers, Urbanization and Economics: Galilean Archaeology and the Historical Jesus." *Society of Biblical Literature 1994 Seminar Papers*, 203–219. Ed. Eugene H. Lovering, Atlanta, GA Scholars Press, 1984.

Reich, Ronny. "The Great Mikveh Debate." *Biblical Archaeology Reveiw* 19 (March/April 1993) 52–53.

____. "The Hot Bath-House (*balneum*), the Mikveh and the Jewish Community in the Second Temple Period." *Journal of Jewish Studies* 39 (1988) 102–107.

____. "More on Miqva'ot." *Biblical Archaelogical Review* 13 (July/August 1987) 59–60.

Rengstorf, H. "*Harmartolos, ktl.*" In *Theological Dictionary of the New Testament*, vol. 1, 317–335. Ed. G. Kittel. Grand Rapids, MI: Eerdmans, 1964.

Ricci, Carla. *Mary Magdalene and Many Others: Women Who Followed Jesus*. Trans. Paul Burns. Minneapolis: Fortress Press, 1994.

Richardson, H. Neil. "Some Notes on 1QSa." *Journal of Biblical Literature* 76 (1957) 108–122.

Riddle, John M. et al. "Ever Since Eve . . . Birth Control in the Ancient World." *Archaeology* (March/April 1994) 29–35.

Riley, Gregory. *Resurrection Reconsidered: Thomas and John in Controversy*. Minneapolis: Fortress Press, 1995.

Robbins, Vernon K. "Foxes, Birds, Burials and Furrows." In *Patterns of Persuasion in the Gospels*, 69–84. Burton L. Mack and Vernon K. Robbins. Sonoma, CA: Polebridge Press, 1989.

Robins, W. "Woman's Place: Jesus Reverses Traditional Understanding." *Church and Society* 82 (1992) 85–88.

Robinson, James M. "The Jesus of Q as Liberation Theologian." In *The Gospel Behind the Gospels: Current Studies on Q*, 259–274. Ed. R. Piper. Leiden: Brill, 1995.

____. "Luke 7:29–30/Matt 21:31b–32." Paper presented to the International Q Project. Claremont, CA, May 1994.

____. *The Problem of History in Mark and Other Markan Studies*. Philadelphia: Fortress Press, 1985.

____. "Q 7:29–30: Third Response." Paper presented to the International Q Project. Claremont, CA, May 1994.

____. "The Q Trajectory: Between John and Matthew Via Jesus." In *The*

Future of Early Christianity: Essays in Honor of Helmut Koester, 173–194. Ed. Birger Pearson. Minneapolis: Fortress Press, 1991.

Robinson, James M., Paul Hoffmann, John S. Kloppenborg, eds. *The Critical Edition of Q.* Minneapolis: Fortress Press; Leuven: Peeters, 2000.

Rogers, Susan Carol. "Female Forms of Power and the Myth of Male Dominance: A Model of Female/Male Interaction in Peasant Society." *American Ethnologist* 2 (1975) 727–756.

____. "A Woman's Place: A Critical Review of Anthropological Theory." *Comparative Studies in Society and History* 20 (1978) 123–162.

Rohde, Erwin. *Psyche: The Cult of the Souls and Belief in Immortality among the Greeks.* New York: Harcourt, Brace; London: Kegan Paul, Trench, Trubner, 1925.

Rollin, Sue. "Women and Witchcraft in Ancient Assyria (900–600BC)." In *Images of Women in Antiquity*, 34–45. Eds. Averil Cameron and Amélie Kuhrt. Detroit: Wayne State University Press, 1983.

Rose, H. J. "Ghost Ritual in Aeschylus." *Harvard Theological Review* 43 (1950) 257–280.

____ . "Heracles and the Gospels." *Harvard Theological Review* 31 (1938) 113–142.

Rostovtzeff, M. I. and C. Bradford Welles. "A Parchment Contract of Loan from Dura-Europus on the Euphrates." In *Yale Classical Studies*, vol. 2, 1–78. Ed. Austin M. Harmon. New Haven: Yale University Press, 1931.

Ruether, Rosemary Radford. *Sexism and God-Talk: Toward a Feminist Theology.* Boston: Beacon Press, 1993.

Rush, Alfred C. *Death and Burial in Christian Antiquity.* Washington DC: Catholic University Press of America, 1941.

Safrai, Hannah. "Women and the Ancient Synagogue." In *Daughters of the King: Women and the Synagogue*, 39–49. Ed. Susan Grossman and Rivka Haut. Philadelphia; New York; Jerusalem: Jewish Publication Society, 1992.

Safrai, S. "Home and Family." In *The Jewish People in the First Century*, vol. 2, 728–792. Eds. by S. Safrai, et al. Philadelphia: Fortress Press; Assen/Maastricht: Van Gorcum, 1987.

____ . "Pilgrimage to Jerusalem at the End of the Second Temple Period." In *Studies on the Jewish Background of the New Testament*, 12–21. Eds. O. Michel, et al. Assen, The Netherlands: Van Gorcum, 1969.

Saldarini, Anthony. *Matthew's Christian-Jewish Community.* Chicago: University of Chicago Press, 1994.

____ . *Pharisees, Scribes, and Sadducees in Palestinian Society: A Sociological Approach.* Wilmington, Delaware: Michael Glazier, 1988.

____ . "Political and Social Roles of the Pharisees and Scribes in Galilee." *Society of Biblical Literature 1988 Seminar Papers*, 200–209. Ed. David J. Lull. Atlanta, GA: Scholars Press, 1988.

____ . "The Social Class of the Pharisees in Mark." In *The Social World of Formative Christianity and Judaism. Essays in Tribute to Howard Clark Kee*, 69–77. Eds. Jacob Neusner, et al. Philadelphia: Fortress Press, 1988.

Sanders, E. P. *The Historical Figure of Jesus.* London: Penquin Press, 1993.

____ . *Jesus and Judaism.* Philadelphia: Fortress Press, 1990.

____. *Jewish Law from Jesus to the Mishnah*. Philadelphia: Fortress Press, 1990.

Sandifer, D. Wayne. "The Humor of the Absurd in the Parables of Jesus." In *Society of Biblical Literature 1991 Seminar Papers*, 287–297. Ed. Eugene Lovering. Atlanta, GA: Scholars Press, 1991.

Satlow, Michael. "Reconsidering the Rabbinic *ketubah* Payment." In *The Jewish Family in Antiquity*, 133–151. Ed. Shaye J. D. Cohen. Atlanta, GA: Scholars Press, 1993.

Sawicki, Marianne. "Magdalenes and Tiberiennes: City Women in the Entourage of Jesus." *In Transformative Encounters: Jesus and Women Re-viewed.* Ingrid Rosa Kitzberger, Ed. Leiden: Brill, 2000.

____. *Seeing the Lord: Resurrection and Early Christian Practices*. Minneapolis: Fortress Press, 1994.

Scanzoni, Letha and Nancy Hardesty. *All We're Meant to Be: Biblical Feminism for Today*. Reprint; Nashville: Abingdon Press, 1986.

Schaberg, Jane. "(The) Feminist (Contribution to) Experience of Historical Jesus Scholarship." *Continuum* 3 (1994) 266–285.

____. *The Illegitimacy of Jesus. A Feminist Theological Interpretation of the Infancy Narratives*. San Francisco: Harper and Row, 1987.

____. "The Infancy of Mary of Nazareth." In *Searching the Scriptures*, vol 2, 708–727. Ed. Elisabeth Schüssler Fiorenza. New York: Crossroad, 1994.

____. "Luke." In The *Woman's Bible Commentary*, 275–292. Ed. Carol A. Newsom and Sharon H. Ringe. Louisville, KY: Westminster/John Knox, 1992.

Schierling, Marla J. "Women as Leaders in the Markan Community." *Listening* 15 (1980) 250–256.

Schiffman, Lawrence H. "Laws Pertaining to Women in the Temple Scroll." In *The Dead Sea Scrolls: Forty Years of Research*, 210–228. Ed. Devorah Dimant and Uriel Rappaport. Leiden: Brill, 1992.

Schmidt, Thomas. *Hostility to Wealth in the Synoptic Gospels*. Sheffield: JSOT Press, 1987.

Schmitt, John J. "Women in Mark's Gospel." *Bible Today* 19 (1981) 228–33.

Schnackenburg, Rudolf. *The Gospel According to John*. 3 Volumes.
New York: Crossroad, 1982.

____. *Jesus in the Gospels: A Biblical Christology*. Louisville, KY: Westminster/John Knox, 1995.

Schneiders, Sandra M. *Women and the Word: The Gender of God in the New Testament and the Spirituality of Women*. New York; Mahwah: Paulist Press, 1986.

Scholer, David. "Women." *Dictionary of Jesus and the Gospels*, 880–887. Downers Grove, IL: Intervarsity Press, 1992.

Schottroff, Luise. "Itinerant Prophetesses: A Feminist Analysis of the Sayings Source Q." In *The Gospel Behind the Gospels: Current Studies on Q*, 347–360. Ed. Ronald A. Piper. Leiden: Brill, 1995; Institute for Antiquity and Christianity Occasional Papers 21, August 1991.

____. *Let the Oppressed Go Free: Feminist Perspectives on the New Testament*. Louisville, KY: Westminster/John Knox, 1992.

____. *Lydia's Impatient Sisters: A Feminist Social History of Early Christianity*. Trans. Barbara and Martin Rumscheidt. Louisville, KY: Westminster, 1995.

____. "The Saying Source Q." In *Searching the Scriptures*, vol. 2, 510–534. Ed. Elisabeth Schüssler Fiorenza. New York: Crossroad, 1994.

____. "Women as Followers of Jesus in New Testament Times: Exercise in Social-Historical Exegesis of the Bible." In *The Bible and Liberation: Politics and Social Hermeneutics*, 418–427. Ed. N. K. Gottwald. Mary Knoll, NY: Orbis Books, 1983.

Schottroff, Luise and Wolfgang Stegeman. *Jesus and the Hope of the Poor*. Trans. Matthew O'Connell. Maryknoll, NY: Orbis Books, 1986.

Schuller, Eileen M. "4Q372 1: A Text About Joseph." *Revue de Qumran* 55 (1990) 349–376.

____. *Post-Exilic Prophets*. Willmington, Delaware: Michael Glazier, 1988.

____. "The Psalm of 4Q372 1 Within the Context of Second Temple Prayer." *Catholic Biblical Quarterly* 54 (1992) 67–79.

____. "Women in the Dead Sea Scrolls." In *Methods of Investigation of the Dead Sea Scrolls and the Khirbet Qumran Site: Present Realities and Future Prospects*, 115–131. Eds. Michael O. Wise, et al. New York: New York Academy of Sciences, 1994.

Schultz, S. "*Porne, ktl.*" ." In *Theological Dictionary of the New Testament*, vol. 6, 579–95. Ed. G. Kittel. Grand Rapids, MI: Eerdmans, 1964.

Schüssler Fiorenza, Elisabeth. *But She Said: Feminist Practices of Biblical Interpretation*. Boston: Beacon Press, 1992.

____. *In Memory of Her: A Feminist Theological Reconstruction of Christian Origins*. New York: Crossroad Press, 1983; 1994.

____. *Jesus, Miriam's Child, Sophia's Prophet: Critical Issues in Feminist Christology*. New York: Crossroad, 1994.

____. *Jesus and the Politics of Interpretation*. London and New York: Continuum, 2000.

____. "The Rhetorics and Politics of Jesus Research: A Critical Feminist Perspective." In *Jesus, Mark and Q: The Teaching of Jesus in its Earliest Records*, 259–282. Eds. Michael Labahn and Andreas Schmidt. Sheffield: Sheffield Academic Press, 2001.

____, ed. *Searching the Scriptures, vol. 2: A Feminist Commentary*. New York: Crossroad, 1994.

____. *Sharing Her Word. Feminist Biblical Interpretations in Context*. Boston: Beacon Press, 1998.

____. "Text and Reality – Reality as Text: The Problem of Feminist Historical and Social Reconstruction Based on Texts." *Studia Theologica* 43 (1989) 19–34.

Schwank, B. "Neue Funde in Nabatäerstädten und ihre Bedeutung für die neutestamentliche Exegese." *New Testament Studies* 29 (1983) 429– 435.

Schweizer, Eduard. *The Good News According to Matthew*. Trans. David E. Green. Atlanta, GA: John Knox Press, 1975.

Scott, Bernard Brandon. "The Empty Jar." *Forum* 3 (1987) 77–81.

____. *Hear Then the Parable: A Commentary on the Parables of Jesus*. Minneapolis: Fortress Press, 1989.

Scott, James C. *Domination and the Arts of Resistance: Hidden Transcripts*. New Haven and London: Yale University Press, 1990.

____. *Weapons of the Weak: Everyday Forms of Peasant Resistance.* New Haven and London: Yale University Press, 1985.

Scott, Joan W. "Gender: A Useful Category of Historical Analysis." In *Coming to Terms: Feminism, Theory, Politics*, 81–100. Ed. Elizabeth Weed. New York and London: Routledge, 1989.

Scroggs, R. "Woman in the New Testament." *Interpreter's Dictionary of the Bible*, Suppl. vol., 966–968. Nashville, TN: Abindgon, 1976.

Seeley, David. "Blessing and Boundaries: The Interpretation of Jesus'Death in Q." *Semeia* 55 (1991) 131–146.

____. "Jesus' Death in Q." *New Testament Studies* 38 (1992) 222–234.

____. *The Noble Death: Graeco-Roman Martyrology and Paul's Concept of Salvation.* Sheffield: JSOT Press, 1990.

____. "Rulership and Service in Mark 10:41–45." *Novum Testamentum* 35 (1993) 234–250.

Seim, Turid Karlsen. *The Double Message: Patterns of Gender in Luke-Acts.* Nashville: Abingdon Press, 1994.

____. "Roles of Women in the Gospel of John." In *Aspects on the Johannine Literature*, 56–73. Edited by L. Hartman and B. Olsson. Uppsala: Almqvist and Wiksell, 1986.

____. "The Gospel of Luke." In *Searching the Scriptures*, vol. 2, 728–762. Ed. Elisabeth Schüssler Fiorenza. New York: Crossroad Press, 1994.

Sellew, Philip. "Death, Body and the World in the Gospel of Thomas." *Studia Patristica*, vol. 31, 530–534. Ed. Elizabeth A. Livingstone. Leuven: Peeters, 1996.

Selvidge, Marla. "And Those Who Followed Feared." *Catholic Biblical Quarterly* 45 (1983) 396–400.

Sergio, Lisa. *Jesus and Women: An Exciting Discovery of What He Offered Her.* EPM Publications, 1975.

Sheffield, Julian. "The Father in the Gospel of Matthew." ." In *A Feminist Companion to Matthew*, 52–69. Ed. Amy Jill Levine. Sheffield: Sheffield Academic Press, 2001.

Silberman, Lou. "The Queen of Sheba in Judaic Tradition." In *Solomon and Sheba*, 65–84. Ed. James B. Pritchard. London: Phaidon Press, Ltd., 1974.

Silva, Moisés. "Bilingualism and the Character of Palestinian Greek." In *The Language of the New Testament: Classic Essays*, 205–226. Ed. Stanley A. Porter. Sheffield: Sheffield Academic Press, 1991.

Sim, David C. "What About the Wives and Children of the Disciples? The Cost of Discipleship from Another Perspective." *Heythrop Journal* 35 (1994) 373–390.

____. "Women Followers of Jesus: The Implications of Luke 8:1–3." *Heythrop Journal* 30 (1989) 51–62.

Simon, Marcel. *Heracle et le Christianisme.* Paris: University of Strasbourg, 1965.

Skupinska-Lovset, Llona. *Funerary Portraiture of Roman Palestine: An Analysis of the Production in Its Culture-Historical Context.* Gotab: Kungälv, 1983.

Slee, Nicola. "Parables and Women's Experience." *Modern Churchman* 26 (1984) 20–31.

Small, David B. "Late Hellenistic Baths in Palestine." *Bulletin of the American Schools of Oriental Research* 266 (1987) 59–74.

Smelik, K. A. D. "The Witch of Endor: 1 Samuel in Rabbinic and Christian Exegesis Till 800 A. D." *Vigiliae christianae* 33 (1977) 160–179.

Smith, Dennis E. "The Historical Jesus at Table." In *Society of Biblical Literature Seminar Papers*, 466–486. Ed. David Lull. Atlanta, GA Scholars Press, 1989.

____. "Social Obligation in the Context of Communal Meals: A Study of the Christian Meal in 1 Corinthians in Comparison with Graeco-Roman Meals." Th.D. Dissertation. Harvard Divinity School, 1980.

____. "Table Fellowship and the Historical Jesus." In *Religious Propaganda and Missionary Competition in the New Testament World: Essays Honoring Dieter Georgi*, 135–162. Ed. Lukan Bormann, et al. Leiden; New York; Köln: Brill, 1994.

____. "Table Fellowship as a Literary Motif in the Gospel of Luke." *Journal of Biblical Literature* 106 (1987) 613–38.

Smith, Jonathan Z. *Drudgery Divine: On the Comparision of Early Christianities and the Religions of Late Antiquity*. Chicago: Chicago University Press, 1990.

____. "Good News is No News: Aretalogy and Gospel." In *Christianity, Judaism and Other Greco-Roman Cults: Studies for Morton Smith at Sixty*, vol. 1, 21–38. Ed. Jacob Neusner. Leiden: Brill, 1975.

____. *Map is Not Territory*. Chicago: Chicago University Press, 1978.

____. *To Take Place. Toward Theory in Ritual.* Chicago: Chicago University Press, 1987.

Smith, Mark S. *The Early History of God: Yahweh and the Other Deities in Ancient Israel.* San Francisco: Harper and Row, 1990.

Smith, Morton. "Palestinian Judaism in the First Century." In *Israel: Its Role in Civilization*, 67–81. Ed. Moshe Davis. New York: Harper and Brothers, 1956.

____. "Prolegomena to a Discussion of Aretalogies: Divine Men, the Gospels and Jesus." *Journal of Biblical Literature* 90 (1970) 174–199.

Snyder, Graydon F. *Ante Pacem: Archaeological Evidence of Church Life Before Constantine.* Mercer University Press, 1985.

Solodukho, Yu. A. "Slavery in the Hebrew Society of Iraq and Syria in the Second Through the Fifth Centuries A.D." In *Soviet Views of Talmudic Judaism: Five Papers by Yu. A. Solodukho in English Translation*, 1–9. Ed. Jacob Neusner. Leiden: Brill, 1973.

Spencer, Scott F. "The Ethiopian Eunuch and His Bible: A Social Science Analysis." *Biblical Theology Bulletin* 22 (1992) 155–165.

Spicq, C. "Le vocabulaire de l'esclave dans le Noveau Testament." *Revue Biblique* 85 (1978) 201–226.

Stagg, Evelyn and Frank. *Woman in the World of Jesus*. Philadelphia: Westminster, 1978.

Starr, Chester G. "An Evening with the Flute-Girls." *La parola del passato* 33 (1978) 401–410.

Steck, Odil Hannes. *Israel und das gewaltsame Geschick der Propheten.* WMANT 23; Neukirschen-Vluyn: Neukirchner Verlag, 1967.

Stegemann, Ekkehard and Wolfgang Stegemann. *The Jesus Movement: A Social History of Its First Century*. Trans. O. C. Dean. Minneapolis: Fortress, 1999.

Stein, S. "The Influence of Symposia Literature on the Literary Form of the Pesah Haggadah." *Journal of Jewish Studies* 8 (1957) 13–44.

Stemberger, Günter. *Jewish Contemporaries of Jesus: Pharisees, Sadducees and Essenes.* Trans. Allan W. Mahnke. Minneapolis: Fortress Press, 1995.

Stephens, Shirley. *A New Testament View of Women.* Nashville, TN: Broadman Press, 1980.

Strack, H. L. and P. Billerbeck. *Kommentar zum neuen Testament.* 6 vols. Munich: C. H. Beck, 1922–56.

Strange, James F. "Late Hellenistic and Herodian Ossuary Tombs Found at French Hill Jerusalem." *Bulletin of the American Schools of Oriental Research* 219 (1975) 39–67.

Strelan, Rick. "To Sit Is To Mourn: The Women at the Tomb (Matthew 27:61)." *Colloquium* 31/1 (1999) 31–45.

Strubbe, J. H. M. "Cursed Be He That Moves My Bones." *In Magica Hiera: Ancient Greek Magic and Religion*, 33–39. Eds. Christopher A. Faraone and Dirk Obbink. New York and Oxford: Oxford University Press, 1991.

Swartley, Willard M. "The Role of Women in Mark's Gospel: A Narrative Analysis." *Biblical Theology Bulletin* 27 (1997) 16–22.

Swidler, Leonard. *Biblical Affirmations of Women.* Philadelphia: Westminster, 1979.

____ . "Jesus Was a Feminist." *Catholic World* 212 (1971) 177–183.

____ . "Leonard Swidler's Response to A.-J. Levine's Review." *Journal of Ecumenical Studies* 26 (1989) 717–719.

____ . *Women in Judaism. The Status of Women in Formative Judaism.* Metuchen, NJ: Scarecrow Press, 1976.

____. *Yeshua: A Modern for Moderns.* Kansas City: Sheed and Ward, 1988.

Tannehill, Robert C. "The Disciples in Mark: The Function of a Narrative Role." In *The Interpretation of Mark*, 134–157. Ed. W. Telford. Philadelphia: Fortress Press; London: SPCK, 1985.

Tatum, W. Barnes. *John the Baptist and Jesus.* Sonoma, CA: Polebridge Press, 1994.

Telford, William R. "The Pre-Markan Tradition in Recent Research." In *The Four Gospels: Festschrift for Frans Neirynck*, vol. 2, 693–723. Ed. F. van Segbroeck, et al. Leuven: University Press, 1992.

Tetlow, Elizabeth M. *Women and Ministry in the New Testament.* New York/Mahwah: Paulist Press, 1980.

Theissen, Gerd. "Itinerant Radicalism: The Tradition of Jesus Sayings from the Perspective of the Sociology of Literature." *Radical Religion* 2 (1975) 84–93.

____ . "Review: Kathleen E. Corley, *Private Women, Public Meals*." *Journal of Theological Studies* 46 (1995) 631–634.

____ . *Social Reality and the Early Christians: Theology, Ethics and the World of the New Testament.* Trans. Margaret Kohl. Minneapolis: Fortress Press, 1992.

____ . *The Sociology of Early Palestinian Christianity.* Philadelphia: Fortress Press, 1978.

Theissen, Gerd and Annette Merz. *The Historical Jesus: A Comprehensive Guide.* Minneapolis: Fortress Press, 1998.

Thistlethwaite, Susan Brooks. *Sex, Race and God: Christian Feminism in Black and White.* New York: Crossroad, 1989.

Thompson, George and Walter G. Headlam. *The Oresteia of Aeschylus*, vol. 2. Cambridge: Cambridge University Press, 1938.

Tolbert, Mary Ann. "Mark." In *The Woman's Bible Commentary*, 263–274. Ed. Carol A. Newsom and Sharon H. Ringe. Louisville, KY: Westminster/John Knox, 1992.

Torjesen, Karen Jo. *When Women Were Priests: Women's Leadership in the Early Church and the Scandal of their Subordination in the Rise of Christianity*. San Francisco: HarperCollins, 1993.

Toynbee, J. M. C. *Death and Burial in the Roman World.* Ithaca, NY: Cornell University Press, 1971.

____. *A Study of History*, vol. 4. London: Humphrey Milford; Oxford University Press, 1939.

Trautman, C. "Salomé l 'incrédule: récits d'une conversion." In *Ecritures et traditions dans la littérature copte*, 61–72. Cashiers de la bibliothéque copte 1; Louvain: Peeters, 1983.

Treat, Jay C. "The Two Manuscript Witnesses to the Gospel of Peter." In *Society of Biblical Literature 1990 Seminar Papers*, 191–199. Ed. David E. Lull. Atlanta, GA: Scholars Press, 1990.

Trenchard, Warren C. *Ben Sira's View of Women: A Literary Analysis*. Chico, CA: Scholars Press, 1982.

Treu, K. "Die Bedeutung des Griechischen für die Juden im römischen Reich." *Kairos* 15 (1973) 123–144.

Tuckett, Christopher. "Feminine Wisdom in Q?" In *Women in the Biblical Tradition*, 112–128. Ed. George J. Brooke. Lewiston: Edwin Mellen Press, 1992.

Tzaferis, V. "Crucifixion: The Archeaological Evidence." *Biblical Archaeology Review* 9.1 (1985) 44–53.

____ . "Jewish Tombs at and Near Giv'at ha-Mivtar." *Israel Exploration Journal* 20 (1970) 18–32.

Ubieta, Carmen Bernabé. "Mary Magdalene and the Seven Demons in Social-Scientific Perspective." *In Transformative Encounters: Jesus and Women Re-viewed*, 203–223. Ingrid Rosa Kitzberger, Ed. Leiden: Brill, 2000.

Urbach, E. E. "Laws Regarding Slavery as a Source for Social History of the Period of the Second Temple, the Mishnah and Talmud." In *Papers of the Institute of Jewish Studies London*, vol. 1, 1–94. Ed. J. G. Weiss. Jerusalem: Magna Press, 1964.

Vaage, Leif E. *Galiean Upstarts: Jesus' First Followers According to Q*. Valley Forge, PA: Trinity Press International, 1994.

____ . "More Than a Prophet, and Demon-Possessed: Q and the 'Historical John." In *Conflict and Invention: Literary, Rhetorical, and Social Studies on the Sayings Gospel Q*, 181–202. Ed. John S. Kloppenborg. Valley Forge, PA: Trinity Press International, 1995.

Van der Horst, Pieter W."Jewish Funerary Inscriptions: Most are in Greek." *Biblical Archaeology Review* 18.5 (1992) 46–57.

Van der Ploeg, J. P. M. "Slavery in the Old Testament." *Supplements to Vetus Testamentum* 22 (1971) 72–87.

Vermes, Geza. *The Changing Faces of Jesus*. New York: Viking Compass, 2001.

____. *Jesus the Jew. A Historian's Reading of the Gospels.* Philadelphia: Fortress Press, 1973.

____ . "Sectarian Matrimonial Halakhah in the Damascus Rule." In *Post-Biblical Jewish Studies*, 50–56. Leiden: Brill, 1975.

Vermeule, Emily. *Aspects of Death in Early Greek Art and Poetry.* Berkeley: University of California Press, 1979.

Veyne, Paul. "The Household and Its Freed Slaves." In *A History of Private Life: From Pagan Rome to Byzantium*, 71–93. Ed. Paul Veyne. Trans. Arthur Goldhammer. Cambridge, MA; London: Belknap Press of the Harvard University Press, 1987

____. "Slavery." In *A History of Private Life: From Pagan Rome to Byzantium*, 51–69. Ed. Paul Veyne. Trans. Arthur Goldhammer. Cambridge, MA; London: Belknap Press of the Harvard University Press, 1987.

Von Kellenbach, Katharina. *Anti-Judaism in Feminist Writings.* Atlanta, GA: Scholars Press, 1994.

Wainwright, Elaine Mary. *Towards a Feminist Reading of the Gospel According to Matthew.* Berlin; New York: Walter de Gruyter, 1991.

Walker, Wm O. "Jesus and the Tax Collectors." *Journal of Biblical Literature* 97 (1978) 221–38.

Waller, Elizabeth. "The Parable of the Leaven: Sectarian Teaching and the Inclusion of Women." *Union Seminary Quarterly Review* 35 (1979–80) 99–109.

Watson, Paul E. "The Queen of Sheba in Christian Tradition." In *Solomon and Sheba*, 115–151. E. James B. Pritchard. London: Phaidon Press Ltd., 1974.

Weber, Hans Ruedi. *Jesus and the Children: Biblical Resources for Study and Preaching.* Geneva: World Council of Churches, 1979.

Weeden, Theodore J. *Mark–Traditions in Conflict.* Philadelphia: Fortress Press, 1971.

Weems, Renita. *Just a Sister Away. A Womanist Vision of Women's Relationships in the Bible.* Sand Diego, CA: Lura Media, 1988.

Wegner, Judith Romney. *Chattel or Person? The Status of Women in the Mishnah.* New York: Oxford University Press, 1988.

____ . "Philo's Portrayal of Women – Hebraic or Hellenic? In *"Women Like This": New Perspectives on Jewish Women in the Graeco-Roman World.* Ed. Amy-Jill Levine. Atlanta, GA: Scholars Press, 1991.

Westermann, William L. *The Slave Systems of Greek and Roman Antiquity.* Philadelphia: American Philosophical Society, 1955.

Wicker, Kathleen O'Brian. "Mulierum Virtutes." In *Plutarch's Ethical Writings and Early Christianity*, 106–134. Ed. Hans Dieter Betz. Leiden: Brill, 1978.

Wiedemann, Thomas. *Adults and Children in the Roman Empire.* New Haven; London: Yale University Press, 1989.

____. *Greek and Roman Slavery.* Baltimore, MD: Johns Hopkins University Press, 1981.

Williams, Larry and Charles S. Finch. "The Great Queens of Ethiopia." In *Black Women in Antiquity*, 12–35. Ed. Ivan Van Sertima. New Brunswick and London: Transaction Books, 1988.

Wink, Walter. *Engaging the Powers: Discernment and Resistance in a World of Domination.* Minneapolis: Fortress Press, 1992.

____. "Neither Passivity Nor Violence: Jesus' Third Way (Matt 5:38–41/Luke 6:29–30)." *Forum* 7 (1991) 5–28.

Wire, Antoinette Clark. "Gender Roles in a Scribal Community." In *A Social History of the Matthean Community: Cross-Cultural Disciplinary Approaches*, 87–121. Ed. David L. Balch. Minneapolis: Fortress Press, 1991.

Witherington, Ben III. "On the Road With Mary Magdalene, Joanna and Other Disciples – Luke 8:1–3." *Zeitschrift für die neutestamentliche Wissenschaft* 70 (1979) 243–248.

____ . "Rite and Rights for Women – Galatians 3:28." *New Testament Studies* 27 (1981) 593–604.

____ . "Women (NT)." *Anchor Bible Dictionary*, vol. 6,957–961. New York; London: Doubleday, 1992.

____. *Women in the Ministry of Jesus: A Study of Jesus' Attitudes to Women and Their Roles as Reflected in His Earthly Life.* Cambridge: Cambridge University Press, 1984.

Wolf, Eric R. *Peasants*. Englewood Cliffs, NJ. Prentice Hall, 1966.

Wright, Benjamin G. "Jewish Ritual Baths – Interpreting the Digs and the Texts: Some Issues in the Social History of Second Temple Judaism." In *The Archaeology of Israel: Constructing the Past, Interpreting the Present*, 190–214. Eds. Neil Asher Silberman and David Small. Sheffield: JSOT Press, 1997.

Wright, N. T. *Jesus and the Victory of God.* Minneapolis: Fortress Press, 1996.

Yadin, Y., et al. "Babatha's *Ketuba*." *Israel Exploration Journal* 44 (1944) 75–99.

____ . "Epigraphy and Crucifixion." *Israel Exploration Journal* 23 (1973) 18–22.

Yamaguchi, Satoko. "Revisioning Martha and Mary. A Feminist Critical Reading of a Text in the Fourth Gospel." D. Min Thesis. Episcopal Divinity School, 1996.

Yardeni, Ada. *Nahal Se'elim Documents*. Jerusalem: Israel Exploration Society and the Ben Gurion University in the Negev Press, 1995.

____ . and Greenfield, Jonas C. "A Receipt for a Ketubba." In *The Jews in the Hellenistic-Roman World: Studies in Memory of Menahem Stern*, 197–208. Ed. I. M. Gafni, et al. Jerusalem: Zalman Shazar Center for Jewish History and the Historical Society of Israel, 1996.

Young, Brad H. *Jesus the Jewish Theologian*. Peabody, MA: Hendrickson, 1995.

Young, Serinity. *An Anthology of Sacred Texts By and About Women*. New York: Crossroad, 1993.

Zanker, Paul. *The Power of Images in the Age of Augustus*. Ann Arbor: University of Michigan Press, 1990.

Zeitlin, Solomon. "Slavery During the Second Commonwealth and the Tannaitic Period." In *Solomon Zeitlin's Studies in the Early History of Judaism: History of Early Talmudic Law*, vol. 4, 225–269. Ed. Solomon Zeitlin. New York: KTAV Publishing House, 1978.

Zias, J. and E. Sekeles. "The Crucified Man from Giv'at ha-Mivtar: A Reappraisal." *Israel Exploration Journal* 35 (1985) 22–28.

Indices

Ancient Texts

New Testament

Old Testament

Apocrypha and Pseudipigrapha

New Testament Apocrypha

Mishnah, Talmud, and Related Literature

Philo and Josephus

Qumran

Early Christian and Greco-Roman Literature

Papyri

Modern Authors